Management and Organization Theory

The Jossey-Bass
Business & Management Series

The Instructor's Guide for *Management and Organization Theory* includes a test bank, PowerPoint slides, key terms, discussion questions, and course activities. The Instructor's Guide is available free online. If you would like to download and print out a copy of the guide, please visit: www.wiley.com/college/miles

Management and Organization Theory also has a Student Guide available free online. It includes study notes and key terms. If you would like to download and print out a copy of the Student Guide, please visit: www.wiley.com/college/miles

Birgit den Oute

Management and Organization Theory

A Jossey-Bass Reader

Jeffrey A. Miles

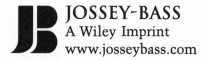

JOSSEY-BASS
A Wiley Imprint
www.josseybass.com

Published by Jossey-Bass
A Wiley Imprint
One Montgomery Street, Suite 1200, San Francisco, CA 94104-4594—www.josseybass.com

Jossey-Bass books and products are available through most bookstores. To contact Jossey-Bass directly call our Customer Care Department within the U.S. at 800-956-7739, outside the U.S. at 317-572-3986, or fax 317-572-4002.

Wiley also publishes its books in a variety of electronic formats and by print-on-demand. Some material included with standard print versions of this book may not be included in e-books or in print-on-demand. If the version of this book that you purchased references media such as CD or DVD that was not included in your purchase, you may download this material at http:// booksupport.wiley.com. For more information about Wiley products, visit www.wiley.com.

Library of Congress Cataloging-in-Publication Data
Miles, Jeffrey Allen.
    Management and organization theory : a Jossey-Bass reader / Jeffrey A. Miles.—First edition.
        p. cm.—(The Jossey-Bass business and management reader series)
    Includes bibliographical references and index.
    ISBN 978-1-118-00895-9 (pbk); ISBN 9781118196588 (ebk); ISBN 9781118196595 (ebk); ISBN 9781118196601 (ebk)
    1. Management. 2. Organization. I. Title.
    HD31.M4357 2012
    302.3'501—dc23
                                                                                        2011047502

Printed in the United States of America

FIRST EDITION
PB Printing 10 9 8 7 6 5 4 3 2 1

Contents

To Patrick—thank you so much for all your love,
support, encouragement, and wisdom

Acknowledgments

I graciously thank Kathe Sweeney, executive editor in the business and management and public administration teams at Jossey-Bass. Kathe launched this project with great enthusiasm and energy, and she helped sustain my enthusiasm and energy throughout the project. I also thank Kathe for helping me write at speeds that I did not believe were possible for me to reach.

I graciously acknowledge Lisé Johnson, executive editor at Wiley. Lisé is always so positive, optimistic, supportive, and energetic that she inspires me every time I talk with her. She is never-endingly devoted to ensuring that every one of her projects is the best that it can be; and fortunately, she has the never-ending drive and motivation to make that happen.

Thank you so much to the talented editorial team at Wiley: Dani Scoville, editorial program coordinator; Nina Kreiden, senior production editor; Michele Jones, copyeditor; Xenia Lisanevich, editor; and Elizabeth Forsaith, proofreader. Their passion, enthusiasm, dedication, and conscientiousness are amazing and so inspiring. I have completely enjoyed working with them.

Introduction

The purpose of this book is to educate students, faculty members, researchers, practicing managers, and consultants about the past and future directions of the forty most important theories in the field of management and organization. Those who are new to the field can use this book as a valuable tool to learn about its depth and scope, and those who have experience with management and organization theories can refresh their knowledge about those they already know and also learn about new theories that are not in their repertoire.

After reading this book you will be able to: (1) name and describe the forty most important management and organization theories; (2) know both the strengths and weaknesses of each theory; (3) conduct your own research studies by examining one or more of the hundreds of suggestions for further research presented in the book; (4) locate measures and questionnaires from online sources for measuring important variables in each theory; (5) know the five most important references for each of the theories; and (6) help your organization be more effective by applying the major concepts from each theory in your organization.

Theories

Theories are very useful tools that help us accomplish many important outcomes and objectives in an academic field of study. They help us to: (1) organize our thoughts and ideas about the world; (2) generate and explain relationships and interrelationships among individuals, groups, and entities; (3) improve our

1

predictions and expectations about people, groups, and organizations; and (4) achieve better understanding of the world (Hambrick, 2007).

There is little agreement on a single, universal definition of theory (Abend, 2008). This lack of consensus may explain why it is so difficult to develop strong theories in the social and behavioral sciences (Sutton & Staw, 1995). For this book, I define theory as a statement of constructs and their interrelationships that shows how and why a phenomenon occurs (Corley & Gioia, 2011). A theory can be any coherent description or explanation of observed, experienced, or documented phenomena (Gioia & Pitre, 1990).

Good theories must contain four essential elements: (1) what, (2) how, (3) why, and (4) who, where, and when (Whetten, 1989). I explain each of these four essential elements in the next sections.

"What" Elements of a Good Theory

Theories help us explain phenomena or patterns. In theory development, researchers observe and then write about interesting phenomena and facts. When documenting, describing, and explaining these phenomena and facts, researchers must select and include the most important factors. These important factors have been called constructs or concepts, and are the "what"—the major building blocks, the primary elements—in good theories.

Researchers cannot include all possible factors derived from their observations, so they must decide which factors are the "right" factors to be included in a theory and which should be excluded. Researchers should strive to include all possible factors (be comprehensive), but should also strive to include only those factors that provide additional value to the theory (be parsimonious). Generally, researchers tend to include many factors in the early stages of theory development and then, through research studies and findings, delete unnecessary or irrelevant constructs.

"How" Elements of a Good Theory

After a list of constructs has been identified in a theory, the next step in theory building is to describe how the constructs are related and interrelated. Usually, researchers describe these relationships in text form and then operationalize them by drawing diagrams or models of them. In creating a conceptual diagram of a theory, researchers draw a box for each construct and then draw arrows showing how specific factors might influence other constructs in the theory. The arrows among boxes in a conceptual diagram help delineate patterns and flows of direct and indirect influences of constructs on other constructs in the theory.

After a theory is initially depicted in a diagram, further research is then relied on to test out the actual relationships among all the constructs. Constructs and their relationships and interrelationships are retained in theories when research supports them, but are removed when research does not support them.

"Why" Elements of a Good Theory

Taken together, the what and how elements of a theory make up the domain, or the subject of the theory. The "why" parts of a theory help explain the relationships among the what and how elements. More specifically, the why elements help explain underlying psychological, economic, and social dynamics of the constructs and the proposed relationships of those factors.

The why parts of a theory include the researcher's assumptions. These assumptions are the theoretical glue that holds together all the parts of the theory. In good theory, the researcher clearly describes the logic used to explain why the elements of the theory fit together as they do. Good theories help expand and broaden our knowledge by providing compelling and logically stated reasons that justify the whys underlying the what and how parts of a theory.

Researchers combine the what and how elements of a theory into a model from which testable propositions are derived. Propositions are statements that explain why the constructs of a theory influence each other as they do. The basic elements of a theory are constructs, and the propositions explain the relationships and influences among those constructs.

Researchers test out the propositions of a theory in research studies to determine if real-world or laboratory data support them. Some researchers refer to propositions in a research study as hypotheses. In a research study, researchers create a working, or operational, definition of a construct, which is called a variable. The variables are measured and data are collected using survey instruments. Researchers then use statistical methods to assess the strength of the research variables and hypotheses in their study in order to support or refute the constructs and the propositions in a theory. Through careful, logical, and systematic research studies, researchers can find support for the constructs and the propositions in a theory or can revise and restate the theory when support for its constructs and propositions is not found.

The "Who, Where, and When" Elements of a Good Theory

The what, how, and why elements of a theory will never hold for all possible conditions. Researchers need to specify the boundaries and constraints that limit the generalizability of theories. For example, the limitations of a theory might include temporal, contextual, and geographical factors. For instance, will the theory hold for American women working in the summer and also hold for Chinese men working in the winter?

When first developing a theory, researchers are unlikely to be able to specify all of the possible who, where, and when factors. However, through careful and logical thought, they should be able to specify an initial list of boundaries and constraints for a theory. Subsequent research studies and their findings are then used to test those boundaries and constraints and to offer additional ones that were not initially stated by the theorist. Subsequent research studies and findings are also used to eliminate boundaries and constraints when no research support is found for them to stay in the theory.

In addition to containing the four essential elements, good theories must also contain well-created constructs. This next section describes good constructs.

As noted, a theory is a system of constructs that are related to each other by propositions (Bacharach, 1989). Constructs tend not to be real observations. Instead, they are conceptual abstractions of phenomena that cannot be directly observed. Constructs are often deliberately and consciously invented by researchers for a specific task or purpose, to represent categories of individual observations. Constructs are robust, conceptual generalizations or summations of actual, real-world observations. Constructs are strong, useful categories that are invented by researchers to artificially separate real observations into clear, distinct categories. For example, a researcher might make note of all the widely diverse entities in the world and then divide those entities into three arbitrarily created, but extremely useful, constructs—animal, vegetable, and mineral. In another example, a scientist might document all the elements in the world and then create three constructs to categorize all those elements—gases, liquids, and solids (Suddaby, 2010).

Strong and useful theories tend to have well-developed constructs. Constructs that are clear and useful comprise four basic elements: (1) definitions, (2) conditions, (3) relationships, and (4) coherence. A good construct definition should capture the essential properties and characteristics of the constructs as concisely as possible. A strongly written construct should accurately capture the essence of the phenomena without using circular language. (An example of circular language would be stating that a transformational leader transforms organizations.) A well-written construct definition should be as simple, or parsimonious, as possible and use just enough of the right words to accurately describe the construct.

Good theories delineate the conditions or constraints of their constructs. In the hard sciences, constructs tend to be universally applicable, so theorists tend not to set very many conditions on their constructs. In the social sciences, however, most constructs are not universally applicable, so good theorists spell out the conditions, or boundaries and limitations, of their constructs. Examples of conditions on constructs include space, time, and values. A value of a constraint may be that the constraint is from the employee's point of view or from the manager's point of view, but not from both points of view.

Good theorists also specify the relationships among other similar constructs. Rarely are constructs created in a vacuum. Instead, most constructs are derived from, or related to, other similar constructs. A good theory should carefully describe how its constructs are similar to and different from others, and even distinguish its constructs from other uses of the same term in other related theories.

Finally, good constructs should be coherent, meaning that the definitions, conditions, and relationships of the constructs make sense and hang together well as a whole: they all fit together in a logical and consistent manner.

The Importance of Theories

Theory is the most basic and fundamental building block in scholarly research (Corley & Gioia, 2011). Anyone who wants to become knowledgeable about the field of management and organization research must learn about the most important theories in the field.

In the areas of management and organization, all the top journals require that all manuscripts contribute to the development and advancement of theory (Colquitt & Zapata-Phelan, 2007; Hambrick, 2007). Every paper must have a section about the origins and current state of the theory that is being examined in order to explain relationships among variables of interest. It is not enough for a researcher simply to state how a paper contributes to our knowledge or our understanding. Instead, every author of every research paper must state how theory is better off or more advanced because of the findings of that research study.

Most of the top journals, such as the Academy of Management journals, require manuscript submissions to do one or more of the following: (1) challenge existing theory; (2) clarify or improve existing theory; (3) synthesize and integrate existing theories into fresh new theories; and (4) identify and describe new theoretical problems or observations that will lead to the search and creation of new theories (LePine & Wilcox-King, 2010). Articles or manuscripts that clarify or challenge existing theory are often made up of reviews and examinations of existing theory. These articles often reveal inconsistencies in theories or illuminate assumptions that result in the launching of new ways of thinking and new conversations about theoretical constructs. Manuscripts that identify new theoretical problems often provide evidence that existing theories are deficient in trying to explain particular phenomena, and help create fundamental shifts in our understanding. Research that synthesizes and integrates existing theories often provides structure that did not exist before, for example, by repositioning constructs among new antecedents and consequences in a way that generates new communication and attention from scholars. Without such theoretical improvements, manuscript submissions will simply not be accepted by the best refereed academic journals.

In addition to helping researchers make contributions to journals and to the field, theories also help practicing managers perform their jobs better. They help managers better describe, understand, predict, and control behavior in organizations. The more that practicing managers know and apply theories, the better able their organizations may be to make progress toward achieving their mission, strategies, and goals.

Theories about organizations and groups of organizations can also help policymakers create and administer organizations more effectively. Some of the theories in this book examine how entire organizations or systems of organizations interact and interrelate with each other. When people who create and set policy know and understand these theories, then their decisions and actions can help those organizations or systems of organizations operate more effectively and efficiently and better accomplish their goals.

Organizations

All the theories in this book examine some aspect of attitudes and behaviors of individuals or groups or some aspect of entire organizations or groups or systems of organizations. Therefore, it is important and necessary to establish a definition for organizations. There is no one definition of organizations that is agreed on by all researchers. For this book, I define organizations as deliberate arrangements and conscious coordinations of people to achieve a common goal or set of goals. Organizations have a distinct purpose and a deliberate structure, and they accomplish specific goals through the work and behavior of people. An organization is not a random group of people who come together by chance; rather it is a consciously and formally established entity that is designed to accomplish certain goals that its members would be unable to reach by themselves. It is a managed system designed and operated to achieve a mission, vision, strategies, and goals.

Management

Almost all the theories in this book also examine some aspect of management. Management is a process that happens inside of, or as a part of, organizations. The term "management" has three different definitions: (1) the process that managers follow to accomplish organizational vision, mission, strategies, and goals; (2) a specific body of knowledge that examines various methods used by managers and organizations; and (3) the individuals in organizations who guide and direct the actions of others to accomplish organizational goals. The theories explored in this book that examine management processes may do so in reference to one, two, or all three definitions; most often, however, a theory will examine only one of the three.

Management can be described as the process of accomplishing organizational mission, strategies, goals, and objectives through the use of people (human resources), money (financial resources), things (physical resources), and data (informational resources). The people in an organization can be employees or other individuals such as consultants who work part-time, full-time, on a contract basis, or in some other relationship with the organization. The money used in an organization can be any sort of financial resource or capital that the organization uses toward achieving desired organizational outcomes. The things in an organization can include physical resources, such as equipment, computers, desks, chairs, tables, lamps, and even the building where the organization resides. The data or knowledge in an organization can be any sort of information, such as databases or archives that are used by the organization to help accomplish desired organizational goals.

A manager's job is to achieve high performance relative to the organization's desired outcomes. Good managers accomplish desirable organizational outcomes both effectively and efficiently. An effective manager constantly and consistently accomplishes organizational mission, strategies, goals, and objectives. An efficient manager accomplishes organizational outcomes with minimal waste of human, financial, and physical resources, making the best possible use of money, time, materials, and people.

The job of managing is typically broken down into four main functions: (1) planning, (2) organizing, (3) directing, and (4) controlling. The planning function of management involves analyzing the current situation and anticipating the future; determining the vision, mission, strategies, goals, and objectives; and determining the resources needed to achieve those desired outcomes. It also includes selecting tasks that employees perform, indicating when and how those tasks should be done, and coordinating employee activities.

The organizing function of management involves assembling and coordinating the human, financial, physical, informational, and other resources that the organization uses to achieve its desired outcomes. Organizing activities include attracting qualified people to the organization, specifying job responsibilities and assigning specific tasks to employees, arranging and coordinating work assignments and activities, and creating conditions that facilitate the coordination of all the resources to achieve maximum organizational success.

The directing function of management involves influencing employees to perform as well as possible. Directing activities include leading, motivating, and communicating with employees as individuals, in groups, and as an organization as a whole. Effective directing involves guiding and inspiring employees to new, high levels of achievement while accomplishing the vision, mission, strategies, and goals of the organization. Directing activities can also include setting a good example for employees, serving as a role model for appropriate and desired company behavior, and showing others the way to job and career success in the company.

The controlling function of management involves monitoring employee progress toward outcome success and making appropriate changes when necessary. Controlling activities include setting performance standards; monitoring individual, group, and organizational progress toward attaining established goals; providing feedback and information to employees about progress toward goal attainment; identifying problem areas by comparing actual performance levels to performance standards; and solving performance problems once they have been identified, such as by improving employee motivation. Additional controlling functions include maintaining a budget, cutting costs and reducing waste, and taking employee disciplinary action when necessary.

How the Theories Were Selected

An important part of writing this book was selecting the management and organization theories that would be included. I began the process of theory selection by making a list of all the theories that have been published in articles contained in the EBSCO Business Source Complete database of management and organization journals. Next, I reduced this list of theories by following the decision rules stated by Miner (1984, 2003) in his classic works on establishing the validity and usefulness of management and organization theories. First, the theories had to be at least ten years old. Miner (2003) noted that it takes roughly ten years for a theory to generate sufficient research to emerge as an important theory in the management and organization area. Second, the theories have all been found to be useful in understanding, explaining, and predicting the functioning of organizations or the behavior of people in them. The theories selected for this book have received the most research attention and are the subjects of the most publications, most interest, and most discussion of all the theories. Third, the theories all have been shown to have clear implications for practice and application in some area of management and organization functioning. They all are excellent means of effectively analyzing and solving management and organization problems and challenges. Fourth, the theories have all generated significant research, have become well established, and have been thoroughly examined, analyzed, and tested by researchers.

I created my own fifth decision rule for selecting the best theories for this book: the theories had to be both "classic" and "current." My definition of a classic theory is one that has stood the test of time and has become well established, well known, and influential. My definition of a current theory is one that has an active, ongoing research stream in the major management and organization journals to which a researcher could contribute in the present.

Why I Wrote This Book

I wrote this book for many reasons, the first of which is a selfish one. When I was a student, I wished that there was such a book to help me quickly and easily see and understand the major management and organization theories. Unfortunately, there was no such book, so I was left to my own devices. Since that time, no one has written such a book, so I finally decided to just go ahead and write one myself. I describe my other reasons in the following sections.

Review of the Literature

When I conducted the research for this book, I searched the literature for all the relevant books and articles I needed for each of the forty theories. I printed out each of the journal articles, as I prefer to have the actual articles in my hands rather than to read them off a monitor. I also went to the library and checked out each of the books needed for each theory. In total I collected over fifty linear feet of journal articles (if I made one giant stack of all of the articles) and 122 books! This was a massive amount of material to organize and store, so I ended up taking a spare room in my house and stacking the articles and books for each theory on the floor, putting a label with the name of each theory on top of each stack. The result was a massive set of forty stacks of articles and books.

When I looked at these forty stacks, I realized that this was an excellent review of the field of management and organization. I saw the collection of forty theories as a sort of picture puzzle that enabled me to see the entire field of research in this academic field all in one place and at one time. I began to mentally move the theory puzzle pieces around in my mind. I tried to imagine how the pieces fit together, how they overlapped, how some pieces seemed smaller and some larger than the others. I also realized that there seemed to be some holes among the pieces where further research needed to be done to bring the pieces together and to integrate the theories. It is my goal that this book will enable you to see the overall field of management and organization in the same way I did.

Ideas for Further Research

One of the most important parts of this book is the collection of over four hundred ideas (ten or more ideas for each of the forty theories) for further research. I don't know how many times I have heard from students and faculty over the years that they can't think of anything about which they want to conduct a research study. Therefore, one of my goals was to provide the most up-to-date research ideas for each of the theories. These ideas were all derived from the "suggestions for future research" sections of the latest three years of journal articles for each of the forty theories. The suggestions for further research in this book should be an excellent starting point for anyone trying to find a great research idea for his or her own research project, thesis, or dissertation.

Five Most Important Works for Each Theory

Anyone who wants to become knowledgeable about theories in the field of management and organization or who wants to earn a degree in the field will need to know the names of the most significant works associated with the most important theories. Therefore, this book includes the five most frequently cited works for each theory, or what are called the seminal works for each theory. When I was earning my degrees, I had to find these works myself, which took a great deal of time, so I wanted to be sure to include this information in this book to save you the time and trouble of finding these seminal works yourself.

Survey Instruments for Each Theory

Probably the second-most-frequent comment I've heard from students is "How do I measure variables in my theory?" For this reason, I was sure to include hundreds of survey instruments, questionnaires, and measures for the most important constructs for each theory. All the instruments in this book are available through almost every academic database, such as EBSCO.

Implications for Managers

Academia has often been criticized for writing theories that have no relevance to the real world. I was a practicing manager myself, so I was careful to provide a section on the implications for managers for each of the forty theories in this book. My goal was to provide managers with a short summary of the major implications of each theory that they could immediately take back to work and apply on the job that day.

Organization of the Book

Each of the theories in the book will be briefly reviewed and examined in about six pages. For ease of reference, they are presented in alphabetical order. The discussion of each theory will follow a simple format, or template, made up of six sections:

1. Brief description of the theory
2. Criticisms and critiques of the theory
3. Measuring variables in the theory
4. Suggestions for further research
5. Major references to know for the theory
6. Implications of the theory for practicing managers

Brief Description of the Theory

Each theory is briefly described in a few easy-to-read pages. The short description of each theory identifies and explains the major constructs in the theory and describes the most important relationships and interrelationships of those constructs. The brief description will not be a thorough and exhaustive explanation of every aspect of the theory, but will be a quick review of the most important, helpful, and useful aspects of the theory.

Criticisms and Critiques of the Theory

The theory description is followed by a short discussion of the major criticisms and critiques of the theory. It may seem strange to some readers to have a section of criticisms for each theory, because the theories are such useful tools for analyzing and solving management and organization issues and problems. However, every useful tool has both strengths and weaknesses, and these theories are no different. To use an analogy, a hammer is a very useful tool; it has many strengths, such as enabling us to efficiently and effectively drive in and remove nails. However, hammers also have some weaknesses: for example, if you don't pay attention when using them, you can smash your thumb. Despite these weaknesses, we wouldn't stop using hammers; they are still very useful tools. The same is true for the theories presented in this book. Even though they all have some weaknesses, we wouldn't stop using them to help analyze and solve our important management and organization problems and challenges.

Also, each of the theories in this book has been extensively studied and has been found to be highly successful and valuable for organizations, so although the criticisms and weaknesses of each theory are important, they are not major enough to prevent use of the theory by researchers or practicing managers. The discussion of the weaknesses of each theory should be used as a guide for determining limitations and constraints when applying or using the theory.

A final point here is that being an expert in a field means that one knows both its strengths and its weaknesses. This means that if you want to be an expert in the field of management and organization theories, you will need to know both their strengths and their weaknesses.

Measuring Variables in the Theory

The next section of each theory discussion is a list of published survey measures or instruments. Theories describe and explain the relationships and interrelationships of constructs. However, when people conduct research, they convert constructs into measurable variables. The measures for those variables are called survey instruments. This section provides references for published survey instruments for the theory. The survey instruments include the actual questions or items in those instruments. You can locate the survey instruments through an academic database such as EBSCO Business Source Complete, and then use them to conduct your own research into a theory.

Suggestions for Further Research

As I noted earlier, one of the most difficult aspects of conducting original academic research in the area of organization and management is creating an original research idea. This section of each theory discussion will list ten or eleven areas where further research can be conducted by students and faculty.

Major References to Know for the Theory

Every person who wants to become an expert in the field of organization and management must learn the most important references for the most important theories. This section of each theory discussion provides a quick way to learn the most important, or seminal, references for each theory. These are not exhaustive or totally comprehensive lists, but they are a very helpful and easy way to learn some of the most important references. The lists were derived from the most-often-cited references for each theory or from the references most often used by the authors of the theories themselves in their own research. These sections contain five seminal references for the theory.

Implications of the Theory for Practicing Managers

All forty of the theories presented in this book are extremely practical and useful for solving management and organization problems, issues, and challenges. Indeed, Lewin (1945) noted that "nothing is as practical as a good theory" (p. 129). Therefore, the last section of each theory discussion is a short explanation of the implications of applying the theory to situations with real employees in real-life organizations.

In summary, this book is an excellent tool for teaching, research, and practice that can be used by students, teachers, researchers, consultants, and practicing managers in their quest to know, understand, apply, and advance the most important theories in the field of management and organization research.

1

Absorptive Capacity Theory

Absorptive capacity theory examines the extent to which a firm can recognize the value of new external information, assimilate it, and apply it toward achieving organizational goals (Cohen & Levinthal, 1989, 1990). The theory assumes that absorbing new knowledge can help an organization become more innovative and flexible and achieve higher levels of performance than it would without absorbing new knowledge. The theory also assumes that firms that have higher abilities for absorbing new knowledge will have a competitive advantage over firms with lower abilities.

A firm's technical knowledge tends to come from four sources. (1) The firm conducts its own research and development (R&D). (2) The firm derives new knowledge from its own current manufacturing operations. (3) The firm borrows new knowledge from other organizations or other sources. (4) The firm purchases new knowledge, such as through buying new equipment, hiring new knowledgeable people, or paying a consultant to train individuals in the use of a new method.

The theory assumes that organizations require a knowledge base to be able to absorb and use new knowledge. Firms that have no knowledge base may never be able to absorb new knowledge, no matter how they obtain it or how much they spend to obtain it. Firms that have never developed a knowledge base are said to be "locked-out" for subsequent knowledge and technological developments, a situation that can result in the creative destruction of an organization (Schumpeter, 1942).

The possession of prior knowledge is helpful for organizations in two ways. First, creating an absorptive capacity for new

1

knowledge in one period will help the absorption of new knowledge in the next period. Second, the successful use of new knowledge can be self-reinforcing and can motivate a firm to continue to absorb new knowledge indefinitely. Firms with higher absorptive capacities tend to proactively search for and absorb new knowledge regardless of current performance, but firms with lower absorptive capacities tend to reactively scrounge for new knowledge in response to some failure or decline in performance.

In order to recognize, assimilate, and use new knowledge, firms must have a knowledge base that is relatively similar to the new knowledge that is being processed. However, the new knowledge must be fairly diverse in relation to the firm's existing knowledge base in order for the new knowledge to be applied in new, helpful ways. Most organizational innovations come from borrowing ideas from other people, rather than through inventing them (March & Simon, 1958). However, the firm must have some idea of how the borrowed new knowledge can be applied to current methods for the process to be successful.

There are two factors that will affect an organization's incentives to acquire new knowledge: (1) the quantity of knowledge available to absorb and exploit and (2) the difficulty and costs involved in absorbing that new knowledge. Some types of new knowledge and expertise are more expensive to assimilate than others. Therefore, firms will tend to absorb new knowledge when doing so is inexpensive and will tend not to do so when it is expensive. However, a potential mediator of those two influences is the firm's interdependence with its rivals. The more that competitors tend to benefit from absorbing and using new knowledge, the less a firm will be motivated to increase its absorption of new knowledge.

A firm's ability to find and use new knowledge depends on the absorptive capacity of its employees. However, a firm's absorptive capacity is not just the sum of its individual members' absorptive capacities. Organizations depend on knowledgeable individuals to assess and evaluate the potential positives and negatives of new knowledge. These people can serve as "gatekeepers" who can prevent or facilitate the absorption of new knowledge. These individuals must be excellent transmitters, disseminators, and disciples of new methods, who champion and advocate the use of new knowledge in the firm. Organizations rely on these strong, knowledgeable, "boundary spanners" to help absorb and utilize new knowledge.

Zahra and George (2002) reconceptualized part of the theory. They took the steps of recognizing the value of new knowledge and assimilating and applying it, and created four capabilities or dimensions: (1) acquisition, (2) assimilation, (3) transformation, and (4) exploitation. (They refer to acquisition and assimilation as "potential" absorptive capacity; transformation and exploitation are "realized" absorptive capacity.) The acquisition capability refers to the firm's prior expenditures; prior knowledge base; and intensity, speed, and direction for obtaining new knowledge. The assimilation capability refers to the firm's routines and processes that enable it to assess, interpret, understand, and learn new knowledge. The transformation capability refers to the firm's ability to add, delete, recombine, and reconfigure the new knowledge for use in the company. The exploitation capability refers to the firm's ability to actually change its routines and processes and use the new knowledge. Zahra and George separated potential versus realized absorptive capacity because some firms may have strong potential to absorb new knowledge, but are then unable to actually use that knowledge (Baker, Miner, & Eesley, 2003).

Murovec and Prodan (2009) demonstrated that there can be two kinds of absorptive capacity: demand-pull and science-push. Demand-pull refers to new knowledge derived from market sources (for example, customers, competition, and suppliers). Science-push refers to new knowledge derived from research and scientific sources (such as books, journals, conferences, trade shows, and other academic sources). Organizations will need to assimilate new knowledge from both sources if they want to be as effective and innovative as possible.

Criticisms and Critiques of the Theory

The theory has been criticized for not adequately defining the term "absorptive capacity" or for using various differing definitions (Murovec & Prodan, 2009; Volberda, Foss, & Lyles, 2010). Some researchers have used the term without providing a definition (for example, Glass & Saggi, 1998; Keller, 1996). Also, most often the concept of absorptive capacity has been defined according to R&D aspects and not according to other organizational aspects.

As noted earlier, Murovec and Prodan (2009) found that there are two different kinds of absorptive capacity: demand-pull and science-push. As a result of this finding, they argued that researchers should not use a single-construct survey to measure absorptive capacity.

Todorova and Durisin (2007) criticized the Zahra and George (2002) reconceptualization of the theory, saying that the changes did not build enough on the original work. First, they criticized the reformulation for removing the step of "recognizing the value" of new knowledge. Todorova and Durisin recommended that the first step in the process of absorbing new knowledge should be recognizing the value of that knowledge. They emphasized the importance of this step in that firms often fail to identify and absorb new knowledge because they are hindered by their existing knowledge bases, inflexible capabilities, and path dependencies (Gavetti & Levinthal, 2000; Tripsas & Gavetti, 2000). Todorova and Durisin thus recommended that "valuing new knowledge" should be put back into the theory as was originally formulated by Cohen and Levinthal (1989, 1990).

Second, Todorova and Durisin (2007) criticized the reformulation of the theory for stating that transformation was a consequence of assimilating new knowledge. Instead of specifying that acquisition and assimilation of new knowledge lead to transformation and exploitation of new knowledge, Todorova and Durisin argued for a more complex relationship among acquiring, assimilating, transforming, and exploiting new knowledge. Todorova and Durisin argued that these four steps can influence each other and do not occur linearly from one to the other.

As a result, Todorova and Durisin (2007) remarked that the "neat" new concepts of potential and realized absorptive capacity would have to be removed from the theory (p. 775). Zahra and George (2002) argued that potential absorptive capacity (acquisition and assimilation) leads to realized absorptive capacity (transformation and exploitation). However, if one acknowledges the existence of a complex relationship among acquiring, assimilating, transforming, and exploiting new knowledge, the concepts of potential and realized absorptive capacity would not work.

Third, Todorova and Durisin (2007) argued that the theory should be reconceptualized as an ongoing process that involves feedback loops. They argued that Cohen and Levinthal's original formulation of the theory (1989, 1990) emphasized the accumulation of knowledge over time and the absorption of new knowledge into current routines and processes. Therefore, Todorova and Durisin argued for the inclusion of feedback loops in which the successful process of absorbing new knowledge looped back and influenced future absorption actions.

Measuring Variables in the Theory

Absorptive capacity measure. Cadiz, D., Sawyer, J. E., & Griffith, T. L. (2009, December). Developing and validating field measurement scales for absorptive capacity and experienced community practice. *Educational and Psychological Measurement, 69,* 1035–1058.

Absorptive capacity measure. Jimenez-Barrionuevo, M. M., Garcia-Morales, V. J., & Molina, L. M. (2011). Validation of an instrument to measure absorptive capacity. *Technovation, 31,* 190–202.

Absorptive capacity measure. Camison, C., & Fores, B. (2010). Knowledge absorptive capacity: New insights for its conceptualization and measurement. *Journal of Business Research, 63,* 707–715.

Absorptive capacity scale. Flatten, T. C., Engelen, A., Zahra, S. A., & Brettel, M. (2011). A measure of absorptive capacity: Scale development and validation. *European Management Journal, 29,* 98–116.

Absorptive capacity measures. Kotabe, M., Jiang, C. X., & Murray, J. Y. (2011). Managerial ties, knowledge acquisition, realized absorptive capacity and new product market performance of emerging multinational companies: A case of China. *Journal of World Business, 46,* 166–176.

Suggestions for Further Research

1. Explore the idea that the faster the pace of technological change, the greater the impact of absorptive capacity on a firm's profitability.

2. Examine the trade-offs between complementary versus supplementary resources in absorbing new knowledge.
3. Compare the costs and benefits of obtaining both types of new knowledge from various sources (for example, licensing, contracting).
4. Explore the influence of firm size on firms' absorptive capacities and the effects on organizational outcomes.
5. Examine both the positive and negative effects of absorption of spillovers and other sources of absorption on firm performance.
6. Compare and contrast the influences of intraindustry, interindustry, and scientific absorptive capacity on organizational outcomes.
7. Examine a range of types of knowledge (for example, domestic versus foreign) and the influence of those types on absorption and use.
8. Explore and empirically test the similarities and differences among organizational learning and absorptive capacity models.
9. Study the influence of absorptive capacity on what individuals know and what they can do, and how absorptive capacity influences their interactions.
10. Examine the influence of ownership type, R&D investment levels, and alliance ties with foreign firms on absorptive capacity.

References to Know

Cohen, W. M., & Levinthal, D. A. (1989, September). Innovation and learning: The two faces of R&D. *Economic Journal, 99*(397), 569–596.

Cohen, W. M., & Levinthal, D. A. (1990, March). Absorptive capacity: A new perspective on learning and innovation. *Administrative Science Quarterly, 35*(1, Special Issue), 128–152.

Lane, P. J., Koka, B. R., & Pathak, S. (2006). The reification of absorptive capacity: A critical review and rejuvenation of the construct. *Academy of Management Review, 31,* 833–863.

Lane, P. J., & Lubatkin, M. (1998). Relative absorptive capacity and interorganizational learning. *Strategic Management Journal, 19,* 461–477.

Zahra, S. A., & George, G. (2002). Absorptive capacity: A review, reconceptualization, and extension. *Academy of Management Review, 27,* 185–203.

1

Implications of the Theory for Managers

Absorptive capacity theory examines how firms recognize the value of new knowledge, assimilate it, and use it toward achieving organizational goals. Firms that are able to absorb and use new knowledge will have a competitive advantage over those that aren't.

Your job as a manager is to help your firm better absorb and use new knowledge to accomplish your organizational goals. First, you'll need to build a strong knowledge base by helping everyone see and understand what your organization currently does. Second, set up a knowledge culture in which everyone sees the importance of learning about and incorporating new knowledge that can help the company better reach its goals. Third, find ways for the organization to monitor the environment and identify better and newer ways of doing things. Fourth, select knowledgeable people who can adapt and modify the new knowledge for your organization. Fifth, create teams of people who can promote acceptance and use of the new knowledge. Last, monitor the progress of the new knowledge, keep track of what went well and what didn't, and use that information to keep the cycle going for finding and absorbing new knowledge into your organization to make it the best that it can be. This theory examines why some firms perform better than others. This book will examine other theories that use this same approach but employ a different variable, such as the dynamic capabilities, resources, and knowledge of a firm.

2

Actor-Network Theory

Actor-network theory (also called the "sociology of translation") takes the view that all entities (human and nonhuman) take form and acquire their characteristics through their relations with other entities in the location in which they circulate (Callon, 1986; Callon & Latour, 1981; Latour, 1999; Law, 1994, 1999).

Translation refers to (1) the process of making two different things the same, (2) how network builders attract potential new actors, and (3) offering new interpretations of interests and directing attention (Latour, 1987; Law, 1999). In the theory, "the social" (existing and new networks, stakeholder relations, communication patterns, and so on) are what must be explained and should not be assumed. In a course of action, a variety of actors (human and nonhuman) may change or divert the original intent (Bryson, Crosby, & Bryson, 2009). Translation has four "moments" (Callon, 1986): (1) "problematization" (how to become indispensable), (2) "profit-sharing" (how allies are locked in place), (3) "enrollment" (how roles are defined and coordinated), and (4) "mobilization" (are the spokespersons representative?).

The theory has been described as a "semiotics of materiality" (Law, 1999, p. 4). Semiotics has to do with studying what things mean or examining when one thing stands for something else. Materiality refers to something having body or substance. According to the theory, entities (human or nonhuman) have materiality or substance only through their "assemblage of relations" with other entities, or what the theory calls "relational materiality."

The term "network" in the name of the theory does not have the same meaning as the term "network" as in the Internet or a social network. The term network was created for the theory before the creation of the Internet. Due to the current confusion over the term, the author (Latour, 1999) wishes that the theory had a different name.

In the theory, network refers to the "framing" and "summing up" of interactions and relations through various methods, into a very local, practical, narrow focus. The term refers to the transformations, translations, or transductions among entities in relations or interactions with each other. When someone examines "the social" (society, societal forces), he or she is not examining the "big picture" but is looking at the small, local, immediate, connected picture of entities in relations among one another—exactly the opposite of the Internet or social network definition (Latour, 1999). In the theory, there are only networks, with nothing in between the networks. There is only the local summing up, which produces either "local totalities" or "total localities."

The term "actor" in the theory does not have the typical meaning of the word used by most people. The authors typically use the term "actant" in the theory, which distinguishes the concept from the lay term "actor." The theory does not focus on what an actant does. Instead, the theory focuses on "what provides the actants with their actions, with their subjectivity, with the intentionality, with their morality" (Latour, 1999, p. 18).

The theory stresses the process through which actants coordinate their efforts and actions among one another. As behaviors are performed by both humans and nonhumans, the entities adjust and react to each other in a fluid way. For example, a person may adapt or be adjusted to a wheelchair that she is using, and in turn the wheelchair reacts, may adjust, or be adjusted to the people involved with it (sitting in it, pushing it, repairing it, and so on). One of the most controversial aspects of the theory is that actors themselves can be networks (Oppenheim, 2007).

The theory stresses that it does not try to explain the behavior of social actors. Instead, it takes the approach that actors already know what they do and how they are influenced by social forces. Researchers thus have to learn what actors do, and why and how they do it. The difficult part for researchers is to learn from actors about their behaviors without imposing artificially created categories, constructs, and so on onto their world-building behaviors.

The theory stresses that the vocabulary of researchers has contaminated their ability to simply let actors build their own space and to observe actors in the process of acting (Chateauraynaud, 1991; Lee & Brown, 1994).

The authors wish that a hyphen between the words "actor" and "network" had not been included in the theory. Sometimes the authors, such as Law and Hassard (1999), do not use a hyphen when stating the theory's name. The hyphen may have been meant to join the two terms "actor" and "network" rather than to divide or separate them. On one level, the hyphen suggests that the theory examines the ongoing debate between the power of individual agents (actors) versus the power of social forces (the network), which is exactly the opposite of what the theory tries to accomplish (Latour, 1999). The hyphen also focuses attention on the fact that the theory assumes that both humans and nonhumans can be agents who take action in their location. The hyphen helps perpetuate the belief that the theory focuses on "outside/ out there" versus "inside/in there" perspectives, which it does not. The theory recommends avoiding arbitrary labels and instead focusing on what is "there" and not labeling whether that is "out there" or "in there."

The theory advocates eliminating dichotomous, "either-or" terms—agency/structure, micro/macro, old/new, inside/outside, and so on—because they are doubly dissatisfying. For example, one of the classic debates in sociology has been over "agency" versus "structure." "Agency" means that individuals determine their own actions. "Structure" means that society at large determines behaviors. Theorists have fought for decades over which side is the "right" answer in the debate. In trying to find a winner, researchers tend to narrow their focus on one side, then find that approach dissatisfying, so then turn their focus to the other side, but then again are dissatisfied. Instead, of taking these "either/ or" approaches, the theory advocates considering both sides at once. The researcher should concentrate on both sides as merely being a "circulating entity" that shapes and reshapes its form as behaviors are performed.

Criticisms and Critiques of the Theory

The theory has been criticized for trying to distance itself from modern scientific practices and methodologies (Savage, 2009).

The theory recommends using only a narrative, descriptive format for observing actors in their natural location. However, in order to describe unique and important events for scientific journals, researchers must use the standard scientific methods that the theory dislikes. In addition, the theory offers no methodology for distinguishing bad or ineffective descriptions from good or effective ones.

2

Although some critics have applauded the theory for challenging fundamental research methods and theories, for changing "matters-of-fact" into "matters-of-concern" (Latour, 2004), and for challenging methods of conventional organizational thinking (Alcadipani & Hassard, 2010; Calas & Smirich, 1999; Reed, 1997; Whittle & Spicer, 2008), they have complained about Latour's recommendations (1996, 2005) to use only descriptive methodology (Krarup & Blok, 2011). Critics have argued that a great deal will be lost if researchers forgo the use of more sophisticated or advanced research methodologies in favor of only describing what they see. Critics argue that researchers are able to effectively "reconstruct" behaviors in their research without "deconstructing" them (Krarup & Blok).

The theory has been applauded for including nonhuman actants. However, the theory has also been criticized for being biased toward nonhuman actants over human ones (Habers & Koenis, 1996; Krarup & Blok, 2011; Newton, 1999, 2002). Also, the theory has been criticized for treating organizations as merely black boxes of actant networks that can be opened for full description (Hanseth, Aanestad, & Berg, 2004; Krarup & Blok, 2011).

In the theory, the concept of "folding" refers to a type of acting that produces sociotechnical relations that connect one place and time with another. Any technology can be seen as a hybrid of folds, layers, and compilations that develop over time and place. For example, how people view guns has changed over time. Critics have argued that Latour tends to focus on the folds and foldings of objects in society, but tends not to discuss how human morality, convictions, and so on fold in society over time (McLean & Hassard, 2004).

Critics have argued that the entire world cannot be reduced to "responsible description." The theory stresses that description is all that matters, but critics argue that explanations and causes are equally important for researchers to uncover (Young, Borland, & Coghill, 2010). Callon and Latour (1981) admit that sometimes explanations do make their way into their simple descriptions of behaviors.

Critics also have argued that the theory had its advantages when it sought to describe only technoscientific issues of humans and machines. However, the theory seems to be insufficient when it has been extended to examine the entire field of sociology (Walsham, 1997). Critics recommend that pure description alone will not suffice compared to typical scientific methods.

2

Measuring Variables in the Theory

Ethnographic interview question formation.   Smith, L. (2010, Spring). Always judged: Case study of an interview using conversation analysis. *Clinical Law Review, 16,* 423–450.

Various methods. Kraal, B. J. (2007, November). *Actor-network inspired design research: Methodology and reflections.* Proceeding of the International Association of Societies for Design Research, Hong Kong.

Ethnographic interviews and questions. Gee, M. K., & Ullman, C. (1998). *Teacher/ethnographer in the workplace: Approaches to staff development.* Grayslake, IL: College of Lake County National Workplace Literacy Program. (ERIC Document Reproduction Service No. ED 423721)

Suggestions for Further Research

1. Examine the methods through which firms decide to include or exclude entities in their networks.
2. Explore how efficient enrollment and alignment of actors in networks can lead to desired and undesired outcomes.
3. Look at how adding and removing actors from the network could align or misalign the organization and influences on outcomes.
4. Create a typology of the types of items and issues that organizations hold as "matters of fact" rather than as "matters of concern."

5. Explore a firm's ability to distinguish between matters of fact and of concern and the influence of that ability on organizational outcomes.
6. Examine who and what has the most and least influence on organizations and who and what has the most and least influence on them in return.
7. Look at how decisions regarding whom to influence and whom to let influence your organization affect organizational performance.
8. Examine individual differences in influencing and being influenced by humans versus nonhumans on desired behaviors and outcomes.
9. Explore the extent to which removing "either-or" dichotomies in one's focus or network leads to improved organizational performance.
10. Examine how more effective translation (problematization, profit sharing, enrollment, mobilization) leads to better actor outcomes.

References to Know

Callon, M. (1986). Some elements of a sociology of translation: Domestication of the scallops and the fishermen of St. Brieuc Bay. In J. E. Law (Ed.), *Power, action, and belief: A new sociology of knowledge* (pp. 196–223). London: Routledge.

Latour, B. (1988). *The pasteurization of France* (A. Sheridan & J. Law, Trans.). Cambridge, MA: Belknap Press.

Latour, B. (1993). *We have never been modern* (C. Porter, Trans.). Cambridge, MA: Harvard University Press.

Latour, B. (1999). On recalling ANT. In J. Law & J. Hassard (Eds.), *Actor network theory and after* (pp. 15–25). Oxford: Blackwell.

Latour, B. (2005). *Reassembling the social: An introduction to actor-network-theory.* Oxford: Oxford University Press.

Implications of the Theory for Managers

Actor-network theory examines how the characteristics and forms of entities (humans and nonhumans) are created and changed through their continual relations with other entities. In the theory, humans influence objects and objects influence humans, through an ongoing process of negotiation and translation. The theory examines such topics as how you influence technology and how technology influences you (for example, how you think, talk, and act when you have your favorite technologies, versus when you don't have them).

The theory advocates getting rid of categories and groups that might be holding you back, and instead focusing on the fluid and intensive generation of what could happen for your organization. The theory would say that using arbitrary categories, such as customer versus noncustomer, user versus nonuser, competitor versus noncompetitor, is typical for most organizations, but could be getting in the way of your success. For example, don't think of people as users or nonusers of your product. Think about how everyone out there is influenced by your product and how your product is influenced by him or her. People may not have directly bought your product, but they might be influenced by it because they are involved with family, friends, neighbors, and strangers who use your product. Try getting rid of the arbitrary categories that your company uses, or at least try broadening them a little, and see how your thoughts and attention are immediately changed as a result. This change in focus could help you see and address your problems and challenges in new and, one hopes, helpful ways.

The theory recommends not taking for granted the way that you currently do things in your organization. Instead, take note of what you are doing now and think of better ways that people and machinery can work together to accomplish your goals. For example, having rows of desks all facing toward the front can stress the power hierarchy in your firm. You can challenge that power structure by arranging desks to face each other or by creating a communal "hot desk" that would convey a totally different view of power and space in your organization (Grint, 1998).

3

Agency Theory

Since the late 1700s, theorists have discussed the problem of corporate owners hiring others as stewards of their wealth. Managers of other people's money cannot be expected to watch over it with the same zeal as the owner, so managerial negligence will always be present in the affairs of a company (Smith, 1776/1952).

According to agency theory, an agent or agency is hired by one or more person(s), called the principal(s), under a contract and is compensated by the principal to achieve desired outcomes for the principal. Because the agent is acting on behalf of the principal, the principal gives away some decision-making authority to the agent.

Agency relationships occur in a wide variety of situations and contexts that involve the delegation of authority—for example, clients and service providers (for example, doctors, lawyers, dentists, insurance and real estate agents), citizens and elected representatives, employers and employees, and stockholders and company managers (Kiser, 1999). In all of these examples, the former is the principal, and the latter is the agent. According to a review by Eisenhardt (1989), agency theory has been used by scholars in a wide variety of fields, such as accounting, economics, finances, political science, organizational behavior, and sociology.

There are five central elements that describe the principal-agent relationship: (1) there are different types of issues regarding agents (for example, laziness, reliability, trustworthiness); (2) the agent's actions influence the principal's desired outcomes; (3) random factors in addition to the agent's actions influence the outcomes; (4) there is some sort of outcome; and (5) there is asymmetrical information (Petersen, 1993).

Arrow (1985) advanced two models of asymmetrical information: the hidden action model and the hidden information model. In the hidden action model, the principal does not observe the actions taken by the agent, but only observes the outcome of those actions. In the hidden information model, the principal observes the agent's actions, but does not know vital information needed to perform those actions.

According to agency theory, the principal tends to have imperfect information with which to evaluate the agent, which leads to information asymmetry. Marketers seeking business for the agent may tend to overstate skills, abilities, and talents, and may overpromise when seeking new business (Davies & Prince, 2010). This overselling by agents can lead to principals' choosing the wrong agency for the task, which has been called "adverse selection."

In addition, agents can also underdeliver on their promised outcomes in order to obtain the maximum compensation for the least amount of effort, which has been called the "moral hazard" (Ellis & Johnson, 1993). The more autonomy that the agent has, and the greater the amount of specialized knowledge and information required to do the job, the more significant this moral hazard becomes (Holmstrom, 1979).

Agency theory is concerned with resolving two problems that can occur in the agency relationship (Eisenhardt, 1989). The first is the problem of risk sharing, which can arise when the principal and the agent have different risk preferences. The second problem is called the "agency problem." There is the potential for managers to misbehave if the interests of the company owners and the agent managers diverge (Dalton, Hitt, Certo, & Dalton, 2007). If the principal and the agent both seek to maximize their own self-interests in this relationship, then the agent may not always act in the best interests of the principal (Jensen & Meckling, 1976).

It is generally impossible for the principal to ensure that the agent will always act in the best interests of the principal. However, there are three main ways to help minimize the agency problem: (1) board independence (the main role of the board is to monitor the behavior of managers); (2) market for corporate control (mischievous managers are controlled by an active merger and acquisition market); and 3) agent equity ownership (managers share ownership of the company and thus help advance shareholder interests) (Dalton et al., 2007).

Unfortunately, each of these methods does not come without costs incurred for the principal (Jensen, 1983). Agency costs come from many sources: recruitment, adverse selection, specifying principal preferences, establishing incentives, moral hazard, stealing, side deals, monitoring and policing, bonding and insurance, and hiring agents to oversee other agents (Shapiro, 2005). Sometimes the costs associated with regulating and controlling agents may not be worth the benefits of improved agent behavior (Mitnick, 1998).

The unit of analysis in agency theory is the contract that governs the relationship between the principal and the agent (Eisenhardt, 1989). Research focused on the type of contract has produced the best outcomes for the principal. This research has taken into account that people act rationally within limits, are self-interested, and tend to avoid risk. For example, researchers have examined whether outcome-based contracts are better or worse than contracts based on agent behavior.

There are two main branches of agency theory: positivist agency theory, and principal-agent theory (Jensen, 1983). Researchers with the positivist perspective have focused on (1) identifying situations in which the principal and the agent desire opposing outcomes and (2) describing governance mechanisms that control and regulate these principal and agent differences, especially for large public corporations (Berle & Means, 1932). For example, equity ownership by managers can help align the interests of owners and managers (Jensen & Meckling, 1976), efficient capital and labor markets can be used as information mechanisms to prevent self-serving behavior on the part of top executives (Fama, 1980), and the board of directors can serve as an information system that stockholders can use to monitor inappropriate behavior of top executives (Fama & Jensen, 1983).

Principal-agent researchers have focused on a general theory of the principal-agent relationship that can be applied to all kinds of "acting for" relationships. This line of work is characteristic of formal theory, and involves precise specification of assumptions, logical deduction, and mathematical proof. Principal-agent research examines which kinds of contracts are the most efficient under various conditions, such as outcome uncertainty, outcome measurability, risk aversion, and goal conflict.

Criticisms and Critiques of the Theory

Agency theory has made a major impact on management and organization research, yet it is controversial (Eisenhardt, 1989). The theory has been used by scholars in a wide variety of fields, and researchers exhibited early optimism about its use to further the understanding of organizational behavior (Eisenhardt). However, this optimism is clearly waning (Nyberg, Fulmer, Gerhart, & Carpenter, 2010).

Research has shown that the agency problem (conflicts arising from divergence between agents' and principals' desires and goals) is real and intractable (Lan & Heracleous, 2010). However, a large and growing body of empirical research has failed to support the efficacy of the ways to mitigate the agency problem (Dalton, Daily, Certo, & Roengpitya, 2003; Dalton et al., 2007). A review of fifty-four studies examined the influence of independent directors on boards and found no influence on company performance. In addition, a similar review of thirty-one studies found that separating leadership roles of board chairperson and CEO had no influence on corporate performance (Ghoshal, 2005).

The positivist view of agency theory has enriched research areas, such as economics (Jensen, 1983), and has inspired considerable research attention (Barney & Ouchi, 1986). Unfortunately, the positivist view has been criticized by organization researchers for being minimalist (Hirsch, Michaels, & Friedman, 1987; Perrow, 1986) and by microeconomists for being tautological and for lacking rigor (Jensen, 1983).

Agency theory has been criticized because its overly simplistic assumptions do not reflect the real-world business environment, and because empirical research has failed to support its basic tenets. Researchers are now not only seeking ever finer incremental adjustments to the theory but also asking for reexamination of the theory so that research can move into new and different directions (Lan & Heracleous, 2010).

Some critics have complained that agency theory does not make significant contributions to management and organization theory and research. On the one hand, Ross (1973) argued that agency problems were universal. On the other hand, Perrow (1986) claimed that agency theory did not address any clear organizational problems. Hirsch and Friedman (1986) viewed agency theory as excessively narrow, focusing primarily on organizational stock price.

For economists, agency theory may be revolutionary, as research in this area had focused only on organizations as "black boxes" until agency theory opened up the inside activities of the black box to examination. However, organization scholars tend not to see the obvious worth of agency theory for solving management and organizational problems.

Measuring Variables in the Theory

Information asymmetry scale. Jaworski, B. J., & Young, S. M. (1992). Dysfunctional behavior and management control: An empirical study of marketing managers. *Accounting, Organizations and Society, 17,* 17–35.

Budgetary slack measure and information asymmetry measure. Dunk, A. S. (1993). The effect of budget emphasis and information asymmetry on the relation between budgetary participation and slack. *Accounting Review, 68,* 400–410.

Supply risk sources questionnaire and risk management techniques questionnaire. Zsidisin, G. A., & Ellram, L. M. (2003, Summer). An agency theory investigation of supply risk management. *Journal of Supply Chain Management, 39*(3), 15–27.

Moral hazard measure. Tuttle, B., Harrell, A., & Harrison, P. (1997, Spring). *Journal of Management Information Systems, 13*(4), 7–27.

Suggestions for Further Research

1. Examine the influence of physical, social, temporal, or experiential barriers that separate principals and agents and how they affect agency relationships.
2. Explore broader types of agency or "acting for" relationships, such as the division of labor, the acquisition of experience,

the access to knowledge, and the desire to collectively enjoy economies of scale.

3. Look at newer ways, such as virtual methods, to monitor and control agent behavior, including selection, monitoring, and sanctioning processes.

4. Examine new types of agent mischief, such as white-collar crime, and retributory justice behaviors in agency relationships.

5. Explore the effect of a range of regulating agent behaviors (from totally rigid to completely flexible) on principal-desired outcomes.

6. Conduct a cost-benefit analysis of the various types of agent monitoring, controlling, and bonding in relation to organizational outcomes.

7. Test Ghoshal's assertion (2005) that if you combine agency theory with game theory and negotiation analysis, you will have a better real-world picture than if you use agency theory alone.

8. Compare nonprofit and for-profit organizations in terms of the effectiveness of ways to mitigate the agency problem.

9. Examine the extent to which individuals conduct a cost-benefit analysis of individual versus corporate interests when making decisions.

10. Explore individual attitudes (such as guilt, anxiety, regret, and denial) when agents make decisions on behalf of principals.

References to Know

Dalton, D. R., Hitt, M. A., Certo, S. T., & Dalton, C. M. (2007). The fundamental agency problem and its mitigation. In J. F. Walsh & A. P. Brief (Eds.), *Academy of Management Annals* (Vol. 1, pp. 1–64). Mahwah, NJ: Erlbaum.

Eisenhardt, K. M. (1989). Agency theory: An assessment and review. *Academy of Management Review, 14,* 57–74.

Fama, E. F., & Jensen, M. C. (1983). Separation of ownership and control. *Journal of Law and Economics, 26,* 301–325.

Jensen, M. C. (1983). Organization theory and methodology. *Accounting Review, 58,* 319–339.

Jensen, M. C., & Meckling, W. H. (1976). Theory of the firm: Managerial behavior, agency costs, and ownership structure. *Journal of Financial Economics, 3,* 305–360.

Implications of the Theory for Managers

According to agency theory, one or more person(s) called the principal(s) either can't or don't want to perform necessary business activities. The principal hires an agent or agency to perform those activities on the principal's behalf.

Agency theory assumes that everyone always acts according to his or her own best interests. Thus an agent will act to maximize his or her own self-interests at the expense of the principal's interests. This forces the principal to take action to keep the agent in line.

The principal can do any number of things to keep the agent performing properly, such as creating a contract with the agent, monitoring the agent's behaviors, buying some type of insurance, and hiring another agent to watch the agent. All these methods to curtail bad agent behavior take time and money away from the principal's resources. If the costs of regulating the agent's behavior are worth the money, then the principal should continue. However, if the costs of regulating the agent's behavior are not worth the money, then the principal should stop trying to regulate the agent's mischievous behavior and should perform the desired actions himself or herself.

One of the roles of effective managers is regulating the behaviors of agents acting for the organization. Examine areas in your organization where agents act on behalf of principals. Explore the mechanisms in place that help keep agents acting in the best interests of principals, such as rules of conduct or performance evaluations. Improve your methods for controlling agents where problems might occur, and add ways to control agents where no controls are in place so that your agents don't damage your organization.

4

Agenda Setting Theory

Originally, agenda setting theory examined the correlation between the frequency and duration of mass media coverage of a story and the extent to which people believed that an issue or story was important (Kosicki, 1993; MacKuen, 1981; McCombs, 2004). Initially, there was concern that the mass media would have powerful, pervasive, "hypodermic needle–like" effects that would change public attitudes and behaviors (for example, Lasswell, 1927; Lippman, 1922). However, research revealed that mass media influences are strong but not totally dominating (Klapper, 1960; Miller, 2007). Over time, agenda setting research has moved from examining small, short-term attitudinal changes to looking at long-term social impact caused by the mass media and other policymakers. Overall, agenda setting theory ultimately looks at how social change occurs in society (Rogers, Dearing, & Bregman, 1993).

Agenda setting theory examines (1) why information about some issues, but not others, is available to the public; (2) how public opinion is changed; and (3) why some issues are examined through social policy actions, but other issues are not (Dearing & Rogers, 1996).

Agenda setting research has shown that when people are asked to identify the significant problems facing the country, they tend to list issues that have received extensive news coverage by mass media outlets (Iyengar, 1990). These findings have been quite robust for all types of mass media coverage (television, newspapers, radio, and so on) for both local and national issues and in both field and laboratory settings.

An agenda is a set of issues, or political controversies, that fall within a range of legitimate concern and that are presented in order of importance (Cobb & Elder, 1983; Dearing & Rogers, 1996). Agenda setting research examines the possibility that people have their own personal agenda set by the mass media agenda (Rogers et al., 1993).

Cohen (1963) wrote that the mass media tended not to be very successful in telling people what to think, but that the mass media were remarkably successful in telling people what they should think about. McCombs and Shaw (1972) concluded that research on agenda setting theory supported the view that the mass media tell people not only what to think about but how to think about it, and that they thus tell people what to think.

Agenda setting theory has typically referred to research in four areas: (1) media agenda setting, (2) public agenda setting, (3) policy agenda setting (Rogers et al., 1993), and (4) corporate agenda setting. Media agenda setting refers to mass media news agencies determining which issues to promote and discuss. Public agenda setting refers to those issues that have relative importance to the members of the general public. Policy agenda setting refers to governmental bodies or elected officials determining which issues are important and thus promoting and discussing those issues. Similarly, corporate agenda setting refers to issues that big companies think are important.

There are two levels of agenda setting. The first level examines how the salience (or importance) of issues (such as corporate reputation) portrayed by the mass media influences the salience of issues for the public. The key variable is public attention to issues. The second level examines how the media's portrayed attributes of the important issues influence the public's perceived attributes of those same issues (McCombs & Evatt, 1995; McCombs, Shaw, & Weaver, 1997). The key variable here is comprehension, both substantive and evaluative (also called cognitive and affective). News media convey more than just facts to the public. They also convey feelings and tone, which influence public cognitions about important issues (McCombs & Ghanem, 2001).

Agenda setting research (for example, Staw & Epstein, 2000) has examined a large number of corporate issues where mass media coverage (frequency, depth, and tone) has influenced public perceptions. A corporate issue has been defined as a controversial inconsistency that (1) is based on gaps in stakeholder perceptions, (2) involves legitimate circumstances affecting the organization, (3) is about what corporate performance is or ought to be, and (4) has a current or future impact on the organization (Wartick & Mahon, 1994). Examples of corporate reputational variables include financial performance, product quality, treatment of employees, community involvement, and environmental performance (Fombrun, 1998; Fombrun, Gardberg, & Sever, 2001).

In addition, agenda setting research has examined organizations as powerful corporate political actors who actively shape policy agendas at all levels of government and shape public opinion about issues that they deem important and helpful for business interests (Berger, 2001). Organizations can influence agendas through funding, lobbying, giving testimony, and advertising and public relations (Schattschneider, 1960; Schlozman & Tierney, 1986; Useem, 1980), and by helping employees form and use optimal agendas that will help the organization become more successful and effective (McKelvey, 1981).

Framing is an essential part of agenda setting theory (Zhou & Moy, 2007). Entman (1993) described framing as essentially involving both selection and salience. Framing means selecting aspects of a perceived reality and making them more salient to the audience in such a way that it promotes (1) a particular issue definition, (2) a specific causal interpretation, (3) a certain moral evaluation, and (4) a recommended solution (Entman). Framing an issue makes it more salient. Salience means to make an issue more noticeable, meaningful, or memorable to audiences (Entman). Increasing the salience of an issue enhances the probability that people will perceive the issue and believe that the issue is important and meaningful to them, thus making them more likely to mentally process the issue and remember it (Fiske & Taylor, 1991). Related to framing is the concept that Iyengar and Kinder (1987) called the "priming effect," which refers to people's tendency to more easily recall issues that have received extensive news media coverage. Extended coverage tends to enhance the salience and significance of the issue, as reported by survey respondents.

Weaver (1977, 1980) examined the need for some people to have the media orient them and provide background information about a specific topic, a concept called "need for orientation." The higher the level of a person's interest in an issue and the more uncertain he or she is about the topic, then the higher that person's need for the media to provide more information about that agenda item.

According to agenda setting theory, a key strategy for policy setters desiring change depends on (1) problem definition, (2) framing, and (3) issue perceptions when shaping policy conflicts (Baumgartner & Jones, 1993; Pralle, 2006; Rochefort & Cobb, 1994). The key to getting attention and mobilizing the public to take action around a proposed solution depends on shifting the way an image is discussed and understood. For example, policymakers must transform an issue from merely being a "condition" that can be tolerated to a "problem" that must be dealt with immediately (Kingdon, 1984; Stone, 1988). Issue redefinition can generate movement for issues that have broken down and languished. However, most issue redefinition is slow, with only incremental shifts occurring, and usually requires substantial amounts of resources for larger shifts to occur (Leech, Baumgartner, Berry, Hojnacki, & Kimball, 2002).

More recent agenda setting research has shown that in addition to accessibility, the content of news stories is a primary determinant of media agenda setting influences (Miller, 2007). People pay attention to the content of news stories that specifically arouses their negative emotions, particularly sadness and fear, which can then lead them to believe that an issue is of national importance.

Criticisms and Critiques of the Theory

Critics have argued that a weakness of agenda setting theory is its bias toward aggregate-level analyses of public opinion (McCombs et al., 1997). Iyengar (1988) argued that people are not passive receptors of mass media content. Instead, people actively interpret, elaborate, and evaluate media content.

Critics have complained that the process of framing is a scattered conceptualization that lacks clear conceptual definitions and relies on context-specific operationalizations (Brosius & Eps, 1995; Entman, 1993; Scheufele, 1999).

Matthes (2009) listed many areas that need further research attention. First, the concept of framing must be further refined.

The frequently cited definition of framing by Entman (1993) includes moral evaluations of issues, which may not be ideal for theory advancement. Some researchers have not even made a distinction between agenda setting, framing, and priming (Iyengar & Kinder, 1987; McCombs et al., 1997; Zhou & Moy, 2007).

Second, there is a clear debate between researchers who favor a generic definition of frame and those who prefer an issue-specific definition. Researchers must specify how general a frame has to be in order for it to qualify as a generic frame. Many studies define frames from the aspect of a single news article, which may be successful for that specific study, but may not generalize beyond that article.

Third, most research on frames within the agenda setting literature has been descriptive. This research is helpful, but has not advanced the definition of frames. More nondescriptive research is needed if the definition of frames is to be further refined.

Fourth, very little research has examined visual aspects of frames. Instead, research has focused mostly on textual or verbal aspects of frames. Focusing only on verbal analyses loses a great deal of information that may be vital for better defining and understanding how framing works in agenda setting approaches.

Fifth, there has been a problem with research methods for many of the studies in the agenda setting area. Specifically, many studies suffer from reliability and validity problems in their research methodology. More rigorous statistical methods should be followed and better reporting should be done in future research if the theory is to advance.

Critics have argued that the concept of salience has multiple definitions that will prevent theory development (Takeshita, 2005). Some researchers (for example, McCombs & Shaw, 1972) describe agenda setting as the transfer of salience from the media to the public. According to this view, salience is the same as importance. Coming from a cognitive psychology perspective, however, some researchers refer to salience as meaning easily available and accessible from memory (Takeshita, 2005).

Measuring Variables in the Theory

Political knowledge scales. Shaker, L. (2009, Winter). Citizens' local political knowledge and the role of media access. *Journalism and Mass Communication Quarterly, 86,* 809–826.

Motivations for using the Internet scale. Roy, S. K. (2009). Internet uses and gratifications: A survey in the Indian context. *Computers in Human Behavior, 25,* 878–886.

Suggestions for Further Research

1. Extend the theory to corporate boards or leaders as agenda setters for corporate issues.
2. Examine the influence of information-seeking behaviors on the effects of agenda setting.
3. Explore demographic differences in social and nonsocial media usage, information seeking, and agenda setting in terms of their influence on knowledge of and attitudes about salient issues.
4. Analyze the full causal processes involved in first- and second-level agenda setting, priming, framing, accessibility, and salience.
5. Explore media bias effects and the effect of individual difference variables on media usage, media expertise, media trust, and issue knowledge.
6. Examine the extent to which the public are victims of the "primordial power" of the media versus the extent to which the public actively set the media's agenda.
7. Explore how and by whom agendas are set and changed across the four types of agenda setting (public, media, firm, and policy).
8. Look at how the public, media, and corporations handle multiple competing frames for the same and varied issues.
9. Explore the concept of multimedia multitasking and its influence on agenda setting.
10. Look at how media users set frames and prime the media to focus on specific agenda items.

References to Know

Dearing, J. W., & Rogers, E. M. (1996). *Communication concepts 6: Agenda-setting.* Thousand Oaks, CA: Sage.

McCombs, M. (1981). The agenda setting approach. In D. D. Nimmo & K. R. Sanders (Eds.), *Handbook of political communications* (pp. 121–140). Thousand Oaks, CA: Sage.

McCombs, M. (2004). *Setting the agenda: The mass media and public opinion.* Cambridge: Polity Press.

McCombs, M., & Shaw, D. (1972, Summer). The agenda-setting function of mass media. *Public Opinion Quarterly, 36,* 176–187.

Weick, K. E. (1992, September). Agenda setting in organizational behavior. *Journal of Management Inquiry, 1,* 171–182.

Implications of the Theory for Managers

Agenda setting theory examines how mass media and other policy-makers (1) help set people's own individual agendas about important issues and (2) help shape people's perceptions and thoughts about those issues. Successful organizations more often proactively work to shape the public's and their own employees' perceptions of important issues compared with less successful organizations.

For example, an organization can focus public attention on itself to help ensure that people are even thinking about the organization and its efforts. It can then work to help shape those public thoughts about the organization. For instance, policymakers can help frame issues by defining the problem in a way that is beneficial for the organization, diagnosing the causes of the problem, helping people make moral and ethical judgments about the problem, and suggesting remedies for the problem.

Your task as a successful manager is to help set the right agenda for the vision, mission, and goals of your organization. Specifically work with members of your organization to: (1) define problems in ways that benefit your organization, (2) frame issues in ways that help support organizational efforts, such as viewing situations positively or negatively, and (3) shape perceptions about important issues, such as setting a high urgency level for some issues and setting a low urgency level for others.

4

5

Attachment Theory

Attachment theory examines an individual's sense of the optimal balance between closeness to and distance from key people in his or her life (Ainsworth, 1967; Ainsworth & Bowlby, 1991; Bowlby, 1969, 1973, 1980). The theory attempts to explain the nature of the affective bonds that people make with each other (Smith, Murphy, & Coats, 1999). It assumes that early childhood experiences of attachment to caregivers have long-term effects on social relationships and the stress regulation of adults (Adshead, 2010). Attachment theory is a theory of psychosocial development that was based on animal models, such as that of Lorenz (1935), who examined how baby animals imprint on their mothers. Harlow and others (for example, Suomi, Harlow, & Domek, 1970) examined how monkeys reared in isolation from their mothers suffered severe emotional and social problems as adults, never formed an attachment ("privation"), grew up to be aggressive, and had difficulty interacting with other monkeys.

An attachment is a deep and enduring emotional bond between people that persists across time and space (Ainsworth, 1969; Bowlby, 1969). Attachments can be reciprocal, but are often one-way. They involve specific behaviors, such as wanting to spend time in the proximity of the person with whom one has an attachment when one feels upset, scared, or threatened (Bowlby, 1969). In an adult-child attachment relationship, an adult can respond to the needs of a child through being sensitive and by attending to the child's needs. Attachment behaviors appear to be universal across all cultures.

Bowlby (1969, 1973, 1980) theorized that people have thousands of early attachment experiences that influence their working mental models of the self and of other people in later life. The mental models that people form influence their thoughts, emotions, and behaviors in relationships with others in many ways. Research has shown that if an adult has developed an extremely negative view of attachment relationships, positive experiences with a partner or therapist can help bring about a reconstruction of a poor attachment mental model (Bowlby, 1988).

Ainsworth, Blehar, Waters, and Wall (1978) identified three styles of attachment that infants form with their mother: secure, anxious-ambivalent (or resistant), and avoidant. The styles were derived from behaviors exhibited by children left alone with a stranger for a short time, called the "strange situation." In secure attachment, the child is distressed when the mother leaves, is avoidant of the stranger alone but friendly with the mother present, and is happy when the mother returns. In anxious-ambivalent (resistant) attachment, the infant shows intense distress when the mother leaves, avoids the stranger, and resists the mother or pushes her away when she returns. In avoidant attachment, the child shows no distress when the mother leaves, plays normally with the stranger, and ignores the mother when she returns.

Bartholomew and Horowitz (1991) developed a 2×2 matrix of adult attachment. On one axis is the model of self: positive or negative (or dependence: low or high); on the other axis is the model of other: positive or negative (or avoidance: low or high). The four cells in the matrix are (1) secure (positive, positive); (2) preoccupied (negative, positive); (3) dismissing (positive, negative); and (4) fearful (negative, negative).

A person's attachment model can influence his or her career and workplace functioning (Lee & Hughley, 2001; van Ecke, 2007; Wolfe & Betz, 2004; Wright & Perrone, 2008). People who had secure attachments tend to see others as trusting and themselves as worth loving, and are able to control and cope with stressful events (Bartholomew & Horowitz, 1991; Buelow, Lyddon, & Johnson, 2002). Those who had preoccupied attachments trust others but not themselves, have low self-esteem, need reassurance and praise, pull away when getting feedback, and choose jobs based on salary, which can lead to low job and career satisfaction. Those with dismissing attachments are independently motivated because others cannot be trusted to meet their needs, do not seek emotional support from others during stress, tend not to accept criticism, compulsively work to avoid relationships with others, tend to work longer and harder than others, but believe that work interferes with their personal life. Those with fearful attachments do not trust others, have low self-esteem, tend not to self-disclose, have low intimacy and romantic involvement, tend to have poor social and emotional coping skills, tend not to seek emotional support from others during stress, and tend not to take orders well from bosses (Buelow et al., 2002; Hawkins, Howard, & Oyebode, 2007; Renfro-Michel, Burlew, & Robert, 2009).

Research also shows that attachment models can be related to ethical behavior and standards (Albert & Horowitz, 2009). In a study examining both managers and consumers in three culturally different samples, individuals with secure and preoccupied attachment models tended to believe that ethical transgressions were wrong. However, those with a dismissing attachment model were most likely to exploit, cheat, or deceive others, and displayed the greatest indifference to unethical situations.

Attachment models were also found to be related to leadership (Davidovitz, Mikulincer, Shaver, Izsak, & Popper, 2007; Popper & Mayseless, 2003; Popper Mayseless, & Castelnovo, 2000). For example, leaders who had attachment anxiety tended to be more self-serving, exhibiting poorer leadership qualities in task-oriented situations. Leaders with attachment-related avoidance had lower prosocial motives to lead, and tended not to act as a secure provider for followers, which tended to lead to poor follower socio-emotional functioning and poorer long-range mental health.

Attachment models were found to be related to helping others, turnover intentions, and emotional regulation (Richards & Schat, 2011). Mikulincer, Shaver, Gillath, and Nitzberg (2005) found that securely attached individuals were more likely to show greater compassion and to help a person in distress compared to those with less securely attached mental models.

Criticisms and Critiques of the Theory

Attachment theory has been criticized for a number of aspects (Field, 1996). First, the primary area of investigation has examined only behaviors that occur during momentary separations that are stressful for an individual. An example of this is Ainsworth's "strange situation" approach (1967, 1969; Ainsworth & Bell, 1970) in which children are examined regarding how they behave toward strangers in isolation from their mother. The theory requires a broader understanding of attachment processes over a range of time periods and a range of stressors. Second, the theory has been criticized for having circular reasoning in that attachment is defined by the behaviors of the attachment figure during an impending separation.

A third problem with the theory is that basically anything wrong with the child's behavior is the mother's "fault." The theory does not examine the wide range of attachments that people form and the impact of those on attitudes and behaviors across a person's lifetime, such as with father, siblings, friends, teachers, coaches, spiritual and religious leaders, guidance counselors, bosses and supervisors, coworkers, and so on. A fourth problem is that the theory has tended to examine only overreactive behaviors and not covert or attitudinal behaviors. The theory should therefore be extended to examine a wide range of outcomes stemming from a wide range of attachments to a wide range of figures throughout a person's life.

Harris (1998, 2009) has criticized the theory with regard to the nature versus nurture debate. The theory has a "nurture assumption" that kind, caring, loving parents always produce kind, caring, loving children. Harris (1998) argued that the theory ignores many other important influences on an individual's subsequent behaviors, such as peer group, neighborhood, environment, and genetics. Critics have argued that good parenting can make up for poor genetics; however, a lack of nurturing can seriously harm nature's best efforts (Harris, 1998). Lastly, Rutter (1979) argued that it is the quality of the relationship bond with the mother that is important, not merely the time spent with her.

Measuring Variables in the Theory

Relationship status scale. Bodie, G. D., Burleson, B. R., Gill-Rosier, J., McCullough, J. D., Holmstrom, A. J., Rack, J. J., Hanasono, L., & Mincy, J. (2011). Explaining the impact of attachment style on evaluations of supportive messages: A dual-process framework. *Communication Research, 38,* 228–247.

Meaning and purpose in the workplace scale. Mitroff, I. I., Denton, E. A., & Alpaslan, C. M. (2009, March). A spiritual audit of corporate America: Ten years later (Spirituality and attachment theory, an interim report). *Journal of Management, Spirituality and Religion, 6,* 27–41.

Work encouragement, organizational trust, and citizenship scales. Lin, C.-P. (2010). Modeling corporate citizenship, organizational trust, and work engagement based on attachment theory. *Journal of Business Ethics, 94,* 517–531.

Motives for exploration scales. Martin, A. M., III, Paetzold, R. L., & Rholes, W. S. (2010). Adult attachment and exploration: Linking attachment style to motivation and perceptions of support in adult exploration. *Basic and Applied Social Psychology, 32,* 196–205.

Relationship variables scales. Paulssen, M. (2009). Attachment orientation in business-to-business relationships. *Psychology & Marketing, 26,* 507–533.

Self-report measure of adult attachment. Fraley, R. C., Waller, N. G., & Brennan, K. A. (2000). An item response theory analysis of self-report measures of adult attachment. *Journal of Personality and Social Psychology, 78,* 350–365.

Social group attachment scale. Smith, E. R., Murphy, J., & Coats, S. (1999). Attachment to groups: Theory and measurement. *Journal of Personality and Social Psychology, 77,* 94–110.

5

Suggestions for Further Research

1. Examine how individual differences in adult attachment styles affect assorted relationship processes and outcomes.
2. Explore how people become attached to others in the workplace and at home and how those attachments change over time.
3. Look at how employee attachment styles influence helping others and the employee's commitment to stay with the organization over time.

4. Examine how attachment styles can affect employees taking time off to care for sick children or parents.
5. Explore how people use and maintain a hierarchy of attachment figures during a range of stressful situations.
6. Study the extent to which adults can change and improve their attachment mental models to improve their functioning.
7. Explore how attachment histories influence the forming and maintenance of supervisor-supervisee relationships.
8. Uncover moderators and mediators of the relations between attachment and work behaviors and attitudes.
9. Explore ways that employees regulate their cognitive, affective, and behavioral actions at work due to their attachment styles.
10. Examine the relationship between relationship efficacy and career-related self-efficacy, and the impact of attachment on them.
11. Examine personal and interpersonal factors that cause people to accept insecure leaders and comply with destructive influences.

References to Know

Ainsworth, M.D.S. (1967). *Infancy in Uganda: Infant care and the growth of love.* Baltimore, MD: Johns Hopkins University Press.

Bowlby, J. (1969). *Attachment and loss: Vol. 1. Attachment.* New York: Basic Books.

Bowlby, J. (1988). *A secure base: Clinical applications of attachment theory.* London: Routledge.

Feeney, J. A., & Shaver, P. R. (Eds.). (1999). *Handbook of attachment: Theory, research, and clinical applications.* New York: Guilford Press.

Mikulincer, M., & Shaver, P. R. (2007). *Attachment in adulthood: Structure, dynamics, and change.* New York: Guilford Press.

Implications of the Theory for Managers

Attachment theory examines how the types of attachments formed with caregivers early in life can influence important attitudes and behaviors of people throughout their lifetime. Based on the treatment received from important others, children tend to form positive or negative views of themselves (as being warm, loving, caring, capable, trusting, or as being mean, uncaring, calculating, and cold) and tend to form positive or negative views of others (as being trustworthy, loving, supportive, or as being deceitful, vengeful, unsupportive, and so on).

People's mental view of attachments can influence a number of their important workplace attitudes and behaviors, such as the level of closeness that they want to maintain with other people, the level of interpersonal support and praise that they want from their boss and from others, their leadership ability, their view of ethical behaviors and standards, their ability to handle stress, and their desire to seek emotional support from others during stressful situations.

Some managers tend to treat all their employees the same way when it comes to attention, praise, support, nurturing, caring, and so on. Attachment theory would recommend that you get to know each of your employees individually in order to design a unique interpersonal relationship with them. For each employee, find out his or her optimal levels of interpersonal relationship closeness, praise and attention, feedback and criticism, and emotional support during crisis situations. You may have to ask your employees about what type of supervisor-supervisee relationship works best for them. Then, work with your employees to create the kind of interpersonal relationship that helps them work at their best levels.

5

Remember that employees' views about relationships were created early in their lifetime and typically do not change without professional help. Therefore, don't try to change your employees. Instead, try to deliver the best interpersonal relationship that you can to meet each of your employees' current individual needs and expectations.

6

Attribution Theory

Attribution theory examines the ways that people determine retrospective causes for their own and for others' behavioral outcomes (Kelley, 1967, 1973; Weiner, 1985, 1986, 2010). The theory seeks to explain how people's perceived causes for their past successes or failures contribute to their current and future attitudes, motivation, and expectations for future successes or failures (Weiner, 1974). People tend to automatically ask "why" when noticing behavioral outcomes even when they have not been prompted to do so (Wong & Weiner, 1981).

The theory has two related sides: intrapersonal causal attribution and interpersonal causal attribution (Weiner, 2000). The intrapersonal process examines how a person determines the cause of her own successful or unsuccessful performance and how that perceived cause influences her subsequent attitudes and performance. The intrapersonal attribution process has seven phases: (1) outcome, (2) outcome-dependent affect, (3) causal antecedents, (4) causal ascriptions, (5) causal dimensions, (6) psychological consequences, and (7) behavioral consequences.

The intrapersonal attribution process begins with an outcome. Due to cognitive limitations, people can't pay attention to all of their behavioral outcomes (Weiner, 2000). People tend to pay attention to unusual, unexpected, or negative outcomes more than expected outcomes. If a person notices a behavioral outcome, then there are three possible affects (or feelings) that can occur as a result: positive (happy), unexpectedly negative, and negative (frustrated and sad).

A person's answer to the "why" question can be influenced by many sources, called "causal antecedents," such as past history of success or failure, social norms, and expectations. The causal antecedents influence "causal ascriptions" or "causal categories." Causal categories for the behavioral outcome could be perceived in one of two ways: in terms of achievement or of affiliation. Causal categories that are achievement related are ability, effort, task difficulty, luck, mood, fatigue, illness, and the like. Causal categories that are affiliation related are physical characteristics, personality, availability of the target, and so on.

People tend to select a causal dimension when trying to determine the reasons for others' behaviors or of others' outcomes. There are three causal dimensions: locus, stability, and controllability. Locus, or location, refers to whether the cause of the behavior or outcome was internal or external to the person. Stability refers to whether the cause tends to be stable or changing over time. Controllability refers to whether or not a person can control his or her behaviors or outcomes.

The result of an action can be due to factors within the person or due to factors in the environment (external to the person) (Heider, 1958; Rotter, 1966). Heider noted that behavioral outcomes are a result of three possible causes: ability, task difficulty, and effort. He saw ability and effort as reasons internal to the person, task difficulty as external to the person. Rotter acknowledged one internal cause (skill or ability), and one external cause (luck or chance).

Weiner et al. (1971) wrote about four main causes of achievement outcome: ability, effort, task difficulty, and luck. Ability and effort were seen as internal to the person, and task difficulty and luck were seen as external to the person. The result was a 2 × 2 matrix: one axis was locus of control: internal or external; the other axis was stability: stable or unstable. Thus a person could attribute his or her behavioral outcomes to (1) ability (internal, stable); (2) task difficulty (external, stable); (3) effort (internal, unstable); or (4) luck (external, unstable). Later formulations of the theory added two more possible causal dimensions: controllability/intentionality and globality (Weiner, 2000). Controllability/intentionality referred to whether or not the person could control his or her behavior. Globality was referred to as stability of achievement across situations.

6

The causal dimension that a person assigned to his or her behavioral outcome then influences cognitive and affective consequences for that person. For example, an outcome that was attributed to effort and hard work might lead to feelings of pride, high self-esteem, and high self-efficacy, accompanied by great expectations for future success. However, an outcome that was attributed to poor performance might lead to future expectations of hopelessness and failure. In addition, a person who blamed himself for not controlling something that was within his ability might experience feelings of guilt and shame. Finally, the psychological consequences experienced then lead to behavioral consequences for future performance, such as striving to achieve or not.

Individuals may not be entirely accurate when they attempt to attribute the causes for others' behavior. People tend to emphasize internal causes for others' behaviors even in light of important external environmental factors (Jones & Harris, 1967). Ross (1977) called this the "fundamental attribution error" and Jones (1979) called it the "over-attribution effect," although this effect has been shown to disappear over time (Burger, 1991; Truchot, Maure, & Patte, 2003). Another error in attribution is the "blame the victim" phenomenon in which people attribute the cause of a person's unfortunate circumstance to internal reasons rather than to external ones (Ryan, 1976). The "actor-observer" effect is another attribution error. This effect most often occurs in cases of negative behaviors; people tend to attribute their own behavior to external causes but attribute the behavior of others to internal causes (Jones & Nisbett, 1971). Last, there is a "self-serving attribution bias," which means that individuals tend to take responsibility for good behavioral outcomes and to deny responsibility for poor ones (Bradley, 1978; Miller & Ross, 1975; Riess, Rosenfeld, Melburg, & Tedeschi, 1981).

6

There is now considerable evidence that the self-serving bias also exists in groups and organizations in that they take credit for success, but blame failure on aspects of their environment. This phenomenon has been called a "group-serving bias" (Forsyth & Schlenker, 1977; Johns, 1999; Salancik & Meindl, 1984; Staw, McKechnie, & Puffer, 1983). There are two types of group-serving bias: (1) attributions that distinguish among contributions made by each individual group member and (2) attributions that focus on contributions of groups as a whole (Goncalo & Duguid, 2008).

People tend to make internal or external attributions about another person on the basis of three separate pieces of information: distinctiveness, consensus, and consistency (Kelley, 1967). Distinctiveness means that the person responds similarly in other types of situations. Consensus means that others typically respond the same way as this person. Consistency means that a similar response is produced in similar situations. Research has shown that people tend to attribute the cause of someone's behavior to external factors when all three (distinctiveness, consensus, and consistency) are high. However, people tend to attribute the cause of someone's behavior to internal factors when consensus is low, distinctiveness is low, but consistency is high (DiVitto & McArthur, 1978; Orvis, Cunningham, & Kelley, 1975).

The second side of attribution theory is the interpersonal attribution process (Weiner, 2000). The interpersonal process has four steps: (1) event, (2) cause or type, (3) responsibility antecedent, and (4) behavioral reaction. The event can be any sort of achievement or failure, stigmatizing condition, need for help, or aggressive act of another. The cause can be lack of effort, behavioral or psychological condition, or addictive condition. After perceiving the event and determining a cause or type, the individual then ponders responsibility antecedents, which lead to one of two conclusions: that the event was (1) the responsibility of the other person (which results in behavioral reactions to reprimand, condemn, neglect, or retaliate against that individual) or (2) not the responsibility of the other person (which results in behavioral reactions to help the person and not to reprimand, condemn, or retaliate against the person).

Attribution theory has had a resurgence (Martinko, Harvey, & Dasborough, 2011) and has been applied to such topics as leadership (Ellis, Ilgen, & Hollenbeck, 2006; Lam, Huang, & Snape, 2007; Martinko, Harvey, & Douglas, 2007); corporate reputation (Sjovall & Talk, 2004); entrepreneurship (Chattopadhyay, 2007); anti- and prosocial behavior (Greitemeyer & Weiner, 2008); individual entitlement (Harvey & Martinko, 2009); organizational performance (Jeong, 2009; Tessarolo, Pagliarussi, & Mattos da Luz, 2010); and stigma (Hegarty & Golden, 2008).

Criticisms and Critiques of the Theory

Attribution theory has been criticized for the number of causal dimensions. Researchers have argued that there could be more or fewer than the three causal dimensions of locus, stability, and controllability (Weiner, 1985). Anderson (1983) argued for six causal dimensions: locus, stability, globality, controllability, intentionality (the cause reflects an intention to behave), and changeability (the person can change the factors that determined the outcome). Weiner (1985) also argued that the causal dimensions are highly intercorrelated and may not be distinct from each other.

The theory has been criticized for focusing exclusively on causal determinants of outcomes. Buss (1978) criticized the theory for not adequately distinguishing "causes" for behavior from "reasons" for behavior. He argued that causes are things that bring about change, but that reasons are things for which a change is brought about, such as goals, purposes, and so on.

Critics have complained that the theory has not adequately defined a behavioral "outcome." Buss (1978) argued that researchers must distinguish between behaviors or actions that are performed by a person and occurrences that happen to a person. He argued that theorists have attempted to force a causal framework on all outcomes that people experience, whether those outcomes were the result of actions taken by a person or were occurrences that the person merely experienced.

Measuring Variables in the Theory

6

Effort, ability, task, strategy, and luck attribution scales. Dixon, A. L., Spiro, R. L., & Jamil, M. (2001, June). Successful and unsuccessful sales calls: Measuring salesperson attributions and behavioral intentions. *Journal of Marketing, 65,* 64–78.

Motives scales. De Stobbeleir, K.E.M., Ashford, S. J., & De Luque, M.F.S. (2010). Proactivity with image in mind: How employee and manager characteristics affect evaluations of proactive behaviors. *Journal of Occupational and Organizational Psychology, 83,* 347–369.

Attribution style questionnaire. Martinko, M. J., Moss, S. E., Douglas, S. C., & Borkowski, N. (2007). Anticipating the inevitable:

When leader and member attribution styles clash. *Organizational Behavior and Human Decision Processes, 104,* 158–174.

Suggestions for Further Research

1. Examine the similarities and differences between individual and group-based attributions and their influence on each other.
2. Explore the influence of group-based attributions on a broad range of behaviors in the field versus in the laboratory.
3. Look at the influence of individual and organizational differences, such as culture, on attributions.
4. Examine how factors that strengthen individual identification with the group can promote or deter attributions.
5. Explore the extent to which homogeneity and heterogeneity of group members can positively or negatively influence group-level attributions.
6. Study the extent to which the turnover rate influences group-level attributions that can influence behavioral measures.
7. Look at the influence of followers' attributional styles on their evaluation of leader effectiveness.
8. Examine the influence of collective attributions on team identity, performance, and effectiveness.
9. Study how collective attributions influence organizational performance during crisis versus typical situations.
10. Explore the influence of time on individual and collective attributions and its influence on attitudes and behaviors.

6

References to Know

Kelley, H. H. (1967). Attribution theory in social psychology. In D. Levine (Ed.), *Nebraska symposium on motivation* (Vol. 15, pp. 192–238). Lincoln: University of Nebraska Press.

Kelley, H. H., & Michela, J. L. (1980). Attribution theory and research. *Annual Review of Psychology, 31,* 457–501.

Rotter, J. B. (1966). Generalized expectancies for internal versus external control of reinforcement. *Psychological Monographs, 80,* 1–28.

Weiner, B. (1985). An attributional theory of achievement motivation and emotion. *Psychological Review, 92,* 548–573.

Weiner, B. (1986). *An attributional theory of motivation and emotion.* New York: Springer.

Implications of the Theory for Managers

Attribution theory examines how people tend to automatically determine the cause of their own and others' behaviors. The theory looks at how people tend to determine that the causes of behaviors are either internal to the person (for example, effort or ability) or external to the person (for example, luck or task difficulty). Managers tend to automatically determine the cause of their own and their employees' behaviors and then base their treatment of their employees on those causal attributions.

As a manager, you need to remember that employees tend to make attribution errors. For example, if employees perform successfully, they tend to give themselves credit for their success. However, if employees perform poorly, they tend to blame factors outside themselves (such as their boss) for their failure. You need to be aware of this attribution error and help employees determine the correct causes for their performance levels.

You also need to be aware that managers too tend to make attribution errors. If an employee performs successfully, managers tend to attribute that success to themselves (and not to the employee). However, if an employee performs poorly, then managers tend to blame the employee (and not take responsibility for their employee's poor performance). Work to reduce attribution errors by taking the blame when poor performance is your fault and helping employees perform at higher levels.

6

7

Balance Theory

The main idea in balance theory (also known as consistency theory) is that maintaining a harmonious balance of sentiments is the implicit goal in interactions with other people (Heider, 1946, 1958; Newcomb, 1953, 1968). A major assumption of the theory is that people tend to organize their thoughts, beliefs, attitudes, and behaviors in meaningful, sensible, and consistent ways (Heider, 1946; Osgood & Tannenbaum, 1955; Festinger, 1957; Zajonc, 1960).

According to the theory, people are aware of their surroundings and of the events that take place in their environment (their life space) through a process of perception. People are affected by their environment and cause changes in their environment. People have wants and sentiments with regard to others, have a sense of belonging with others, and hold others accountable to certain standards. All of this determines the roles that other people play in a person's life space and how that individual reacts to other people (Heider, 1958).

A key concept in the theory is "sentiments" (Heider, 1958). Sentiments are the positive or negative valuations that an individual has toward other people or objects. A sentiment refers to the way a person p feels about something, such as another person o or an object x.

Positive sentiments reflect "liking" and negative sentiments reflect "disliking." Sentiments include emotions, thoughts, behavioral intentions, and qualities of the other person or object. The sentiment is thought of as the connecting link between two people or between a person and an object. The theory assumes that

7

people sometimes make decisions based on affective sentiments instead of rational thoughts (Peterson, 2006).

People are particularly aware of the sentiments that others in their life space have toward them. For instance, people tend to notice whether others in their life space tend to like or dislike them. Moreover, if we notice that a person p likes or dislikes a person o, then we also know that person o plays an important role in person p's life that could affect person p's thoughts and behaviors.

According to balance theory, people tend to form balanced, or harmonious, states in their interactions with other people. In a balanced state, people and objects seem to fit together without stress and with no pressure to change. For example, a balanced, positive state arises when p likes o (+1), p likes x (+1), and o likes x (+1). In this case, the p-o-x triad is all positive (+1, +1, and +1). A balanced state can also be all negative, such as when p dislikes o (−1), p dislikes x (−1), and o dislikes x (−1). In this case, the p-o-x triad is all negative (−1, −1, and −1). Supposing you like me (positive, or +1), and you like your new friend (positive, or +1), but I don't like your new friend (negative, or −1). The result is (+1 times +1 times −1), which mathematically has a negative result, and shows that the situation is not balanced. On the other hand, if I also like your new friend (positive, or +1), then the result would be (+1 times +1 times +1), which would have a positive, or balanced, result.

The theory examines interpersonal interaction within a person's environment or situation, which constantly changes. Thus the current and future environment or situation can change a person's perceptions of interpersonal interactions. For example, Zajonc (1968a) found that mere repeated exposure of a person to an object tends to enhance that person's attitude toward that object. The term "mere exposure" simply means that the object was accessible to the person's perception.

People may change their perceptions of another person when there is a chance for future contact or interaction with that person. Thus interpersonal perceptions may change when there is a chance for reciprocity regarding sentiments with the other person, compared to when the other person will remain an abstract, separated stranger (Insko & Adewole, 1979).

As noted, balance theory posits that people strive to achieve balanced sentiments in their interactions with others. In general, people tend to align their attitudes more toward others whom they like, compared to those they don't like (Chaiken & Eagly, 1983; Sampson & Insko, 1964). However, if balance cannot be achieved, then people will feel uncertain and unstable about their interpersonal relations, which can lead to feelings of tension, a desire to change, negative affect, and physiological arousal (Burdick & Burnes, 1958; Festinger & Hutte, 1954; Jordan, 1953; Osgood & Tannenbaum, 1955; Taylor, 1967; Tsai & Levenson, 1997). For example, people may experience discomfort, or what Festinger (1957) called "dissonance," when they should have made a different choice, such as in buyer's remorse. People will actively move to avoid dissonant thoughts to create a state of consonance, or balance.

The theory offers two remedies for restoring balance to unbalanced situations: (1) a change in sentiments or (2) a change in the unit relationship, or leaving the relationship (Heider, 1958). For example, Hovland, Janis, and Kelley (1953) argued that if a person thinks positively about a speaker, but that speaker says something offensive, then the listener may develop more negative feelings toward the speaker in order to restore balance. Treadway, Ferris, Duke, Adams, and Thatcher (2007) described how a supervisor was in an unbalanced situation when giving a favored supervisee a poor performance review. The supervisor could restore balance to the situation by distancing the favored supervisee from the poor performance.

Researchers have debated whether balance processes are implicit or explicit (Insko, Sedlak, & Lipsitz, 1982). Balance processes may involve explicit attention to environmental stimuli, such as toward other people and other objects. However, it is unlikely that people will specifically go through the thought processes of "I like you" and "you like me" and so forth. Insko et al. argued that balance processes can be highly overpracticed and so may occur more or less automatically without explicit attention and cognitions. In contrast, Cacioppo and Petty (1981) argued that complex balance processes always require ample time or motivation for thought.

Criticisms and Critiques of the Theory

Balance theory was originally criticized for examining no more than three entities (*p*, person one; *o*, person two; and *x*, the object of interest) (Cartwright & Harary, 1956). This view was criticized for being too simplistic and for not examining the wide number of people and objects experienced by individuals in real life. Later formulations extended the theory to an infinite number of people and objects (for example, Cartwright & Harary). However, those views became so cognitively complicated that later uses of the theory returned to the original three-part formulation (Homburg & Stock, 2005).

Some theorists have argued that balance theories are just wrong. For example, it may just be more pleasant to agree with someone else than to disagree with him or her. Zajonc (1968b) concluded that attraction and agreement effects are damaging to the principles of balance theory.

Critics have argued that the theory tends to examine positive interactions more than negative ones. For example, Newcomb (1968) restricted the balance-imbalance distinction only to those cases where p likes o, thus ruling out some of the possible combinations of p, o, and x. Further, some researchers have used only positive scales, such as pleasantness (Jordan, 1963), instead of using scales with a wider range of cognitions.

The theory has also been criticized for its assumption that people always want stress-free, balanced interpersonal interactions (Osgood & Tannenbaum, 1955). Some people, instead, actively seek to create imbalance or to find unbalanced situations because they enjoy the stresses and strains caused by the imbalance.

The theory has been criticized in its oversimplification of "balanced" versus "unbalanced." According to the theory, people are either balanced or not. Later formulations have created ranges of balance or imbalance, such as in Cartwright and Harary's "degree of balance" (1956), to improve on the theory.

Critics have examined the time that it takes for people to form perceptions of balance or imbalance. Cacioppo and Petty (1981) found that people spontaneously direct their attention to others when judging pleasantness. The authors found that people devoted the shortest amount of time to assessing attraction (p-o), more time to assessing agreement or disagreement (p-x compared to o-x), and even more time to assessing balance or imbalance (p-o-x). Cacioppo and Petty concluded that three different and independent judgmental tendencies may be occurring, which would be detrimental to a balance theory explanation.

Measuring Variables in the Theory

Balance theory items in a sales context. Homburg, C., & Stock, R. M. (2005, May). Exploring the conditions under which sales-person work satisfaction can lead to customer satisfaction. *Psychology & Marketing, 22,* 393–420.

Consistent/inconsistent, pleasant/unpleasant, and discordant/harmonious scale items. Insko, C. A., & Adewole, A. (1979). The role of assumed reciprocation of sentiment and assumed similarity in the production of attraction and agreement effects in *p-o-x* triads. *Journal of Personality and Social Psychology, 37,* 790–808.

Interpersonal attraction scales. McCroskey, J. C., & McCain, T. A. (1974). The measurement of interpersonal attraction. *Speech Monographs, 41,* 261–266.

Interpersonal attraction scales. McCroskey, L. L., McCroskey, J. C., & Richmond, V. P. (2006, February). Analysis and improvement of the measurement of interpersonal attraction and homophily. *Communication Quarterly, 54,* 1–31.

Fan identification scale items. Trail, G. T., & James, J. D. (2001, March). The motivation scale for sport consumption: Assessment of the scale's psychometric properties. *Journal of Sport Behavior, 24,* 108–127.

Suggestions for Further Research

1. Examine customer attitudes toward celebrities and sports figures, products and services, and their manufacturers.
2. Explore balanced and unbalanced perceptions of fans regarding off-the-job behaviors of politicians, sports figures, and celebrities.
3. Look at how people treat separate individuals as a single entity in balance-process perceptions, especially in negative balance states.
4. Compare balance processes for individual others versus for group others.
5. Explore the ability of customers to substitute desired and undesired products and services to rebalance their situation.

7

6. Examine the differences among Fournier's fifteen brand relationships (1998) with customers in balance processes.
7. Look at hierarchical or multilevel balance perceptions of others and of objects, such as valuing family over work, versus the traditional single level of perceptions.
8. Explore how focusing messages (for example, advertising and marketing) on those in unbalanced states may move them to new balanced states and behaviors (for example, purchasing decisions).
9. Look at the extent to which people must receive supportive communication in order to maintain a balanced state.
10. Examine the range of balance and imbalance levels on the ease or difficulty with which people's behaviors can be changed.
11. Explore individual difference variables in preferences for maintaining unbalanced versus balanced states.

References to Know

Heider, F. (1946). Attitudes and cognitive organization. *Journal of Psychology, 21,* 107–112.

Heider, F. (1958). *The psychology of interpersonal relations.* Hoboken, NJ: Wiley.

Insko, C. A. (1984). Balance theory, the Jordan paradigm, and the Wiest tetrahedron. In L. Berkowitz (Ed.), *Advances in experimental social psychology* (Vol. 18, pp. 89–140). New York: Academic Press.

Newcomb, T. M. (1953). An approach to the study of communicative acts. *Psychological Review, 60,* 393–404.

Newcomb, T. M. (1968). Interpersonal balance. In R. P. Abelson, W. J. Aronson, T. M. McGuire, T. M. Newcomb, M. J. Rosenberg, & P. H. Tannenbaum (Eds.), *Theories of cognitive consistency: A source book* (pp. 28–51). Chicago: Rand McNally.

7

Implications of the Theory for Managers

A major assumption in balance theory is that people tend to organize their thoughts, beliefs, attitudes, and behaviors in meaningful, sensible, and consistent ways. People tend to keep liking other people and things that they already like, and tend to keep disliking other people and things that they already dislike. This tendency can have a major impact on any change efforts that you'd like to make in your workgroup or organization. People also tend to make their judgments of "like" or "dislike" fairly quickly, often without much thought.

When attempting to make changes, find out where your employees already have positively or negatively balanced thoughts. For example, an employee may like another employee because they both dislike keeping a neat work area or both dislike double-checking their work. Changing such employee thoughts can be difficult. If you are going to change the work habits of these employees, then you will probably have to separate these two individuals and expose them to new people who have different views than they do. Just the "mere exposure" to another person over time can help improve someone's perceptions of or attitudes toward that person.

In addition, think about what positively or negatively balanced thoughts you might have that could be preventing you from growing and making positive changes in your life. For example, you might not want to play on the company softball team because Joe loves the company softball team, and you don't like Joe. In order for you to play on the company team, you will need to do one of two things: wait for Joe to leave the team, or change your thoughts about Joe, so that you can rebalance your thoughts positively about playing on the team. Stay aware of how you balance your attitudes toward other people and other things.

7

8

Control Theory

Control theory, or cybernetic theory, examines self-regulating systems, both mechanistic and humanistic. The theory's central ideas have been around for many decades (for example, Cannon, 1929), but Wiener (1948) is generally attributed with establishing control theory as a distinct body of thought. Control theory has had a major impact on a diverse number of fields, such as management, engineering, applied mathematics, economics, and health care.

According to control theory, the feedback loop is the basic unit of cybernetic control (Carver & Scheier, 1982). The feedback loop contains four elements: (1) a referent standard, (2) a sensor, (3) a comparator, and (4) an effector. Many people have used the example of a thermostat to describe how the four parts of the feedback loop work together (Klein, 1989). When a thermostat controls the temperature of a room, the referent standard is the thermostat's set temperature, the sensor is the device that monitor's the room's temperature, the comparator is the mechanism that compares the room's current temperature with the set temperature, and the effector is a device that can change the temperature of the room, such as a furnace or air conditioner.

In the feedback loop process, the sensor (also called input behavior) continually compares the actual room temperature with the set room temperature. If the comparison shows no discrepancy between the set temperature and the actual temperature, then the system takes no action to change the room temperature, and merely continues to monitor the room. However, if the comparison reveals a discrepancy between the set room temperature and the actual room temperature, then the system takes action. If the actual room temperature is below the set temperature, then the effector (also called output behavior) will turn on the furnace to warm up the room until the desired temperature is reached. If the actual room temperature is above the set temperature, then the effector will turn on the air conditioner to cool off the room until the desired temperature is reached.

Feedback loops can be either positive or negative (Powers, 1973). A feedback loop is negative when a signal is given to an employee that his performance is below the standard. In that situation, the employee would take action to improve his performance so that his actual performance reaches the performance standard. A feedback loop is positive when a signal is given to an employee that his performance should continue to depart from the performance standard. For the most part, in human behavior, there are rarely times when a positive feedback loop is used to help shape behavior away from a performance standard, although this is often the case for mechanical systems.

Control theory has two primary elements that help describe human behavior: a cognitive element and an affective element (Carver & Scheier, 1981). In the cognitive element, individuals have goal standards for their performance, they process how well they are currently performing their task, and they compare their performance level to their goal standard. In the affective element, if individuals perceive a discrepancy between their desired performance level and their actual performance level, then they make behavioral changes that arise from their desire to resolve the performance discrepancy.

In the workplace, employees perform more than one task at a time, which means that they will have feedback loops for every task they perform. According to control theory, all of these feedback loops are organized in a hierarchy of importance for individuals. Through trial and error, the means that are used to reduce performance discrepancies in the most important feedback loops are then used to reduce discrepancies in the less important feedback loops (Powers, 1973).

For example, a salesperson might be assigned to increase new sales contacts, a job that can comprise more than one task, such as finding potential customers and then making initial contacts. According to control theory, there would be a separate feedback loop for each task and for each task's lower-level behaviors, such as searching for customers and finding addresses or phone numbers (Klein, 1989). The final result is a cascading set of feedback loops that starts with the most important performance goal for the salesperson (that of selling more company products). The human body is full of hierarchies of cascading feedback loops that regulate bodily functions from the most important down to the least important, such as from keeping the heart beating and the lungs breathing down to scratching an itch (Powers, 1973).

Criticisms and Critiques of the Theory

Control theory has been effective at explaining purposeful human behavior. Many researchers have tried to extend the cybernetic aspects of mechanical behavior to human behavior while trying to preserve the conceptual simplicity in the original cybernetic principles (Fellenz, 1997). However, control theory has been repeatedly criticized as being too mechanistic for explaining human behavior. Many critics have concluded that although control theory is appropriate for mechanistic systems, it is inappropriate to apply it to human behavior (Locke, 1991).

Control theory researchers have predominantly focused on negative feedback loops and ignored positive feedback loops. In mechanical systems, both negative and positive feedback loops are prevalent and useful. However, for humans in real-life situations, negative feedback loops seem to receive primary focus at the expense of the benefits of shaping behavior away from past performance standards.

A major criticism of control theory is that action is taken only to change or improve behavior when a discrepancy is detected. Many times in human behavior, innovations and changes are made without any detected discrepancies. There can be many reasons why behaviors are changed besides detection of discrepancies, but control theory does not account for these other reasons.

Control theory does not offer much explanation about the origins and difficulty levels of performance standards. The theory basically ignores how and why performance standards are set in the first place. It is silent about who sets performance standards,

8

when they get set, how they are set, and when they are changed, and about the influences of all of those on resultant performance levels.

Control theory had its origins in cybernetic systems and was expanded to human systems. Due to this mechanistic setting, control theory ignored the meaning of the information that was sent to the system about performance discrepancies. The signal that was sent was merely data stating that actual performance met the performance standard or was above or below the standard. No information was sent regarding the meaning of that current state. However, the meaning of information is particularly important for people. Humans need to know both that the performance standard was met or not and what that means for the individual, the organization, and other stakeholders (Fellenz, 1997).

Measuring Variables in the Theory

Action-state orientation scale. Diefendorff, J. M., Hall, R. J., Lord, R. G., & Strean, M. L. (2000). Action-state orientation: Construct validity of a revised measure and its relationship to work-related variables. *Journal of Applied Psychology, 85,* 250–263.

Action Control Scale (ACS-90). Kuhl, J. (1994). Action versus state orientation: Psychometric properties of the Action Control Scale (ACS-90). In J. Kuhl & J. Beckmann (Eds.), *Volition and personality: Action versus state orientation* (pp. 47–59). Seattle: Hogrefe & Huber.

Treatment Self-Regulation Questionnaire (TSRQ). Levesque, C. S., Williams, G. C., Elliot, D., Pickering, M. A., Bodenhamer, B., & Finley, P. J. (2007). Validating the theoretical structure of the Treatment Self-Regulation Questionnaire (TSRQ) across three different health behaviors. *Health Education Research, 22,* 691–702.

General Causality Orientations Scale (GCOS). Deci, E. L., & Ryan, R. M. (1985). The general causality orientations scale: Self-determination in personality. *Journal of Research in Personality, 19,* 109–134.

8

Self-Regulation Questionnaire (SRQ-A). Ryan, R. M., & Connell, J. P. (1989). Perceived locus of causality and internalization: Examining reasons for acting in two domains. *Journal of Personality and Social Psychology, 57,* 749–761.

Self-Regulation Questionnaire (SRQ). Brown, J. M., Miller, W. R., & Lawendowski, L. A. (1999). The self-regulation questionnaire. In L. VandeCreek & T. L. Jackson (Eds.), *Innovations in clinical practice: A source book* (Vol. 17, pp. 281–289). Sarasota, FL: Professional Resource Press.

Input control, behavior control, output control questionnaire. Snell, S. A. (1992). Control theory in strategic human resource management: The mediating effect of administrative information. *Academy of Management Journal, 35,* 292–327.

Suggestions for Further Research

1. Examine how, when, and why individuals override or change current behavioral standards in favor of new standards.
2. Explore how people change and create hierarchies of performance standards.
3. Investigate the most effective ways to give performance discrepancy feedback to individuals.
4. Examine how people coordinate individual and group performance standard hierarchies.
5. Study the most effective ways to take action to reduce performance discrepancies.
6. Explore the effects of symmetry or asymmetry of positive versus negative performance discrepancies on performance for the same and for different tasks.
7. Examine the effectiveness of input control, behavior control, and output control in different types of organizational settings and contexts.
8. Investigate the point at which people give up on changing their performance when a discrepancy is perceived to be too large to correct.
9. Examine the parallel use of both positive and negative feedback loops to shape human behavior toward desired performance standards.

8

10. Investigate the strategic use of purposefully setting easy or difficult-to-reach performance standards in terms of the effectiveness of positive or negative feedback loops and their impact on task performance.

References to Know

Carver, C. S., & Scheier, M. F. (1981). *Attention and self-regulation: A control theory approach to human behavior.* New York: Springer.

Carver, C. S., & Scheier, M. F. (1982). Control theory: A useful conceptual framework for personality—social, clinical, and health psychology. *Psychological Bulletin, 92,* 111–135.

Carver, C. S., & Scheier, M. F. (1990). Principles of self-regulation: Action and emotion. In E. T. Higgins & R. M. Sorrentino (Eds.), *Handbook of motivation and cognition* (Vol. 2, pp. 3–52). New York: Guilford Press.

Carver, C. S., & Scheier, M. F. (1999). Themes and issues in the self-regulation of behavior. In R. S. Wyer Jr. (Ed.), *Advances in social cognition: Vol. 7. Perspectives on behavioral self-regulation* (pp. 1–105). Mahwah, NJ: Erlbaum.

Klein, H. J. (1989). An integrated control theory model of work motivation. *Academy of Management Review, 14,* 150–172.

Implications of the Theory for Managers

The main idea in control theory is that people are motivated to behave when they see that there is a discrepancy between their standard for performance and their actual performance level, according to a feedback loop process. Your task as a manager is to facilitate and enhance this discrepancy perception for your employees.

First, set performance standards with your employees. They need to know specifically what they are supposed to do and how they are supposed to do it. Work with your employees and set up specific, measurable performance standards for all the important tasks that they perform.

Second, establish a system for monitoring employee performance levels. Your employees need to know how well they are performing their important tasks. Work with them to create a system that monitors and tracks the specific performance levels for each important task that your employees perform.

Third, create a system for comparing the performance standard with your employees' actual performance level. According to control theory, people are motivated when they see discrepancies between desired and actual performance. Your task as a manager is to help your employees see any discrepancies between their desired and their actual performance levels.

Finally, if a discrepancy exists between employee performance standards and actual performance levels, the most important step is to find out why there is a discrepancy and then take action to reduce it. For example, maybe your employees need further instructions on how to perform the task, need better equipment, or need training and education. Work with your employees to find out how to help them perform according to performance standards.

8

9

Diffusion of Innovations Theory

Diffusion of innovations theory examines the process through which information is communicated to people or organizations over time that can lead to the use of an innovation (Bass, 1969; Rogers, 1983). An innovation can be a good, service, practice, or idea that people perceived to be new (Rogers, 1983, 2004). The newness does not depend so much on the creation date of the item, but refers more to the newness of the application for helping address a need or for solving some sort of problem. Newness also refers to people having a positive reaction to using the item themselves; they may have known about an item before, but may have never thought about using it themselves.

The characteristics of an innovation can help explain its adoption rate. Innovations tend to be adopted more quickly when they (1) have a relative advantage over existing methods; (2) are compatible with existing values, past experiences, and current needs; (3) are simple to understand; (4) can be tried out or played with by potential adopters; and (5) are observable, such that adopters can see the results for themselves.

Diffusion is the process through which an innovation is communicated, or shared, through communication channels over time to people in a social system. Communication involves people exchanging and creating information that results in collective understanding about the innovation. Communication channels include face-to-face, electronic, and other forms of information sharing. Communication about innovations tends to involve two-way communication among people, rather than one-way communication from a source to an audience (Rogers & Kincaid, 1981).

The theory includes the innovation-decision process, which comprises five stages: (1) knowledge, (2) persuasion, (3) decision, (4) implementation, and (5) confirmation (Rogers, 1983). In the knowledge stage, the individual becomes aware of the innovation. Some researchers (for example, Coleman, 1966) have argued that individuals tend to be passive in this stage, whereas others see individuals as seeking out innovations. Hassinger (1959) argued that individuals tend not to expose themselves to communication about innovations without first having experienced a need or interest in those innovations. Individuals can be early or late "knowers" of information about innovations. Rogers (1983) described early knowers as having more education, social status, exposure to mass media, channels of interpersonal communication, change agent contact, social participation, and cosmopolitan orientation, compared to late knowers.

The diffusion of innovation takes time, so not everyone adopts the innovation at the same moment. Previously, researchers disagreed over names for people who adopted innovations early or later, but Rogers's labels (1962) became the dominant terminology. Rogers showed that the curve of adoption follows an S shape that rises from the lower left to the upper right. The lower-left slope of the S demonstrates that the adoption rate starts out slowly, then rapidly increases as the innovation is quickly adopted. The upper part of the S curve represents the extended time that it takes for late individuals to adopt the innovation. Bass (1969) also proposed a now classic "saddle-shaped" innovation adoption curve, and other shaped curves are possible.

The term "innovativeness" refers to the degree to which an individual or organization adopts relatively early compared to others (Rogers, 2002). Rogers (1983) created five ideal categories of adopters: (1) innovators (venturesome, 2.5 percent of people); (2) early adopters (respectable, 13.5 percent); (3) early majority (deliberate, 34 percent); (4) late majority (skeptical, 34 percent); and (5) laggards (traditional, 16 percent). The "innovativeness-needs paradox" describes how the people who could most benefit from the adoption of an innovation are often the ones who last adopt it. Individuals or organizations who are oriented beyond their community have been called "cosmopolitans" and tend to adopt early, whereas individuals or organizations who are oriented toward their immediate community have been called "locals" and adopt later (Gouldner, 1957; Merton, 1957; Robertson & Wind, 1983.

As more and more people adopt an innovation, the adopters exert pressure or influence on others to also adopt the technology. Rogers (1983) called this phenomenon "the diffusion effect." However, "overadoption" can occur when pressures rise so high that reluctant individuals go ahead and adopt an innovation that they should not adopt.

According to the theory, innovations are diffused through organizations in five stages: (1) agenda setting, (2) matching, (3) redefining or restructuring, (4) clarifying, and (5) routinizing. At each stage, there are specific events, actions, and decisions that occur, and later stages cannot take place until previous stages have been completed. Typically, organizations move steadily through the five stages, although sometimes the process moves slowly. However, it is possible for one or more stages of the process to be skipped or for organizations to "backtrack" instead of moving directly through all five stages.

The first two stages, agenda setting and matching, take place during the "initiation" or initial part of adopting an innovation. The initiation part includes all of the information gathering, conceptualizing, forecasting, visualizing, and planning that lead up to the decision to adopt the innovation. Agenda setting involves one or more people in the organization who have identified a problem and then seek an innovation to help solve that problem. The second stage of the process is matching. In reality, most organizations tend to focus on solutions, then once those solutions are found, focus on applying them to specific problems (March, 1981). Thus most organizations continually scan for innovations, then try to match promising innovations to relevant problems.

If the first two stages of the process are successful, then the organization decides to adopt the innovation. Implementing the newly adopted innovation involves stages three through five of the process. The third stage is called "redefining" or "restructuring." Typically the innovation won't fit the organization exactly, so it must be modified to fit the organizational culture, structure, or other aspect. The organization itself also can be changed to fit the innovation, such as when a new division is created to monitor and maintain the innovation.

9

The fourth stage, clarifying, involves helping everyone understand the purpose, meaning, and functions of the innovation, as the innovation goes into wider use. This stage involves identifying and correcting misunderstandings and side effects that can arise as people adopt the innovation.

The fifth stage, routinizing, involves making the innovation a habit or routine for everyone. The purpose of this stage is to help ensure that the innovation becomes a part of the organizational identity and to prevent any efforts to reject or "deimplement" the innovation in favor of prior methods.

Rogers (2004) described recent trends in diffusion of innovation research. For example, a "critical mass" (or "tipping point") is the point at which so many people have adopted an innovation that adoption continues because it becomes self-sustaining (Mahler & Rogers, 1999). The theory has moved from examining linear communication of messages from one individual to another to focusing on communication among potential adopters of an innovation via social networks of individuals, groups, and organizations (Peres, Muller, & Mahajan, 2010). Finally, research about the theory has examined the process of "re-invention," exploring how an innovation evolves, changes, and is transformed by adopters during the diffusion process.

Criticisms and Critiques of the Theory

A basic assumption of the diffusion of innovations theory is that all new methods are helpful and productive and should therefore be adopted. Little space in the theory is devoted to the methods that organizations use to screen out or filter bad ideas from implementation. Some innovations may not fit an organization's culture, mission, or values, and so should not be adopted. Critics have argued that more attention should be devoted to examining how organizations decide not to use innovations.

The theory has also been criticized for assuming that all adoptions of innovations produce positive results (Goss, 1979). Rogers himself (1983) agreed that researchers have not spent enough time examining the consequences of adoption of innovation. During the innovation adoption process, decision makers should discuss and predict the advantages and disadvantages of adopting the new technology, but this is seldom done. Typically, decision makers only examine the positive aspects of innovation adoption, which can lead to disastrous results. The theory has devoted some time to negative consequences of adoptions, but more attention is needed.

The theory has been criticized for assuming that all good innovations are adopted. It has tended to ignore the fact that some excellent innovations have not been adopted. The theory has not examined why these innovations have been overlooked, despite poor innovations having been adopted. Rogers (1983) gave the example of the failure of the fast Dvorak keyboard (with the most frequently used letters in the middle of the keyboard) to be adopted, whereas the much slower QWERTY keyboard remains in almost exclusive use.

The theory has been criticized for describing people who adopt innovations later, or never at all, in negative ways, such as with the term "laggards." The theory ignores the positive aspects of maintaining and valuing traditional ways and methods for doing things and rejecting newer, untested methods that could damage or destroy cultures and societies.

The theory has tended to focus only on technological innovations to the exclusion of other types of innovations. This may have occurred because Rogers (1983) specifically described the "hardware" and "software" aspects of technological innovations and ignored other types of innovations.

Measuring Variables in the Theory

Perceived attributes scale. Pankratz, M,. Hallfors, D., & Cho, H. (2002). Measuring perceptions of innovation adoption: The diffusion of a federal drug prevention policy. *Health Education Research, 17,* 315–326.

Intraorganizational diffusion and other measures. Pae, J. H., Kim. N., Han, J. K., & Yip, L. (2002). Managing intraorganizational diffusion of innovations: Impact of buying center dynamics and environments. *Industrial Marketing Management, 31,* 710–726.

Cosmopolitan-local orientation scale. London, M., Cheney, L. A., & Tavis, R. L. (1977). The relationship between cosmopolitan-local

9

orientation and job performance. *Journal of Vocational Behavior, 11,* 182–195.

Innovation awareness scale. Borrego, M., Froyd, J. E., & Hall, T. S. (2010, July). Diffusion of engineering education innovations: A survey of awareness and adoption rates in U.S. engineering departments. *Journal of Engineering Education, 99,* 185–207.

Suggestions for Further Research

1. Examine negative influences of current adopters on future adopters, and of future adopters on past adopters.
2. Explore the differences between adopting functions as compared to adopting devices that perform versions of that function.
3. Look at the differences in adoption rates for innovations with current versus deferred benefits, such as for safety or medical prevention.
4. Create better heuristic devices for estimating the adoption rates of new technologies and innovations compared to current methods.
5. Refine the concepts of "adopters," "innovators," and "imitators."
6. Examine how aspects of the social system's structure and social norms influence adoption or rejection of innovations.
7. Look at the attributes of competing innovations and their influence on adoption or rejection of those innovations.
8. Examine the point at which a critical mass occurs that results in sustainable innovation adoption.
9. Explore the influence of the age of the innovation, the percentage of adopters, and the number of adopters in the system on adoption.
10. Examine the diffusion patterns of innovations across industries and across nations for global businesses.

References to Know

Bass, F. M. (1969). A new product growth model for consumer durables. *Management Science, 15,* 215–227.

Rogers, E. M. (1983). *Diffusion of innovations* (3rd ed.). New York: Free Press.

Rogers, E. M. (2002). Diffusion of preventive innovations. *Addictive Behaviors, 27,* 989–993.

Rogers, E. M. (2002). The nature of technology transfer. *Science Communication, 23,* 323–341.

Rogers, E. M. (2004). A prospective and retrospective look at the diffusion model. *Journal of Health Communication, 9,* 13–19.

Implications of the Theory for Managers

Diffusion of innovations theory examines the process through which information is communicated to people or organizations over time that can lead to the use of an innovation. The better-performing managers don't sit by and let innovations come to them. Instead, they actively seek out innovations and other new solutions that might help them solve their problems or perform more effectively. Stay on top of the innovations in your field by reading trade journals, accessing networking sites, talking with experts, and attending trade shows.

The success of an innovation adoption depends on how it is implemented. Individuals and groups will discuss the innovation in order to understand and make sense of it, which can help or hurt the implementation of the innovation in your organization. Actively work with new adopters to ensure that they understand how and why an innovation has been adopted. Responsively address their concerns and answer their questions so that the innovation is effectively used and is not rejected. Like individuals, organizations often adopt innovations at a specific point on the adoption curve, such as early or late compared to their peers. To be more effective and more competitive, examine whether or not you should change the point at which you typically adopt innovations.

10

Dynamic Capabilities Theory

Dynamic capabilities theory examines how firms integrate, build, and reconfigure their internal and external firm-specific competencies into new competencies that match their turbulent environment (Teece, Pisano, & Shuen, 1997). The theory assumes that firms with greater dynamic capabilities will outperform firms with smaller dynamic capabilities. The aim of the theory is to understand how firms use dynamic capabilities to create and sustain a competitive advantage over other firms by responding to and creating environmental changes (Teece, 2007).

Capabilities are a collection of high-level, learned, patterned, repetitious behaviors that an organization can perform better relative to its competition (Nelson & Winter, 1982; Winter, 2003). Organizational capabilities are called "zero-level" (or "zero-order") capabilities, as they refer to how an organization earns a living by continuing to sell the same product, on the same scale, to the same customers (Winter, 2003, p. 991).

Dynamic capabilities are called "first-order" capabilities because they refer to intentionally changing the product, the production process, the scale, or the markets served by a firm (Winter, 2003). An organization has dynamic capabilities when it can integrate, build, and reconfigure its internal and external firm-specific capabilities in response to its changing environment. For example, whereas organizational capabilities have to do with efficient exploitation of existing resources, dynamic capabilities refer to efficient exploration and implementation of new opportunities (March, 1991).

A firm has a capability if it has some minimal ability to perform a task, regardless of whether or not that task is performed well or poorly (Helfat et al., 2007). A firm does not actually have to use a capability in order for it to have that capability. However, on average, firms have to use their capabilities in order to sustain their ability to use them. In other words, there is a "use it or lose it" assumption about a firm's capabilities over time (Helfat & Peteraf, 2009).

According to Helfat et al. (2007), a dynamic capability is "the capacity of an organization to purposefully create, extend, and modify its resource base" (p. 4). The resource base of an organization includes its physical, human, and organizational assets (Eisenhardt & Martin, 2000). Dynamic capabilities are learned and stable patterns of behavior through which a firm systematically generates and modifies its way of doing things, so that it can become more effective (Macher & Mowery, 2009; Zollo & Winter, 2002). For example, operating routines develop from the accumulation of experience through the repeated execution of similar tasks over time (Argote, 1999).

According to Teece (2007), a firm's history and prior paths help determine its current tangible and intangible positions and asset bases, which lead to organizational processes. The firm uses its sensing capabilities to identify opportunities. Once they are identified, the firm invests in ("seizes") these opportunities to improve its organizational capabilities. Then the firm actually recombines or reconfigures its organizational capabilities into new capabilities that better fit its environment. These new capabilities can help a firm create new paths, positions, and asset bases, which can lead to a sustained competitive advantage for the firm relative to other firms.

Helfat et al. (2007) identified two yardsticks for calibrating a firm's capabilities: technical (internal) fitness and evolutionary (external) fitness. Technical fitness refers to how well a capability performs its function divided by its cost. A dynamic capability is not something that a firm has or does not have. This measure can show that the dynamic capabilities of some firms may be more or less technically fit compared to other firms. Evolutionary fitness refers to how well a capability enables the firm to make a living outside the company relative to other firms by creating, extending, or modifying its resource base. Dynamic capabilities help a firm achieve evolutionary fitness (Teece, 2007).

Pavlou and El Sawy (2011) created a framework for a proposed model of dynamic capabilities. According to the framework, the firm (1) uses its sensing capabilities to spot, interpret, and pursue opportunities that it perceives from internal and external stimuli; (2) uses its learning capabilities to determine what organizational capabilities must be revamped, rebuilt, or reconfigured into new knowledge; (3) uses its integrating capabilities to collectively understand and to make the necessary changes to its operational capabilities; (4) uses its coordination capabilities to implement and use the reconfigured operational capabilities; and (5) continues to scan external and internal stimuli (Ettlie & Pavlou, 2006; Pavlou & El Sawy, 2006).

The dynamic capabilities approach has tended to incorporate Schumpeterian rents in its explanation of sustainable competitive advantage (Teece et al., 1997). However, Parayitam and Guru (2010) have argued that dynamic capabilities can lead to both Ricardian and Schumpeterian rents for a firm. According to Schumpeter (1911/1934), an entrepreneur will make profits (rents) because of innovations (strategies) as long as other entrepreneurs are not able to copy those innovations. In other words, profits emerge when innovations are new, and profits disappear when innovations are copied; profits can reappear if new innovations are created. According to Ricardo (1817), profits (rents) occur because of scarcity of resources or capabilities, such as land, that are available to the entrepreneur but not available to his or her competitors. Thus the entrepreneur will have lower operating costs compared to those of other entrepreneurs, which will result, simply speaking, in a competitive advantage for the entrepreneur. As pointed out by Penrose (1959), turbulent environments may change the significance of resources for organizations. Future research should integrate both types of rents into the dynamic capabilities approach (Parayitam & Guru, 2010).

Criticisms and Critiques of the Theory

Dynamic capabilities theory has been criticized for not properly defining the term "dynamic capabilities," for constantly changing the definition, and for outright contradictions in the definition (Arend & Bromiley, 2009; Collis, 1994; Zahra, Sapienza, & Davidsson, 2006). The term dynamic capabilities has often been described in vague and ambiguous ways—for example, as "routines to learn routines"—that are tautological and impossible to operationalize (Eisenhardt & Martin, 2000). Di Stefano, Peteraf, and Verona (2010) argued that a lack of clarity over basic terms will impede further progress for the theory.

The theory has been criticized for being a tautology. Some researchers have identified firms as having dynamic capabilities by their success (Arend & Bromiley, 2009). For example, some researchers tautologically state that dynamic capabilities lead to success and that successful firms have dynamic capabilities. Critics have argued that two instances of such a tautology were *In Search of Excellence* (Peters & Waterman, 1982) and *Good to Great* (Collins, 2001). In addition, some critics have complained that poor-performing firms also can have dynamic capabilities, or "continuous morphing" properties (Rindova & Kotha, 2001, p. 1264) that do not lead to success, such as Yahoo! and Excite. Some critics have argued that just because a firm does not change does not demonstrate that a firm lacks the dynamic capabilities to change (Arend & Bromiley, 2009).

Critics have argued that compared with other similar terms, the term dynamic capabilities does not provide added value in explaining why some firms are successful and others are not. For example, the following terms address similar issues: absorptive capacity, intrapreneurship, strategic fit, first-mover advantage, organizational learning, and change management (Arend & Bromiley, 2009). Some critics are even skeptical that the concept of dynamic capabilities even exists (Winter, 2003). Because so much research has described dynamic capabilities as abstract capabilities, many researchers believe that managers' deliberate efforts to develop and strengthen dynamic capabilities may not be effective (Winter).

Critics have argued that there are many ways to adapt to a rapidly changing environment and that the development of dynamic capabilities is but one way to do so. For example, Winter argued that it is possible for a firm to make appropriate changes to adapt to a rapidly changing environment as needs arise, or employ what he called an "ad hoc" approach to change. Winter (2003) also argued that ad hoc problem solving may even be a better, cheaper approach than investing in dynamic capabilities. Ad hoc problem solving involves only spending money as needs arise. In contrast, developing a firm's dynamic capabilities can involve trying to anticipate every possible need for change and investing significant monies toward each of those potential change areas. The development of dynamic capabilities most often involves sunk costs, whereas the costs for ad hoc changes are often only temporarily deployed and can eventually be returned to their prior uses (Dunning & Lundan, 2010; Romme, Zollo, & Berends, 2010). Few studies have measured the costs and benefits of developing dynamic capabilities to address this issue.

10

The theory has received considerable criticism for problems with measuring dynamic capabilities (Williamson, 1999). Pavlou and El Sawy (2011) noted that there was a lack of a measurement model for the theory. Galunic and Eisenhardt (2001) argued that the existence of dynamic capabilities was often just assumed without specifying exact components. Most often, researchers have used distant proxies, or only vaguely related items, to measure dynamic capabilities (for example, Arend & Bromiley, 2009; Henderson & Cockburn, 1994). Most researchers have used only short-term, cross-sectional tests, although the theory requires long-term, longitudinal, time-series data for proper analysis.

Measuring Variables in the Theory

Dynamic capabilities measures. Pavlou, P. A., & El Sawy, O. A. (2011). Understanding the elusive black box of dynamic capabilities. *Decision Sciences, 42,* 239–273.

Alliance capabilities measures. Kale, P., & Singh, H. (2007). Building firm capabilities through learning: The role of the alliance learning process in alliance capability and firm-level alliance success. *Strategic Management Journal, 28,* 981–1000.

Operational capabilities measures. Wu, S. J., Melnyk, S. A., & Flynn, B. B. (2010). Operational capabilities: The secret ingredient. *Decision Sciences, 41,* 721–754.

Suggestions for Further Research

1. Explore the conditions where firms have dynamic capabilities to change but decide not to change.

2. Examine the comparative advantages versus costs of developing long-term versus short-term dynamic capabilities to change.
3. Look for a solution that optimizes the trade-offs between dynamic capabilities and operational capabilities.
4. Examine the trade-offs between dynamic capabilities and improvisation under a range of turbulent environmental conditions.

10

5. Study the process of sensing, learning, integrating, and coordinating capabilities in firms, as compared to divisions.
6. Create ways to better measure the activities required in sensing, learning, integrating, and coordinating capabilities.
7. Examine the contribution of capabilities as a function of industry and market maturity.
8. Explore the extent to which an activity can be regarded as a dynamic capability if conducted in a single firm as opposed to in an industry.
9. Look at how firms find a balance between replication and renewal regarding resource availability and environment fit.
10. Examine and document the feedback and search processes that firms use to make themselves more dynamic and competitive.

References to Know

Eisenhardt, K. M., & Martin, J. A. (2000). Dynamic capabilities: What are they? *Strategic Management Journal, 21,* 1105–1121.

Helfat, C. E., Finkelstein, S., Mitchell, W., Peteraf, M., Singh, H., Teece, D., & Winter, S. G. (Eds.). (2007). *Dynamic capabilities: Understanding strategic change in organizations.* Oxford: Blackwell.

Teece, D. (2007). Explicating dynamic capabilities: The nature and microfoundations of (sustainable) enterprise performance. *Strategic Management Journal, 28,* 1319–1350.

Teece, D. (2009). *Dynamic capabilities and strategic management: Organizing for innovation and growth.* New York: Oxford University Press.

Teece, D., Pisano, G., & Shuen, A. (1997). Dynamic capabilities and strategic management. *Strategic Management Journal, 18,* 509–533.

Implications of the Theory for Managers

Dynamic capabilities theory examines how firms integrate, build, and reconfigure their internal and external firm-specific competencies into new competencies. Firms that are best able to reinvent and match their competencies with the demands of their changing environment will outperform their competitors.

Your task as a manager is to help your firm sense, learn, integrate, and coordinate capabilities. Help your firm sense the changes that are going on in your industry and environment. Read trade journals, articles, magazines, Web sites, and other sources to stay on top of changes that are occurring for your company and for your industry. Work with others to determine your organizational capabilities that will need to be reworked into new capabilities that will better help your firm meet the demands of your turbulent environment. Once that is completed, work with others to help everyone make sense of the new capabilities and develop a plan of action to implement and use the newly created capabilities. Next, design and implement a plan to integrate the new capabilities within the current organizational processes and get the new capabilities up and running. Finally, keep the process going, as the best firms will need to continuously keep up with the changing demands of their turbulent business environment if they want to succeed.

10

11

Efficient Market Theory

Individuals invest (buy assets or securities) in the stock market in order to make money. The premise is to buy low and sell higher than the price that was originally paid. Although that idea sounds reasonable, the prevailing view is that "you can't beat the market" because the market is efficient and so will always win. The concept of market efficiency had been anticipated as early as 1900 by Bachelier in his mathematics dissertation. Cowles (1933) found that there was no discernable evidence of any ability to outguess the market.

The efficient market approach has been the central position in finance for more than forty years. Fama (1970) defined an efficient market as one in which security prices always reflect available information. In a completely efficient market, the price of the security fully reflects all possible information about the security. Jensen (1978) wrote that there was no other proposition in economics that had more solid empirical support than the efficient market approach.

Fama (1970) described three types of available information that could affect price levels: weak forms, semi-strong forms, and strong forms. Weak information refers only to past price or prior stock performance. Semi-strong information refers both to past price information and also to publicly available information, such as announcements of stock splits, annual company reports, new security issues, and so on. The semi-strong form has received the most research attention. For example, there are no undervalued or overvalued securities, so trading rules are not capable of producing superior returns. Strong information refers to all information known to anyone at any time about the security, including private information. Work by Seyhun (1986) provides evidence that insiders profit from trading on information not already incorporated into prices.

Researchers began to look at price changes in the market in order to attempt to create a universal method that could be used to explain and predict those price changes. The problem of an optimal search procedure was first explored by Pearson (1905). If prices wander randomly, then this poses a major challenge to market analysts who try to predict the future path of security prices.

Pearson proposed the problem of trying to find a drunk who had been left out in a field. The drunk was able to walk in any random direction for any random distance. Pearson's solution was that the most probable place to find the drunken man was some-where near his starting point. This problem has become known as the random walk model. The model describes the way that stock prices change unpredictably as a result of unexpected information appearing in the market. The stock prices do not change unexpectedly; it is the news or information about those securities that changes unexpectedly, which is then reflected in the price.

The best evidence that markets are efficient comes from studying specific events that occur for an individual organization (Fama, 1991). The first study that examined events was by Fama, Fisher, Jensen, and Roll (1969), which examined stock splits. Other specific events that have been examined include earnings (for example, Ball & Brown, 1968); capital expenditure (for example, McConnell & Muscarella, 1985); divestitures (for example, Klein, 1986); and takeovers (for example, Jensen & Ruback, 1983). The results of these event studies indicate that, on average, stock prices adjust quickly and efficiently to company information, such as investment decisions, dividend changes, changes in capital structure, and corporate control decisions made by a specific company (Fama, 1991).

According to the random walk approach, the day of the week should not influence the level of stock returns. However, researchers have examined possible "day of the week effects" that go against the random walk approach. Rozeff and Kinney (1976) documented the January Effect whereby returns tended to be higher in January compared to other months. Cross (1973) and

Keim and Stambaugh (1984), for example, examined the Monday Effect (or the Weekend Effect) whereby returns on Monday were different, or unexpectedly negative, compared to other weekdays. Holiday (the trading day before a holiday) and turn-of-the-month effects (the last and first three days of the month) have also been documented as showing higher returns at those times, over time and across countries. Even the weather has been found to be related to stock prices, with sunshine positively related to prices and clouds negatively related. In sum, these phenomena have been called anomalies because they cannot be explained by efficient market theory. These anomalies suggest that information alone is not moving market prices.

One of the assumptions of efficient market theory is that investors always act rationally when confronted with new information. However, more recent work has incorporated the findings of social and behavioral scientists and adopted a psychological perspective. Research findings in the psychological literature show that individuals have limited information-processing abilities, are often biased and prejudiced, are prone to making mistakes, and tend to rely on the opinions of others in their decision making. All of these human weaknesses go against the random walk approach in efficient markets.

De Bondt and Thaler (1985) discovered that stock market prices could "overreact" to unexpected and dramatic news events. This result occurred because investors tend to overreact to new information and ignore base-rate performance levels for their investments. De Bondt and Thaler's work marked the start of behavioral finance.

Important advances have been made by bridging different theoretical lenses from finance, economics, and the behavioral sciences (Okhuysen & Bonardi, 2011). Significant progress was made by using cognitive and emotional factors to understand individual decisions, such as investor actions. The development of these behavioral approaches over the last ten years has been extremely rapid and has generated many new insights and new research areas (Subrahmanyam, 2007).

For example, behavior-based financial research has examined psychological aspects of investors, such as mood, level of over- or underconfidence, level of over- or underreaction, tolerance for risk, first impressions, high and low status, "herd mentality," and level of certainty when making decisions. For instance, more confident investors may overreact more compared to less confident investors. Grinblatt and Keloharju (2001) found that distance, language, and culture influenced stock trades.

Further incorporation of psychological aspects of decision makers should offer even more contributions to the finance literature. However, the jury is still out about whether traditional, and neoclassical, finance research can be integrated successfully with behavioral finance (Shiller, 2006).

Criticisms and Critiques of the Theory

11

Undoubtedly, efficient market theory has made invaluable contributions to the understanding of the securities markets. The theory is simple and elegant, but the quest to obtain a universal theory that completely explains changes in asset prices remains elusive (Dimson & Mussavian, 2000).

A significant amount of research has uncovered exceptions to efficient market theory in that information alone is not moving market prices. There is now sufficient evidence to show that security prices could deviate due to psychological factors, fads, and noise trading. Noise trading refers to making investment decisions without being "rational" or without using all available means and instruments to be fully informed before buying or selling. In general, most typical individuals are noise investors.

Shiller (2003) wrote that we have to distance ourselves from the presumption that the markets are efficient and that price changes always reflect genuine information. In order to move forward, researchers need to consider other variables that can influence prices, such as human foibles and arbitrary feedback situations. The task for researchers is to integrate the concepts in the neoclassical approach in efficient market theory with concepts from the behavioral finance and behavioral psychology literatures.

Measuring Variables in the Theory

Opinion leadership scale and information-seeking scale. Reynolds, F. D., & Darden, W. R. (1971). Mutually adaptive effects of individual communication. *Journal of Marketing Research, 8,* 449–454.

Uncertainty orientation scale. Smith, J. B., & Bristor, J. M. (1994). Uncertainty orientation: Explaining differences in purchase involvement and external search. *Psychology and Marketing, 11,* 587–607.

Impact of event scale. Horowitz, M., Wilner, N., & Alvarez, W. (1979, May). Impact of event scale: A measure of subjective stress. *Psychosomatic Medicine, 41,* 209–218.

Suggestions for Further Research

1. Examine the level of information comfort needed for people to purchase securities.
2. Explore the influence of information-seeking and information-avoiding behavior on individual securities purchases and sales.
3. Look at an individual's range of behaviors, from underreacting to overreacting to information, and its influence on his or her buying or selling of securities.
4. Examine individual difference variables and their influence on people's tendency to overreact, underreact, and not react at all to information about securities.
5. Explore how an individual's level of uncertainty orientation can influence differences in his or her purchase involvement and external product search.
6. Study the effects of individual difference in reaction to specific events and the impact of those on the buying and selling of securities.
7. Investigate the patterns of investor risk tolerance; for example, risk tolerance tends to rise after higher market returns and fall after lower market returns.
8. Examine the symmetry of investor risk tolerance; for example, risk tolerance in foresight may or may not be different from risk tolerance in hindsight.
9. Look at the extent to which investor risk tolerance may be compartmentalized rather than generalized, such as for reaching specific goals like retirement, children's education, and extravagant living.
10. Investigate to what extent investors tend to overreact or not to new information in their purchasing and selling and to their forecasts of future events, whether good or bad.

11

11. Examine the relationship between over- and underconfidence and over- and underreacting to new information.

References to Know

Bachelier, L. (1900). *Théorie de la speculation (Speculation theory).* Paris, France: Gauthier-Villars.

De Bondt, W.F.M., & Thaler, R. (1985). Does the stock market overreact? *Journal of Finance, 40,* 793–805.

Fama, E. F. (1970). Efficient capital markets: A review of theory and empirical work. *Journal of Finance, 25,* 383–417.

Fama, E. F. (1991). Efficient capital markets: II. *Journal of Finance, 46,* 1575–1617.

Jensen, M. C. (1978). Some anomalous evidence regarding market efficiency. *Journal of Financial Economics, 6,* 95–102.

Implications of the Theory for Managers

According to the efficient market theory, investors make completely rational short-term decisions in order to maximize their personal wealth. Unfortunately, this point of view has really taken hold with many managers and employees today. People simply want the greatest reward for the least effort and in the shortest amount of time.

Most investors are concerned only with short-term profits. The same can be true of most managers and most employees. The length of time that most people consider nowadays is only about three months, or the length of the next quarter in the year. For many, this short-term focus has arisen because managers and employees have been evaluated and rewarded solely on the basis of their previous quarter's performance. As a result, managers and employees virtually never think about their long-term performance or that of their company. They never think about how they should invest in the long term in order to reap the highest long-term returns.

Unfortunately, this short-term mentality is taking its toll on overall employee, manager, and company performance. Everyone needs to invest in both the short term and the long term in order to achieve maximum performance. However, this refocus will only happen if performance evaluation measures are changed such that employees are rewarded for both short- and long-term performance. Such a change is not likely to happen in most organizations.

According to efficient market theory, individuals always act completely rationally, and instantaneously obtain, absorb, and use all available information. Your task as a manager is to help both your employees and the public act rationally when buying or selling your company's stock. Help them understand the importance of investing for the long term and of not overreacting by selling company stock when hearing about possible temporary bad news for the marketplace or for your organization.

Many managers hope that their employees will act this way on the job as well. Unfortunately, many times employees aren't rational, behave for no obvious reason, and exhibit the same biases, prejudices, and limitations on the job as they do when they buy and sell securities. Today's best managers understand that their employees aren't totally rational robots who always perform efficiently and expertly. The best managers understand the behavioral and psychological aspects (such as tolerance for risk, over- and underconfidence, and over- and undercertainty) that can affect employee decisions on the job.

11

12

Ethical Theory

Ethical theories give advice about how people ought to be and how they ought to behave (Brady & Hart, 2007). Ethical theories state the conditions under which an action is "right" or "moral" (Moore, 2007). Most often, an ethical theory will state that behavior is right if and only if a specific condition occurs or exists. Different ethical theories offer rival accounts of the condition that must occur for behavior to be right. Some ethical theories only state what the condition is for a behavior to be "wrong." In general, there is no one universally accepted ethical theory. Instead, there are competing versions of ethical theories.

Ethical theories have been around for a very long time, so there are many versions of and variations on them. The main classifications and divisions of these theories are also subject to debate (Louden, 1996). However, ethical theories tend to fall into two different lines of thought: (1) ethics of character, which examine what sort of people we should be; and (2) ethics of conduct, which examine what sort of actions people should perform. Ethical theories in the ethics of character area focus on virtues or the goodness of an agent's character for determining the rightness of actions, instead of on universal laws (Buckle, 2002; Santas, 1993). Examples of approaches in this area are those of Plato, Aristotle, and Confucius (Brewer, 2005; Sim, 2010). For example, according to Confucius, it is rare for a person who has a strong sense of filial and fraternal responsibility to defy authority or to initiate a rebellion against the government. A behavior is considered to be right if it is what a virtuous person would do in the same circumstance (Sandler, 2010).

Ethical theories in the ethics of conduct view tend to fall within two main areas of thought: (1) teleological (consequentialism) and (2) deontological (nonconsequentialism) (Broad, 1959; Louden, 1996). A third type of ethical theory in this area is called "intuitionism" (Crane et al., 2011). Some researchers have believed that intuitionism should be classified as teleological (for example, Bentham, Mill, and Sidgwick); some have thought that it could be either teleological or deontological (Rawls, 1971).

Theories based on the teleological or consequentialism approach believe that people ought to focus their actions so as to maximize the value or values to be gained as a result (or consequence) of those actions (Hull, 1979). The term "teleological" is derived from the Greek word "telos," which means aim or purpose. Ethical behavior here refers to the "goodness" or "badness" of the consequences of people's actions alone as what makes those actions right or wrong. According to this view, there is nothing intrinsically good or bad about the actions themselves. An action is morally right if doing it would bring about the best possible consequences if everyone performed that action whenever he or she were in that sort of situation.

Ethical theories in this category often refer to the utility, or cost versus benefit, of behavior, so they are often called utilitarian theories (Hume, 1740/2000; Bentham, 1789/1996; Mill, 1863/1998). There are a number of utilitarian approaches: hedonism (Jeremy Bentham, John Stuart Mill, Harriet Taylor Mill); eudemonism (Paul Kurtz); agathism (G. E. Moore); agapeism (Joseph Fletcher); and values pluralism (Fritzsche & Becker, 1984). Theories in this area can be act utilitarian (solely based on outcomes), or rule utilitarian (rules revised based on situational circumstances). Rawls's theory of justice (1971) advocates that resource allocators should act with equity, fairness, and impartiality.

The second area of thought within the ethics of conduct view is called deontological. The term "deontological" is derived from the Greek word "deon," which means duty, obligation, or necessity. The term deontological was coined in the mid-1900s. Ethical theories in this category refer to ethical behavior as something that a person has a moral obligation or duty to perform (Hull, 1979; Louden, 1996). Deontologists are often absolutists, but some hold that what is morally right depends on the situation.

12

Deontologists are completely against outcome-based reasons, and can argue that a morally "right" action can have bad consequences, and a morally "wrong" action can have good consequences.

There are two types of deontologists: act (moral obligations depend on the situation, such as "I ought not to lie in this situation"), and rule (duty applies in every situation, such as following the Ten Commandments or the Golden Rule in every situation). Kant (1724–1804) proposed a set of moral, philosophical, and ethical tenets to guide society that focus on moral intentions and duties. Kant's "categorical imperative" (1785/1993) serves as the ultimate moral norm that society must follow. People should make moral decisions in which the outcomes could be accepted by everyone as universal law (Place, 2010).

The third kind of ethics in the ethics of conduct area is called intuitionism (Arnold, Audi, & Zwolinski, 2010; Ross, 1930). Intuitionism refers to ethical standards that are immediately known without any conscious reasoning to determine them. In other words, as educated humans, people simply know about these ethical standards of behavior. They know and accept these standards without arguing over them or questioning them. Main writers in this area have included Ross, Sidgwick, Moore, Ewing, Nagel, and Parfit. According to this approach, people are moral agents who have core ethical obligations that they must follow.

12

According to the intuitionist perspective (Ross, 1930; Audi, 2004), there are "prima facie duties" or moral obligations for people to perform: (1) justice (distribute benefits and burdens fairly to everyone); (2) noninjury (do no harm); (3) fidelity (keep your promises); (4) reparation (amend all wrongdoing); (5) beneficence (do good deeds for others); (6) self-improvement; (7) gratitude; (8) liberty (enhance everyone's freedom and autonomy); and (9) obligations of manner (be respectful of others).

A recurring topic in ethical theory research has been the examination of how people handle ethical dilemmas (Schminke, Ambrose, & Noel, 1997). A number of taxonomies exist that examine possible ethical frameworks that underlie ethical decisions (for example, Brady, 1985; Kohlberg, 1984; Velasquez, 1992). Brady's taxonomy (1985, 1990) compared process-oriented formalism (often associated with Kantian ethics) with outcome-oriented utilitarianism (often associated with Mill and Bentham). For example, researchers have examined gender differences in ethical frameworks (Schminke, 1997) and explored perceptions of gender-based ethical differences (Ambrose & Schminke, 1999; Schminke & Ambrose, 1997), such as that men are often perceived as being more utilitarian and women as being more formalist (Schminke, Ambrose, & Miles, 2003).

Criticisms and Critiques of the Theory

Ethical theories have been criticized for a number of reasons. Many critics have argued that although ethical theories sound plausible, in reality they offer little help to people making actual decisions. Hodgson (2001) wrote that there is no moral knowledge that ethical experts can give to actual human beings who are in need of it when facing concrete and significant ethical decisions.

Critics argue that a major problem with ethical theories is that they compete with each other. Ethics textbooks are filled with examples of ethical dilemmas with illustrations of conflicts among applications of ethical theories for the same situation. In class, students are often asked to argue for a direction of action in accordance with either of two different ethical approaches that conflict with each other. Considering that researchers themselves continue to struggle over how to reconcile conflicting ethical theories (Kelly, 2005), critics argue that we cannot expect less knowledgeable individuals to make much progress at reconciling competing theories when faced with ethical dilemmas in organizations.

Measuring Variables in the Theory

Measure of ethical viewpoints scale. Schminke, M., & Wells, D. (1999). Group processes and performance and their effects on individuals' ethical frameworks. *Journal of Business Ethics, 18,* 367–381.

Ethical orientation vignettes. Schminke, M. (1997). Gender differences in ethical frameworks and evaluation of others' choices in ethical dilemmas. *Journal of Business Ethics, 16,* 55–65.

Responses to ethical dilemma items. Schminke, M., & Ambrose, M. L. (1997). Asymmetric perceptions of ethical frameworks of

12

men and women in business and nonbusiness settings. *Journal of Business Ethics, 16,* 719–729.

Ethical climate questionnaire. Victor, B., & Cullen, J. B. (1988). The organizational bases of ethical work climates. *Administrative Science Quarterly, 33,* 101–125.

Ethical climate index. Arnaud, A. (2010). Conceptualizing and measuring ethical work climate: Development and validation of the ethical climate index. *Business and Society, 49,* 345–358.

Suggestions for Further Research

1. Examine how people apply (or do not apply) ethical theory concepts when faced with real-world situations on the job.
2. Explore circumstances in which people resort to social consensus rather than apply ethical theory reasoning when faced with ethical dilemmas.
3. Create a typology of task and situation types and ethical theory perspectives for real-world decision-making situations.
4. Extend research on individual difference variables and ethical decision making for real organizational issues and problems.
5. Explore cross-cultural influences on preferences for ethical theories and their influence on behaviors.
6. Look at when and why empathetic concern (such as measured by an ethical climate index) may be inversely related to perceived performance.
7. Examine the relationship between individual political behavior and perceptions of moral awareness.
8. Explore how organizations can meet the needs of multiple stakeholders following competing ethical theory perspectives.
9. Conduct quantitative and qualitative analyses of an ethics-based theory of the firm.
10. Uncover the essential factors that lead to the establishment of corporate social responsibility and sustainable practices.

12

References to Know

Aristotle. (2009). *Nicomachean ethics* (W. D. Ross, Trans.). New York: World Library Classics.

Kant, I. (1993). *Groundwork of the metaphysics of morals* (3rd ed.). (J. W. Ellington, Trans.). Indianapolis, IN: Hackett. (Original work published 1785)

Mill, J. S. (1998). *Utilitarianism* (R. Crisp, Ed.). Oxford: Oxford University Press. (Original work published 1863)

Rawls, J. (1971). *A theory of justice.* Cambridge, MA: Belknap Press.

Ross, W. D. (1930). *The right and the good.* Oxford: Oxford University Press.

Implications of the Theory for Managers

Ethical theories give advice about how people ought to be and how they ought to behave. These theories state the conditions under which an action is "right." The theories typically offer arguments for their own view of ethical behavior, but do not provide assistance for resolving conflicts among multiple ethical theories. Researchers have tried for extensive periods of time to resolve conflicts among ethical theories, so the typical individual will not be able to resolve conflicts among competing theories on their own. As a result, individuals who are knowledgeable about ethical theories can still end up using their own intuition and opinions when deciding how to behave ethically for situations that occur in real organizations (Derry & Green, 1989).

Unfortunately, ethical theories can only provide information about how to behave ethically in general. However, managers have to make decisions in order to take action, and they often end up resorting to "social consensus" to help them decide what to do. Following social consensus means to adopt the approach that typically appeals to the social values accepted in one's society. The belief is that these values provide enough foundation for taking action on a particular task. Although this approach might work for simple, everyday problems, it tends not to work for more ambiguous, complex social issues. For example, this approach is unlikely to be helpful for situations in which no clear social consensus exists (Derry & Green, 1989).

Ideally, individuals in organizations should be able to follow the advice given by ethical theories. More specifically, employees should be able to identify situations that have ethical implications. For example, an employee might realize that there is an ethical problem if her boss asks her to "cut corners" in order to deliver a product on time to a customer. Individuals should be able to apply the principles of one or more ethical theories to their situation. The result should be that the employee's behavior is consistent with ethical theory. For instance, the employee would find a way to deliver a quality product on time to that customer, rather than cut corners.

Talk with your employees about situations that may have ethical implications for them in your organization. Discuss solutions to those situations before employees are faced with them in real life. Whenever possible, reward employees for applying the principles of ethical theories.

12

13

Field Theory

Field theory was characterized as early as the 1920s in the physical sciences (Maxwell, 1921). The view proposed that it was not the charges or the particles in physical matter but the field in the space between them that was essential for describing physical phenomena (Einstein & Infeld, 1938). According to Einstein, space is a definitely distributed system of forces (gravitational and electromagnetic) that determine what an object with certain properties will do.

The field of physics frequently makes use of a representation of a multitude of factors that influence an event. For example, properties such as temperature, pressure, time, and position in space must be considered. This type of representation is called a "phase space" (Lewin, 1943a). Applied to the social sciences, field theory tries to map out the totality and complexity of the field in which a behavior takes place (Back, 1992). To understand a behavior, it is necessary to understand the present situation—the status quo—in which a behavior occurs, and the forces and conditions acting on an individual at a specific time (Lewin, 1943a).

Lewin defined a field as "a totality of coexisting facts which are conceived of as mutually interdependent" (1946, p. 240). Lewin (1947) believed that a field was in a constant state of change and adaptation, such that change and constancy are relative concepts that occur in varying amounts in any given time for group life. Lewin used the term "quasi-stationary equilibrium" to describe the constantly changing rhythm and pattern of group behavior due to the constantly changing forces or circumstances that act on the group (Burnes, 2004).

The field includes a person in his or her own "life space" (Lewin, 1951). The life space should not be confused with the geographical environment. The life space is only perceptual— that is, it has to be perceived by the individual. The boundary conditions of the field are essential characteristics of the life space. The perceived boundaries depend on aspects of the individual, such as his or her character, motivation, cognitive structure, and so on. In addition, the properties of any event are determined by its relations with the system of events of which it is a component.

Field theory is a useful framework for understanding the cognitive, affective, and behavioral aspects of individuals (Houston, Bettencourt, & Wenger, 1998). The theory begins with the life space, which is composed of all coexisting factors that are relevant for that individual, such as self-perceptions, wants, needs, desires, and so on. An individual's behaviors result as all of the various forces in the life space exert their influence over the individual. Any behavior or any other change in a psychological field depends only on the psychological field at that specific time. Therefore, individual behaviors should be examined only from within the context of the field as a whole (Lewin, 1943a), such as in the area of leadership (Wheatley, 2006).

13

Lewin (1951) considered the term "force field" in which driving and resisting forces determine whether and to what extent changes in behavior occur. In a general way, Lewin proposed three different types of conflict situations: (1) an individual stands midway between two positive forces of equal strength (go to an important business meeting or attend his child's recital); (2) an individual stands between two negative forces of equal strength (study for an exam or fail the exam); and (3) an individual stands between two equally opposing forces (leave home in order to pursue a desired career) (Riordan & Riordan, 1993).

All of the countervailing forces act on the individual, creating psychological tension, which creates motivation for the individual to behave in goal-directed ways that serve to reduce this perceived level of tension (Houston et al., 1998). Objects that have an overall positive force within the field are approached, and objects that have an overall negative force within the field are avoided (Diamond, 1992). The difficult part for the researcher is to quantify the strength, direction, and duration of all these various forces that act on the individual. According to the theory, which forces combine is less important than understanding the final statement (motivational calculus) of how the various positive and negative forces exert influence on an individual to behave in a specific way.

Researchers in field theory have used the term "field" in three overlapping and interrelated ways (Martin, 2003). First is the diagrammatic, topological sense of field that was emphasized by Lewin (1936). In this case, the field is an analytic area of simplified dimensions in which we place people or institutions. Individuals are examined in respect to their position and interrelation with others in the same field. Second is the sense of the field as an organization of forces, such as a magnetic field, which is derived from physics (Bourdieu, 1985, 1988). Third is the sense of the field as an arena or battlefield (Back, 1992).

A central tenet of field theory is that the activities of actors in a field are regulated by their relative positions within the field and their interrelationships with each other. The interrelationships of the actors can lead to shared subjectivities and cultures. Lewin drew diagrams of the forces acting on individuals, which came to be known as "bathtubs" (oval representations of the life space). Diagrams of the life space of group activity, such as the systematizing person-group relations approach (Sjovold, 2007), are still in use today and are reminiscent of Lewin's bathtub drawings. The resurgence of such diagrams in both physical and nonphysical sciences is due in part to advances in mathematics and computer modeling and simulations that make creating such diagrams possible.

13

Field theory has also been applied to organizations (for example, Sauder, 2008). Research has examined the mechanisms specific to field-level organizational changes, giving rise to three general approaches. First, Meyer and colleagues demonstrated how sudden, abrupt changes can disrupt field equilibrium, causing opportunities for new fieldwide norms, boundaries, and hierarchical relationships to emerge (for example, Haveman, Russo, & Meyer, 2001; Meyer, Gaba, & Colwell, 2005). Second, research has examined changes in established organizational logics that give rise to new practices and conventions (for example, Thornton & Ocasio, 1999). Third, research has examined how fields gradually change over time due to general, evolutionary institutional changes (for example, Scott, Ruef, Mandel, & Caronna, 2000).

Unfortunately, these approaches have not fully explained how new field-level actors become incorporated into already well-established and structured organizational fields (Sauder, 2008).

According to field theory, a field exists when it is helpful to describe a set of individuals or organizations regarding their current positions relative to each other. This approach is particularly useful for examining organizations. Organizational fields connect and align organizations, which can result in shared cultures and perspectives. For example, interorganizational fields arise when organizations share suppliers and clients. The organizational field spans and coordinates institutional activities. An organization's actions can be explained by its position in the field relative to every other organization in that field. Every position in the field influences a set of motivations that are subjectively experienced by the organization as telling the organization "what should be done" (Martin, 2003).

Criticisms and Critiques of the Theory

Critics of field theory have complained that it is not really a theory but just an approach (Gold, 1992). They have argued that field theory does not have the usual set of assumptions and propositions from which empirical hypotheses can be deduced, which makes field theory more like a language, an orientation, or simply a point of view than a proper theory (Jones, 1985).

Part of the confusion about whether field theory is a theory or simply an approach was caused by Lewin himself. He wrote that "field theory is probably best characterized as a method: namely, a method of analyzing causal relations and of building scientific constructs" (1943a, p. 294). However, researchers have declared that field theory is in fact a theory with a body of definitions and axioms from which hypotheses have been derived (for example, Deutsch, 1954).

Critics have complained that field theory is "postperceptual and prebehavioral" (Brunswik, 1943). According to field theory, all of the conditions (both positive and negative forces) that act on the individual or the organization must be known in order to predict how the entity will behave. Lewin called this the "pure case" and referred to Galileo's study of falling bodies as an example. The pure case is a cross section in time that is a snapshot of the forces acting on an entity at a specific moment, but is not static; rather, it is dynamic in that the specific moment continually changes over time.

Critics have complained about the motivational calculus in field theory. Using a calculus to sum all of the positive and negative forces that act on an individual results in our saying that the person merely did what the person wanted to do (Diamond, 1992). In other words, any force could be created to explain away the motivation for the behavior that was taken.

Critics have complained that field theory itself is tautological and unfalsifiable (Diamond, 1992). Field theory requires knowledge of the totality of coexisting forces that act mutually dependently on individuals or on organizations. The theory is also tautological because it states that behavior should be defined as a function of both personality and environment, and that environment is a function of personality and personality is a function of the environment.

According to field theory, every individual or organization should be analyzed according to its position relative to every other entity in the field. Every position in the field influences a set of motivations that are subjectively experienced by the organization and that tell it "what should be done." Unfortunately, field theory stops there and offers little to explain exactly how all of that happens (Martin, 2003).

13

Measuring Variables in the Theory

Deans' ranking scale. Sauder, M. (2008). Interlopers and field change: The entry of *U.S. News* into the field of legal education. *Administrative Science Quarterly, 53*, 209–234.

Family objectives scale. Riordan, D. A., & Riordan, M. P. (1993, April). Field theory: An alternative to systems theories in understanding the small family business. *Journal of Small Business Management, 31*, 66–78.

Suggestions for Further Research

1. Examine the difficulties of studying individuals or organizations that are simultaneously at equilibrium or in flux.

2. Explore nonlinear change at multiple levels over time in organizations.
3. Look at how people create their own motivational calculus of both positive and negative forces acting on them.
4. Study the mechanisms involved in including or avoiding forces that an individual or organization perceives in its life space.
5. Examine how people establish the boundaries of their life space.
6. Explore how a person's life space changes over time and what influences cause those changes.
7. Study the point at which individuals or organizations leave the perceptual state and move into the behavioral state regarding forces acting on them.
8. Create a computer-generated graphical representation of individual or organizational life spaces, including all forces.
9. Examine the similarities and differences among the perceived life spaces of individuals or organizations in the same field.
10. Explore how managers can help strengthen the influence of positive forces and reduce the influence of negative forces for their employees.

13

References to Know

Deutsch, M. (1954). Field theory in social psychology. In G. Lindzey (Ed.), *Handbook of social psychology* (pp. 181–222). Reading, MA: Addison-Wesley.

Lewin, K. (1943). Defining the "field at a given time." *Psychological Review, 50,* 292–310.

Lewin, K. (1951). *Field theory in social science* (D. Cartwright, Ed.). New York: Harper & Brothers.

Martin, J. L. (2003, July). What is field theory? *American Journal of Sociology, 109,* 1–49.

Mey, H. (1972). *Field theory: A study of its applications in the social sciences.* New York: St. Martin's Press.

Implications of the Theory for Managers

Talk with your employees and help them discover their own individual life space. Help your employees understand the boundaries of their life space, see who is in their life space, and know where they stand in relation to all other people in their life space.

Show your employees that both positive and negative forces are acting on them to behave in specific ways. These forces create tension in an employee, which induces him or her to behave in specific ways to reduce this tension. For example, the force to play a video game and the force to finish a report for a client might both be exerting influence on an employee. Help your employees identify these forces, resist the negative forces, and follow the positive forces that help them accomplish desired organizational outcomes. You might also be able to exert positive forces of your own to help counter the negative forces that are pushing on your employees to behave in certain ways and not to behave in others.

If necessary, help your employees change the boundaries of their life space and change their perceptions of who is in their life space. For example, negative individuals might be in their life space, who exert negative forces on the individual to engage in negative behaviors. Help your employee remove these negative forces and possibly replace them with positive individuals who can exert forces on them to behave more positively and with better organizational outcomes. The more that individuals understand the forces acting on them, the better they will understand why they behave as they do.

13

14

Game Theory

Game theory examines the decisions that individual players make in order to win a game against one or more competitors. The players are abstract, intelligent, individual agents who act in pursuit of their own limited goals in an abstract setting. Von Neumann and Morgenstern (1944) based their original model on the analogy of two or more people playing a parlor game, such as chess, poker, or bridge. Game theory examines games of strategy but not games of chance, such as rolling dice. A strategic game involves two or more participants making choices of actions in which each may gain or lose depending on the actions taken by the other player(s). There is some uncertainty, as none of the players knows exactly what the others will do. Game theory has had its greatest impact in economics, but it has also had tremendous influence on management, accounting, biology, finance, law, marketing, and political science.

The basic game theory concepts include player (a rational, self-interested decision-making entity); strategy (a rule that tells a player which action to prefer at each stage of the game); outcome (the result of every possible decision made by the players); payoff (satisfaction obtained from a specific outcome of the game); and equilibrium (the optimal sequence of decisions in the game) (Madhani, 2010; Rasmusen, 1989).

In a typical game, there is a finite number of strategies that can be employed by the players. The perceptions of individual payoffs can be mapped in a matrix of different possible combinations. Among the possible decision alternatives, there may be a winning strategy that offers the optimal payoff to a player, regardless of the actions taken by the opponent.

In some games, there may be no clear winning strategy, so the play continues until an equilibrium is reached. A Nash equilibrium (Nash, 1951) occurs when each player obtains the best result possible based on the actions of his or her opponents. If a game does not reach an equilibrium, then one of the players could have obtained a better outcome by acting differently. The idea of an equilibrium point is the basic ingredient in game theory. The set of equilibrium points is simply the set of all pairs of opposing "good strategies" in a win-lose game.

There are a number of basic assumptions in game theory (Herbig, 1991). There is complete information, in that all the players know all the rules of the game and know the preferences of the other players for all the possible outcomes. Each player is fully informed about all prior choices when making decisions. Each player is intelligent and will act rationally and make decisions trying to maximize his or her payoffs. When faced with uncertainty, each player will make subjective estimates based on the probability of expected payoffs. Each player can put himself or herself in the position of the other players and can reason from their point of view. Behavior is competitive and not cooperative, in that each player acts to obtain his or her own best result. Cooperative behavior could result in less than optimal results for an individual, but better results for all the players. Most games are multimove and dynamic, with the environmental factors and the players' positions changing over time. The game is interdependent in that one player's performance depends on the decisions of the other. No unilateral decisions are possible. The game's outcome is determined by the length of the game. Game theory seeks to establish an equilibrium, or no better result, among the active players.

14

In the general study of game theory, there are seven important divisions based on the number of individual players in the game: (1) one-person games (one person trying to solve a problem); (2) two-person games; (3) three-person games; (4) few-person games (from four to about twenty people, such as committees, clubs, packs, and herds); (5) many-person games (from about twenty to a few hundred people, such as villages, small firms, and tribes); (6) large but finite games; and (7) games with an infinite number of people.

Harsanyi (1967, 1968a, 1968b) examined games of incomplete information. At the beginning of the game, the players have information about themselves, but not about their opponents.

The players then update their knowledge about their opponents based on player actions during the game. More recent work has examined combined or hybrid forms of both cooperative and noncooperative games, such as biform games (Brandenburger & Stuart, 2007).

Criticisms and Critiques of the Theory

Many practitioners are doubtful about the usefulness of game theory for solving everyday business problems. Critics of game theory have generally focused their criticism on several basic assumptions in the theory (Herbig, 1991). For example, a basic tenet of game theory is that the players act rationally when they make decisions. In business settings, it is not always the best practice that is chosen. Irrational motives are often followed at the expense of seemingly rational ones. For instance, decisions can be made based on the emotional preferences of the CEO or on a personal relationship with a sales representative. Irrational actions occur quite frequently in business, such as when trying to mislead or bluff an opponent. The objectives of companies can also vary among competing firms, such as taking a long-term versus a short-term outlook.

Game theory assumes that complete information is known with certainty. In reality, the future is uncertain and unpredictable, and companies and managers are apt to forget information (Thomadsen & Bhardwaj, 2011). Critics argue that game theory predictions are best with perfect information, but less accurate when one player has limited knowledge and information about another player's history and profile. Incomplete knowledge is the rule, rather than the exception, in business. Most firms know a great deal about their own capabilities and goals, but often very little about those of their competitors. Game theory has therefore not been shown to be a useful tool for generating precise prescriptions for managerial behavior, and remains largely a way of describing what happened in a particular situation (Roy, 2003).

An assumption in game theory is that the desired outcome is a choice based on probabilities and not a fixed scenario. For example, the probability of success if option A should be taken is 6/11 and the probability if option B should be taken is 5/11, so a person decides to choose option A. In reality, most organizations

14

do not want their managers to make decisions based on such simplistic probabilities.

Game theory assumes that behavior tends toward competitiveness and maximization of one's own individual position at the expense of others. However, in business there is the consideration of long and lasting relationships with other business entities. In such circumstances, cooperative and mutually beneficial actions can be more helpful to organizations than individual self-maximization decisions.

Game theory can be helpful for simple games with a few players, where the environment is predictable and the decision variables are few, but the theory begins to fall short when the situation becomes more complicated and involves a large number of decision variables. For infinitely large, repeated games, the strategy options become very broad and complex with the possible result that "anything can happen."

Game theory is not very effective at understanding the reasoning behind independent human behavior—for example, how people represent or order their alternatives. Decision makers in the real world frequently do not evaluate uncertain events according to the laws of probability, nor do they always make decisions to maximize their own expected payoffs. Game theory may not be able to fully explain human behavior because people are incapable of fully analyzing complex decision situations when the future consequences are unknown or uncertain.

Camerer (1991) describes what he considers four major shortcomings of game theory with regard to applying it to business situations; he refers to them as (1) the chopstick problem (game theoretical models are too hard to use in real life, as they involve complicated mathematical formulas and calculations); (2) the collage problem (the models form an incoherent collage that results in no general principles); (3) the testing problem (the models are hard to test in real life); and (4) the Pandora's box problem (the models can explain everything, thereby explaining nothing that can be used on a daily basis).

Measuring Variables in the Theory

Decision maker characteristics scale. Scharlemann, J.P.W., Eckel, C. C., Kacelnik, A., & Wilson, R. K. (2001). The value of a smile:

Game theory with a human face. *Journal of Economic Psychology, 22,* 617–640.

Commitment and sacrifice scales. Van Lange, P.A.M., Agnew, C. R., Harinck, F., & Steemers, E. M. (1997). From game theory to real life: How social value orientation affects willingness to sacrifice in ongoing close relationships. *Journal of Personality and Social Psychology, 73,* 1330–1344.

Accuracy of forecast scale. Green, K. C. (2002). Forecasting decisions in conflict situations: A comparison of game theory, role-playing, and unaided judgment. *International Journal of Forecasting, 18,* 321–344.

Suggestions for Further Research

1. Examine the influences of time—continuous, periodic, or fixed amounts, for example—on decisions that players make in games.
2. Explore the influence of complexity and context of decisions and outcomes in game decisions.
3. Study different types of problems (such as complex or simple ones) or combinations of problems in gaming decisions.
4. Look at the similarities and differences between cooperative, noncooperative, and combination games on decisions and outcomes.
5. Examine how static versus dynamic, and constantly revising, changing, or adapting players and conditions, can influence gaming decisions and outcomes.
6. Explore the influence of static versus novel conditions—such as new markets, technologies, and institutions—on gaming behavior and outcomes.
7. Look at the influence of complexity and redundancies versus simple and static conditions on gaming behaviors and outcomes.
8. Examine the influence of the passions and emotions of the players on gaming behaviors and outcomes.
9. Explore the influence of rationality, irrationality, and combinations of the two on gaming decisions and outcomes.

14

10. Examine the influence of a continuum of degrees of payoff satisfaction on gaming decisions and outcomes.
11. Study varying environmental conditions, ranging from predictable with a few unchanging variables to unpredictable with many changing variables, on the decisions and outcomes in games.

References to Know

Kreps, D. (1990). *Game theory and economic modeling.* Oxford: Oxford University Press.

Myerson, R. B. (1997). *Game theory: analysis of conflict.* Cambridge, MA: Harvard University Press.

Nash, J. (1951, September). Non-cooperative games. *Annals of Mathematics, 54,* 286–295.

Schelling, T. C. (1960). *The strategy of conflict.* Cambridge, MA: Harvard University Press.

Von Neumann, J., & Morgenstern, O. (1944). *Theory of games and economic behavior.* Princeton, NJ: Princeton University Press.

Implications of the Theory for Managers

Game theory examines the decisions that individual players make in order to win a game against one or more competitors. The theory offers a number of implications for managers (Fisher, 2008; Miller, 2003). For example, employees will always strive to maximize their own welfare and not yours. An employee spending her company's money has more incentive to spend the money for her benefit and not for her company's benefit.

Compensating employees based on their achievements maximizes their incentive to work, but can force employees to take a lot of unnecessary risks. Ideally, pay your employees based on their effort, not on their outcomes; however, measuring employees' effort is much harder than measuring their outcomes. Pay employees based on their individual performance, because paying them to work based on the efforts of a large group creates incentives for individuals to free-ride on the efforts of others.

Stay with a strategy if you win, but shift your strategy if you lose. If your choice to use an independent, noncooperative strategy

14

turns out to be better than cooperating, then stay with your strategy. If you aren't successful, then change to another strategy.

Bring extra players into the game. For example, if you are in a two-player game, then turn it into a three-player game. It especially helps to bring in a player who you know will be a noncooperator. The extra player may be able to act as a trusted party to enforce the rules of the game.

Take your negotiations to the brink of failure. This can make a credible demonstration to the other parties that you may not always act in your own self-interest, which can give you more power. Remember that what you would get if negotiations fail can often determine what you would get if negotiations succeed.

Set up forms of reciprocity. One of the best facilitators of cooperation among the parties is knowing that you will have to interact with them in the future. Set up such situations of reciprocity either directly or indirectly to enhance future reciprocity.

Show the other players that your commitment to cooperate with them is credible. Do this by restricting your own future options so that you will lose if you defect on cooperation. For example, put yourself in a position that your reputation will suffer if you do not deliver on a promise to another player. Also, genuinely offer trust to help establish trust's being offered in return.

Create a situation from which neither party can independently escape without experiencing a loss. This situation follows the ideas of a Nash equilibrium in that players have no better result, so they will stay with the current solution.

Employees' sense of fairness is a strong motivator for behavior. Distribute goods, responsibilities, jobs, and other valued resources so that there is the least amount of envy. Set up situations in which the decision-making process is agreed on and transparent, and the outcome is obviously fair.

Subdivide large groups into smaller ones. Cooperation within groups is much easier to obtain in smaller groups than in larger ones. However, creating more groups results in greater difficulty achieving cooperation among or between groups.

14

15

Goal Setting Theory

The theory of goal setting rests on the belief that life is a process of goal-oriented action (Locke & Latham, 1990, 2002). Goals can be defined as a result that individuals try to accomplish (Locke, Shaw, Saari, & Latham, 1981). In organizations, people are motivated to direct their attention toward and achieve goals. Goals have both an internal and an external aspect for individuals. Internally, goals are desired ends of achievement; externally, goals refer employees to an object or to a condition being sought, such as a performance level, a sale to a customer, or a promotion (Locke, 1996; Locke & Latham, 2006). The positive relationship between goal setting and task performance is one of the most replicable findings in the management and organization literature (Locke, Shaw, Saari, & Latham, 1981).

According to goal setting theory, the highest levels of performance are usually reached when goals are both difficult and specific. The more difficult a goal assigned to someone, the greater the resulting performance level. When a specific, difficult goal is set for employees, then goal attainment provides those employees with an objective, unambiguous basis for evaluating the effectiveness of their performance (Locke & Latham, 2006).

Goals influence performance levels by affecting the direction of action, the degree of effort exerted, and the persistence of action over time. For example, when an employee is told to improve quality and not make mistakes, that employee will focus his energy on producing a higher-quality product compared to when that employee is merely told to "do his best" on the task. The only exception to this is that for some creative tasks, being

15

specific may not always be possible. People learn from a very early age that if they want to accomplish a goal, then they have to pay attention to the goal and ignore other things, work hard to accomplish the goal, and keep working hard until the goal is reached.

Performance has been shown to be higher when goals are higher, when people are committed to reaching the goal, and when people possess the required ability and knowledge to achieve that goal (Locke, 1968; Locke & Latham, 2006). When giving people goals to perform, be sure that the goal is specific, such as "Sell one hundred computers," or that the goal describes the desired performance level, such as "Complete this list of seven tasks by 5:00 P.M. today"; otherwise, performance may not be higher than when goals are not used.

To improve performance, help ensure that individuals are committed to their goals (Locke, Latham, & Erez, 1988). When assigning easy or vague goals to employees, commitment to accomplishing those goals is not usually a problem. However, for difficult goals, getting employees to commit to goal attainment can be problematic. Higher performance levels usually result when people are committed to reaching specific, difficult goals, compared with when people are not committed to goal attainment. Higher levels of commitment can be reached when an individual believes that reaching the goal is both important and attainable, or at least believes that progress toward reaching the goal is possible.

Goal setting has been shown to result in higher levels of performance when goals are either assigned to individuals or when individuals are allowed to set goals for themselves (Hollenbeck & Brief, 1987). When goals are assigned to individuals by an authority figure, then performance expectations emerge that can focus employee performance on reaching the assigned goal. When individuals set goals for themselves, equally high performance increases have also been found, provided that the purpose or rationale for having a goal was carefully explained by managers or supervisors. However, when a goal is harshly or tersely set without explanation—"Do this or else"—then performance can be substantially lower compared to when goals are self-set.

Goal setting results in the highest performance levels when people are given feedback about how well they are performing (Locke, 1967). For some tasks, performance levels are self-evident,

15

such as when an employee has been assigned to mow a lawn. However, for other tasks, employees might not be able to determine on their own how well they are performing, so it is helpful to periodically inform people about their progress toward their goals.

People with high self-efficacy set higher goals for themselves than do people with low self-efficacy (Locke & Latham, 2006). People with high self-efficacy tend not to be satisfied with lower goals or with lower performance levels for themselves. Managers can help increase employee self-efficacy by providing adequate training and education to improve mastery of necessary skills, finding role models with whom individuals can identify, and expressing confidence and belief in the employee's ability to accomplish the performance goal.

Goal setting effects may be weaker depending on task complexity (Earley, 1985; Jackson & Zedeck, 1982; Wood, Mento, & Locke, 1987). As the complexity of a task increases, so does the required skill and knowledge level of the employee performing that task. People use a greater variety of tactics and strategies when performing complex tasks compared to performing simple, easy tasks. Goal setting effects may be smaller for a complex task if the individual does not discover appropriate strategies and methods while performing the task.

Criticisms and Critiques of the Theory

The theory of goal setting has received testing in both field and laboratory settings that is arguably among the most rigorous and thorough testing of all the theories in management and organizations. Goal setting research studies have examined over forty thousand subjects of all ages and in eight countries performing more than eighty-eight different tasks ranging from one minute to several years in length. Goal setting effects are usually quite high, typically yielding a success rate of 90 percent (Locke, 1996).

15

However, there are some criticisms of goal setting theory (Latham & Locke, 2006; Locke & Latham, 2009; Ordoñez, Schweitzer, Galinsky, & Bazerman, 2009). Critics have complained that goal setting theory has been overprescribed (Ordoñez, et al., 2009). Goal setting has been described as being effective for any type of task in any type of setting, but this may not actually be the case in organizations.

The theory has been criticized for advocating goals that are too specific or too narrow (Ordoñez, et al., 2009). Specific goals can cause individuals to spend too much time focusing on them to the detriment of other important organizational behaviors, such as innovation, creativity, and flexibility. More research is needed to uncover the influences on level of goal specificity on performance level. Staw and Boettger (1990) found that goals that are too narrow can lower performance levels on assigned tasks.

Critics have argued that the theory has ignored the problems caused by too many goals being assigned for task performance (Ordoñez, et al., 2009). Shah, Friedman, and Kruglanski (2002) found that individuals tend to focus only on one goal at a time when assigned multiple goals simultaneously.

Critics of goal setting theory have argued that most research has ignored a time horizon when setting goals (Ordoñez, et al., 2009). For example, if short-term goals are set, then managers will most often only focus on short-term performance at the expense of long-term performance. Cheng, Subramanyam, and Zhang (2005) found that focusing on meeting only quarterly performance goals can result in firms not investing in long-term research and development efforts.

Critics have argued that there may not be a positive, linear relationship between goal difficulty and task performance as advocated by the theory. If goals are too challenging, then undesired organizational outcomes can occur, such as unethical behavior and unnecessary risk taking in order to accomplish goals (Larrick, Heath, & Wu, 2009; Ordoñez, et al., 2009).

Finally, critics of the theory contend that there can be unexpected undesirable consequences for employees when assigned goals are not reached (Ordoñez, et al., 2009). For example, when employees don't reach goals they can have lower attitudes, lower self-perceptions, and lower self-efficacy beliefs (Galinsky, Mussweiler, & Medvec, 2002; Mussweiler & Strack, 2000).

Measuring Variables in the Theory

Goal orientation scales. Zweig, D., & Webster, J. (2004). Validation of a multidimensional measure of goal orientation. *Canadian Journal of Behavioural Science, 36,* 232–243.

Goal acceptance and goal commitment scales. Renn, R. W., Danehower, C., Swiercz, P. M., & Icenogle, M. L. (1999, March). Further examination of the measurement properties of Leifer & McGannon's (1986) goal acceptance and goal commitment scales. *Journal of Occupational & Organizational Psychology, 72,* 107–113.

Measures for ten goal setting components. Lee, C., Bobko, P., Earley, P. C., & Locke, E. A. (1991). An empirical analysis of a goal setting questionnaire. *Journal of Organizational Behavior, 12,* 467–482.

Multiple factor scales measuring goal commitment. Hollenbeck, J. R., Klein, H. J., O'Leary, A. M., & Wright, P. M. (1989). Investigation of the construct validity of a self-report measure of goal commitment. *Journal of Applied Psychology, 74,* 951–956.

Goal commitment scale. Klein, H. J., Wesson, M. J., Hollenbeck, J. R., Wright, P. M., & Deshon, R. P. (2001). The assessment of goal commitment: A measurement model meta-analysis. *Organizational Behavior and Human Decision Processes, 85,* 32–55.

Achievement goal measures. Hulleman, C. S., Schrager, S. M., Bodmann, S. M., & Harackiewicz, J. M. (2010). A meta-analytic review of achievement goal measures: Different labels for the same constructs or different constructs with similar labels? *Psychological Bulletin, 136,* 422–449.

Suggestions for Further Research

1. Examine the effectiveness of goal setting in dynamic or interactive environments and settings, compared to static, unchanging situations or environments.
2. Explore the effects of short-term versus long-term goals, and examine the influence of combining both short- and long-term goals on task performance.
3. Look at the use of self-commitment versus other-commitment on task performance.
4. Examine the use of goal visualization for tasks of varying difficulty (for example, easy, moderate, difficult) and the influences of goal setting on task performance.

15

5. Investigate the influence of single versus multiple goals on resultant performance levels.
6. Consider the influence of individual, group, and combined individual and group goals on task performance.
7. Examine the effects of direct versus vicarious goal attainment on task performance.
8. Study the effects of conscious versus subconscious goals and task performance.
9. Explore the influence of active versus passive goal priming and goal framing on task performance.
10. Examine the influence of activating and deactivating goals over time on task performance.

References to Know

Locke, E. A. (1996). Motivation through conscious goal setting. *Applied & Preventative Psychology, 5,* 117–124.

Locke, E. A., & Latham, G. P. (1984). Goal setting: A motivational technique that works. Englewood Cliffs, NJ: Prentice Hall.

Locke, E. A., & Latham, G. P. (1990). *A theory of goal setting and task performance.* Englewood Cliffs, NJ: Prentice Hall.

Locke, E. A., & Latham, G. P. (2002, September). Building a practically useful theory of goal setting and task motivation: A 35-year odyssey. *American Psychologist, 57,* 705–717.

Locke, E. A., & Latham, G. P. (2005). Goal setting theory: Theory building by induction. In K. G. Smith & M. A. Hitt (Eds.), *Great minds in management: The process of theory development.* (pp. 128–150). New York: Oxford University Press.

15

Implications of the Theory for Managers

According to goal setting theory, using performance goals can result in higher levels of employee performance compared to when not using performance goals, because goals help employees (1) direct attention to important behaviors and outcomes, (2) increase effort, (3) improve persistent behavior toward reaching desired performance levels, and (4) foster development of action plans and performance strategies. Setting goals for employees is most likely to improve task performance under the following conditions: the goals are specific, measurable, and sufficiently difficult; employees have the ability to perform the desired task; feedback is provided showing progress toward goal attainment; rewards are given for goal attainment; the supervisor or manager is supportive of the goal setting process; and goals are accepted by employees and viewed as important.

When setting goals, be careful not to set goals that are too high, as employees can feel demoralized and defeated when they perform far below the goal. Don't set too many goals for employees, as they tend to focus on only one or two goals at a time and thus may overlook other goals. Be sure to set the right time orientation for employees to reach their goals. If you don't specify a time frame or the time frame is ambiguous, then employees will tend to focus on short-term goals and avoid long-term goals. Be careful to stress that goal accomplishment should only be done through ethical behaviors, and that unethical behaviors will not be tolerated in your organization.

15

16

Image Theory

Image theory focuses on an individual making a decision in the context of a relationship or organization with a presumption that the decision may remain or may later be changed. Image theory was proposed as an alternative to traditional decision-making theory and as a descriptive psychological theory of decision making (Mitchell & Beach, 1990).

Images can be defined as information structures representing different kinds of information about what the decision maker is doing, how and why he or she is doing it, and what kind of progress is being made (Beach & Mitchell, 1987). Image theory uses the term "image" to refer to the schemata involved in decision making (Mitchell & Beach, 1990). Schemata refer to cognitive frameworks that help decision makers organize their world and provide meaning and structure to incoming information that aids in the decision-making process.

Image theory offers a portrait of behavioral decision processes. The traditional view of decision making is that decisions are made deliberately and systematically. Image theory, in contrast, views decisions as being made intuitively and automatically. According to image theory, people most often make decisions using simple, easy, nonanalytic, and rapid processes for each decision, even when the decision has considerable importance to the decision maker.

Image theory posits that there are three types of images: the value image, the trajectory image, and the strategic image. The value image comprises the decision maker's principles, such as morals, ethics, values, ideals, standards of equality, justice,

16

loyalty, and goodness, taken together with his or her moral, civic, and religious beliefs. The value image represents the "self-evident truths" for which the decision maker stands. It helps the decision maker determine which goals are worthy of pursuit and which are not.

The trajectory image refers to the future state that the decision maker is trying to achieve, the agenda that the decision maker is trying to follow. The strategic image comprises the various plans, strategies, and tactics that have been adopted for achieving the trajectory image. For example, a person might want to keep his or her job, avoid bankruptcy, get tenure, or set a new record of achievement.

The three images can then be further broken down into those components that are relevant to the current decision and those that are not. The relevant parts of the three images make up the frame of the current decision. The frame helps establish the context and provides standards that constrain the decision.

Image theory holds that the three types of images are used in two kinds of decisions: adoption decisions and progress decisions. Adoption decisions involve adopting or rejecting candidate components for images. They require that the candidates at least be compatible with the existing components of the images. For instance, candidate goals must be compatible with the decision maker's principles and with the other goals in the trajectory image.

According to image theory, the decision process itself consists of two stages: screening and choice. Screening consists of eliminating unacceptable candidates. Choice consists of selecting the most promising candidates from among the survivors of the screening process. The decision maker screens or filters possible options, and a decision is then followed if a possible option survives. However, if there are no survivors to implement, then the decision maker has to find more options and pursue other interests. If more than one option survives, then the decision maker has to make a choice among the possible decision options to implement.

The screening process narrows down possible decision options. Screening focuses on what is wrong with a possible option and is based on violations of the decision maker's standards and values. Screening does not balance out what is good and bad about a possible option, but tends to focus only on how an option violates standards, morals, and principles. The number of violations

16

that it takes to reject a decision option is called the rejection threshold.

Adoption decisions and progress decisions are made using either or both of two kinds of decision tests: the compatibility test and the profitability test. Compatibility is based on whether a decision candidate fails to violate the existing images. Profitability is the degree to which a decision option offers attractive consequences upon its successful achievement. The profitability test involves evaluating the relative merits of the acceptable decision options and the subsequent choice and implementation of the best alternative. The profitability test can be either compensatory or noncompensatory and is usually more complex and comprehensive than the compatibility test. Usually the attributes of each possible option that are considered in the screening process are not used in the compatibility or profitability tests, as all of the options were found to be acceptable in the screening process.

Progress decisions examine whether each plan in the strategic image is making progress toward attaining the goals of the trajectory image. Progress decisions are, in a way, a special type of adoption decisions. If the current course of action is making progress toward reaching the trajectory image, even in only minimal amounts, then the decision maker usually continues with the status quo. However, if there is significant incompatibility between a decision maker's current image and his or her trajectory image, then decision making proceeds with rapid and instinctive activity to reject the current strategy and to take action in a new and different direction. There appears to be a natural bias for decision makers to view current events in a positive or optimistic way and to overweigh evidence that indicates that the status quo and the trajectory image remain compatible (Beach & Mitchell, 1990).

Researchers have begun to apply image theory concepts to non-decision-making areas (Bissell & Beach, 1996; Richmond, Bissell, & Beach, 1998), such as supervision and job satisfaction. Dunegan (2003) examined the influence of compatible leader image on follower satisfaction and commitment levels. Mady and Gopinath (2008) examined the influences of image theory components on customer service satisfaction and quality perceptions. Dunegan advocated that image theory can be successfully applied to a multitude of managerial and organizational behaviors and

16

processes, such as fairness situations (Gilliland, Benson, & Schepers, 1998).

Criticisms and Critiques of the Theory

The concept of images is a vital part of image theory, and much more work needs to be done that fully explores images themselves. Research on image theory has not fully examined the nature of images—what they are, how they are created, and how they change over time. Image researchers have forfeited work on images and have instead focused on the screening mechanism in the theory.

Beach and Mitchell (2005) stated that the focus on the screening method rather than on images themselves was intentional, driven by concerns for marketing the theory in order to make it more popular with journals and researchers. Beach and Mitchell stated it was easier to conduct more rigorous research on the screening method, which would increase both the attention paid to the theory and the likelihood of publication.

Beach and Mitchell (2005) wrote that they tailored the research to meet the needs of two different audiences. They tailored the numbers and equations aspect of the screening process to meet the needs of decision researchers. They tailored the practical concepts to meet the less rigorous needs of human resource researchers, which they stated was a specific marketing attempt to gain as much widespread knowledge of and attention to image theory as possible. They noted that acceptance of the theory can now enable researchers to focus on a broader array of its features.

The compatibility factor of image theory needs to be further examined. Although the compatibility factor is simple and intuitively appealing, there have been few studies that have even measured it, and there haven't been enough studies that have examined it as a predictor of decision behaviors (Beach & Mitchell, 1987; Dunegan, 1995).

Measuring Variables in the Theory

16

Image compatibility. Dunegan, K. J. (1995). Image theory: Testing the role of image compatibility in progress decisions. *Organizational Behavior and Human Decision Processes, 62,* 79–86.

Leader-image compatibility scale. Dunegan, K. J. (2003, Winter). Leader-image compatibility: An image theory view of leadership. *Journal of Business and Management, 9,* 61–77.

Object attractiveness. Beach, L. R., Puto, C. P., Heckler, S. E., Naylor, G., & Marble, R. A. (1996). Differential versus unit weighting of violations, framing, and the role of probability in image theory's compatibility test. *Organizational Behavior and Human Decision Processes, 65,* 77–82.

Suggestions for Further Research

1. Apply image theory aspects to non-decision-making tasks, contexts, and situations in organizations.
2. Examine the range of tolerance for deviations between actual and ideal workplace behaviors.
3. Explore the influence of time constraints on each of the aspects of image theory.
4. Look at how rejection thresholds are created and changed when people screen decision options.
5. Examine the process through which decision makers create, maintain, and revise their value images.
6. Explore the influence of biases and prejudices on the compatibility and profitability processes in decision making.
7. Study how decision makers balance both violations and non-violations on different types of judgment and decision responses.
8. Examine the threshold level of progress toward accomplishing goals to determine how and when decision makers decide to change their current course of action.
9. Explore the stability and fluidity of the three types of images over time.
10. Examine the influence of individual difference on the creation and use of the three types of images.
11. Look at the cognitive rigor and time required to make decisions according to image theory.

References to Know

Beach, L. R. (1990). *Image theory: Decision making in personal and organizational contexts.* Chichester, England: Wiley.

16

Beach, L. R. (1998). *Image theory: Theoretical and empirical foundations*. Mahwah, NJ: Erlbaum.

Beach, L. R., & Mitchell, T. R. (1990). A contingency model for the selection of decision strategies. *Academy of Management Review, 3,* 439–449.

Mitchell, T. R., & Beach, L. R. (1990). ". . . Do I love thee? Let me count . . ." Toward an understanding of intuitive and automatic decision making. *Organizational Behavior and Human Decision Processes, 47,* 1–20.

Seidl, C., & Traub, S. (1998). A new test of image theory. *Organizational Behavior and Human Decision Processes, 75,* 93–116.

Implications of the Theory for Managers

Image theory holds that decision makers monitor the status quo and forecast expected progress toward desired goals. If the decision maker's image of the status quo differs too much from his or her image of the desired state, and if there is little hope that the situation will correct itself, then the decision maker must either accept the poor situation or take action to change the situation. The perceived incompatibility between the current situation and the desired situation is what motivates the decision maker to take action.

Employees decide to devote their time and energies to organizations for many reasons—for example, because they trust and believe in the mission and goals of an organization. Image theory can help you understand and influence the decisions that your employees make. Image theory posits that employees base their decisions on three images: (1) the value image (which reflects the employee's personal values); (2) the trajectory image (which reflects the employee's ideal self); and (3) the strategic image (which reflects the actions the employee takes to become the ideal self).

Employees look for the actions that will give them the most return on their investment to become their ideal self. Once employees have found a good fit or balance of effort and reward, they tend to try to maintain that situation. Employees tend to be "cognitive misers" who try to maintain a desirable status quo. They

16

have little need to reevaluate or change the current situation unless they see a trajectory image that is better for them.

Your task as a manager is to help employees uncover a new trajectory image for themselves that will take them to new and better places. To do this, gather information about the employee's value image (personal values and beliefs) by talking with the employee. Work with the employee to uncover her ideal self, or trajectory image, of where she wants to go. Create a mutual strategy with the employee to develop a path to help the employee reach her ideal self in her job, in her organization, and in her career as a whole. Finally, follow up with your employee over time and fine-tune her images and trajectory toward a new status quo.

Thus, according to image theory, as a manager, you too should have a careful and specific idea about what the future should be like (an ideal image). You should also carefully monitor the progress being made to reach the ideal state. Finally, you must take action to change things if you perceive that progress toward the ideal state is not being made.

16

Institutional Theory

Institutional theory addresses the central question of why all organizations in a field tend to look and act the same (DiMaggio & Powell, 1983). The core concept of institutional theory is that organizational structures and processes tend to acquire meaning and achieve stability in their own right, rather than on the basis of their effectiveness and efficiency in achieving desired ends, such as the mission and goals of the organization (Lincoln, 1995). In the initial stages of the organizational life cycle, there is considerable variety in organizational forms. Over time, however, there is startling homogeneity in organizational structures and practices.

Institutional theory posits that institutions are a critical component in the environment. Institutions have been defined as "regulative, normative, and cognitive structures and activities that provide stability and meaning for social behavior" (Scott, 1995, p. 33). Examples of institutions include laws, regulations, customs, social and professional norms, culture, and ethics. Institutions exert a constraining influence over organizations, called isomorphism, that forces organizations in the same population to resemble other organizations that face the same set of environmental conditions (Hawley, 1968).

Institutions exert three types of isomorphic pressure on organizations: coercive, normative, and mimetic (DiMaggio & Powell, 1983). Coercive isomorphism refers to pressure from entities who have resources on which an organization depends. Mimetic isomorphism refers to the imitation or copying of other successful organizations when an organization is uncertain about what to do. Normative isomorphism refers to following professional standards and practices established by education and training methods, professional networks, and movement of employees among firms.

New organizational forms typically do not emerge on the basis of the availability of an unused resource. Instead, new organizational forms emerge once they are viewed by society as legitimate (Aldrich & Fiol, 1994). Legitimacy refers to the extent to which an organization's actions are socially accepted and approved by various internal and external stakeholders (Kostova, Roth, & Dacin, 2008) and are consistent with widely held norms, rules, and beliefs (Sonpar, Pazzaglia, & Kornijenko, 2009). When organizations submit to institutional pressures and conform to social norms for certain organizational structures and processes, they are rewarded by earning increased legitimacy, resources, and survival capabilities for their operations (Oliver, 1997; Yang & Konrad, 2010).

Institutional theory posits that institutionalized activities occur due to influences on three levels: individual, organizational, and interorganizational (Oliver, 1997). On the individual level, managers follow norms, habits, customs, and traditions, both consciously and unconsciously (Berger & Luckmann, 1967). On the organizational level, shared political, social, cultural, and belief systems all support following traditions of institutionalized activities. On the interorganizational level, pressures from government, industry alliances, and expectations from society define what is socially acceptable and expected organizational behavior, which pressures organizations to look and act the same (DiMaggio & Powell, 1983).

Institutional theorists are especially interested in examining those organizational structures and practices that have no obvious economic or technical purpose. For example, an organization might retain an unreliable supplier merely out of habit, or because it "has always done it that way." An action has become "institutionalized" when the reason for its existence is merely that "everybody else is doing it too." Institutional theorists argue that many organizational actions are so taken for granted that managers no longer question why a specific action was started or why a specific action should continue (Oliver, 1997).

Institutional theorists have gone astray, such as in the misinterpretation of DiMaggio and Powell's classic "iron cage" paper

(1983). DiMaggio and Powell argued that organizations become isomorphic within their institutional environments. Institutional researchers erroneously took this work to mean that (1) organizations become isomorphic with each other, so over time, all become identical to each other; and (2) organizations are only passive to the elements and forces in their environments (Suddaby, 2010).

In response, DiMaggio (1988) attempted to get institutional theorists back on track. He argued that organizations are not prisoners of their environmental forces. He stressed that organizations often act in creative ways to change their institutional environments, in a process that he labeled "institutional entrepreneurship."

As a result of this change in theoretical focus, institutional theorists investigated how organizations can act as change agents. For example, Oliver (1991) examined the range of ways in which organizations can conform or resist. More specifically, in response to institutional pressures and expectations to conform, organizations can adopt the following strategies (in ascending order of active organizational resistance): acquiescence, compromise, avoidance, defiance, or manipulation.

Institutional entrepreneurs are actors who create new organizations or transform existing ones (DiMaggio, 1988; Garud, Hardy, & Maguire, 2007). The actors can be individuals, groups, organizations, or groups of organizations, but they must both initiate and implement divergent changes (Battilana, Leca, & Boxenbaum, 2009).

Institutional theory research underwent a significant change in the late 1970s and early 1980s. Prior to that time, classical institutional theorists examined such issues as coalitions, competing values, influence, power, and informal structures (Greenwood & Hinings, 1996). Selznick (1957) is often cited as a source of the "old" approach. The new (neo) institutional theorists examine organizations at the field level amid both competitive and cooperative exchanges with other organizations, and focus on legitimate and "taken for granted" structures and processes.

Suddaby (2010) proposed four areas of research that appear to be the promising avenues for future institutional theory: categories, language, work, and aesthetics. Heugens and Lander (2009) examined three ongoing disputes among institutional theorists. First is the quarrel regarding the supremacy of structure over agency. This debate examines whether organizational structures and processes emerge due to macro societal forces or due to organizations' taking action to create them. Second is the continuing debate over the influence of conformity on organizational performance. Third is the examination of the influence of within-field variability on the extent to which organizations adopt structures and practices that are similar to their peers, and the rate at which they do so.

Criticisms and Critiques of the Theory

Although there is considerable agreement in the institutional theory literature on the necessity and benefits of legitimacy, there are exceptions. For example, Kraatz and Zajac (1996) found little evidence supporting the constraints of legitimacy. Phillips and Zuckerman (2001) argued that it is the middle-status players who feel the need to act legitimately. High-status players have the reputational capital to deviate from the norm, and low-status players have to do whatever it takes to survive, whether legitimate or not.

Some researchers have questioned the reasoning behind moving from classic institutional theory and solely toward new institutional theory (Koelble, 1995; Selznick, 1996). The old and new approaches both have their advantages and disadvantages, and should be integrated into modern institutional theory.

Another criticism of institutional theory has had to do with the way that institutions have been measured. Peters (2000) argued that researchers have overlooked the problem of appropriately measuring institutions. Suddaby (2010) argued that institutional research moved from treating organizations as "passive dopes" to "hypermuscular supermen" (p. 15). Any change, no matter how slight, is treated as "institutional," and any change agent is regarded as an "institutional entrepreneur." Dacin, Goodstein, and Scott (2002) warned that institutional research should only value instances of significant, profound, field-level change, and not merely incremental changes.

Critics have argued that the processes underlying institutionalization have not been examined (Phillips, Lawrence, & Hardy, 2004). Institutional theory has tended to focus on the effects of institutionalization rather than on the process through which organizations become institutionalized. This has resulted in a view of organizations merely as "black boxes" with nothing of value inside.

17

Measuring Variables in the Theory

Professional commitment scale. Suddaby, R., Gendron, Y., & Lam, H. (2009). The organizational context of professionalism in accounting. *Accounting Organizations and Society, 34,* 409–427.

Subsidiary performance measures. Slangen, A.H.L., & Hennart, J.-F. (2008, November). Do foreign greenfields outperform foreign acquisitions or vice versa? An institutional perspective. *Journal of Management Studies, 45,* 1301–1328.

Programmability measure and span of control measure. Eisenhardt, K. M. (1988). Agency- and institutional-theory explanations: The case of retail sales compensation. *Academy of Management Journal, 31,* 488–511.

Suggestions for Further Research

1. Explore how organizations experience isomorphic pressures, make sense of them, and learn to manage them over time.
2. Investigate the temporal dynamics in which the benefits of legitimacy might increase or decrease for organizations.
3. Examine how isomorphic pressures accelerate and coordinate collective actions of organizations over time.
4. Study the underlying reasons why spontaneous, organizational field-level isomorphic changes occur, such as minimizing collective regrets (Landman, 1993) or bolstering threatened collective identities (Hardy, Lawrence, & Grant, 2005).
5. Explore how organizations can differentiate themselves from their competitors yet remain within the "range of acceptability" (Deephouse, 1999).
6. Examine differences in the ways that cooperative and competitive forces produce isomorphism.
7. Look at how field-level factors moderate isomorphic processes in organizational fields.
8. Measure various isomorphic processes and examine the relative impact that each of those processes has on organizational outcomes.

9. Examine the extent to which isomorphic forces are stronger in fields where organizations regularly interact with state agencies.
10. Explore the extent to which template diffusions proceed more rapidly or slowly in organizational fields that operate in relative isolation from or inclusion with other fields.
11. Investigate how human decision makers initiate and sustain institutional changes to the organizational field and environment.

References to Know

DiMaggio, P., & Powell, W. W. (1983). The iron cage revisited: Institutional isomorphism and collective rationality in organizational fields. *American Sociological Review, 48,* 147–160.

Meyer, J., & Rowan, B. (1977, September). Institutionalized organizations: Formal structure as myth and ceremony. *American Journal of Sociology, 83,* 340–363.

Powell, W. W., & DiMaggio, P. J. (1991). *The new institutionalism in organizational analysis.* Chicago: University of Chicago Press.

Scott, W. R. (1995). *Institutions and organizations.* Thousand Oaks, CA: Sage.

Zucker, L. G. (1977). The role of institutionalization in cultural persistence. *American Sociological Review, 42,* 726–743.

Implications of the Theory for Managers

Institutional theory examines why and how organizations tend to look and act the same over time. One reason for the similarity among organizations is that some organizational structures and methods are so commonplace that nobody ever challenges them. Nobody ever wonders why they were started in the first place, and nobody ever asks if they should be discontinued. Everyone just thinks of them as the only possible way of doing business.

One of the reasons for this similarity and conformity is that organizations tend to follow only those organizational structures and practices that have been made legitimate by other organizations. Managers can get caught in this same trap of only doing what "everyone else is doing." They may keep doing the same old thing due to norms, habits, customs, and traditions, both consciously and unconsciously. They may be forced to go along due to company rules, standard operating procedures, and field-tested methods. Managers may be uncertain about what to do, so they simply copy what has already been successfully done by someone else. They may simply keep doing what they learned in school, what their professional standards dictate, or what they learned working for another company.

If you want to make significant changes and take your group, division, or company in significantly new directions, then simply following the crowd will not be a successful strategy. If you want to become an "institutional entrepreneur," then you will have to take some risks and try new methods that have not been field-tested or legitimized by other managers or by other companies. Greater risks can offer greater returns for you and your company, but breaking new ground is not for the fainthearted. Consider your own personal risk-tolerance level when deciding whether to go where no manager has gone before, as opposed to staying with methods that have been shown to yield good results.

18

Knowledge-Based Theory

The main idea of the knowledge-based theory of the firm is that organizations exist in the way that they do because of their ability to manage knowledge more efficiently than is possible under other types of organizational structures (Conner, 1991; Kogut & Zander, 1992, 1993, 1996; Conner & Prahalad, 1996; Foss, 1996; Grant, 1996a, 1996b; Madhok, 1996; Nahapiet & Ghoshal, 1998; Nickerson & Zenger, 2004). In other words, organizations are social entities that use and store internal knowledge, competencies, and capabilities that are vital for the firm's survival, growth, and success (Hakanson, 2010). The theory emphasizes the organizational need for superior coordination and integration of learning by employees inside the organization (Kogut & Zander, 1992; Nelson & Winter, 1982).

Theorists have not yet agreed on a single definition of knowledge (Balconi, Pozzali, & Viale, 2007). Indeed, some researchers do not distinguish between information and knowledge (Nonaka, 1994). According to Winkin (1996), data are turned into information, information is turned into knowledge, and then knowledge is confronted with wisdom. Gorman (2002) classified knowledge into four types: declarative (knowing what), procedural (knowing how), judgment (knowing when), and wisdom (knowing why). Balconi et al. presented a synthesis of some typologies: know-what, know-why, know-how, and know-who.

The theory makes a strong distinction between tacit knowledge (what a person knows only inside his or her own mind) and explicit knowledge (what is in the public domain) (Nelson & Winter, 1982; Polanyi, 1966). An oft-quoted example of tacit knowledge is riding a bicycle (Phelan & Lewin, 2000). Tacit knowledge is a valuable resource for organizations because it cannot be easily acquired, and trying to copy it is often costly, assuming that someone with the desired knowledge can even be located. Tacit knowledge cannot be easily written down and documented (or codified), so it can only be learned through observation of experts and subsequent practicing of skills (Kogut & Zander, 1992; Grant, 1996b).

Unfortunately, researchers have not reached agreement on defining tacit knowledge (Ancori, Bureth, & Cohendet, 2000; Hakanson, 2007). For the most part, researchers have agreed that tacit knowledge is revealed only through watching someone use his or her skills and abilities. Articulation is the process through which tacit knowledge is made explicitly known to everyone. Codification is the process through which articulated knowledge is fixed, recorded, standardized, and disseminated to people in the organization (Hakanson, 2007). Some researchers believe that tacit knowledge cannot be articulated (Grant & Baden-Fuller, 1995; Reed & DeFillipi, 1990). Soo, Devinney, Midgley, and Deering (2002) argued that once tacit knowledge is articulated, then it stops being knowledge and becomes merely data. However, other researchers argue that all tacit knowledge can be translated into explicit knowledge (Schulz & Jobe, 2001). Hakanson (2007) created a typology that defined important terms in the theory: explicit knowledge (know-why and know-what), internalized knowledge (explicit knowledge that is not being used), procedural knowledge (knowledge of skills and capabilities), and tacit knowledge (articulate and inarticulate).

How organizations manage their stores of knowledge can determine their success or failure. For example, firms that are more effective than other organizations at finding, absorbing, and exploiting new knowledge from both their internal and external environments will tend to perform better than their competition (Martin-de-Castro, Delgado-Verde, Lopez-Saez, & Navas-Lopez, 2011). Liebeskind (1996) argued that firms that can protect their explicit knowledge will perform better than those that can't protect it. Organizations can protect their knowledge by designing jobs where individuals can't see the "whole picture" of a process, using employment contracts and confidentiality agreements to slow the spread of company secrets, and imposing costs on employees for leaving the company, such as through deferred compensation (pension plans, stock options, and so on).

The theory assumes that organizations are all heterogeneous, knowledge-bearing entities that apply knowledge to the production of their goods and services (Foss, 1996). Firms organize the way that they do because they are depositories of productive knowledge. The knowledge stocks contribute to differential efficiencies and help some firms realize competitive advantages over other firms. The knowledge stocks also help explain why some organizations are more diversified and innovative than others (Foss, 1996). This assumption goes against older theories of the firm that see organizations as merely a bundle of contracts that govern efficient allocation of property rights (Kogut & Zander, 1992). The theory also assumes that knowledge—created, stored, and used—is the most strategically important of an organization's resources (Grant, 1996b). Knowledge is such an important resource because all human productivity is dependent on knowledge, and all technology is merely the embodiment of knowledge.

The theory assumes that knowledge is created, stored, and used by individuals and not by organizations as a whole. Coordinating and integrating this knowledge held by diverse individuals is a difficult task for managers. Grant (1996b) described four mechanisms for integrating specialized knowledge held by individuals: (1) rules and directives (procedures, plans, policies, and practices); (2) sequencing (time-patterned schedules); (3) routines (complex organizational patterns of behavior); and (4) group problem solving and decision making (social communication involving discussing, sharing, and learning and then taking action).

These four mechanisms for coordinating and integrating individual-level knowledge all depend on the existence of "common knowledge." Common knowledge refers to those elements of knowledge of which everyone in the organization should be aware. Common knowledge is important in an organization because it enables everyone to share knowledge that is *not* common. Different types of common knowledge include language, symbolic communication (literacy, numeracy, software programs), shared specialized knowledge, shared meaning (shared metaphors, analogies, and stories), and recognition and

18

mutual adjustment with other employees (Grant, 1996b). Complex hierarchies in organizations can impede the sharing of common knowledge when knowledge is stored in separate and distant levels within the hierarchy.

Research examining knowledge-based theory has focused on (1) exploitation of organizational capabilities, (2) creation of new knowledge capabilities, and (3) knowledge exchange processes within knowledge-based (epistemic) communities (Hakanson, 2010).

A critical debate underlying research has to do with what is called the locus of knowledge—whether the individual or the collective is the source of new value for organizations (Felin & Hesterly, 2007; Nahapiet & Ghoshal, 1998). Most researchers have focused on a collective locus of knowledge (for example, Adler, 2001; Brown & Duguid, 2001; Kogut, 2000; Nahapiet & Ghoshal, 1998; Nelson & Winter, 1982; Tsoukas, 1996). However, a few researchers have focused on the individual locus of knowledge (for example, Grant, 1996b; Simon, 1991).

In this knowledge-based economy, there also has been a move to examine a firm's knowledge assets, or intellectual capital (Dean & Kretschmer, 2007). Intellectual capital has not been well defined and is in need of a better theoretical framework (Cabrita & Bontis, 2008). A firm's intellectual capital includes human capital, structural capital, and relational capital (Martin-de-Castro et al., 2011). Intellectual capital is related to a firm's ability to create and apply its knowledge base.

Criticisms and Critiques of the Theory

Knowledge-based theory has been criticized for not adequately defining the term "knowledge" (Balconi et al., 2007; Kogut & Zander, 1993). Original formulations of the theory treated knowledge as an objective company resource like other company properties. However, more recent formulations of knowledge treat the concept as something that is learned, shared, produced, and utilized through a community of people. Later discussions were more careful to distinguish between knowledge and knowing (Polanyi, 1966), but researchers still disagree on how knowledge is conceptualized and operationalized (Ancori et al., 2000; Hakanson, 2007).

An additional criticism of the theory was over the idea that organizations are social communities of people. These communities have boundaries that enable knowledge to be more prevalent inside organizations compared to outside them. However, this aspect of the theory was not well described in early writings, so it has received criticism as a result.

The theory has also been criticized for its assumption that knowledge inside a firm can be shared and used more cheaply than knowledge among firms. Critics argue that to examine this statement, the theory needs some sort of individual choice mechanism, but note that there are no individual choice mechanisms in organizational capabilities approaches (Foss, 2003). The theory is thus vulnerable to critiques from those who follow a comparative contracting perspective (Foss, 1996; Williamson, 1999).

Measuring Variables in the Theory

Organizational emphasis on knowledge management, centralization of IT decisions, top managers' knowledge, and other scales. Kearns, G. S., & Sabherwal, R. (2007). Strategic alignment between business and information technology: A knowledge-based view of behaviors, outcome, and consequences. *Journal of Management Information Systems, 23,* 129–162.

Codifiability, teachability, and complexity scales. Kogut, B., & Zander, U. (1993). Knowledge of the firm and the evolutionary theory of the multinational corporation. *Journal of International Business Studies, 24,* 625–645.

Suggestions for Further Research

1. Examine how firms use incentives and productivity to facilitate knowledge usage and sharing.
2. Explore how firm exit leads to loss of socially embedded tacit knowledge.
3. Look at the impact of decreased invention and innovation before and after mergers and acquisitions.
4. Examine individual-level variables, such as knowledge hoarding, self-interest, and individual inertia, on knowledge structures.

5. Explore the range of a firm's intellectual capital and its influence on creating a sustained competitive advantage.
6. Study the range of communication devices that can be used to share knowledge within and among organizations and their influence on firm performance.
7. Examine how firms integrate and coordinate knowledge by embedding knowledge into software and other technologies.
8. Explore whether firms that obtain and share new knowledge through social networking technologies are more successful than firms that do not.
9. Examine the effectiveness of face-to-face versus social network displays of tacit knowledge and their influence on knowledge sharing.
10. Look at the similarities and differences in "knowing how" and "knowing about" in communities of practice versus individual learning and training programs.

References to Know

Grant, R. M. (1996b, Winter). Toward a knowledge-based theory of the firm. *Strategic Management Journal, 17*(Special Issue), 109–122.

Kogut, B., & Zander, U. (1992). Knowledge of the firm, combinative capabilities, and the replication of technology. *Organization Science, 3,* 384–397.

Kogut, B., & Zander, U. (2003). A memoir and reflection: Knowledge and an evolutionary theory of the multinational firm 10 years later. *Journal of International Business Studies, 34,* 505–515.

Nonaka, I. (1994). A dynamic theory of organizational knowledge creation. *Organization Science, 5,* 14–37.

Polanyi, M. (1966). *The tacit dimension.* New York: Doubleday.

Implications of the Theory for Managers

According to knowledge-based theory, an organization can succeed only to the extent of its ability to obtain, generate, store, and use knowledge better than its competitors. The term "knowledge" includes everything that your employees know: know-how, know-what, know-who, know-when, and know-why.

Your task as manager is to make the best possible use of your employees' knowledge base toward accomplishing your company's mission, strategies, and goals. Some of your employees' knowledge is explicit, or in the public domain, and so is available to everyone. However, some of your employees' knowledge is tacit—that is, it exists only in their minds. Your job as a manager is to help bring out the knowledge that resides inside the brains of your employees, so that it can be documented, shared, and used by others in the company, a process called codification.

18

Codifying the tacit knowledge of your employees is not an easy process, and often requires employees to watch a knowledgeable person demonstrate his or her skills and abilities. You will need to provide opportunities for employees to observe and learn from knowledgeable employees in action. Next, you will need to provide practice opportunities for employees to try out and refine their newly learned skills. Without practice, they will not retain their newly learned skills and abilities, and the knowledge will be lost.

Finally, you need to protect employee knowledge from leaving the company by retaining key knowledgeable employees, offering deferred compensation to keep people from leaving, and using confidentiality agreements or other methods to inhibit employees from revealing company secrets to other organizations.

19

Media Richness Theory

The major premise of media richness theory is that a person's performance in a communication situation tends to be a function of the fit between the characteristics of the communication medium and the characteristics of the task to be performed (Daft & Lengel, 1984, 1986). In other words, people who use the best-fitting communication channel for their tasks will be more effective than people who use the wrong-fitting communication channel. For instance, you shouldn't propose marriage or fire an employee using a text message, and you should send a formal engraved invitation to invite your future in-laws to your wedding.

The communication process involves sharing meaning and information with others. Communication is conducted using one or more communication media, such as talking, letters, memos, and telephone. Communication media can have varying levels of "richness," which refers to their potential information-carrying capacity (Daft & Lengel, 1984). Media richness also can refer to a medium's capacity to transmit multiple cues and rapid feedback to the recipient of the communication (Russ, Daft, & Lengel, 1990).

Bodensteiner (1970) created a hierarchy of communication media that ranked four different media classifications. Daft and Lengel (1984) adapted this hierarchy and created a continuum of media richness for four media channels with four media characteristics: (1) feedback, (2) channel, (3) source, and (4) language. Their continuum rated media from highest to lowest in terms of level of richness: face-to-face (most social presence), telephone, personal written, formal written, and formal numeric (least social presence). A later reformulation of the continuum (Lengel & Daft, 1988) rated media from highest to lowest in terms of richness as physical presence (face-to-face), interactive media (telephone, electronic media), personal static media (memos, letters, personally tailored computer reports), and interpersonal static media (flyers, bulletins, generalized computer reports). Face-to-face communication was described as the most rich communication medium because it has the capacity for social presence, direct experience, multiple information cues, immediate feedback, and personal focus. Telephone communication is less rich because it has less direct feedback, fewer cues (no body language, head nodding, eye contact, and so on). Personal written media (such as memos, notes, and reports) are less rich than telephone due to limited cues and slow feedback. Impersonal written media (such as flyers, bulletins, and reports) are the least rich (most lean) due to impersonal focus, limited information cues, and no feedback.

According to the theory, ambiguity is a key concept for determining the best communication medium to use for each type of task (Daft & Lengel, 1986; Daft & Macintosh, 1981; Weick, 1979). Messages that are more ambiguous require using richer communication media in order to be effective. Messages are ambiguous, or equivocal, when they can be interpreted in many different ways. Meaning and understanding in these situations must be created, negotiated, and shared among people. Richer communication media, such as face-to-face communication, tend to be more effective for ambiguous messages. Face-to-face communication allows for discussion of ideas, immediate feedback, and using both words and body language to convey meaning.

However, messages are unambiguous, or unequivocal, when only one interpretation is possible and when there is already consensus about the meaning and interpretation of the message. Messages that are less ambiguous only require using a lean (or less rich) communication medium in order to be effective. Lean communication media include memos, letters, e-mails, and text messages.

Research has shown that managers who are more skilled at using the right communication medium for specific tasks tend to be more effective than managers who are less skilled (Lengel & Daft, 1988; Russ et al., 1990). Communication messages also involve a level of uncertainty. Selecting the right communication medium depends on the level of uncertainty and ambiguity of the message. Uncertainty typically refers to the absence of information in the message (Shannon & Weaver, 1949). More effective managers tend to use the face-to-face medium for highly equivocal and uncertain communications, but use written media for clear, objective, unequivocal, and more certain communications (Daft, Lengel, & Trevino, 1987; Russ et al., 1990).

Carlson and Zmud (1999) examined how users' perceptions of media can change over time with continued usage of a medium. In an approach they referred to as "channel expansion," they focused on four user experiences that are particularly relevant for shaping users' media perceptions—namely, experience with the channel, the message topic, the organizational context, and the communication coparticipants.

More recent research has enhanced the description of the capabilities of communication-rich media. For example, Lan and Sie (2010) have explored four user perceptions of the components of media richness: content timeliness, content richness, content accuracy, and content adaptability. Content timeliness means that the medium is time sensitive and allows for immediate feedback. Content richness means that the medium includes various media types (such as text, graphics, and video). Content accuracy means that the message can be explicitly expressed or easily comprehended. Content adaptability means that the message can be adapted to other formats or modes.

Some media selection research has moved away from aggregate constructs like media richness and social presence in favor of specific media characteristics, such as synchronicity, channel capacity, and reprocessability (Mohan et al., 2009). Synchronicity refers to whether communication occurs in real time or with a delay. Channel capacity means that the medium can transmit a high variety of cues. Reprocessability means that a message can be reexamined in the current situation. Other research has looked at differences among media users with regard to space and time, employing, for example, a 2 × 2 matrix of same and different time and same and different location (Robert & Dennis, 2005).

Criticisms and Critiques of the Theory

Media richness theory has generally been supported when tests were conducted on the so-called traditional media, such as face-to-face, telephone, letters, and memos (Daft et al., 1987; Lengel & Daft, 1988; Russ et al., 1990). However, the theory has not stood up well when tested on newer media, such as e-mail, voice-mail, and text messaging (for example, Suh, 1999). In opposition to the theory, Rice (1983) found that communication media usage was weakly associated with social presence in new media.

The theory has been criticized for focusing exclusively on individual (such as managerial) choice and not accounting for situational and social factors that could affect adoption and usage of communication media. Widespread, or critical mass, usage of a medium can facilitate adoption and use of communication technology (Markus, 1987). Researchers have explored how attitudes and behaviors toward media usage are partially socially constructed (Fulk, 1983; Fulk, Steinfeld, Schmitz, & Power, 1987; Schmitz & Fulk, 1991). In addition, social pressures, such as sponsorship, socialization, social control, and social norms, can result in public adoption and use of communication technologies (Markus, 1994). However, even the research on social influences has not been consistent (Davis, Bagozzi, & Warshaw, 1989; Rice, 1983).

Other critics have commented that the theory assumes that people are passive receptacles of whatever information is sent to them. Following the work of Habermas (1979, 1984, 1987), researchers have explored the view that people are intelligent, active assessors of the truth, completeness, sincerity, and contextuality of the messages that are sent to them (Ngwenyama & Lee, 1997), so there are societal and cultural influences on media choice and usage.

Kock (2005, 2009) argued for a media naturalness approach. The media naturalness approach follows that the more a communication medium is less like face-to-face communication, then the more cognitive effort, ambiguity, and physiological arousal there are when using the medium.

Robert and Dennis (2005) found a paradox that goes against the main idea of the theory. They argued that the use of rich communication media (high in social presence) can increase motivation of the user, but can hinder the user's ability to process the information received; the use of lean communication media (low in social presence) can decrease motivation of the user, but can facilitate the user's ability to process the information received in the communication.

Measuring Variables in the Theory

Media richness variable items. Brunelle, E. (2009). Introducing media richness into an integrated model of consumers' intentions to use online stores in their purchase process. *Journal of Internet Commerce, 8,* 222–245.

Media richness scale. Vickery, S. K., Droge, C., Stank, T. P., Goldsby, T. J., & Markland, R. E. (2004). The performance implications of media richness in a business-to-business service environment: Direct versus indirect effects. *Management Science, 50,* 1106–1119.

Media richness scale. Suh, K. S. (1999). Impact of communication medium on task performance and satisfaction: An examination of media-richness theory. *Information and Management, 35,* 295–312.

Media richness and culture items. Guo, Z., Tan, F. B., Turner, T., & Xu, H. (2008, December). An exploratory investigation into instant messaging preferences in two distinct cultures. *IEEE Transactions on Professional Communication, 51,* 396–415.

Media gratification items. Ramirez, A., Jr., Dimmick, J., Feaster, J., & Lin, S.-F. (2008, August). Revisiting interpersonal media competition: The gratification niches of instant messaging, e-mail, and the telephone. *Communication Research, 35,* 529–547.

Capabilities of media richness. Lan, Y.-F., & Sie, Y.-S. (2010). Using RSS to support mobile learning based on media richness theory. *Computers and Education, 55,* 723–732.

Suggestions for Further Research

1. Examine the influence of media richness and the instructor's teaching style and pedagogy on online learning.
2. Explore the relationships among media richness and audience interest and engagement with regard to media-based learning.
3. Look at the influence of social presence and media richness on motivation to help others locally and remotely.

19

4. Examine the influence of media richness on customer stakeholder involvement and engagement in desirable business activities.
5. Look at the influence of communication media on receivers' attitudes, understanding, knowledge, and behavior changes.
6. Explore how media perceptions change over time with experience, practice, and training and how those perceptions influence desired outcomes.
7. Examine media effects on forthrightness and truthfulness when conducting performance evaluations and other functions.
8. Look at how the use of rich and lean media for technology-dependent tasks influences group attitudes, behaviors, and effectiveness.
9. Explore media richness effects on individual and group trust or mistrust, cooperation or competition, and outcomes.
10. Explore people's duration and frequency of personal versus impersonal communication across the continuum of media richness in work versus nonwork settings.

References to Know

Daft, R. L., & Lengel, R. H. (1984). Information richness: A new approach to managerial behavior and organization design. In B. Staw & L. L. Cummings (Eds.), *Research in organizational behavior* (Vol. 6, pp. 191–233). Greenwich, CT: JAI Press.

Daft, R. L., & Lengel, R. H. (1986). Organizational information requirements, media richness and structural design. *Management Science, 32,* 554–571.

Daft, R. L., Lengel, R. H., & Trevino, L. K. (1987). Message equivocality, media selection, and manager performance: Implications for information systems. *MIS Quarterly, 11,* 355–366.

Daft, R. L., & Macintosh, N. B. (1981, June). A tentative exploration into the amount of equivocality of information processing in organizational work units. *Administrative Science Quarterly, 26,* 207–224.

Trevino, L. K., Lengel, R. H., & Daft, R. L. (1987). Media symbolism, media richness and media choice in organizations: A symbolic interactionist perspective. *Communication Research, 14,* 553–575.

19

Implications of the Theory for Managers

Media richness theory examines the effectiveness of using various communication media on desired organizational outcomes. You and your employees can use a variety of communication media— face-to-face, telephone, e-mail, and text—to accomplish your necessary tasks. The media you choose can have a significant impact on your own and your employees' attitudes and behaviors. The communication media that will enable you all to perform the most effectively can be determined by a variety of factors, such as cost, convenience, social factors, situational factors, employee demographics, culture, and even the image that you want to present for your organization. Don't take your media usage for granted. Establish an effective communication plan for your organization, addressing such issues as whether standardization is helpful or not for your firm. Work with your employees to select the media that will best enable them to accomplish their job tasks successfully. Discuss communication methods and options with your employees and let them have a say in helping select the tools that can result in the most effective attitudes and behaviors for you, your work group, and your organization. Work together with your employees to establish communication policies on such conduct as using social media, surfing the web, and texting while on the job.

19

20

Mental Models Theory

Mental models are simplified knowledge structures, or cognitive representations, that people use to make sense of and interact with the world around them (Gentner & Stevens, 1983; Johnson-Laird, 1983). The theory of mental models examines how managers use mental models to influence their decision making and strategic choices in order to accomplish organizational mission, strategies, and goals. The theory assumes that those organizations that are better able to construct and use accurate mental models of their business environment will be more successful than organizations that are not able to do so. The theory also assumes that managers who have both a fuller and more accurate understanding of their organization's capabilities and of the key principles of their business environment will have higher performance outcomes than managers who don't have such knowledge (Cockburn, Henderson, & Stern, 2000; Gary & Wood, 2011).

The concept of mental models has a long history and can be traced back to the work of Kelvin, Boltzmann, and Maxwell (Johnson-Laird, 2006) and also to Craik (1943) and Peirce (1931–1958). The theory can be summarized in three principal predictions: (1) people typically build mental models of what they believe to be true; (2) people usually construct only one mental model, rather than multiple mental models; and (3) people tend to consider data and information and to make decisions and choices from within their one mental model. People form mental models of complicated systems so that they can understand what the system contains, how the system works, and why the system works (Zhang, 2010).

Managers are not able to fully know and understand their environment because they have limited sensory and information-processing capabilities. For this reason, managers use simplified mental models to understand and make sense of the world around them (Cyert & March, 1992; March & Simon, 1958). Mental models are merely cognitive representations of reality and are not mental depictions of reality (Kiesler & Sproull, 1982). Although mental models help organizations make sense of a large amount of information, they can also lead to erroneous conclusions, assumptions, and actions. Mental models are subjective, so different organizations can create different mental representations of the same environmental situation and information. The creation of differing mental models about the same set of information can even occur within an organization (Dean & Sharfman, 1993; Dutton, 1993; Haley & Stumph, 1989).

Doyle and Ford (1998) defined a mental model as a relatively enduring, limited, internal conceptual representation of an external system, with the same structure as that of the perceived system. According to the theory, organizations tend to create and adhere to only one mental model at a time, through five main processes: (1) construction of multiple mental models based on perceived information, historical information, and current knowledge; (2) integration of the multiple models; (3) formulation of conclusions based on the integrated models; (4) falsification of conclusions; and (5) taking action based on the single, consolidated model (Bara, Bucciarelli, & Lombardo, 2001).

The theory assumes that most people have not been trained to make logical decisions following complicated rules of logic and inference (Johnson-Laird, 1983). Instead, most people simply depend on their native ability to understand and use premises. The theory posits that people are able to reason on the basis of content and discussions, rather than purely on formal rules of logic (Westbrook, 2006). People use the information that they perceive around them to build mental models. Using these mental models, they formulate conclusions that they believe to be true. They then test the validity of their presumptions based on the fact that there are no other models available that refute their beliefs. In other words, people create and follow a particular mental model merely because no one has shown them that another possible model exists.

Because organizations tend to rely on one mental model, they often fail to consider possibilities that lie outside the boundaries of their model, which can have grave consequences. For example, operators of the Three Mile Island nuclear reactor focused on the model that there was a leak, instead of on the simpler reality that a valve was stuck open. Using a mental model helps organizations focus, but focusing often inhibits organizations from searching for alternative actions and solutions. For example, when an organization is deciding to take action or not, the organization will often construct a mental model about that action and will create an alternative model in which it does not take that action. The organization will tend to search for more information that supports taking the action, and will tend to avoid searching for more information that supports not taking the action. Organizations will tend not to consider alternative courses of action, especially when no one has stated their possibility. Organizations also tend to avoid considering opportunity costs among various alternatives when deciding on a course of action (Friedman & Neumann, 1980).

A great deal of research needs to be conducted to uncover how mental models are formed. Research has shown that people with good memories tend to pay attention to their environment and form mental models more easily than people with poor memories (Westbrook, 2006). People with poor memories tend not to form mental models, and instead focus on memorizing details (Von Hecker, 2004).

The mental models approach has received a large amount of attention in the teamwork area. Team mental models refer to cognitive representations of key aspects of a team's environment that are shared among team members (Mohammed, Ferzandi, & Hamilton, 2010). Numerous studies have shown positive support for the influence of shared mental models on team performance variables (for example, Mathieu, Maynard, Rapp, & Gilson, 2008). Team mental models enable team members to (1) describe (interpret information in the same way); (2) predict (share expectations about upcoming events); and (3) explain (share causal accounts for events) (Mohammed et al., 2010).

Criticisms and Critiques of the Theory

The theory has been criticized for not adequately defining the term "mental model" (Doyle & Ford, 1999). Fetzer (1999) wrote that the term mental model is so vague that it is impossible to test whether people use mental models or not. Turner and Belanger

(1996) noted that the term mental model is confusing because it is used in various ways by different disciplines.

The theory has also been criticized because the term mental model is too similar to other terms. For example, there has been confusion over using the term "cognitive map" as a synonym for mental model. Tolman (1948) used the term cognitive map to refer to a mental representation, or navigational aid, used by people and animals to find their way through mazes and geographical locations. Axelrod (1976) used the term cognitive map to refer to the extensiveness of an expert's cognitive knowledge. In addition, Eden, Jones, and Sims (1979) used the term cognitive map to refer to an elicitation process designed to help people change their ways of thinking. Doyle and Ford (1999) argued that the field's willingness to accept ambiguity regarding the term mental model has inhibited refinement and advancement of the theory. Westbrook (2006) noted that mental models are similar to the preferences, actions, and tools used when people make decisions.

In addition, researchers who prefer formal logic to mental models for reasoning have seriously criticized mental models theory (Fetzer, 1993, 1999). According to the theory, people tend not to make information explicit when they use mental models. Fetzer (1999) argued that this merely means that people use "rules of thumb," but that it does not mean that people avoid using logical rules when making deductions.

Fetzer (1999) also argued that mental models theory does not hold up when it comes to validation of a currently used mental model. According to the theory, people believe that their mental model is true only because they have no better model available to replace it. The theory requires that people think long and hard about other possible models, which may never result in any other models' being discovered. Fetzer argued that not knowing about any better models does not mean that they do not exist, nor does it provide evidence that the current model is valid. People merely believe that their model is valid because they want to believe that it is valid.

Measuring Variables in the Theory

Opportunity costs scale. Friedman, L. A., & Neumann, B. R. (1980). The effects of opportunity costs on project investment decisions: A replication and extension. *Journal of Accounting Research, 18,* 407–419.

Organizational change process questions. Santos, M. V., & Garcia, M. T. (2006). Organizational change: The role of managers' mental models. *Journal of Change Management, 6,* 305–320.

Mental model measures. Smith-Jentsch., K. A., Mathieu, J. E., & Kraiger, K. (2005). Investigating linear and interactive effects of shared mental models on safety and efficiency in a field setting. *Journal of Applied Psychology, 90,* 523–535.

Task work and teamwork mental model scales. Lim, B.-C., & Klein, K. J. (2006). Team mental models and team performance: A field study of the effects of team mental model similarity and accuracy. *Journal of Organizational Behavior, 27,* 403–418.

Suggestions for Further Research

20

1. Examine the formation, maintenance, and evolution of mental models over time.
2. Explore the range of inaccuracies in mental models and their influence on organizational performance.
3. Look at why organizations develop causal blind spots in their mental models and why they sustain such inaccuracies.
4. Create a range or typology of mental model misperceptions and identify which types of misperceptions are the most damaging.
5. Examine the similarities and differences among mental models, images, decision rules, and strategies, and their influence on organizational performance.
6. Explore similarities and differences between individual and organizational mental models.
7. Examine how and why subunits of organizations can develop mental models that conflict with that of their organization and the impact of those models on performance.
8. Look at the process through which people find evidence that supports the maintenance of their current mental model or that results in their abandoning or adapting their current mental model.

9. Explore individual difference variables in people's ability to use mental models to summarize complex situations.
10. Compare using mental models to using formal rules of logic for making organizational decisions and strategy choices.
11. Explore the formation of team mental models over time through the stages of: orientation, differentiation, and integration, and their influence on team performance.

References to Know

Gentner, D., & Stevens, A. L. (Eds.). (1983). *Mental models.* Hillsdale, NJ: Erlbaum.

Johnson-Laird, P. N. (1980). Mental models in cognitive science. *Cognitive Science, 4,* 71–115.

Johnson-Laird, P. N. (1983). *Mental models.* Cambridge, MA: Harvard University Press.

Johnson-Laird, P. N. (2006). Models and heterogeneous reasoning. *Journal of Experimental and Theoretical Artificial Intelligence, 18,* 121–148.

Johnson-Laird, P. N., & Byrne, R. (1991). *Deduction.* Mahwah, NJ: Erlbaum.

20

Implications of the Theory for Managers

Mental models theory examines the processes through which people and organizations make sense of their environment by creating simplified knowledge structures, called mental models. When organizations have a well-developed, shared mental model, then everyone is better able to agree about what we are doing, understand why we are doing it, and anticipate what we are likely to do next. Having a well-formulated, shared mental model enables everyone to be "on the same page" and to describe, explain, and predict his or her environment better than members of organizations without well-developed mental models.

The task for management is to ensure that there is a well-formulated mental model. Take the time to specifically discuss your organization or work group's mental model with your employees. Determine if everyone really is on the same page and seeing the "big picture" in the same way, and if there isn't agreement, work to help everyone see the world in the same way.

Organizations tend to take their mental model for granted as being true without gathering information or data and testing whether or not their mental model is valid. The job for management is to actively seek out and test alternative mental models to ensure that the organization is following the right path relative to its environment and situation. Organizations that take their mental model for granted can be outperformed by their competitors who work to refine and adapt their mental model based on changing environmental conditions. Don't be left behind. Work with your employees to agree on and refine your mental model in response to current environmental and situational factors affecting your organization. Don't just follow what's always been done before. Instead, respectfully question why things are being done the way they are. If the only reason is that "we've always done it that way," then you probably need to work together to find new mental models.

20

21

Organizational Ecology Theory

Organizational ecology theory examines how organizational populations change and develop over time through stages of founding, growth, transformation, decline, and death (Hannan & Freeman, 1977, 1989). The theory addresses the forces of social, political, and economic systems that (1) increase organizational diversity, for example, creating new organizational forms, and (2) decrease organizational diversity, for example, driving away certain organizational forms via competition. The theory also looks at the dynamics within organizational populations (Hannan & Freeman, 1989).

Aldrich and Ruef (2006) reported that there are literally hundreds of thousands of organizations in the world, varying in size from tiny to enormous. Hannan and Freeman (1977) asked the question, "Why are there so many (or so few) different kinds of organizations?" (p. 7). To answer this question, Hannan and Freeman borrowed from Hawley's work on human ecology (1950, 1968) and explored a population ecology of organizations. However, they extended Hawley's work in two ways: (1) using explicit competition models showing how organizations change in structure depending on their environmental pressures, and (2) using niche theory to examine how organizations change in dynamic environments.

Organizational ecology theory was designed to address five issues: (1) the reasons for the wide variety of organizational forms in existence, (2) the distribution of those various organizational forms throughout differing environments, (3) the influence of environment on the distribution of organizational forms, (4) the rate of change of organizational forms (Reydon & Scholz, 2009), and (5) how short-run processes combine to produce organizational characteristics over long periods of time (Hannan & Freeman, 1989).

When someone decides to start a new business, he or she has to decide the niche in which the organization will operate (Baum & Singh, 1994a; Hannan, Carroll, & Polos, 2003; Peli & Nooteboom, 1999). Hutchinson (1978) defined a niche as the set of environmental conditions in which a population reproduces itself. A niche comprises the environmental conditions that allow a population to sustain or even grow its numbers (Hannan & Freeman, 1989). An organizational niche refers to the productive capacities and resource requirements that organizations use within their population. Populations are defined as multiple organizational niches in a multidimensional resource space (Baum & Singh, 1994a, 1994b). Organizations with similar characteristics can be grouped together in the same population (Monge & Poole, 2008). Competition for resources tends to increase as the number of organizations in a niche increases, or becomes more dense, as organizations fight against each other to obtain necessary resources. However, competition can be less if organizations have nonoverlapping niches (Baum & Singh, 1994a, 1994b; Hannan & Freeman, 1989). Niche width refers to the environmental range from which organizations can obtain resources in order to survive (Scheitle, 2007; Sorenson, McEvily, Ren, & Roy, 2006).

The main idea in most of the work that examines single populations is "density dependence selection" (Hannan & Freeman, 1987, 1988). Population density drives two processes: legitimation and competition (Freeman & Audia, 2006). As legitimacy rises, the number of organization foundings increases and the number of failures decreases, and the population of organizations grows. However, competition among those organizations then increases, which can lead to organization deaths. If the number of organizations that the environment can support varies over time, then the number of organizations that can survive in that environment can also vary over time (Lomi, Larsen, & Freeman, 2005).

Theorists have examined reasons why some organizations die while others survive and thrive. At least five reasons have been examined as to the mortality of organizations: age, size, strategy, relational density, and linkages. The death rate of organizations tends to decrease as they age (Baum & Oliver, 1991; Carroll & Delacroix, 1982; Carroll, 1983; Freeman, Carroll, & Hannan, 1983). Newly born organizations suffer a "liability of newness" (Stinchcombe, 1965; Hannan & Freeman, 1984), in that they have to learn how to survive, and must create successful patterns of operations despite having limited resources (Singh, Tucker, & House, 1986; Hannan & Freeman, 1989). Slightly older organizations can suffer a "liability of adolescence" in that they can survive for a time on their initial store of resources, but then their failure rate tends to follow an inverted U-shaped pattern as they age (Bruderl & Schussler, 1990; Fichman & Levinthal, 1991). Older organizations can suffer a "liability of obsolescence" if their operations are highly inertial and unchanging and become increasingly misaligned with their environment (Baum, 1989; Ingram, 1993; Barron, West, & Hannan, 1994).

Research has found that organization survival rate is related to organization size (Basil, Runte, Basil, & Usher, 2011; Baum & Oliver, 1991; Freeman, Carroll, & Hannan, 1983; Núñez-Nickel & Moyano-Fuentes, 2006; Singh, Tucker, & House, 1986). The organization death rate tends to decline with organization size. Little organizations can suffer from a "liability of smallness," as it can be more difficult for them to raise capital, recruit and train a workforce, and cover administrative costs, compared to large organizations (Aldrich & Auster, 1986).

Regarding organizational strategies, organizations are referred to as "specialists" if they can survive only within a limited range of resources. However, firms are referred to as "generalists" if they can survive using a wide range of resources (Hannan & Freeman, 1977). Empirical research has shown that organizations that are more generalist in nature tend to last longer than organizations that specialize. Generalist organizations tend to have more resources than they need for routine operations, and only operate at full capacity when responding to unanticipated environmental demands (Sorenson et al., 2006). Generalist organizations also tend to introduce more new products and reach beyond their typical market segments than do specialist organizations (Sorenson et al., 2006). However, the strength of generalizing versus specializing can be influenced by the typical duration of environmental fluctuations (Freeman & Hannan, 1983, 1987; Hannan & Freeman, 1989). Finally, organizations that develop

21

ties or linkages to well-established societal institutions tend to live longer than organizations that do not do so (Baum & Oliver, 1991).

Researchers have posited that organizations follow a growth process from young to mature and from small to large through a process of five stages: creativity, direction, delegation, coordination, and collaboration (Greiner, 1972; Strauss, 1974). Transitioning from one stage to another increases the organization's vulnerabilities and weaknesses, increases its probability of failure, and exposes it once again to the liability of newness (Hannan & Freeman, 1984).

The theory has moved from addressing the question, "Why are there so many different kinds of organizations?" (Hannan & Freeman, 1977) to "How and why does the number of organizations of a certain kind vary over time?" (Carroll & Swaminathan, 1991). Key research questions in the theory relate to organization density (the number of organizations in a population) and the legitimation of organizational forms within a population. As a result of these questions, the theory has moved away from using evolutionary terminology, or has treated evolutionary terminology merely as a metaphor for evolution (Reydon & Scholz, 2009).

Criticisms and Critiques of the Theory

21

The theory has been criticized for claiming that it follows a Darwinian (1859/2003) perspective on evolution. Scholz and Reydon (2010) argued that the survival or death of an organization because it possesses better or worse traits for its environment does not constitute a Darwinian biological evolutionary perspective. Biological approaches posit that better-fitting organisms have more offspring because their traits enable them to live longer and have more reproductive cycles compared to worse-fitting organisms. Scholz and Reydon argue that this biological approach does not apply well to organizations.

The theory has been criticized for its confusion with regard to the level of analysis (Reydon & Scholz, 2009). Theorists contend that the level of analysis in organizational ecology theory is populations, or collectives of organizations, that evolve, such that older organizations die off and newer organizations are born that only resemble their "parent" organizations. However, critics have argued that the actual unit of analysis is the individual organizations and the forces that influence them, which makes organizational ecology theory no different from most other research programs that examine individual organizations (Reydon & Scholz, 2009). As a result of this confusion, the field of organizational ecology has shifted its focus away from the origins of different kinds of organizations and toward the distribution and abundance of different kinds of organizations.

Critics have argued that there is confusion over the precise definitions of organization "births" and "deaths," which are vital to the theory (Young, 1988). Hannan and Freeman (1989) posited that inertial pressures prevent most organizations from changing their structures and strategies. Thus every time that organizations make major changes, they are referred to as being entirely new organizations. Further, Young (1988) argued that when two organizations merge, it makes no sense to consider both old organizations as having died and a new organization as having emerged. If we say that one organization has died and one has survived, then which one should be selected as the survivor? Freeman, Carroll, and Hannan (1983) considered this situation a gray area for the theory.

The theory has been criticized for ignoring equilibrium assumptions in biological theories (Young, 1988). Hawley's theory (1950, 1968) rigorously relied on the adaptation of human communities to ecological settings. An equilibrium is said to exist when individuals living under the same environmental conditions have acquired a similar form. However, Hannan and Freeman (1989) posited that equilibrium assumptions do not seem appropriate for organizational analysis.

Young (1988) argued that the theory needs a taxonomy of organizations in order to apply biological concepts that use a taxonomy of organisms. There have been attempts at creating a typology or taxonomy of organizations (McKelvey, 1982; Rich, 1992), but they have not met with widespread acceptance or implementation. McKelvey argued that a classification system for organizations is necessary before making population-level inferences.

Measuring Variables in the Theory

Satisfaction with present community scale. Carpenter, E. H. (1977, Fall). The potential for population dispersal: A closer look at residential locational preferences. *Rural Sociology, 42,* 352–373.

Suggestions for Further Research

1. Examine why large organizations are more immune to failure than are small organizations.
2. Explore firm value relative to the extent that the organization takes risks in introducing new products and reaching into new markets.
3. Compare the influence of structural inertia on specialist and generalist organizational behavior.
4. Examine processes through which organizations become specialists or generalists and how those processes influence organizational actions.
5. Look at the tipping point where introduction of new products and entrance into new markets helps or hurts organizations.
6. Explore how "spin-off" organizations help or hurt the reputation and performance of parent and grandparent firms over time.
7. Examine the demographics of individuals who leave parent firms and move to spin-off companies and the impact of such departures on outcomes.
8. Explore penalties that parent organizations experience when they fight the founding of spin-off organizations.
9. Look at the benefits of examining firm density at the pre-entry stage versus the after-entry stage and organization success.
10. Examine the time required to form a new organization and the dangers of the founding of competing organizations for a new organization.
11. Explore why and how some firms are better able to transition from preproduction to production stages.

References to Know

Amburgey, T. L., & Rao, H. (1996). Organizational ecology: Past, present, and future directions. *Academy of Management Journal, 39,* 1265–1286.

Hannan, M. T., & Freeman, J. (1977, March). The population ecology of organizations. *American Journal of Sociology, 82,* 929–964.

Hannan, M. T., & Freeman, J. (1984). Structural inertia and organizational change. *American Sociological Review, 49,* 149–164.

Hannan, M. T., & Freeman, J. (1989). *Organizational ecology.* Cambridge, MA: Harvard University Press.

Singh, J. V., & Lumsden, C. J. (1990). Theory and research in organizational ecology. *Annual Review of Sociology, 16,* 161–195.

Implications of the Theory for Managers

Organizational ecology theory examines how organizations change and develop over time. According to the theory, organizations move through stages of founding, growth, transformation, decline, and death. When organizations are young and small, they are particularly vulnerable to failure. They are also more vulnerable when they transition from one stage to another. Large, mature organizations can also be vulnerable to failure if they develop too many new products and enter too many new markets too quickly for their environment to support. Be aware of the current growth stage of your organization, and stay aware of the potential dangers facing your organization at each stage of its development and growth.

21

Organizations go through four stages of growing pains: crisis of leadership, crisis of autonomy, crisis of control, and crisis of red tape. Help your organization survive its growing pains by expecting these crises, and work to move your firm past each crisis point, so that your organization can grow into a strong, stable, mature organization.

22

Organizational Justice Theory

Organizational justice theory examines individuals' perceptions of fairness in their employment relationship (Colquitt, Greenberg, & Zapata-Phelan, 2005). The topic of organizational justice has become one of the most popular and most researched areas in the fields of organization and management. In management and organization research, the terms "justice" and "fairness" are often used interchangeably, such as when referring to "organizational justice" and "organizational fairness" perceptions.

Researchers have debated about the number of different types of justice that are important in fairness perceptions. Some researchers have focused on one type (an overall perception of fairness), two types (distributive justice and procedural justice), three types (adding interactional justice), and four types (separating interactional justice into both interpersonal justice and informational justice).

The first type of fairness that was examined in the social sciences was distributive justice, which looks at people's perceptions of the fairness of outcomes that they received. One of the early theories of justice (equity theory) posited that the fairest allocations are those that reward people in proportion to their contributions (Adams, 1963, 1965). Additional allocation rules that were shown to be fair were based on equality and need.

The second type of justice is called procedural justice, and it refers to people's perceptions of the fairness of the procedures used to determine the outcomes that they receive (Greenberg, 2009). Work by Thibaut and Walker (1975, 1978) found that individuals were more accepting of unfavorable outcomes as long as the process used to allocate those outcomes was fair. For example, when people have a say or a voice in a process, they tend to believe that it was fair even if they did not receive the most fair outcome as a result of that process (Shapiro, 1993). According to the "fair process effect" (Folger & Cropanzano, 1998), under fair process conditions (for example, consistent, representative, unbiased procedures), even unfavorable outcomes can be perceived by individuals as being fair.

The third type of justice that was examined by researchers was interactional justice. Work by Bies and others found that individuals appraise the fairness of the interpersonal treatment they receive during decision-making procedures and outcome distributions (for example, Bies, 2005; Bies & Moag, 1986; Bies & Shapiro, 1987). Fairness perceptions were found to be higher when people believed that they were treated with dignity and respect, and when information was shared and adequate explanations were given regarding allocation of important resources (Bies, 1987). Initially, there was some debate about whether interactional justice was distinct from procedural justice. Most researchers today believe that interactional justice and procedural justice are distinct concepts (Ambrose & Arnaud, 2005).

Colquitt (2001) subdivided interactional justice into two separate components: informational justice and interpersonal justice. Colquitt, Conlon, Wesson, Porter, and Ng (2001) presented empirical support for the validity of this subdivision. Informational justice refers to fairness perceptions that the decision maker is truthful and provides adequate justifications for decisions. People believe that they are an important part of the organization when officials take the time to thoroughly explain the reasons behind justice decisions. Interpersonal justice refers to treating people with dignity and respect. People believe that they deserve to be treated well and feel that things are unfair when they are not treated well.

Organizational justice is an important part of interpersonal relations among people in the workplace. Employees monitor the fairness of processes, outcomes, and interpersonal treatment in their organizations. When employees see that their organization is being fair, then four important individual needs are met for them: the need for belonging, the need for meaning, the need for positive self-regard, and the need for control (Cropanzano, Byrne, Bobocel, & Rupp, 2001). Organizational justice helps (1) fulfill people's desire for important attachments to others in their organizations, (2) bring employees closer together and have a strong sense of pride in their organization, (3) fulfill employees' need for things to be "done right" and with a sense of morality, and (4) enable employees to have a more positive view of themselves and who they are in their organization.

Organizational justice research examines what individuals assess when they make fairness judgments. Two different approaches have been used by organizational justice researchers to identify the objects of employees' fairness assessments: (1) the event paradigm and (2) the social entity paradigm (Choi, 2008). Research in the event paradigm contends that employees evaluate the fairness of a specific event, such as a pay raise, a performance appraisal, or a smoking ban (for example, fairness theory, Folger & Cropanzano, 2001). Under this approach, people assess the fairness of each isolated event on the basis of what should, would, or could have happened to them.

Research in the social entity paradigm contends that employees assess the fairness of the organization as a whole (for example, the fairness of supervisors or of the organization) (for example, fairness heuristic theory, Lind, 2001). Under the social entity approach, people develop ideas about the level of fairness that they expect to receive from a boss or from an organization as a whole, and these ideas guide future behavior and attitudes. This view holds that people establish a baseline level of fairness expected from a person or an entity and that this baseline can be revised upward or downward as events unfold. For the most part, organizational justice has examined these two paradigms separately, without attempts at integration.

Some researchers have suggested weaknesses in examining each of the three or four types of organizational justice separately (Ambrose & Schminke, 2009). Instead, they argue for the use of one general justice construct. Their view is that an employee's overall justice perception may be more important in influencing subsequent attitudes and performances than would any one of the three or four types of justice alone.

22

Criticisms and Critiques of the Theory

Organizational justice is one of the most popular and most researched areas in the field of organization and management. However, organizational justice has not gone without criticism. A four-factor view of justice has been found to be inconsistent with some justice research. For example, many research studies report extremely high correlations between procedural and distributive justice, which suggests that for some individuals, processes and outcomes are not seen as separate, distinct constructs. Instead, some individuals may view organizational justice from a one-factor perspective (Colquitt, 2001). For example, a study by Martocchio and Judge (1995) found such a high correlation between procedural, distributive, and interactional justice items that the researchers combined all three into one organizational justice variable.

Some researchers (for example, Cropanzano & Ambrose, 2001) believe that procedural and distributive justice are more similar to each other as constructs than most researchers are willing to believe or acknowledge. This may be the case because people's procedural evaluations may in large part be based on outcomes received, and because a single event can be seen as a process in one context and as an outcome in another. For example, believing that a performance appraisal system is fair because it gives employees an opportunity to voice their views can be seen as a fair outcome, even though opportunity to voice one's concerns is an example of a fair process.

A persistent and ongoing problem in organizational justice research has been the use of inconsistent and poor measurement instruments. Some organizational justice studies attempt to measure one type of justice that seems to measure another type (Greenberg, 1990). For example, Fryxell and Gordon (1989) used a measure of distributive justice (which assessed the ability to express ideas during a grievance procedure) that would usually be used to measure procedural fairness instead of outcome fairness.

Measuring Variables in the Theory

Procedural, distributive, interpersonal, and informational justice scales. Colquitt, J. A. (2001). On the dimensionality of organizational justice: A construct validation of a measure. *Journal of Applied Psychology, 83,* 386–400.

Procedural, distributive, and interactional justice scales. Niehoff, B. P., & Moorman, R. H. (1993). Justice as a mediator of the relationship between methods of monitoring and organizational citizenship behavior. *Academy of Management Journal, 36,* 527–556.

Fairness zones of tolerance scales. Gilliland, S. W. (2008). The tails of justice: A critical examination of the dimensionality of organizational justice constructs. *Human Resource Management Review, 18,* 271–281.

Retaliatory justice scale. Scarlicki, D. P., & Foler, R. (1997). Retaliation in the workplace: The roles of distributive, procedural, and interactional justice. *Journal of Applied Psychology, 82,* 434–443.

Suggestions for Further Research

1. Compare the measures of each of the types of justice for assessing fairness perceptions of specific events and for assessing fairness perceptions of overall social entities.
2. Examine the influence of both specific event and social entity perceptions simultaneously on fairness perceptions.
3. Further examine the idea that all four types of justice are conceptually distinct from each other.
4. Explore the influence of fairness on evaluations of the self compared with group and organizational identities.
5. Examine the range and scope of justice violations and contexts on fairness perceptions and performance.
6. Study the similarities and differences between primary and third-party perceptions of fairness for the individual and the group.
7. Examine the influence of presence, location, and psychological distance on the formation of fairness judgments.
8. Explore types of justice violations, such as religious or spiritual versus secular, on individual and group perceptions of justice.
9. Look at the influences of time, time control, and time limits on fairness perceptions.

22

10. Examine individual differences in tolerance for justice violations.
11. Explore the relationship between fairness beliefs and social position, such as social advantage and disadvantage.

References to Know

Greenberg, J. (1987). A taxonomy of organizational justice theories. *Academy of Management Review, 12,* 9–22.

Greenberg, J. (1990). Organizational justice: Yesterday, today, and tomorrow. *Journal of Management, 16,* 399–432.

Greenberg, J. (2010). Organizational justice: The dynamics of fairness in the workplace. In S. Zedeck (Ed.), *APA handbook of industrial-organizational psychology* (Vol. 3, pp. 271–337). Washington, DC: American Psychological Association.

Greenberg, J., & Colquitt, J. A. (Eds.). (2005). *Handbook of organizational justice.* Mahwah, NJ: Erlbaum.

Lind, E. A., & Tyler, T. R. (1988). *The social psychology of procedural justice.* New York: Plenum Press.

Implications of the Theory for Managers

Employees want to be treated fairly by their managers and by their organizations; if they are not treated fairly, then their attitudes and performance may be negatively affected. For example, employees will assess the fairness of the procedures used to allocate important resources. You can improve employees' fairness perceptions of these processes by giving them a voice in the decision-making process, consistently following and applying rules, accurately using information in the decision-making process, correcting any errors that might occur during the decision-making process, and trying to prevent and guard against any biases or prejudices that might exist.

Employee fairness perceptions will most likely be higher when managers act fairly in their resource allocations. However, this may not be the case if employees do not believe that a manager is fair, even if he or she really is fair. As a manager, you should not only be fair but also look fair to employees (Greenberg, 1988). You need to go out of your way to demonstrate how fair you are when allocating important resources, such as by showing employees the information that was included and the process that was followed that made the outcome decision fair. If employees perceive procedures to be unfair, then they may reject the entire system in the organization and believe it to be unfair.

Employees care about how they are treated during resource allocation decision-making processes. You can improve employees' fairness perceptions by treating employees with dignity and respect; showing when, how, and what information was used during decision-making processes; and providing full and adequate explanations about how and why important resource allocations were made. Employees tend to feel more valued when someone in their organization thoroughly explains the rationale behind resource allocations, and this can result in more productive employee attitudes and behaviors.

22

23

Planned Behavior Theory

The main theme in planned behavior theory is that the best way to predict and explain a person's behaviors is through that person's behavioral intentions. The theory assumes that (1) people tend to behave rationally and to systematically make use of information that is available to them when deciding to act or not to act, (2) people's actions are guided by conscious motives and not by unconscious motives, and (3) people consider the implications of their actions before they decide to act or not to act (Ajzen & Fishbein, 1980; Fishbein & Ajzen, 1975).

Based on these assumptions, the theory was originally called the theory of reasoned action (Ajzen & Fishbein, 1980). According to the theory, a person's attitude and subjective norms influence his behavioral intentions. The person's behavioral intentions then influence his behavior. Attitude refers to the person's favorable or unfavorable appraisal of the behavior. Subjective norm refers to the perceived social pressure from other individuals to perform or not perform the behavior. Intentions refer to the motivational factors that influence a person's behavior. Intentions indicate how willing a person is to attempt a behavior, and how much effort he is likely to exert toward that behavior. In general, the stronger the intention to perform a behavior, the more likely a person is to perform that behavior (Ajzen, 1991).

The theory of reasoned action has had much research success. Madden, Ellen, and Ajzen (1992) reported that the theory has been widely used to model the prediction of behavioral intentions and behavior. In a meta-analysis, Sheppard, Hartwick, and Warshaw (1988) noted that the theory predicts both behavioral intentions and behavior quite well, and is useful for identifying where and how to change an individual's behaviors.

Later research found that an important variable was missing from the theory of reasoned action, namely, perceived behavioral control (PBC). For example, Bandura, Adams, Hardy, and Howells (1980) provided empirical evidence that a person's behavior is strongly influenced by her level of self-confidence (her self-perception that she has the ability to perform a behavior). On the basis of these research findings, PBC was added to the theory of reasoned action, and the theory was renamed the theory of planned behavior (Ajzen, 1985).

According to the theory, a behavioral intention can be expressed as a behavior only if that behavior is under the perceived control of the individual, meaning that the person perceives himself as having complete control over deciding to perform that behavior or not (Ajzen, 1991). For example, a person may strongly desire to perform a behavior, but may not have the necessary opportunities or resources (for example, knowledge, skills, abilities, information, time, money, equipment, and cooperation of others) to actually perform it (Kuhl, 1985; Liska, 1984; Sarver, 1983; Triandis, 1977). Both behavioral intentions and PBC directly predict performance of a behavior (Ajzen, 1991, 2001).

Ajzen and Madden (1986) were the first to completely test the theory of planned behavior. Research findings have consistently shown that attitude, subjective norm, and PBC influence behavioral intention, which then influences performance of behavior. However, findings have been mixed regarding the direct influence of PBC on behavior. Some research has found direct support for the effect of PBC on behavior, but others have found that PBC only influences behavior indirectly through intentions. Ajzen and Madden (1986) found a direct influence of PBC on behavior with low-level perceptions of control, but found indirect influence of PBC on behavior with high-level perceptions of control.

Ajzen (1991) wrote that we might expect motivation to behave and perceived control over that behavior to have interactive effects on behavior. Research has predominantly found no support for such an interaction (Ajzen, 1991; Ajzen & Driver, 1992; Ajzen & Madden, 1986; Beck & Ajzen, 1991; Doll & Ajzen, 1992). Schifter and Ajzen (1985) found marginally significant support for an interaction.

23

Research has shown that the intention-behavior relationship is consistent, but only moderate in strength (Armitage & Conner, 2001; Hagger, Chatzisarantis, & Biddle, 2002). This finding may mean that individuals can have strong intentions but fail to transfer them into actual behaviors (Harris & Hagger, 2007). Researchers have tried to find moderator variables that could help strengthen the conversion of intentions into behaviors: temporal stability (Conner, Sheeran, Norman, & Armitage, 2000), need satisfaction (Harris & Hagger, 2007), implementation intentions (Orbell, Hodgkins, & Sheeran, 1997), intention stability (Sheeran, Orbell, & Trafimow, 1999), anticipated regret and descriptive norms (Sheeran & Orbell, 1999; Sheeran & Taylor, 1999), personality (Rhodes, Courneya, & Hayduk, 2002), self-regulatory volitional components (Orbell, 2003), and attitude-intention strength and age (Hagger et al., 2002).

Researchers have argued that the theory does not account for all of the possible ways that social influence can be exerted over intentions to behave (for example, Conner & Armitage, 1998; Terry & Hogg, 1996). Moan and Rise (2006) examined three types of normative influences: injunctive norms (social approval and disapproval of others' behaviors), descriptive norms (behaviors that others are doing), and moral norms (behaviors that are right or wrong to perform).

The theory continues to be applied to a variety of topics, such as management development (McCarthy & Garavan, 2006), consumer behavior (Wang, Hong, & Wei, 2010), e-commerce (Ganesh & Barat, 2010), binge drinking (French & Cooke, in press), and vaccinations (Askelson et al., 2010).

Criticisms and Critiques of the Theory

Armitage and Conner (2001) offered several criticisms of the theory, with regard to the following topics: self-reported measures, control, behavioral intentions, and subjective norms. The theory tends to rely on self-reported behavioral measures. A number of studies have shown that self-reports of behaviors are unreliable compared to more objective behavior measures (Armitage & Conner, 1999a, 1999b; Norwich & Rovoli, 1993; Pellino, 1997). There is confusion over the constructs of PBC and self-efficacy. Ajzen (1991) argued that PBC and self-efficacy were

23

interchangeable, but other researchers have argued the opposite (Bandura, 1986, 1992; de Vries, Dijkstra, & Kuhlman, 1988; Terry, 1993). A number of different ways have been used to measure behavioral intentions (Warshaw & Davis, 1985). The subjective norm factor has been shown to be the weakest predictor of intentions in the theory (Godin & Kok, 1996; Sheppard et al., 1988; van den Putte, 1991), so some researchers have deliberately removed it from their analyses (Sparks, Shepard, & Frewer, 1995). Weak support for subjective norm factors may merely be due to researchers' using only single-item measures for the construct.

In a meta-analysis of research using the theory, Sutton (1998) reported that the theory explained only between 40 and 50 percent of the variance in intention and between 19 and 38 percent of the variance in behavior. Also, after Sutton controlled for the usual components in the theory, self-identity was found to explain an incremental 6 percent of the variance for intention, or 9 percent when past behavior was also controlled (Rise, Sheeran, & Hukkelberg, 2010).

In addition, Sutton (1998) described nine criticisms of planned behavior theory: (1) intentions may change over time; (2) intentions may be provisional (intentions expressed on a questionnaire may only be hypothetical compared to real life); (3) the theory violates the principle of compatibility (intentions and behaviors must be measured in the same way regarding action, target, time, and context); (4) the theory violates scale correspondence (the same scale format has typically not been used for all survey items); (5) the theory uses unequal numbers of response categories for intention and behavior (yes-no questions were used for some variables, 1–7 scores for others); (6) there is random measurement error in the measures for intention and behavior; (7) range or variance in intention or behavior is restricted (ranges of scores may be different for subjects compared to the general population); (8) marginal distributions of the measures do not match (differing variable score ranges were used); and (9) intentions alone may not be the sufficient cause of behavior.

The theory assumes that human behavior is reasoned, deliberate, and mindful. However, other research has shown that behavior can instead be effortless, unintentional, uncontrollable, automatic, and conscious or unconscious (Ajzen & Fishbein,

2000; Bargh, 1996; Bargh, Chen, & Burrows, 1996; Posner & Synder, 1975; Wegner & Bargh, 1998).

Kraft, Rise, Sutton, and Roysamb (2005) have suggested that further research needs to be conducted on PBC. They found that PBC should be conceived of as two separate but related constructs: self-efficacy and controllability.

Measuring Variables in the Theory

Prior behavior, attitude, subjective norm, perceived behavioral control, behavioral intention, and future behavior scales. Elliott, M. A., Armitage, C. J., & Baughan, C. J. (2003). Drivers' compliance with speed limits: An application of the theory of planned behavior. *Journal of Applied Psychology, 88,* 964–972.

Subjective norms and perceived behavioral control scales. Cordano, M., & Frieze, I. H. (2000). Pollution reduction preferences of U.S. environmental managers: Applying Ajzen's theory of planned behavior. *Academy of Management Journal, 43,* 627–641.

Self-efficacy and behavioral intentions scales. Carr, J. C., & Sequeira, J. M. (2007). Prior family business exposure as intergenerational influence and entrepreneurial intent: A theory of planned behavior approach. *Journal of Business Research, 60,* 1090–1098.

Attitude, subjective norm, intention, moral norms, self-identity, and past and future behavior scales. Moan, I. S., & Rise, J. (2006, December). Predicting smoking reduction among adolescents using an extended version of the theory of planned behavior. *Psychology and Health, 21,* 717–738.

Suggestions for Further Research

23

1. Examine the extent to which intentions may change due to situational factors, which may influence subsequent behaviors.
2. Explore the range of knowledge from naïve to expert for behavioral change and its influence on the intention-behavior relationship.

3. Compare and classify the strength of all known moderators of the attitude-behavior relationship.

4. Explore the boundaries and types of research where the theory has not been shown to predict or explain behavior.

5. Further clarify the concept of PBC versus self-efficacy and its relationship to the ease or difficulty of performing the behavior.

6. Look at how people form, maintain, and change reference groups when assessing subjective norms.

7. Examine the effect of preference for local versus online businesses on behavioral intentions and actual performance of behaviors.

8. Explore the influence of cultural, societal, and individual differences on behavioral, normative, and control beliefs.

9. Study single versus dual processing and automatic and non-automatic thoughts and their influence on intentions and behaviors.

10. Examine the ability of change management interventions to change group norms and to influence intentions and behavior.

References to Know

Ajzen, I. (1988). *Attitudes, personality, and behavior.* Chicago: Dorsey.

Ajzen, I. (1991). The theory of planned behavior. *Organizational Behavior and Human Decision Processes, 50,* 179–211.

Ajzen, I., & Fishbein, M. (1980). *Understanding attitudes and predicting social behavior.* Englewood Cliffs, NJ: Prentice Hall.

Fishbein, M., & Ajzen, I. (1975). *Belief, attitude, intention and behavior: An introduction to theory and research.* Reading, MA: Addison-Wesley.

Sheppard, B. H., Hartwick, J., & Warshaw, P. R. (1988). The theory of reasoned action: A meta-analysis of past research with recommendations for modifications and future research. *Journal of Consumer Research, 15,* 325–343.

Implications of the Theory for Managers

According to planned behavior theory, the best way to explain or predict an employee's behaviors is by looking at his or her intentions to behave. Employee behavior tends to be influenced by three kinds of thoughts: (1) beliefs about the likely consequences of his or her behavior, (2) beliefs about the normative expectations of other people, and (3) beliefs about things that might help or hurt performance of the behavior (for example, opportunities, resources, knowledge, skills, abilities, information, time, money, equipment, and cooperation of others), which give rise to feelings of control or lack of control over being able to perform the behavior. These three kinds of thoughts lead to an employee's intending to perform a behavior; this intention in turn influences whether or not the employee actually performs the behavior.

Your job as a manager is to help improve employee intentions to perform desired organizational behaviors. Help improve employees' perceptions about the likely outcomes when they perform the behaviors. Enhance employees' perceptions about the expectations and behavioral norms of others, such as that a customer would be angry if an important project were not completed on time. Help employees believe that they have control over performing desired tasks. For example, talk with employees about what resources, equipment, and social support they need in order to successfully perform a desired behavior. Specifically discuss behavioral intentions with your employees. Find out their feelings and expectations about performing all of their necessary organizational tasks, and work with them to improve any behavioral intentions that might be lower than needed. Higher employee intentions should translate into higher levels of desired employee behaviors.

23

24

Prospect Theory

Prospect theory attempts to explain decisions that people make under conditions of uncertainty and risk. Before the development of the theory, it was generally believed that people base decisions on a rationally calculated "expected utility" of the risk and return of various choices. However, Kahneman and Tversky (1979; Tversky & Kahneman, 1981, 1992) provided robust evidence that people's actual decision-making methods do not tend to follow such rational calculations.

Markowitz (1952) posited the idea that the objects of choice in decision making are prospects that can be defined as either potential gains or losses. This notion is the cornerstone of Kahneman and Tversky's prospect theory (1979).

There are four important components in prospect theory. First, when people must choose between prospects, they typically frame their choices as gains or losses relative to some reference point, an internal standard with which people compare the objective value of an option. Prospect theory posits that the selection of a reference point is critical when evaluating options. People will classify an option as something positive when the option's value is greater than the reference point, or as something negative when the option's value is less than the reference point. Interestingly, a particular option can be framed as either positive or negative, such that in one case an option can be seen as positive, but in another case, the same option could be seen as a negative.

A positively presented, or framed, option tends to decrease the likelihood that a person will see something as neutral in value.

24

However, a negatively framed option tends to increase the likelihood that a person will see something as neutral in value (Highhouse & Paese, 1996). For example, framing a new policy as a loss (10 percent unemployment will result) tends to put people in the negative domain. However, framing a new policy as a gain (90 percent employment will result) tends to put people in the positive domain. If an outcome is framed as a loss, then people will tend to assume more risk to avoid that negative outcome compared to when the same outcome is framed as a gain.

The notion that framing an outcome can influence subsequent levels of accepted risk was surprising for two reasons (Mercer, 2005). Ideally, people should pay attention to their total wealth or their overall gains and losses, not just to wealth changes relative to some arbitrarily set reference point. Also, people's attitudes toward risk should not be so forcefully determined by whether they are momentarily thinking about potential gains or losses. Yet, according to prospect theory, people tend to follow these ideas when making decisions.

The second component in prospect theory is the subjective value function (Kahneman & Tversky, 1979). According to prospect theory, a decision option is associated with a subjective value for the decision maker that can be expressed as positive or negative deviations (that is, gains or losses) from the decision maker's neutral reference point (that has a subjective value of zero). The subjective value function is S shaped: concave in the positive domain (above the reference point) and convex in the negative domain (below the reference point).

The third component in prospect theory is that individuals show tendencies toward risk aversion when facing gains and show tendencies toward risk seeking when facing losses (Kahneman & Tversky, 1979). Additionally, when people are forced to make a choice in situations where there could be losses, people tend to choose a situation with a probable loss (where there is the possibility that the loss may occur) over a situation with a sure loss (where the loss will definitely occur). The fourth component in prospect theory is that lower probabilities are overweighted and higher probabilities are underweighted (Rieger & Wang, 2006; Tversky & Kahneman, 1992; Wakker, 2003). Overweighting of low probabilities may contribute to the attractiveness of insurance, gambling, and lotteries (Kahneman & Tversky, 1979).

Criticisms and Critiques of the Theory

The original formulation of prospect theory had two major problems. First, the value assessments dealt with gains and losses and not final asset levels. Second, the theory examined basically only one decision at a time, and did not handle well an accumulation of outcomes and experiences. To account for these problems, Tversky and Kahneman (1992) developed a new version of prospect theory called cumulative prospect theory. Cumulative prospect theory extends the original model to uncertain as well as to risky prospects with any number of outcomes.

One problem with prospect theory investigations is that decision prospects are confined to being either negative or positive, but not mixed. Kahneman and Tversky (1979) did not present problems to subjects and ask them to decide whether they viewed the problem as more positive, more negative, or as neutral. Instead, the researchers forced the subjects into believing that the problem was positive or negative.

Levy and Levy (2002) conducted a study with mixed (both positive and negative) prospects and found that the subjective utility function followed a reverse S shape, which was the exact opposite of the S shape supported by prospect theory. In their study, Levy and Levy found that 62 to 76 percent of subjects could not be characterized as following the S-shaped subjective value function.

Researchers have typically investigated the shape of the subjective value function by examining only the positive or the negative sections of the ranges (Swalm, 1966; Kahneman & Tversky, 1979; Tversky & Kahneman, 1992). This approach may be presenting subjects with an unrealistic situation. In real life, virtually all investments, such as stocks, bonds, options, and real estate, present individuals with a wide and uncertain range of outcomes.

Prospect theory posits that when faced with a risky prospect whose possible outcomes are typically good, then people tend to avoid risk. Conversely, when faced with a risky prospect whose possible outcomes are typically poor, then people tend to be risk seeking. However, this tendency is not well supported by history. For example, most major organizational innovation and change tends not to be produced by misery (March & Shapira, 1987).

24

Risk-taking behaviors tend not to be related to adversity in the simple way that prospect theory would suggest.

Kanfer (1990) pointed out that prospect theory failed to include time as a variable. In response to this criticism, other researchers have proposed variations of prospect theory that include time functions (Steel & Konig, 2006).

Measuring Variables in the Theory

Utility of wealth survey. Markowitz, H. (1952). The utility of wealth. *Journal of Political Economy, 60,* 151–158.

Resistance to change scale. Oreg, S., Barazit, M., Vakola, M., Arciniega, L., Armenakis, A., Barkauskiene, R., Bozionelos, N., Fujimoto, Y., Gonzalez, L., Han, J., Hrebickova, M., Jimmieson, N., Kordacova, J., Mitsuhashi, H., Mlacic, B., Feric, I., Topic, M. K., Ohly, S., Saksvik, P. O., Hetland, H., Saksvik, I., & van Dam, K. (2008). Dispositional resistance to change: Measurement equivalence and the links to personal values across 17 nations. *Journal of Applied Psychology, 93,* 935–944.

Sensation seeking scale. Haynes, C. A., Miles, J.N.V., & Clements, K. (2000). A confirmatory factor analysis of two models of sensation seeking. *Personality and Individual Differences, 29,* 823–839.

Risk attitude scale. Weber, E. U., Blais, A.-R., & Betz, N. E. (2002). A domain-specific risk-attitude scale: Measuring risk perceptions and risk behaviors. *Journal of Behavioral Decision Making, 15,* 263–290.

Suggestions for Further Research

1. Examine how reference points are created and change over time, and how people create different reference points for different types of options.
2. Explore how people naturally decide to frame options as positive or negative and the influence of that framing on subsequent decisions.
3. Look at the reasons why people may change their reference point while making an option evaluation and how that influences subsequent decisions.

24

4. Study how and why people link a current offer with their reference point when evaluating decision options.
5. Examine how prior information from previous decisions influences the weighting of options for current decisions.
6. Explore how people include the winning and losing experiences of important others in the weighting of their own decision options.
7. Study how time pressures influence the weighting and evaluation of decision options.
8. Examine individual differences and preferences to keep or discard reference points when evaluating decision options.
9. Explore the conditions under which people tend to be risk seeking, risk avoiding, or risk neutral; how those change over time; and how they influence the evaluation of decision options.
10. Look at how denial of the degree of risk can influence the comparison of outcomes in relation to a person's reference points.

References to Know

Kahneman, D., & Tversky, A. (1979). Prospect theory: An analysis of decision under risk. *Econometrica, 47,* 263–291.

Tversky, A., & Kahneman, D. (1981). The framing of decisions and the psychology of choice. *Science, 211,* 453–458.

Tversky, A., & Kahneman, D. (1986). Rational choice and the framing of decisions. *Journal of Business, 59,* S251–S278.

Tversky, A., & Kahneman, D. (1992). Advances in prospect theory: Cumulative representation of uncertainty. *Journal of Risk and Uncertainty, 5,* 297–323.

Wakker, P., & Tversky, A. (1993). An axiomatization of cumulative prospect theory. *Journal of Risk and Uncertainty, 7,* 147–176.

Implications of the Theory for Managers

Prospect theory examines the decisions that people make under varying conditions of expected risks or prospects. Taking risks is an important part of managerial activities. Risk is most often described as reflecting a distribution of possible outcomes, their

24

likelihoods, and their subjective values. When making decisions, and when all factors are held constant, decision makers tend to prefer larger expected returns rather than smaller ones. In general, managers also tend to prefer smaller risks rather than larger risks, provided other factors are held constant. Overall, managers expect to be compensated for the possibility of greater variance in expected returns on their investments.

Attitude toward risk is usually described as being a stable property of an individual, typically related to certain aspects of personality, culture, and motivation to achieve. However, a number of variables, such as mood and the way problems are framed, also appear to affect perception of and attitude toward risk (Tversky & Kahneman, 1981). When dealing with a risky alternative whose possible outcomes are generally positive, people appear to be risk averse. However, when dealing with a risky alternative whose possible outcomes are generally negative, people appear to be risk seeking (Kahneman & Tversky, 1979).

In traditional decision-making theory, individuals must make a trade-off between risk and expected return. Managers who are risk averse tend to prefer low risk levels and may sacrifice some expected return in order to reduce variations in potential outcomes. Managers who are risk seeking tend to prefer high risk levels and may sacrifice some expected return in order to increase potential return on their investment. The theory assumes that decision makers always calculate risk levels and then choose among possible risk-return combinations that are available to them. However, in reality, decision makers may not actually behave in this way.

You should realize that your employees can typically use the status quo as a reference point for determining their domain when making decisions. If employees are happy with how things are, then those employees will tend to view options as potential losses. If employees are unhappy with how things are, then those employees will tend to view options as potential gains, which can influence the actions that they take as a result.

Pay careful attention to how you frame decisions when presenting them to employees. Whether problems are framed as positive or negative can significantly affect the level of risk that employees may perceive and can have a substantial impact on the actions that employees may take as a result of perceived risk levels.

24

When employees are trying to avoid losses, they can take riskier actions to avoid anticipated losses entirely, rather than taking less risky options merely to minimize their losses. You yourself may find that you tend to be risk seeking when losses are not serious, but risk averse when potential losses become large and ruinous.

Assist your employees in making better decisions by working with them to help them view risk levels realistically. Check with them to see whether they have a natural tendency to see problems as potentially positive or negative (the glass is half full or half empty), which could affect how they perceive risk levels and decide whether to take action or not. If employees tend always to see situations as positive or negative, work with them to help them broaden their views about the problems they face at work.

Managers tend to look for alternatives in their decision making that help them meet targets and avoid risk, rather than assess or accept risk (March & Shapira, 1987). Managers tend to believe in their ability to control the odds through organizational controls and incentives that help them manage and reduce risk when possible, which can sometimes get them into trouble.

Don't overestimate your ability to beat the odds. Instead, acknowledge your potential decision-making risks and make the best informed decisions that you can.

24

25

Psychological Contract Theory

When employees join organizations, an employment agreement is often made between the organization and the employee. The terms of this employment agreement include what the employee will do and what the employee will receive, and what the organization will do and what the organization will receive in return. When these employment agreements are written down, they are called legal contracts. However, when these exchange agreements are unwritten, they are called psychological contracts. Just as in legal contracts, in psychological contracts, employees expect to receive things from their organization in exchange for actions that they perform or contributions that they make to their company. Employees tend to form these beliefs and expectations automatically.

A psychological contract has been defined as the beliefs a person holds about an exchange agreement between himself or herself and another party (Argyris, 1960; Levinson, Price, Munden, Mandl, & Solley, 1962; Rousseau, 1989, 1995; Schein, 1965). These beliefs form as a result of implicit or explicit promises made between parties, such as when a company offers an employee a job opportunity. In addition, these beliefs include a consideration that has been offered in exchange for the promises (such as accepting a position or forgoing other job offers), which perceptually binds the employee and the organization together (Rousseau & Tijoriwala, 1998).

Psychological contracts are perpetual. Once perceptions emerge, then they tend to remain and evolve over time. Psychological contracts are based on perceived promises. These promises can be any communication of future intentions or actions, such as written documents, discussions, and organizational policies and practices (Rousseau, 1989; Rousseau & Greller, 1994; Morrison & Robinson, 1997).

Psychological contracts vary in strength and generality (Rousseau, 1990, 1995; Rousseau & McLean Parks, 1993). Some contracts may be simple and short term; others may be complex and long term. Employee beliefs about psychological contracts are shaped by preemployment factors (such as motives and values), on-the-job experiences (such as orientation, socialization, and training), and broader societal and cultural aspects of the community or country (such as norms and values) (Dabos & Rousseau, 2004).

Psychological contracts are idiosyncratic. Each individual in an organization has her own unique set of terms in her exchange relationship with the organization (Rousseau, 1995). The expectations held by one party may not be shared by the other party. Exchange expectations may be different for each party due to miscommunication, differing interpretations, and the complexity and ambiguity of assumed obligations. Workers in the same firm with the same boss can have different beliefs regarding their obligations in psychological contracts (Rousseau & Tijoriwala, 1998).

Psychological contracts are ideally perceived to be a mutual agreement (Dabos & Rousseau, 2004). An individual and an organization behave based on the perceived fulfillment of the promises made between the organization and the employee (for example, Argyris, 1960; Blau, 1964; Rousseau, 1989). For example, an employee may work hard for an organization over a number of years with the expectation that the organization will strive to promote that employee in exchange for his hard work.

Psychological contracts are ideally a reciprocal agreement (Dabos & Rousseau, 2004). Reciprocity refers to the agreement between the employee and the organization about the terms of the exchange agreement. Both parties agree that the commitment and contributions made by one party obligate the other to its commitments and responsibilities.

Psychological contracts have mostly been used to describe the perceived relationship between an organization and its employees, and also with contingent workers (McLean Parks, Kidder, &

Gallagher, 1998), among middle managers (Hallier & James, 1997), and between employees and customers (McGaughey & Liesch, 2002). However, recent work has examined the interplay of worker-employer obligations.

25

Psychological contracts are often categorized into four types: transactional, relational, balanced, and transitional (Robinson, Kraatz, & Rousseau, 1994). Transactional contracts focus on highly monetary or economic exchanges. This type of psychological contract tends to be limited in duration with well-specified performance terms. For example, employees work hard in exchange for adequate compensation and benefits and a safe work environment (Thompson & Bunderson, 2003). Relational contracts focus on economic and socioemotional exchanges that are long term and based on mutual trust and loyalty, with incomplete or ambiguous performance terms. Relational contracts are more likely to be long-lasting, open-ended relationships focusing on mutual satisfaction, loyalty, and commitment. Balanced contracts blend features of transactional and relational contracts. Balanced contracts are long term and open ended with well-specified performance terms, and they change over time. Transitional contracts are "no guarantee" contracts that are short-term in duration with few or no explicit performance demands or incentives.

One of the key assumptions in psychological contract theory is individual choice. Both the individual and the organization participate freely in the exchange, and both voluntarily agree to be bound to a specific direction and course of action (Rousseau, 1995). Neither side is coerced or forced to comply with the exchange arrangement. Both parties are free to leave the exchange situation if they desire.

Employees can mentally derive the terms of their psychological contracts in three main ways (Rousseau, 1995). First, employees can receive information through communication with coworkers, supervisors, and other employees about expectations, obligations, and outcomes with the organization. Second, employees can gain information about psychological contract terms by observing others in the organization. Third, the organization can provide formal information about the terms of psychological contracts through compensation and benefit systems, performance reviews, and compensation adjustments.

Criticisms and Critiques of the Theory

25

Psychological contract theory has not gone without criticism. For example, Guest (1998) cited a number of problems with the theory. First, psychological contracts may be neither a theory nor a measure. Instead, they may be a hypothetical construct drawn inappropriately from the legal literature. Guest wondered if the legal metaphor was appropriate. For legal contracts, the terms are openly stated, but for psychological contracts, the terms are only in the mind of possibly one of the parties. If the terms are not open to both parties, then does an agreement really exist?

Second, psychological contracts are difficult to define, and have been defined differently by various scholars. Psychological contracts may be about perceptions, expectations, beliefs, promises, and obligations. Failure to meet expectations may be different from failure to meet obligations.

Third, not much is known about which employees have psychological contracts and which do not. In addition, not much is known about how psychological contracts develop, and whether for some employees they don't develop at all.

Fourth, whereas a legal contract is between two parties that are specifically named in the agreement, in psychological contracts, the parties tend to be one employee and the entire organization. It may be inappropriate to treat an entire organization as a "party" in the contract; this has been referred to as anthropomorphizing the entire organization.

Fifth, researchers have not created an exhaustive list of key dimensions in psychological contracts. Rousseau (1995) mentioned the dimension of performance requirements. Rousseau and McLean Parks (1993) list five dimensions: stability, scope, tangibility, focus, and time frame.

Sixth, little is known about the specific content of psychological contracts. This problem is a specific concern as researchers further explore how psychological contracts change and get renegotiated over time.

Seventh, little is known about the concept of contract violation and how it should be measured. Are contract violations merely broken promises, unmet expectations, unfulfilled obligations, or some other concept?

In sum, although psychological contract theory has many strengths and advantages for management theory, it also has received its share of criticisms and critiques that will need to be resolved for the theory to advance.

25

Measuring Variables in the Theory

Five-item global scale to measure perceptions of contract breach. Robin, S., & Morrison, E. (2000). The development of psychological contract breach and violation: A longitudinal study. *Journal of Organizational Behavior, 21,* 525–546.

Psychological contract scales. Dabos, G. E., & Rousseau, D. M. (2004). Mutuality and reciprocity in the psychological contracts of employee and employers. *Journal of Applied Psychology, 89,* 52–72.

Psychological Contract Inventory (PCI). Rousseau, D. M. (2000). *Psychological contract inventory* (Tech. Rep. No. 2000–2). Pittsburgh: Heinz School of Public Policy and Management, Carnegie Mellon University.

Suggestions for Further Research

1. A key assumption in psychological contract theory is that both parties enter into the exchange relationship voluntarily. Examine other conditions, such as involuntary exchanges, or compare voluntary and involuntary situations in psychological contracts.
2. Examine psychological contracts in other settings, societies, and cultures to see if previous findings will hold in those situations.
3. Examine psychological contracts across various types of individuals, groups, and organizations and examine more than single individuals in single organizations.
4. Compare psychological versus actual contracts and their influence on individual attitudes and behaviors.
5. One of the main ideas in psychological contract theory is that both sides try to be "reasonably fair." Examine settings in which people and organizations are not reasonably fair,

such as when they are specifically being unfair and unreasonable.

6. Examine situations in which psychological contracts were under- or overfulfilled compared to expectations. Will results be different in these settings as compared with situations that merely meet psychological contractual expectations?

7. Examine prosocial and antisocial reasons for breaking psychological contracts.

8. Psychological contracts assume reciprocity in exchange relationships. Examine the influence of varying reciprocity levels on the attitudes and behaviors of those in psychological contracts.

9. Investigate how psychological contracts change or get renegotiated over time.

10. Examine ways that organizations could help lower employee expectations so that psychological contract terms can more often be fulfilled.

References to Know

Robinson, S. L. (1996). Trust and breach of the psychological contract. *Administrative Science Quarterly, 41,* 574–599.

Robinson, S. L., & Rousseau, D. M. (1994). Violating the psychological contract: Not the exception but the norm. *Journal of Organizational Behavior, 15,* 245–259.

Rousseau, D. M. (1995). *Psychological contracts in organizations: Understanding written and unwritten agreements.* Thousand Oaks, CA: Sage.

Rousseau, D. M. (2005). Developing psychological contract theory. In K. G. Smith & M. A. Hitt (Eds.), *Great minds in management* (pp. 190–214). Oxford: Oxford University Press.

Rousseau, D. M., & Tijoriwala, S. A. (1998). Assessing psychological contracts: Issues, alternatives and measures. *Journal of Organizational Behavior, 19,* 679–695.

Implications for Managers

Psychological contract theory examines the exchange beliefs that employees hold about their organizations. Employees tend to automatically form unwritten beliefs and expectations about what they should get from their organization in return for the contributions they make to the organization. Most often these perceptions are not shared with the organization, but exist only in the mind of the employee. As a result, organizations may not provide outcomes that an employee expects. If employees do not receive the outcomes that they were expecting from their organization in their psychological contracts, then low employee attitudes and behaviors can result.

To lessen the chances of employee disappointment, talk to your employees about their unwritten expectations about what they will give to and receive from the organization. When possible, share the organization's unwritten expectations of employees and what it estimates that it can provide in return. When the situation permits, help the organization deliver on unwritten employee expectations. But if such situations are not possible, then work with your employees to change or renegotiate their unwritten exchange beliefs about the organization, so that their expectations can then be fulfilled.

25

26

Resource-Based Theory

Resource-based theory examines performance differences of organizations based on their resources (Peteraf & Barney, 2003). The theory makes two main assumptions: (1) organizations within an industry may differ in their resources, and (2) these resources may not be perfectly mobile across organizations, so organizational differences in resources can be very long lasting (Barney, 1991). The theory seeks to explain how organizations maintain unique and sustainable positions in competitive environments (Hoopes, Madsen, & Walker, 2003). It focuses on efficiency-based differences, instead of on other ways in which organizations could be different, such as market power, collusion, or strategic behaviors (Peteraf & Barney, 2003).

The central idea in resource-based theory is that organizations compete against others on the basis of their resources and capabilities (Barney, 1991; Wernerfelt, 1984). An organization's competitors can be identified by the similarity of their products, resources, capabilities, and substitutes (Peteraf & Bergen, 2003). The theory assumes that organizational decisions to select and accumulate resources are economically rational and subject to limited information, biases and prejudices, and causal ambiguity (Oliver, 1997). Causal ambiguity means that it is not known exactly how a resource leads to above-average performance for an organization.

A resource is defined as anything that could be thought of as a strength for an organization (Wernerfelt, 1984). Resources include any tangible or intangible assets that are semipermanently tied to the organization (Caves, 1980). Examples of resources include brand names; employee knowledge, skills, and abilities; machinery and technology; capital; contracts; and efficient procedures and processes (Wernerfelt, 1984). An organization's resources are seen as strengths that help the organization to better compete and to accomplish its vision, mission, strategies, and goals (Porter, 1981). Capabilities were originally seen as a type of resource, but later research has separated the two concepts. A capability is not observable and is therefore intangible, it cannot be valued, and it moves only as part of the unit where it is housed (Makadok, 2001).

The desirable position for an organization is to create a unique resource situation that makes it more difficult for its rivals to compete (Wernerfelt, 1984). An organization's competitive position relative to other organizations is based on its collection of unique resources and relationships (Rumelt, 1974). An organization has a competitive advantage when it uses a profitable, value-creating strategy that is not being used by competing organizations (Barney, 1991). If competing organizations are not able to learn about that strategy and copy it, then an organization has a sustainable competitive advantage (SCA).

Organizational SCA derives from the resources and capabilities that an organization controls that are valuable, rare, inimitable, and nonsubstitutable (VRIN) (Barney, 1991). Resources are valuable when they help an organization create or implement strategies that improve its efficiency and effectiveness. Resources are rare when more organizations want the resource than are able to obtain it. Resources are inimitable and nonsubstitutable when they are immobile and expensive to imitate or replicate. An organization must have the ability to absorb and utilize its resources in order to obtain a sustainable competitive advantage (Barney & Clark, 2007; Conner, 1991).

A key assumption in resource-based theory is that it focuses on an enterprise level, or business level, of analysis (Peteraf & Barney, 2003). The theory focuses on the resources and capabilities controlled by an organization that underlie performance differences across organizations. Resource-based theory is different from other theories that focus on the dyad level (boss and supervisee), the group level, or the industry level. Also, resource-based theory is not a substitute for other industry-level analytic tools.

The theory focuses on performance differences across firms. Performance differences are viewed as earnings differentials attributable to resources having different levels of efficiency (Barney, 1991; Peteraf, 1993). Superior resources enable an organization to produce better products and satisfy customers more sufficiently than it would with inferior resources. Organizational efficiency means that a firm has lower costs and can create greater value and net benefits compared to inefficient firms. Efficiency is measured in terms of net benefits, or the benefits to an organization that are left after the firm's costs are subtracted.

26

Sustainable competitive advantages and disadvantages can occur immediately, such as through a purchase, or can develop over a period of time (Helfat & Peteraf, 2003). Resource-based theory did not initially focus on whether resources were static or changing. However, more recent research attention has focused on how resources change, adapt, and evolve over time. For example, research has examined how organizations integrate, build, and reconfigure their resources and capabilities in response to rapidly changing environments (Teece, Pisano, & Shuen, 1997). Research has also examined how resources and capabilities can follow a dynamic life cycle in which they grow from birth to death (for example, Helfat & Peteraf, 2003).

Criticisms and Critiques of the Theory

Resource-based theory is elegantly simple and has immediate face validity; its core ideas are appealing and are easily taught and understood (Kraaijenbrink, Spender, & Groen, 2010). However, the theory has been extensively criticized for its many weaknesses.

The theory lacks managerial implications (Priem & Butler, 2001). The theory merely tells managers to obtain VRIN resources, but does not tell managers how to do this (Conner, 2002; Miller, 2003). The theory also assumes that managers have total control over their resources or can predict the value of resources in the future.

Many researchers have argued that the theory is essentially tautological (for example, Bromiley & Fleming, 2002; Lockett, Thompson, & Morgenstern, 2009; Priem & Butler, 2001). Some have argued that resource-based theory defines, rather than hypothesizes, that sustainable competitive advantages and performance are the result of variation in both resources and capabilities across organizations (Hoopes, Madsen, & Walker, 2003).

Another criticism has been that disconfirming resource-based theory is difficult. Any evidence that is found supports the theory that interorganizational variation in resources and capabilities leads to sustainable competitive performance differences. However, when evidence to the contrary is found, it may only mean that the resources or capabilities that were examined did not have value (Hoopes et al., 2003).

Critics have argued that the theory does not pay attention to contexts or organizational situations (Priem & Butler, 2001). The way that an organization acquires resources or deploys its resources is not separated from the organizational context (Oliver, 1997).

The theory has not paid much attention to where organizations obtain their resources (Barney & Clark, 2007). Possible reasons for organizational differences in resources include path dependence, social complexity, and causal ambiguity. However, the process through which organizations develop their resources is deserving of further attention.

A major criticism of the theory is that resources and capabilities are treated as though they are all the same (Kraaijenbrink, Spender, & Groen, 2010), such as whether they are static or dynamic. Although resources and capabilities have been defined differently, they are essentially treated the same, as are all types of resources. No attention has been given to how different resources contribute in different ways to a firm's SCA.

Critics have argued that SCA is not achievable. For example, Fiol (2001) argued that competitive advantages can be achieved only temporarily because the skills and resources required to create strategic advantages are constantly changing.

Finally, critics have argued that VRIN resources are neither necessary nor sufficient to achieve SCA. Empirical research has provided only modest support that they result in a firm's obtaining SCA (for example, Armstrong & Shimizu, 2007; Newbert, 2007). This means that factors in addition to VRIN resources must also be responsible for firms' obtaining SCA or not.

Measuring Variables in the Theory

Strategic evaluation for emerging manufacturing firms. Chandler, G. N., & Hanks, S. H. (1994). Market attractiveness, resource-based capabilities, venture strategies, and venture performance. *Journal of Business Venturing, 9,* 331–349.

Product development alliances measure. Eisenhardt, K. M., & Schoonhoven, C. B. (1996, March-April). Resource-based view of strategic alliance formation: Strategic and social effects in entrepreneurial firms. *Organization Science, 7,* 136–150.

Technology resources measure. Ray, G., Barney, J. B., & Muhanna, W. A. (2004). Capabilities, business processes, and competitive advantage: Choosing the dependent variable in empirical tests of the resource-based view. *Strategic Management Journal, 25,* 23–37.

Production, marketing, and management capabilities measures. Andersen, O., & Kheam, L. S. (1998, April). Resource-based theory and international growth strategies: An exploratory study. *International Business Review, 7,* 163–184.

Suggestions for Further Research

1. Examine the influence of resource characteristics (dynamic to static, active to inactive, firm specific and nonspecific, location bound and unbound) on organizational capabilities and performance variables.
2. Explore the similarities and differences among perceived value, total monetary value, and exchange value of resources (Bowman & Ambrosini, 2000) and their relationship to firm performance.
3. Study the processes that are used to select and absorb new resources into existing resources.
4. Look at the differences between building, acquiring, and deploying resources.
5. Examine how resource attributes, real or perceived, tangible or intangible, contribute to SCA and firm performance.
6. Explore how organizational competencies can range from beneficial to detrimental and related to unrelated, with regard to organizational performance (Newbert, 2007).
7. Study how the value, rareness, inimitability, and non-substitutability of resources change over time, for example, from birth to death, and from relevant to irrelevant to organizational performance.

8. Examine how managers predict future resource needs, such as resource shortages, or how managers make resource decisions, such as switching to alternative resources.
9. Look at the methods that organizations use to conduct the cost-benefit analysis of acquiring new resources or not.
10. Examine the value of different resource bundles regarding their complementarity, synergy, cospecialization, and relatedness to one another and their influence on firm performance.

26

References to Know

Barney, J. B. (1991). Firm resources and sustained competitive advantage. *Journal of Management, 17,* 99–120.

Barney, J. B., & Clark, D. N. (2007). *Resource-based theory: Creating and sustaining competitive advantage.* New York: Oxford University Press.

Barney, J. B., Wright, M., & Ketchen, D. J., Jr. (2001). The resource-based view of the firm: Ten years after 1991. *Journal of Management, 27,* 625–641.

Peteraf, M. A. (1993). The cornerstones of competitive advantage: A resource-based view. *Strategic Management Journal, 14,* 179–191.

Wernerfelt, B. (1984). A resource-based view of the firm. *Strategic Management Journal, 5,* 171–180.

Implications of the Theory for Managers

Resource-based theory posits that an organization can achieve sustainable competitive advantage by controlling resources that are valuable, rare, imperfectly imitable, and nonsubstitutable. Your task as a manager is to help your organization use resources more effectively and efficiently than your competition over time. Help your organization understand how and why its resources are better or worse than those of its main competitors. Explore ways that you can help make your company's current resources better, more efficient, and more cost-effective.

The theory can also be applied to you as an individual. What are the resources that make you valuable to your organization? What are the knowledge, skills, abilities, capabilities, and competencies that you have that make you more valuable to your company than your rivals? What is it about you that makes you indispensable to your organization? If you are deficient in any areas, what training and education can you get that will help make you even more valuable to your company?

Last, you must not only possess resources that are valuable to your company but also make sure that your company knows that you have them. Find ways to continually demonstrate to your company how valuable you are: specifically document how productive you are and how much you are saving the company in time and resources compared to other employees. If you can demonstrate your worth to your company, then you may not be the first one to be let go if times get tough, because you will be seen as a valuable resource that the company wants to keep around for a long time.

26

27

Role Theory

The central idea in role theory is that people are socialized or conditioned to play roles in a way that helps maintain a stable society or social order. Role theory examines (1) behaviors that are characteristic of people within situations or contexts and (2) various processes that produce, explain, or predict those behaviors (Biddle, 1979).

Role theory contains five major underlying propositions (Biddle, 1979). First, some behaviors are patterned and form a role, and are characteristically performed by a person within a situation or context. Second, roles often involve social positions, or are characteristic of a set of persons in the role who share a common identity, such as the role of a teacher, doctor, or nurse. Third, roles often have expectations, meaning that people know when someone is playing a role, and so have expectations about what behaviors that person will perform when playing the role. Fourth, roles persist over time because they are often embedded in larger social systems. Fifth, people must be taught roles, or be socialized into them, and may find joy or sorrow when playing different roles.

Theorists from different fields have made different assumptions about roles. Linton (1936) saw roles as statuses, or patterns of reciprocal behaviors that are socially recognized positions with rights and duties. Parsons (1951) saw roles as being reinforced through sanctions by society's role expectations. Mead (1934) saw taking on roles as development of the self through a socialization process. Moreno (1934) wrote about playing roles and their significance in education and psychology. Merton (1957) wrote that position, or social status, involves an array of roles, or a role-set, with a complement of role relationships. Goffman (1959) saw roles from a dramaturgical or theatrical perspective, as parts to be played by individuals.

Role theory has defined a number of important terms in use by managers in organizations. Role refers to the behaviors characteristic of a person in a specific context. Role conflict refers to incompatibilities among the various societal obligations that people experience, and can occur within roles (intrarole conflict) or among them (interrole conflict). Role ambiguity refers to uncertainty that employees experience about what is expected of them. Role model refers to a person who serves as a behavioral example that others follow.

The concept of role most often refers to the set of behaviors expected of individuals in specific social categories (Montgomery, 1998). Those categories include positions (or statuses) in both formal and informal systems, such as mothers in families, teachers in schools, and nurses in hospitals (Biddle & Thomas, 1979). Society often assigns roles to reflect positive or negative societal values, such as "hard worker," "concerned citizen," or "proud father" (Zurcher, 1983).

Researchers in role theory have predominantly taken one of two perspectives: functionalist or interactionist (Hilbert, 1981). The functionalist perspective sees a role as the set of behavioral expectations that society places on an individual playing a role (Lynch, 2007). From this perspective, a role is an interlocking network of behaviors that is appropriate for someone in a specific social position or with a specific status (Hilbert, 1981). When someone plays or takes a role, he or she must accept a specific set of rights and responsibilities that come with that role (Linton, 1936), as in "noblesse oblige" (the public obligations and responsibilities of the noble class). Roles are created by society as a group, and the expected behaviors for roles tend to be agreed on, such as that a doctor wears a white coat, asks personal health questions that wouldn't be asked under other circumstances, and so on.

The interactionist perspective is concerned with role making, or the ongoing creation of a role by people through social interaction (Turner, 1962). According to the interactionist approach, people constantly create a role by continually testing and retesting their inferences about what others expect of someone playing that role, and then act accordingly, thereby creating the role extemporaneously (Hilbert, 1981). Roles are made through a negotiation process that involves an interaction between a person and his or her social environment (McCall & Simmons, 1978).

Later research has tried to extend role theory beyond the functionalist and interactionist perspectives because the dichotomy has been seen as unnecessary and unproductive (Callero, 1994). For example, roles can be seen as a resource for agency and structure (Callero, 1994; Collier & Callero, 2005). According to this perspective, roles vary according to cultural endorsement, cultural evaluation, social accessibility, and situational contingency. Roles also have four uses: defining self, thinking, acting, and achieving political ends.

Role theory tends to examine only one role at a time, or what is called "single role occupancy." Roles are traditionally thought of as discrete psychological phenomena, such as in "taking off one hat and putting on another" when changing from one role to another (Ashforth & Johnson, 2001). Lynch (2007), however, attempted to stretch the concept of role enactment to cover multiple and overlapping roles through a cognitive typology called "simultaneous role salience." The goal of this approach is to include the tensions within and among roles with societal normative traditions simultaneously. This approach includes the concepts of role flexibility and role permeability (Hall & Richter, 1988). Role flexibility refers to the work hours and location of the role. Role permeability refers to the extent to which a person can be performing one role but concerned about another role (for example, working at the office but worrying about a problem at home). This approach lets people move, change, and combine the borders and boundaries of their simultaneous roles, such as from "student" and "nurse" to "student nurse" and from "mother" and "employee" to "working mom."

Although the influence of roles has been informally elaborated on a great deal, little research has examined mathematical formulation of role theory constructs. To fill this void, Montgomery (2005) used mathematical formulas to specify the processes through which an individual selects behaviors and to show how observers make evaluations and attributions about that individual based on those behaviors.

Criticisms and Critiques of the Theory

Critics of role theory have argued that the theory is weak when it comes to motivational aspects of behavior (Biddle, 1979). The theory does not explain very well why people enact expected behaviors or not. Biddle argued that a motivational component of role theory may not even be necessary.

Role theory has addressed how roles help maintain society and social order. Role theorists have therefore not advanced systematic propositions regarding role theory and social change (Biddle, 1979). Role theory promotes social conformity by endorsing a normative set of behavioral expectations for roles, and advocates that these behaviors are the "proper way to live" (Connell, 1987).

Role theory has been criticized for reifying social ideologies into concrete realities and calling them roles (Jackson, 1998). Role theory merely perpetuates so-called normative behavioral expectations with a feeling that a majority of people agree with such a position. For example, the role of "coach" has all sorts of connotations that may or may not reflect the behaviors that coaches actually perform.

Role theory has been criticized for rationalizing the socialization process of role learning or role acquisition in which people learn what behaviors are expected in specific roles. For example, schools, churches, families, and social institutions help model appropriate and acceptable behaviors that are learned by individuals. Critics argue that this is merely a way of indoctrinating people to accept, believe, and enact according to social norms and values without questioning them, which can lead to the perpetual oppression of some groups of individuals (Callero, 1994; Jackson, 1998).

Role theory has also been criticized because it does not examine an individual's subjective experience while performing a role. The theory largely ignores the experiences of individuals who try to alter the boundaries of their roles and try to change existing social practices, and also ignores the creative nature of individuals as they adapt to their environment on a daily basis. Role theory acknowledges that people respond to role discrepancies, but it does not provide a framework for examining how people create meaning and purpose for their own lives.

Measuring Variables in the Theory

Intrinsic motivation, role conflict, and role ambiguity scales. Coelho, F., Augusto, M., & Lages, L. F. (2011). Contextual factors and the creativity of frontline employees: The mediating effects of role stress and intrinsic motivation. *Journal of Retailing, 87,* 31–45.

Role ambiguity scale. Schuler, R. S., Aldag, R. J., & Brief, A. (1977). Role conflict and ambiguity: A scale analysis. *Organizational Behavior and Human Decision Processes, 20,* 111–128.

Role conflict and role ambiguity scales. Rizzo, J. R., House, R. J., & Lirtzman, S. I. (1970). Role conflict and ambiguity in complex organizations. *Administrative Science Quarterly, 15,* 150–163.

27

Role conflict and role ambiguity scales. Schwab, R. L., Iwanicki, E. F., & Pierson, D. A. (1983). Assessing role conflict and role ambiguity: A cross validation study. *Educational and Psychological Measurement, 43,* 587–593.

Perceived task demands scale. Williams, K. J., & Alliger, G. M. (1994). Role stressors, mood spillover, and perceptions of work-family conflict in employed parents. *Academy of Management Journal, 37,* 837–868.

Suggestions for Further Research

1. Examine how employees manage multiple roles within a single domain (for example, by studying employees who work at home).
2. Explore the influences of role flexibility and role permeability on the managing of multiple roles simultaneously.
3. Look at the influence of individual difference on multiple-role saliencies and performance.
4. Examine how people manage multiple roles across divergent individual differences and societal, cultural, and national boundaries.
5. Explore how organizations are helping and hurting people in meeting the performance demands of conflicting roles.

6. Look at how roles link institutions, societies, cultures, genders, social classes, ethnic groups, and nations.
7. Study the process through which various demographic groups have reshaped their roles in society over time.
8. Explore the relationship between careful or careless delineation of job range and scope and their influence on employee performance and retention levels.
9. Examine the use of meta-roles (roles that govern the use of other roles) for determining the methods by which people decide when and how roles are played.
10. Explore how job complexity influences role conflict and ambiguity, and examine how that influence can affect job outcomes, such as creativity and performance.

References to Know

Biddle, B. J. (1979). *Role theory: Expectations, identities, and behaviors.* New York: Academic Press.

Biddle, B. J. (1986). Recent developments in role theory. *Annual Review of Sociology, 12,* 67–92.

Biddle, B. J., & Thomas, E. (1979). *Role theory: Concepts and research.* Huntington, NY: Krieger.

Turner, R. H. (1990). Role change. *Annual Review of Sociology, 16,* 87–110.

Zurcher, L. A. (1983). *Social roles: Conformity, conflict and creativity.* Thousand Oaks, CA: Sage.

Implications of the Theory for Managers

Role theory examines the processes through which people are conditioned to play roles. The theory examines behaviors that are characteristic of all people who play the same role, and explores the processes that produce, explain, and predict role behaviors. When employees join an organization, they agree to play a role, or perform a job, for that organization. The role they play has specific tasks, duties, and responsibilities that they are expected to accomplish. Oftentimes, those tasks, duties, and responsibilities are spelled out in a job description and are evaluated through a performance assessment process. Within certain boundaries, each employee can make his role his own by performing it in ways that are unique to him but that also meet the requirements of the job.

Your job as a manager is to help clarify the behaviors that constitute your employees' roles. Talk with your employees about their role expectations to ensure that they are clear about exactly what they are supposed to do and when they are supposed to do it. Make sure that there is no doubt, or any role ambiguity, about the behaviors required in the individual employee's role and how the employee will be evaluated. Also, talk to other employees who work with that employee to ensure that they also understand the role of the employee, so that there is no role confusion or uncertainty.

27

Your task as a manager is to ensure that your employees do not have any role conflicts. Role conflict refers to contradictory demands on your employees' time and attention. Role conflict can cause unnecessary stress for employees and can lower job performance. Talk with your employees about role conflicts that they experience within their job (intrarole conflict) and among the various roles they play (interrole conflict), and work with them to reduce conflicts when possible. Help your employees find appropriate role models in your organization, top-performing employees whom they can identify with and learn from.

28

Self-Determination Theory

Self-determination theory examines the extent to which a person's behavior is self-motivated or self-determined. When people satisfy their basic needs, then they tend to have higher levels of performance, health, and well-being compared to when they do not satisfy their basic needs.

A basic need is a perceived void or gap that can lead to health and well-being when satisfied or to pathology and ill-health when not satisfied or filled. A basic need can be physiological (Hull, 1943), such as for air, food, and water, or it can be psychological, such as for love, respect, and appreciation. Self-determination theory posits that people must continually satisfy three basic psychological needs—for autonomy, competence, and relatedness—throughout their lifetime in order to reach optimal functioning levels and to experience ongoing personal growth and well-being (Deci & Ryan, 2000a; Ryan & Deci, 2000a; Ryan & Frederick, 1997).

The need for autonomy refers to people's need to believe that they choose their own actions, such as initiating, regulating, and maintaining their own behavior. People experience a personal sense of freedom when this need is met. The need for competence refers to people wanting to accomplish difficult and challenging tasks in order to obtain desired outcomes. People experience a sense of mastery, success, and control when this need is met. The need for relatedness refers to people's need to establish mutual respect and connectedness with others. People experience a sense of social support from others when this need is met. Ideally, a person will have all three of these needs met at optimal levels throughout their lifetime (Ryan & Deci, 2002).

These three needs are thought to be innate to all people across the globe (Deci et al., 2001; Ryan & Deci, 2000a; Vansteenkiste, Zhou, Lens, & Soenens, 2005). However, the relative importance of the needs and the methods by which a person meets them tend to change over time and throughout his or her life. In addition, the culture in which the individual resides can influence the extent to which he or she focuses on and seeks to meet each of these three basic needs (Ryan & Deci, 2000b). A main idea in the theory is that human pursuit of some life goals can provide relatively direct satisfaction of the three basic needs, which can lead to enhanced well-being (Ryan, Sheldon, Kasser, & Deci, 1996). However, the pursuit of other goals may not result in satisfaction of the three basic needs, which can result in ill-being or ill health. Kasser and Ryan (1993, 1996; Ryan et al., 1999) compared individual focus on meeting intrinsic goals (for example, personal growth, affiliation, community) to individual focus on meeting extrinsic goals (for example, money, fame, image). They found that focusing on intrinsic aspirations could lead to increased well-being, whereas focusing on extrinsic aspirations could lead to depression and anxiety (Vansteenkiste et al., 2004).

A major focus in the theory is the distinction between intrinsic and extrinsic motivation. Intrinsic, or internal, motivation refers to performing an action because doing so is interesting and spontaneously satisfying for the person doing the activity (White, 1959). People are said to be intrinsically motivated when they experience positive feelings just from doing a task itself. Conversely, extrinsic, or external, motivation refers to performing an action because it will result in some outcome that is separate from the activity itself, such as getting a reward or avoiding a punishment (Deci & Ryan, 2008). People who believe that their actions are caused internally have an internal perceived locus of causality. Conversely, people who believe that their actions are caused externally have a perceived external locus of causality (Ryan & Connell, 1989; Sheldon, 2002; Turban, Tan, Brown, & Sheldon, 2007). Focusing on your intrinsic aspirations can lead to your increased well-being, but focusing on your extrinsic aspirations can result in depression and anxiety (Vansteenkiste, Simons, Lens, Sheldon, & Deci, 2004).

There are four different types of extrinsic motivation, which theorists have arranged along a continuum from the most internally regulated to the most externally regulated: (1) integrated regulation, (2) identified regulation, (3) introjected regulation, and (4) external regulation. Integrated regulation means to identify so much with the value of doing an activity that it becomes a habitual part of the self. Identified regulation means that person performs an activity solely because she identifies with the value or meaning of doing that behavior, and so accepts the reason why she has to do it. Intrinsic motivation (or regulation), integrated regulation, and identified regulation are referred to as "autonomous motivation" (Deci & Ryan, 2008; Gagne & Forest, 2008).

In contrast, introjected regulation refers to doing a behavior because of feelings of self-worth, such as guilt and ego involvement. External regulation refers to behaving in a certain way solely to obtain a reward or to avoid a punishment. Both introjected regulation and external regulation are referred to as "controlled motivation" because the motivation to perform comes from outside the self or is less determined by the self than is autonomous motivation.

28

A third type of motivation, called "amotivation" (nonregulated behavior), is impersonal regulation, which is the least self-determined of the different types of motivation. Impersonal regulation results when a person satisfies none of the three basic needs.

A construct called "causality orientation" refers to the extent to which people self-determine their own behavior or allow the environment to regulate their behavior. Causality orientation is made up of autonomous motivation, controlled motivation, and impersonal motivation. Further enhancements to this continuum resulted in the creation of a subtheory, called organismic integration theory.

Newer concepts in the theory include mindfulness and vitality (Deci & Ryan, 2008). Mindfulness refers to a person's open awareness and attention to what is happening within and around him or her (Brown & Ryan, 2003). Mindfulness involves inner reflection, self-examination of need fulfillment, and purposeful movement from a controlled orientation to a more autonomous orientation. Vitality refers to how energy comes from meeting one's basic needs. When people experience vitality, they feel energetic, exhilarated, and empowered to act autonomously and to sustain their efforts when doing important activities.

Criticisms and Critiques of the Theory

Self-determination theory has been criticized in a number of different areas. First, the theory has been called "Pollyannaish," as it focuses primarily on the positive, optimistic, "bright side" of life and tends to ignore the negative, pessimistic, "dark side" realities of most people's actual lives. Deci and Ryan (2000b) responded by saying that the theory also focuses on the anxiety, grief, and hostility that occur when basic needs are not met.

Second, critics argue that the theory assumes that all people have an active, growth-oriented nature. The theory also assumes that people have a human tendency toward health and well-being and seek out necessary nutrients and nutriments. Critics posit that these assumptions may not apply to all people.

Third, the theory has been criticized for positing only three basic needs and not others, such as needs for safety and security, growth, meaning, and self-esteem. Critics have complained that the theory does not adequately define need satisfaction and does not examine when the three basic needs can conflict with each other. Also, the theory does not examine how the three basic needs change over time for an individual.

Fourth, the theory has been criticized for not examining need strength. The theory does not explain how people prioritize their needs and focus on the costs and benefits of satisfying some needs to the detriment of other needs. Critics also contend that the theory does not examine how people tend to be drawn toward situations in which needs are met and move away from situations where needs are thwarted.

There has been criticism over the concept of autonomy in the theory versus the idea of free will. The theory contends that there is no such thing as free will because there are no situations where human behavior is completely independent from external influences. Conversely, critics have argued that human behavior can be caused solely by a person's free will.

Measuring Variables in the Theory

Motivation at work scale. Gagne, M., Forest, J., Gilber, M.-H., Aube, C., Morin, E., & Malorni, A. (2010). The motivation at work scale: Validation evidence in two languages. *Educational and Psychological Measurement, 70,* 628–646.

28

Need satisfaction scale. La Guardia, J. G., Ryan, R. M., Couchman, C. E., & Deci, E. L. (2000). Within-person variation in security of attachment: A self-determination theory perspective on attachment, need fulfillment, and well-being. *Journal of Personality and Social Psychology, 79,* 367–384.

Achievement goal questionnaire. Elliot, A. J., & McGregor, H. A. (2001). A 2 × 2 achievement goal framework. *Journal of Personality and Social Psychology, 80,* 501–519.

Self-determination measures. Lin, C.-P., Tsai, Y. H., & Chiu, C.-K. (2009). Modeling customer loyalty from an integrative perspective of self-determination theory and expectation-confirmation theory. *Journal of Business and Psychology, 24,* 315–326.

Financial incentives as motivator items. Stone, D. N., Bryant, S. M., & Wier, B. (2010). Why are financial incentive effects unreliable? An extension of self-determination theory. *Behavioral Research in Accounting, 22*(2), 105–132.

28

General employment value scale. Van den Broeck, A., Vansteenkiste, M., Lens, W., & De Witte, H. (2010). Unemployed individuals' work values and job flexibility: An explanation from expectancy-value theory and self-determination theory. *Applied Psychology, 59,* 296–317.

Suggestions for Further Research

1. Examine the impact on behavior of criticism from liked and admired sources versus criticism from disliked or hated sources.
2. Explore the effects of disproportionate or unequal levels of competence, autonomy, and relatedness on motivation.
3. Look at the influences of performance feedback from others, ranging from highly supportive to highly discouraging, on an individual's performance level.
4. Explore the effects of a range of social factors (from temporary, for example, rewards, deadlines, and feedback, to permanent, for example, education) and motivational orientation on behavior.

5. Study the effects of situational conscious and subconscious factors as triggers of motivational processes and goal pursuits.
6. Explore a range of task types (interesting to dull) and the influence of intrinsic and extrinsic motivation on outcomes.
7. Examine how people can endorse more than one type of motivation simultaneously when performing a task over time.
8. Explore how well-being derived from self-growth can contribute to improvement in a person's physical health.
9. Manipulate conditions to compare all types of extrinsic motivation as opposed to intrinsic motivation in terms of their impact on performance.
10. Examine how cultures and environments promote intrinsic and extrinsic values and influence individual internal and external orientations.

References to Know

28

Deci, E. L., & Ryan, R. M. (1980). The empirical exploration of intrinsic motivational processes. In L. Berkowitz (Ed.), *Advances in experimental social psychology* (Vol. 13, pp. 39–80). New York: Academic Press.

Deci, E. L., & Ryan, R. M. (1985). *Intrinsic motivation and self-determination in human behavior.* New York: Plenum.

Deci, E. L., & Ryan, R. M. (2000a). The "what" and "why" of goal pursuits: Human needs and the self-determination of behavior. *Psychological Inquiry, 11,* 227–268.

Deci, E. L., & Ryan, R. M. (Eds.). (2002). *Handbook of self-determination research.* Rochester, NY: University of Rochester Press.

Deci, E. L., & Ryan, R. M. (2008). Facilitating optimal motivation and psychological well-being across life's domains. *Canadian Psychology, 49,* 14–23.

Implications of the Theory for Managers

Self-determination theory examines the extent to which a person's behavior is self-motivated or self-determined. If people satisfy their three basic needs for autonomy, relatedness, and competence, then they tend to have higher levels of performance, health, and well-being compared to when they do not satisfy these three basic needs.

One of your goals as a manager is to motivate employees to accomplish desired organizational goals and outcomes. Employees may perform a task simply to comply with the wishes of management and to obtain a reward or avoid a punishment. Behaviors performed under those conditions tend not to be long lasting and usually stop once the threat of punishment or the promise of reward is taken away. Employees may perform a task because they identify with the purpose and reason for doing that task. Behaviors done under those conditions tend to last a moderate amount of time. However, the most desirable condition is one in which employees perform a task because they have internalized the important aspects of the task and have made that task a part of themselves. Under those conditions, employees perform a task because the task itself is interesting and enjoyable.

Talk with your employees about whether they are internally or externally motivated. If possible, find ways to enable employees to spend more time performing tasks that they find internally rewarding, and less time performing tasks that they find only externally rewarding. To improve internal motivation, show employees how specific tasks contribute to meeting the vision, mission, strategies, and goals of the organization. The more that employees can internalize why and how they need to do their jobs, the more that they can find the tasks themselves interesting and satisfying, which can lead to higher levels of health and well-being. Conversely, employees who feel that none of their three basic needs are being met may want to find a new job, as unsatisfied needs can lead to stress, anxiety, depression, and ill health.

28

29

Sensemaking Theory

The basic idea in sensemaking theory is that making sense is an ongoing process that looks at (1) how people notice events, (2) what those events mean, and (3) how consensually created meanings for those events influence present and future behaviors. First, people have to notice an unusual or different set of circumstances for that event to register for them. Second, once people notice an event, then they typically want to know what that event means for them. People want to know, "What's the story here?" when they experience significant events. Third, creating meaning for events can influence current and future actions and can help people stay in touch with their continuing flow of experience. Weick (1979) summarizes the theme of sensemaking with the question, "How can I know what I think until I see what I say?" (p. 133).

According to sensemaking theory, organization members understand, interpret, and make sense of their environment through ongoing conversations with others. Organization members consensually construct accounts that enable them to comprehend their world and act collectively (Weick & Roberts, 1993). Sensemaking involves creating clear questions and creating clear answers to those questions. According to sensemaking theory, reality is an ongoing accomplishment that emerges from mutual collective efforts to create order and make after-the-fact sense of what happened and what is happening now (Weick, 1993).

The world is an unknowable and unpredictable stream of experiences that people are driven to try to know and understand (Weick, Sutcliffe, & Obstfeld, 2005). Unfortunately, people have limits to their sense organs and brain functioning, so they cannot attend to all possible environmental stimuli. Therefore, people have to place this stimuli into some kind of framework that helps them know, understand, explain, and extrapolate (Dunbar, 1981; Goleman, 1985; Starbuck & Milliken, 1988). For example, a "frame of reference" is a generalized point of view that helps people interpret their experience (Cantril, 1941).

The sensemaking process involves three basic components: (1) cues, (2) frames, and (3) the linking together of cues and frames (Weick, 1995). Frames come from past moments of socialization, whereas cues come from current moments of experience. Cues are information from current environments; they trigger a drive to make sense of the situation. Frames are knowledge structures that include rules and values and serve as a guide to understanding. When people create a relation between frames and cues, they create meaning. Meaning comes from the categories and frames from past experiences, the cues and labels from current events, and the connection of frames and cues. The frame alone and the cue alone do not make sense. What makes sense is a cue inside a frame (Weick, 1995).

Weick (1995) described six types of frames: (1) ideologies (vocabularies of society); (2) categories that classify organizational practices (vocabularies of organizing); (3) paradigms (vocabularies of work); (4) theories of action (vocabularies of coping); (5) tradition (vocabularies of predecessors); and (6) stories (vocabularies of sequence and experience).

Seven characteristics distinguish sensemaking from understanding, interpreting, or attributing: (1) sensemaking is grounded in identity construction (individual self-identity and organizational identity are consensually constructed, and meaning is assigned when events occur); (2) it is retrospective (sense and meaning are made about prior events, and they influence current and future behaviors); (3) it is enactive of sensible environments (people's actions help create their environments, and those creations influence meaning and actions); (4) it is social, based on collective action; (5) it is an ongoing, continuous process; (6) it uses extracted cues (context, language, and vocabularies all affect cues and focus attention on events); and (7) plausibility is more important than accuracy (sensible stories about meaning are consensually created but may not actually reflect reality) (Weick, 1995).

Sensemaking involves the general process of mutual and reciprocal scanning, interpreting, acting, and outcomes (Thomas, Clark, & Gioia, 1993). Scanning is an ongoing process of gathering information that might affect an organization (Daft & Weick, 1984; Kiesler & Sproull, 1986; Milliken, 1990). Interpreting involves creating ways of comprehending the meaning of information, and fitting information into mental structures of understanding (Gioia, 1986; Taylor & Crocker, 1981). Taking action involves making organizational changes on some level (Dutton & Duncan, 1987). Outcomes refer to organizational performance differences or changes, especially improvements, based on successful sensemaking processes.

Organizational leaders can influence the sensemaking process by engaging in "sensegiving" behaviors (Whetten, 1984; Maitlis, 2005). Sensegiving means to influence the sensemaking and meaning construction of others toward a preferred definition of organizational reality (Gioia & Chittipeddi, 1991). When leaders engage in sensegiving, they can focus the organization's attention on the need to change perceptions of reality or can focus attention on changing the organizational reality itself. Leaders often engage in sensegiving behaviors when ambiguous, unpredictable issues arise or when events involve numerous stakeholders (Maitlis & Lawrence, 2007).

29

Maitlis (2005) described four different forms of organizational sensemaking based on two criteria, animation and control. Animation refers to the extent to which stakeholders are engaged in sensemaking. Control refers to the extent to which organizational leaders are involved in the sensemaking process. The four types of organizational sensemaking are (1) guided (high animation and high control); (2) restricted (low animation and high control); (3) fragmented (high animation and low control); and (4) minimal (low animation and low control).

The sensemaking literature has largely separated individual sensemaking from social or organizational sensemaking. However, individuals can engage in sensemaking, such as in Sonenshein's sensemaking-intuition model (2007), and in entrepreneurial sensemaking (Cornelissen & Clarke, 2010).

Sensemaking research has not examined a wide range of organizational circumstances. Most research on sensemaking has been conducted under times of organizational crisis or periods of intense pressure. Fewer research studies have examined sense-making processes in typical, ordinary business environments (Maitlis, 2005).

Sensemaking involves the use of frames or frameworks to make sense of new information. Recent sensemaking research has examined paradoxes, or conflicting organizational frames, that can create managerial tension and inhibit successful organizational performance; These conflicting frames include, for example, top-down and bottom-up, engage and disengage, unity and diversification, and change and stability (Luscher & Lewis, 2008).

Criticisms and Critiques of the Theory

Critics of sensemaking theory have argued that the theory is a self-fulfilling prophecy. People merely create the meaning that they want regardless of the environment, and then act and believe as if the world were like that all along. The concept of enactment means that constraints are partly made by a person's own actions (Weick et al., 2005). People are not able to be neutral, objective, isolated observers of events, but are biased participant observers who change their situation just by their very presence. People attend only to the events and cues that reinforce the outcomes that they premeditatedly created.

Critics contend that sensemaking is not about reality, but only about plausible or sensible meaning that may be far from reality. People create stories that are sensible but not "sensable" or actually perceived by their five senses. Critics contend that managers might be better off if they focused on reality rather than on possible, probable, or plausible meanings for events.

Another criticism is that the theory ignores learning processes. The theory posits that managers act, then make sense, then act. The theory stresses that continuous action is more important than pausing to reflect (Weick, 1995). However, critics argue that sensemaking could be enhanced if managers add a reflective step in the process, so that they act, then make sense, then critically reflect, then make sense, then act (Schwandt, 2005). For example, adding a step where managers update their current thinking with the latest information (or doubt the merits of current thinking) might result in more optimal shared meaning (Maitlis & Sonenshein, 2010; Rudolph, Morrison, & Carroll, 2009).

29

Critics have argued that sensemaking stresses action before thinking. Weick (2010) states that action is always just a little ahead of cognition, and that we always act our way to belated understanding. However, critics contend that sometimes thinking before one acts may be the preferable arrangement. Maybe situations would be changed differently if people thought more before they acted, rather than merely reacting after they behaved.

Critics have also contended that sensemaking theory is always retrospective and never forward thinking. Change and uncertainty are noticed, then plausible sense is made of those events, then people move on (Weick, 2010).

Measuring Variables in the Theory

Image, identity, and information processing scales. Gioia, D. A., & Thomas, J. B. (1996). Identity, image, and issue interpretation: Sensemaking during strategic change in academia. *Administrative Science Quarterly, 41,* 370–403.

Employee support measures. Grant, A. M., Dutton, J. E., & Rosso, B. D. (2008). Giving commitment: Employee support programs and the prosocial sensemaking process. *Academy of Management Journal, 51,* 898–918.

29

Empathic questionnaire scales. Ibarra, H., & Andrews, S. B. (1993). Power, social influence, and sense making: Effects of network centrality and proximity on employee perceptions. *Administrative Science Quarterly, 38,* 277–303.

Positive-gain and controllability, information source and use scales. Thomas, J. B., Clark, S. M., & Gioia, D. A. (1993). Strategic sensemaking and organizational performance: Linkages among scanning, interpretation, action, and outcomes. *Academy of Management Journal, 36,* 239–270.

Suggestions for Further Research

1. Compare settling for plausibility in meaning and moving on, versus stopping and uncovering more realistic meaning and understanding.

2. Compare the benefits of acting then thinking, versus thinking then acting in sensemaking.
3. Explore various organizational environmental maps in terms of their degree of correctness and their influence on organizational performance. Examine if an organization can really get to the right place with the wrong map.
4. Look at how individuals manage differences between their individual sensemaking (making sense of their own inner world) and their collective sensemaking (outer world) processes.
5. Study the influence of conflicting organizational frames on performance and other outcomes.
6. Examine the life span of organizational frames—birth, change, adaptation, decline, and replacement—and the impact on organizational performance and other outcomes.
7. Explore the timing of sensemaking, and how sensemaking can be different when done at different time periods for the same events.
8. Look at the meaning, negative or positive, of labels and categories created during sensemaking, and the impact of those meanings.
9. Examine individual difference variables in noticing behavior and their influence on the sensemaking process.
10. Explore the influence of challenging, rather than accepting, organizational frames and the effect of doing so on outcomes.

29

References to Know

Weick, K. E. (1979). *The social psychology of organizing* (2nd ed.). New York: Addison-Wesley.

Weick, K. E. (1988). Enacted sensemaking in crisis situations. *Journal of Management Studies, 25,* 305–317.

Weick, K. E. (1995). *Sensemaking in organizations.* Thousand Oaks, CA: Sage.

Weick, K. E. (2001). *Making sense of the organization.* Oxford: Blackwell.

Weick, K. E., Sutcliffe, K. M., & Obstfeld, D. (2005). Organizing and the process of sensemaking. *Organization Science, 16,* 409–421.

Implications of the Theory for Managers

Sensemaking involves ongoing, after-the-fact, consensually created, plausible stories that rationalize what is currently being done in the organization. Your task as a manager is to help your employees answer the question, "What's the story here?" To do that, you will need to have conversations with your employees to create meaning about important events. Have conversations about the organization's ideology, philosophy, paradigms, traditions, rituals, and stories and help your employees make sense of things when new, different, or disruptive events happen. Show your employees how the organization's frame of reference (such as valuing speed, accuracy, efficiency, cleanliness, or cost-cutting) can serve as a guide for paying attention to important cues, events, and new information that emerge in the environment.

Your employees will not be able to make sense of things on their own. They will depend on you to help them. You may need to act as a "sensegiver" and help show the way for your employees. Help everyone create a sensible and plausible interpretation and understanding of events. Lead the discussion among your employees, and help the group stay in agreement about what is going on and what is driving everyone's behaviors and actions as you all work together to accomplish your organization's vision, mission, strategies, and goals in an ever-changing environment.

29

30

Social Capital Theory

The main idea in social capital theory is that people gain both tangible and intangible resources at the individual, group, and organizational level through social interactions and connections with others (Bourdieu, 1986; Coleman, 1988; Lin, 2001; Putnam, 2000). A key focus in the theory is that social capital resources are embedded within, available through, and derived from social networks of interconnected people, groups, or nations (Bolino, Turnley, & Bloodgood, 2002; Inkpen & Tsang, 2005).

The concept of social capital initially appeared in work that examined the importance of building strong families and local communities (Jacobs, 1965; Loury, 1977). Hanifan (1916) is credited as having first used the term "social capital" and described it as "goodwill, fellowship, mutual sympathy and social intercourse among a group of individuals and families who make up a social unit, the rural community" (p. 130). Nahapiet and Ghoshal (1998) defined social capital as the sum of both actual and potential resources that can be obtained from, or derived from, the network of relationships of which an individual or a social unit is a member. The concept of social capital has gained widespread research attention in a variety of fields, and has been broadened from local influences (Mix, 2011) to CEO compensation (Belliveau, O'Reilly, & Wade, 1996), organizational performance (Baker, 1990; Fischer & Pollock, 2004), geographical regions (Putnam, 1993, 1995, 2000), multinational corporations (Kostova & Roth, 2003), and nations (Fukuyama, 1995).

Social capital approaches have arisen from a number of different and independent sources. For this reason, a wide variety of meanings and interpretations exist for social capital (Fulkerson & Thompson, 2008). A number of researchers have tried to define the boundaries and to argue in favor of one approach over another. Some researchers see social capital as the property of individuals (Portes, 1998). Some see it as the property of both individuals and their social relations (Coleman, 1990; Loury, 1977). Other researchers see social capital as belonging to groups (Bourdieu & Wacquant, 1992). Still others see it as belonging to groups, political units, communities, and nation-states (Putnam, Leonardi, & Nanetti,1993).

The sources of social capital that can be obtained lie within the network of which the individual, the group, or the nation is a member. Social capital is different from other types of capital because it is based on the position or location of the member within the member's network of social relations. Adler and Kwon (2002) described three dimensions of social structure: (1) market relations, (2) hierarchical relations, and (3) social relations. Market relations refer to the bartering or monetary exchange of goods and services. Hierarchical relations refer to exchanging material and security for obedience to authority. Social relations refer to tacit, symmetrical, ongoing mutual exchanges of gifts and favors.

Drawing from the concept of social capital in sociological work that examined the components and benefits of communities (Durkheim, 1960; Simmel, 1971; Tönnies, 1957), research has found that resources made available through social networks tend to come from two main sources (Portes & Landolt, 2000). The first source of social capital is altruistic: (1) giving resources to others because of moral obligations and (2) giving resources to others to maintain solidarity in the same community or region. Altruistic donations are not expected to be paid back. The second source of social capital is instrumental: (1) person-to-person exchanges and (2) larger social-structure resource transactions (such as a loan from a bank). Instrumental resource exchanges are expected to be paid back. There is trust among the parties in these exchanges because the community has the power to enforce that trust.

The possession of social capital can provide many benefits. Researchers have outlined a number of those benefits: more career success, better executive compensation, easier access to jobs, a richer pool of recruits for companies, higher levels of product innovation, more resource exchange, lower turnover rates, lower organizational failure rates, firm growth, enhanced entrepreneurship and the start-up of companies, stronger relationships with suppliers, and higher levels of interfirm learning. In sum, research has shown that the possession of social capital is quite advantageous and lucrative for individuals, groups, organizations, and nations (Adler & Kwon, 2002; Florin, Lubatkin, & Schulze, 2003).

The research on social capital tends to emphasize its positive aspects (Portes, 1998). However, research also has identified at least four negative consequences of social capital: (1) exclusion of outsiders, (2) excess demands on group members, (3) restrictions of individual freedoms, and (4) downward leveling norms (blocking members of minority groups from upward mobility) (Portes & Landolt, 1996; Portes & Sensenbrenner, 1993). Social capital networks tend to be inward focused and offer benefits only to members at the expense of outsiders. Such arrangements can give rise to homogeneous groups, "good old boy" networks, and discriminatory practices (Ritchie & Gill, 2007). There can also be negative aspects of social capital at the organizational level (Inkpen & Tsang, 2005). For example, being overembedded in one's network can inhibit knowledge flow (Uzzi, 1997). Hansen (2002) found that ties to other business units can be helpful but also can be expensive to maintain.

Fulkerson and Thompson (2008) conducted a meta-analysis of the theory and identified six dimensions of social capital: (1) community values (Hanifan, 1916); (2) collective action, social structure, and realization of interests (Coleman, 1988, 1990); (3) trust, reciprocity, and cooperation (Putnam, 2000); (4) individual and group relationship resources (Bourdieu, 1986); (5) civic engagement and voluntary associations (Putnam, 2000); and (6) social ties and networks (Granovetter, 1973). From these six dimensions, Fulkerson and Thompson (2008) created two overarching and competing categories of social capital: (1) resource social capital and (2) normative social capital. Resource social capital mainly refers to mutually shared resources, networks, and social ties. Normative social capital includes norms; trust; reciprocity; civic engagement; and values among friends, family, and community.

30

Criticisms and Critiques of the Theory

Critics have argued that the theory is tautological by definition (Putnam, 1993). For instance, many researchers start by describing the positive or negative effects of social capital, but then state that social capital was responsible for those outcomes. For example, Putnam (2000) pointed out that a town is civic because it has civic participation. Moreover, researchers have tried to show relationships between social capital and changes in communities, but have not been able to say which one caused the other.

Critics also have argued that the concepts of "community" and "social capital" have not been clearly defined and distinguished from each other (Colclough & Sitaraman, 2005). For example, Putnam (2000) used the terms interchangeably. Putnam never actually defined the term community, but called it the "conceptual cousin" (p. 21) of social capital.

Portes (1998) argued that the Coleman/Putnam approach to social capital has not adequately defined the sources of social capital, holders of social capital, or resources that may be considered as social capital. Critics have argued that the term social capital is not better than, or distinct from, other related terms, such as trust, membership, sociability, ties, associations, reciprocity, civic participation, and community (Fischer, 2005; Haynes, 2009).

Critics have complained that social capital really isn't a type of capital (Arrow, 1999). They argue that social capital is something that happens among people and is not something that is possessed by people. Critics have argued that labeling social concepts with the economic term "capital" is incorrect, inappropriate, and misleading (Fine, 2001, 2002a, 2002b).

Critics have argued that the concept of social capital has been inappropriately moved from the individual and community level to the larger state, nation, and world level (DeFilippis, 2002). Critics contend that this movement inaccurately assumes that individual gains and interests are the same and act in the same ways as larger societal gains and interests.

A continuing problem with social capital is that it is nearly impossible to measure. Critics have complained that some very influential research has been based on oversimplified measures and misleading comparisons (Maraffi, 1994; Morlino, 1995).

Foley and Edwards (1999) complained that quantifying attitudes, norms, and social trust at the national level did not result in usable information regarding possession of those attributes at the group level.

As already noted, researchers have tended to emphasize the positive benefits of social capital. However, more recent research has shown that there are trade-offs in social capital, such as that when someone gains, someone else must lose. Thus the more social capital that a community, state, or nation obtains, the more it will also create disadvantageous situations for some people who are on the losing end of the arrangement (for example, Adler & Kwon, 2002).

Measuring Variables in the Theory

General social capital scale. Onyx, J., & Bullen, P. (2000). Measuring social capital in five communities. *Journal of Applied Behavioral Science, 36*, 23–42.

Social Capital Questionnaire (SCQ-G). Kritsotakis, G., Koutis, A., Alegakis, A. K., & Philalithis, A. E. (2008, June). Development of the social capital questionnaire in Greece. *Research in Nursing and Health, 31*, 217–225.

Suggestions for Further Research

1. Examine the extent to which mass media usage leads to local, regional, national, and global civic engagement and disengagement.
2. Explore how grassroots community efforts can help or hurt the creation of new types and kinds of businesses.
3. Look at how organizational networks work together to protect each other and block new competition.
4. Examine how asymmetrical and symmetrical social capital exchanges can help or hurt individuals, groups, and organizations.
5. Explore how social, cultural, and economic forms of capital work together to influence organizational success or failure.
6. Find ways to quantify social capital value creation.

30

7. Study how different network configurations and conditions can lead to different benefits and harms to individuals, groups, and organizations.
8. Examine the various negative aspects of social capital that can occur for individuals, groups, or organizations.
9. Compare the benefits of quality versus quantity of social capital in relation to individual, group, and organizational outcomes.
10. Explore how social capital is shared and used across levels of analysis: individual, group, organizational, and national.
11. Examine how the costs of building and maintaining social capital networks are greater or less than the benefits of social capital obtained.

References to Know

Adler, P. S., & Kwon, S.-W. (2002). Social capital: Prospects for a new concept. *Academy of Management Review, 27,* 17–40.

Bourdieu, P. (1986). The forms of capital. In J. G. Richardson (Ed.), *Handbook of theory and research for the sociology of education* (pp. 241–258). New York: Greenwood Press.

Coleman, J. S. (1988). Social capital in the creation of human capital. *American Journal of Sociology, 94*(Supplement), S95–S120.

Lin, N. (2001). *Social capital: A theory of social structure and action.* Cambridge: Cambridge University Press.

Portes, A. (1998). Social capital: Its origins and applications in modern sociology. *Annual Review of Sociology, 24,* 1–24.

30

Implications of the Theory for Managers

Social capital theory examines how people obtain both tangible and intangible resources at the individual, group, and organizational level through social interactions and connections with others that they would not be able to obtain on their own. Social capital resources are embedded within, available through, and derived from social networks of interconnected people, groups, organizations, or nations.

According to the theory, managers will be more successful if they work with their employees to develop a sense of shared community, compared to managers who do not do so. Communities are composed of social relationships that arise from shared experiences that lead members to feel a bond with other members. Building a sense of community involves helping your employees create a network of trust, cooperation, reciprocity, shared norms and values, mutual caring, and mutual sharing and exchange with each other. You can build organizational communities by assisting your employees in developing shared responsibilities toward each other, helping each other succeed, and supporting each other whenever possible.

Remember that social capital can have both advantages and disadvantages for organizations. The potential dangers of building strong organizational communities can include exclusion of outsiders, excess demands on group members, restrictions of individual freedoms, and discriminatory treatment toward minority groups or other types of groups. Your task as a manager is to help foster the positive benefits of building social capital, but also to help prevent the negative consequences as well. For example, make sure that your organizational communities do not become too exclusive and block new people from joining. Monitor the demands on individuals to ensure that some employees don't become overloaded by task assignments. Check with your employees to make sure that they don't feel stifled and blocked from creating new ideas and innovations. Last, and most important, ensure that organizational communities don't discriminate in any way against other employees.

30

31

Social Cognitive Theory

The major premise of social cognitive theory is that human action is caused by three mutually interacting factors: (1) behavior, (2) cognitive and other personal factors, and (3) the person's external environment. The three factors do not influence each other simultaneously or with equal strength; they also don't influence each other instantly. Time must pass for each of the three factors to exert influence and to receive influence in return. The three factors influence each other bidirectionally, so people are both producers and products of their own environment.

Social cognitive theory represents a break from the behaviorist approach, which posits that environment causes behavior. Behaviorists ignore human functioning because they assume that it is caused by external stimuli. Bandura suggested that not only does the environment cause behavior, but behavior also helps shape the environment, in a process that he called "reciprocal determinism" (1986). Bandura later added his third factor, a person's psychological processes, or cognitions, to the other two factors (environment and behavior) that reciprocally determine human action.

Three aspects of the theory are particularly relevant for organizations: the development of people's (1) cognitive, social, and behavioral competencies through modeling; (2) beliefs about their capabilities so that they will use their knowledge, skills, and abilities effectively; and (3) motivation through goal systems (Bandura, 1988).

According to the theory, people are not just onlookers of their own human body as it wades through environmental events.

31

Instead, people are agents of themselves and of their own experiences. The core features of personal agency are intentionality, forethought, self-reactiveness, and self-reflectiveness. Intentionality refers to proactive commitment to bringing about a future course of action. Forethought means having a future time perspective in which the individual anticipates the likely consequences of his or her prospective actions. Self-reactiveness is the deliberate ability to make choices and plans, shape appropriate courses of action, and motivate and regulate their implementation. Self-reflectiveness refers to self-examination of one's own functioning, or metacognitive ability (Bandura, 2001).

According to the theory, people can learn vicariously through observation of the competencies of others (Bandura, 1997; Wood & Bandura, 1989). Observational learning comprises four constituent processes: attentional, retention, production, and motivational (Bandura, 1986). Attentional process activities include selecting behaviors to observe, accurately perceiving those behaviors, and extracting information about those behaviors. Retention process activities include remembering, storing, and actively rehearsing the self-performance of behaviors retained. Production process activities include performing the newly modeled behaviors and getting feedback about the success or failure of those actions. Motivational process activities include positive incentives to perform the newly learned behaviors, such as past reinforcement, promised reinforcement, external incentives, vicarious incentives, and self-incentives. There are also negative motivations to perform, such as past punishment, threats or promised punishment, and vicarious punishment. Positive reinforcements tend to work better than negative reinforcements (which can often backfire on the punisher).

The theory distinguishes between merely acquiring information and actively performing the new behaviors, because people do not enact everything that they learn. People often enact newly modeled behaviors without immediate rewards, but they may not continue to perform those behaviors in the future without reinforcement to do so (Bandura, 1986). Most of what is modeled is concrete in nature, rather than abstract, as much of what is learned must be performed in a specific way. However, it is possible to learn abstract rules that can then be applied and evaluated in a variety of situations.

31

There is a difference between possessing skills and being able to use them. Successfully using skills requires a strong belief in one's capabilities to exert control over events in order to accomplish desired goals. Two people with the same level of skill may perform differently if their self-beliefs of efficacy enhance or impair their motivation to perform.

People's self-efficacy beliefs can influence their lives in many ways (Bandura, 1988). For example, self-efficacy beliefs are themselves critical determinants of how well people seek out and acquire new skills and abilities. Further, people with high self-efficacy tend to focus on (visualize) how to master tasks, whereas those with low self-efficacy tend to focus on what can go wrong. People's self-efficacy beliefs determine how much effort they will exert and for how long they will exert it toward overcoming obstacles and accomplishing behaviors. The stronger their beliefs, the greater and more persistent their efforts will be. People who evaluate themselves highly tend to have higher levels of self-esteem compared to those who evaluate themselves poorly.

The theory also emphasizes human capacities for self-direction and self-motivation. People tend to be self-directing. They adopt internal performance standards, they monitor their own behavior (self-observe), and they arrange incentives for themselves (self-react) to sustain their efforts until they accomplish their goals. Through a process of self-evaluation, people keep their behavior in line with their standards, and through a process of self-reward, people give themselves positive (praise, pride, a treat) or negative (shame, guilt, embarrassment) reinforcement. People who perform desired behaviors and reward themselves tend to perform better than those who perform behaviors but do not reward themselves. Excessive self-punishment can lead to overcompensation, inactivity (apathy, boredom, and depression), and escape (substance abuse, technological or virtual obsessive fantasy, and even suicide) (Baumeister, 1990; Chatard & Selimbegovic, 2011).

31

Social cognitive theory examines how people can take charge and control over their own life. People can take an active role—be an agent of change—in their self-development, adaptation, and self-renewal (Bandura, 1989). The theory distinguishes among three different modes of agency: direct personal agency, proxy agency, and collective agency (Bandura, 2001). Direct personal agency means to take control and accomplish what one wants, and includes making the best of fortuitous or unfortunate situations. Proxy agency means to get those who have access to resources, power, influence, or expertise to wield it on one's behavior. Collective agency means to work with others to accomplish desired objectives (Bandura, 1997).

Criticisms and Critiques of the Theory

The theory posits that self-efficacy beliefs contribute significantly to a person's level of motivation and performance (Bandura & Locke, 2003). However, Vancouver and associates found that a person's beliefs in her capabilities did not determine her performance or were self-defeating (Vancouver, Thompson, Tischner, & Putka, 2002; Vancouver, Thompson, & Williams, 2001). Vancouver et al. (2001, 2002) found that performance positively influenced self-efficacy perceptions, but that self-efficacy did not influence subsequent performance. Bandura and Locke (2003) conducted a meta-analysis and determined that the findings of Vancouver et al. (2001, 2002) did not uncover problems with the theory, but were merely due to a poorly designed task in their studies' methodology.

An additional problem with the theory may be that the concept of self-efficacy is not distinct from similar constructs: self-esteem, neuroticism, and locus of control. Judge, Erez, Bono, and Thoresen (2002) found high correlations among the four constructs and recommended that researchers further refine their scale measures of these constructs in order to uncover their unique qualities.

Finally, there is serious debate over measuring the construct of self-efficacy (Scherbaum, Cohen-Charash, & Kern, 2006). The theory rejects the trait approach to explaining human behavior, which posits that people are born with specific traits that govern their behavior. Bandura (2002) argued that perceptions of self-efficacy and outcome expectancies depend on specific circumstances in specific environments, and are therefore not global, context-free dispositions that can be measured using a general self-efficacy (GSE) measure.

However, researchers have developed GSE scales that can be used to measure self-efficacy for any task in any setting (for example, Chen, Gulley, & Eden, 2001). Some researchers have

31

argued that GSE moderates the impact of the environment (for example, provides negative feedback) on a person's task self-efficacy perceptions. In addition, some researchers have argued that GSE is not different from other self-evaluations, such as self-esteem, and that it is not predictive of behavior (Bandura, 1997; Stanley & Murphy, 1997).

Measuring Variables in the Theory

General self-efficacy scale. Chen, G., Gulley, S. M., & Eden, D. (2001, January). Validation of a new general self-efficacy scale. *Organizational Research Methods, 4,* 62–83.

Collective efficacy and peer aggression measures. Barchia, K., & Bussey, K. (2011). Individual and collective social cognitive influences on peer aggression: Exploring the contribution of aggression efficacy, moral disengagement, and collective efficacy. *Aggressive Behavior, 37,* 107–120.

Self-efficacy belief in reading and writing scales. Prat-Sala, M., & Redford, P. (2010). The interplay between motivation, self-efficacy and approaches to studying. *British Journal of Educational Psychology, 80,* 283–305.

General perceived self-efficacy scale. Scholz, U., Gutiérrez Doña, B., Sud, S., & Schwarzer, R. (2002). Is general self-efficacy a universal construct? Psychometric findings from 25 countries. *European Journal of Psychological Assessment, 18,* 242–251.

Suggestions for Further Research

1. Examine the obstacles to and enhancers of observational learning.
2. Explore the range of cognitive and physical rehearsal and imaging methods that can be used to enhance performance.
3. Look at the heuristics used to learn decision rules and how people learn to apply or not apply learned rules.
4. Investigate intrinsic motivation and self-efficacy and their impact on performance continuance and cessation.

31

5. Examine the process in which people justify simultaneous positive and negative performance feedback from others.
6. Explore how individuals select salient others to model and how that process changes over time.
7. Look at how people rationalize high levels of internal self-efficacy with high levels of external criticism of performance.
8. Explore how people refrain from doing negative or unethical acts when the impulse to perform them is strong.
9. Examine the influence of social isolation versus social engagement on social learning and behavior enactment.
10. Compare observational learning through various types of communication media (for example, face-to-face and virtual).
11. Look at the range of self-reward behaviors (positive and negative) after behavior (positive and negative) and their influence on future performance of behavior.

References to Know

Bandura. A. (1977). Self-efficacy: Toward a unifying theory of behavioral change. *Psychological Review, 84,* 191–215.

Bandura, A. (1986). *Social foundations of thought and action: A social cognitive theory.* Englewood Cliffs, NJ: Prentice Hall.

Bandura, A. (1991). Social cognitive theory of self-regulation. *Organizational Behavior and Human Decision Processes, 50,* 248–287.

Bandura, A. (1997). *Self-efficacy: The exercise of control.* New York: Freeman.

Bandura, A. (2001). Social cognitive theory: An agentic perspective. *Annual Review of Psychology, 52,* 1–26.

31

Implications of the Theory for Managers

According to social cognitive theory, people behave as they do because of the mutually interacting influences of their environment, their behaviors, and their thought process, or cognitions. People are both producers and products of their own environment. They learn how to behave by watching, remembering, and reproducing the behavior of others. People continue to perform these new behaviors only if they are positively rewarded for doing so.

Your job as a manager is to help your employees model and perform desirable behaviors. Make sure that your employees notice the behaviors of others who are performing the right behaviors in the correct ways. Next, help shape your employees' self-beliefs about their abilities to perform those behaviors. Employees who have positive self-beliefs (self-efficacy) tend to learn and perform new behaviors more easily than employees with low self-efficacy. Talk with your employees about their self-efficacy beliefs and help them see that they can successfully perform the desired behaviors. Next, positively reinforce your employees when they successfully perform the desired behaviors, such as through acknowledgment, praise, or even money if possible. However, be careful when rewarding employees, as different employees tend to value different rewards. For example, some employees enjoy public praise, but some do not. Talk with your employees about how best to reinforce their new socially learned behaviors.

The ideas of this theory also apply to you. Pay attention to what behaviors you are learning by watching others. Be sure that you are modeling the right behaviors of the right people. Watch out for your own negative self-efficacy beliefs. If you start to doubt yourself, then your performance may suffer. Don't let self-criticism injure your performance. Remember to reward yourself when you perform successfully.

31

32

Social Comparison Theory

The central premise of social comparison theory is that people continually use information about other people's opinions and abilities to assess their own opinions and abilities (Festinger, 1954). The theory assumes that people make social comparisons because they have a need to maintain stable and accurate appraisals of themselves compared to other people, and to maintain and protect their self-esteem and self-worth (Aspinwall & Taylor, 1993; Pyszczynski, Greenberg, & LaPrelle, 1985; Taylor & Lobel, 1989; Wood, 1989). The theory posits that people tend to prefer to evaluate themselves compared to objective information and standards. However, if that information is unavailable, vague, or ambiguous, then people also compare themselves to other people (Suls & Wheeler, 2000).

Festinger (1954) originally proposed that people tend to compare themselves to others who are similar to themselves. The reason that similar others are used for comparison is that they provide a more precise and stable basis for evaluation compared to using dissimilar others. However, people can also compare themselves to others who are similar regarding an attribute of interest, even if those others may be different on other dimensions (Goethals & Darley, 1977).

The theory posits that people use others to evaluate their abilities and to find out how they should think and feel. People tend to make social comparisons when they are (1) uncertain about what to think or feel; (2) under conditions of high stress, novelty, or change; and (3) in situations that foster competition (Sharp, Voci, & Hewstone, 2011).

32

Early research resulted in support for a "better than average" effect, which is the tendency for people to view themselves as performing higher than nearly everyone else (Alicke & Govorun, 2005; Hoorens & Buunk, 1993). However, Moore (2007) found that more often than not there is a "worse than average" effect for many conditions, especially for rare behaviors and uncommon abilities. Larrick, Burson, and Soll (2007) found that hard tasks can produce overconfidence but "worse than average" perceptions, whereas easy tasks can produce underconfidence but "better than average" perceptions.

Research has shown that the results of social comparisons can be either contrast or assimilation. Contrast means that evaluation of the self is seen as displaced away from the comparison other, or something that the person should avoid. Assimilation means that the evaluation of the self is displaced toward the similar other, or something to which a person aspires to become. For example, exposure to a role model can inspire a person to improve himself.

Festinger (1954) originally considered only upward comparisons. However, the theory now includes both upward and downward social comparisons (Mahler, Kulik, Gerrard, & Gibbons, 2010; Wood, 1996). Social comparisons to someone who is performing better (an upward comparison) can result in either improved performance (Collins, 1996; Wood, 1989) or impaired performance (Gordijn & Stapel, 2006). Brown, Ferris, Heller, and Keeping (2007) found that role ambiguity, task autonomy, and core self-evaluations led to upward social comparisons in the workplace, and upward comparisons led to high job satisfaction and affective commitment. However, social comparisons to someone who is performing worse (a downward comparison) also can result in either improved performance (Willis, 1981) or impaired performance (Buunk, Collins, Taylor, VanYperen, & Dakof, 1990).

Festinger (1954) originally proposed that social comparisons were deliberate and that people chose not to compare themselves to dissimilar others. However, more recent research has shown that social comparisons can be (1) controlled and deliberate or automatic and spontaneous, (2) conscious or subliminal, and (3) implicit or explicit (Stapel & Blanton, 2004).

The deliberateness of social comparisons was examined by Gilbert, Giesler, and Morris (1995). They found that people can automatically and uncontrollably make social comparisons with other people. They also found that there is a more deliberate stage in which people can change their minds and "undo" social comparisons and then even change their minds back again (Goffin, Jelley, Powell, & Johnston, 2009). The researchers argued that people can gain indirect control over the automatic making of social comparisons by specifically avoiding situations that tend to lead to automatic social comparisons and by reversing unwanted social comparisons.

Recent research has shown that social comparisons can be made explicitly as well as implicitly (Blanton & Stapel, 2008; Schwinghammer & Stapel, 2011). An explicit comparison occurs when a person is provided with a target and is specifically asked to make a comparison between herself and the target. However, a comparison is implicit if a person is not specifically given a target or there is no instruction to make a comparison. For example, an implicit comparison might occur if by chance a coworker's open pay envelope is accidentally placed in a person's mail slot (Stapel & Suls, 2004). Implicit and explicit comparisons can occur simultaneously (Blanton & Stapel, 2008).

Research has shown that the tendency to engage in social comparisons may be an individual difference variable. For example, researchers have found that some individuals rarely engage in social comparisons, whereas others tend to make frequent comparisons (Buunk, Zurriaga, & Peiro, 2010). Individual differences in the sensitivity to social comparisons can be measured with the social comparison orientation scale (Gibbons & Buunk, 1999). Further, individuals who are highly self-critical tend to seek out and make more unfavorable comparisons about their abilities than do individuals who are less self-critical (Santor & Yazbek, 2004). These individuals specifically make these negative comparisons in order to maintain low self-evaluations.

The theory has been extended to include social comparison and outcome evaluation in group contexts (Goodman & Haisley, 2007; Hertel et al., 2008; Levine & Moreland, 1987). In addition, the theory now looks at being the "comparee" versus being the comparer (Koch & Metcalfe, 2011). The theory has also been extended to include both immediate and long-term comparisons and trends (Zell & Alicke, 2009, 2010). Further, the definition of social comparison continues to be extended beyond Festinger's

32

original formulation (1954). Kruglanski and Mayseless (1990) broadened the definition to comparative judgments of social stimuli about a specific content dimension. Buunk and Gibbons (2007) wrote that the definition now includes any process in which individuals relate their own characteristics to those of others.

Criticisms and Critiques of the Theory

Social comparison theory has been criticized for not adequately defining what exactly is compared when one socially compares (Suls, 1986). Festinger (1954) described that people compare only opinions and abilities in social comparison. Suls (1986) argued that people tend not to compare their traits or dispositions with those of other people. For example, he doubted that people compare how hostile or socially sensitive they are compared with other people.

A second criticism of the theory has to do with how much people make comparisons to others. Suls (1986) doubted that people compare all of their abilities and opinions with others, and argued that the range and boundaries of social comparison had not been adequately explored or defined. Following the work of William James (1890), Suls argued that all dimensions are not self-relevant, and that if a person has no stake in a specific area, then he or she will probably not make social comparisons for that area. Theorists have not fully explored heuristics, hierarchies, or other algorithms that are used by individuals to attend to or avoid possible social comparison information.

A third criticism of earlier versions of the theory was that it focused only on voluntary, deliberate comparison processes in which people compared themselves to similar others (Suls, 1986). More recent work has shown that comparisons can be voluntary or involuntary and can be toward similar or dissimilar others.

A fourth criticism addresses the concept of selective utilization of information obtained through comparison. Suls (1986) argued that Festinger's description of social comparison (1954) focused on the selective use of information and not on selective acquisition of information. Critics argue that research should more fully explore exactly when and why individuals selectively use information gained through social comparison.

32

A fifth criticism has to do with the direction of the social comparison (Blanton, 2001; Kruglanski & Mayseless, 1990; Taylor & Lobel, 1989). Festinger (1954) hypothesized that people have a unidirectional drive to upwardly compare themselves to people who are more capable than themselves. A lack of clarity over the direction of the social comparison, whether it be upward, downward, or even lateral, has led to confusion in general predictions made for the theory (Taylor & Lobel, 1989).

Finally, critics have argued about the purpose of individual social comparison. Festinger (1954) argued that people compare themselves in a purposive, deliberate way to similar others. However, others have debated whether self-evaluation or self-validation purposes are more prevalent and more important. Further research should examine when and why social comparisons are performed, and how that information is used or discarded.

Measuring Variables in the Theory

Sensitivity about being the target of a threatening upward comparison scale. Koch, E. J., & Metcalfe, K. P. (2011). The bittersweet taste of success: Daily and recalled experiences of being an upward social comparison target. *Basic and Applied Social Psychology, 33*, 47–58.

Social comparison orientation scale. Gibbons, F. X., & Buunk, B. P. (1999). Individual differences in social comparison: Development of a scale of social comparison orientation. *Journal of Personality and Social Psychology, 76*, 129–142.

Suggestions for Further Research

1. Examine how utilization of social comparison information changes over time for positive- and negative-trending data.
2. Explore how, over time, people increase or decrease effort and time spent on tasks in which they are succeeding or failing.
3. Look at social comparison processes about cognitions, such as an individual's attitudes and opinions, and how they converge or not with those of others.

32

4. Examine how people select and evaluate individuals versus groups to which they compare themselves.
5. Explore differences in being the better or worse comparer in relation to the "comparee" in terms of subsequent attitudes and performance.
6. Examine organizational factors that contribute to social comparisons and to cognitive, affective, and behavioral outcomes.
7. Look at how people assess the magnitude of their discrepancies in relation to others regarding self-regulation behaviors.
8. Examine the possibility of automatic contagion effects on social comparisons among individuals or among group members.
9. Explore the relationship between social comparison discrepancies and emotional responses for individuals and for groups.
10. Look at how emotions and other responses can mediate social comparison processes in the workplace.

References to Know

Buunk, A. P., & Gibbons, F. X. (2007). Social comparison: The end of a theory and the emergence of a field. *Organizational Behavior and Human Decision Processes, 102,* 3–21.

Festinger, L. (1954). A theory of social comparison. *Human Relations, 7,* 117–140.

Goethals, G. R. (1986). Social comparison theory: Psychology from the lost and found. *Personality and Social Psychology Bulletin, 12,* 261–278.

Suls, J., & Wheeler, L. (Eds.). (2000). *Handbook of social comparison.* New York: Plenum/Kluwer Academic.

Wood, J. V. (1996). What is social comparison and how should we study it? *Personality and Social Psychology Bulletin, 22,* 520–537.

Implications of the Theory for Managers

People have a need to maintain stable and accurate knowledge of themselves. One way that they do this is by comparing their opinions and abilities with those of others. People prefer to have objective standards with which to compare themselves with others,

32

but if that information isn't available, then they will socially compare themselves to others.

Specifically help your employees fill their need to have knowledge about their attitudes and their abilities. Provide your employees with accurate, objective information about their performance whenever you can. Don't wait until performance review time to go over this information with your employees when it may be more difficult, or even too late, to correct performance problems. Instead, keep your employees up-to-date about their performance in real time when possible. Throughout the year, deliberately keep your employees apprised of their performance compared to objective standards, and identify and solve performance problems as soon as you notice them.

Remember that employees prefer to compare themselves to objective standards, but if those aren't available, then they will compare themselves to other people. Help shape this process by making sure that employees compare themselves to the right people in the right ways. Employees may improve their performance if they compare themselves upwardly to higher-performing employees and see that their own performance is lacking. However, employees may lower their performance level if they compare themselves downwardly to lower-performing employees and see that their performance exceeds that of others. Help focus your employees' attention on higher-performing employees so that they can be inspired to learn from and apply effective methods and processes used by effective employees.

32

33

Social Exchange Theory

The major idea in social exchange theory is that parties enter into and maintain exchange relationships with others with the expectation that doing so will be rewarding (Blau, 1968; Gouldner, 1960; Homans, 1958). The theory is limited to examining actions that are contingent on rewarding reactions from others (Blau, 1964), and examines two-sided, mutually contingent, and mutually rewarding processes called "transactions" and relationships called "exchanges" (Emerson, 1976). The theory assumes that self-interested parties transact or exchange with self-interested others in order to accomplish outcomes that neither could achieve on his or her own (Lawler & Thye, 1999), and that these exchanges would cease as soon as they are not perceived to be mutually rewarding by both parties (Blau, 1994). Homans (1961) wrote that the exchange of benefits, or giving something to a recipient that is more valuable to the recipient than it is to the giver, is the underlying basis for human behavior.

According to the theory, each party has something of value that the other wants. The two parties decide what to exchange and in what quantities. The resources exchanged can be economic or social or both. Economic resources include tangible items, such as goods, money, assets, information, advice, or services. Social resources include intangible items, such as social amenities, friendship, and prestige. The value of outcomes received during a social exchange is in the eye of the beholder. However, according to Blau (1968), the most rewarding outcomes in social exchange relationships (for example, social approval and respect) do not have any material value for which a price could be determined.

33

Discourse on social exchange dates as far back as Aristotle's *Nicomachean Ethics,* and included distinctions between social and economic exchanges (Blau, 1968). More recent research that contributed to the formulation of social exchange theory includes Blau (1955, 1960, 1964), Emerson (1962), Homans (1958, 1961), and Thibaut and Kelley (1959).

There are similarities and differences between economic and social exchanges. Social and economic exchanges are similar in that they both include expectations that future returns will be received for current contributions made. However, in economic exchanges, the returns on one's investment are more clearly known and often specified, such as in a written contract, whereas in social exchanges, the returns on one's investment are unspecified and often voluntary. Economic exchanges tend to occur on a quid pro quo (this for that) basis, whereas social exchanges do not. Economic exchanges are based on transactions in the short term; social exchanges are based on relationships in which both parties trust that the other will fairly meet their obligations in the long term (Holmes, 1981). Social exchanges tend to include short-term inequities or asymmetries between the trading parties, whereas economic exchanges tend to be more equitable and symmetrical.

Social exchange relationships involve uncertainty over whether parties will reciprocate contributions or not. As a result, trust between parties is an important part of social exchange theory. Demonstrating trust to the other party may be difficult during the initial stages of exchange. Typically, social exchanges evolve slowly, with lower-value exchanges occurring initially, then larger-value exchanges occurring when higher levels of trust develop. Trust can be generated in two ways: (1) through regular and consistent reciprocation with the other party for benefits received from them, and (2) through the gradual expansion of exchanges with the other party (Blau, 1964).

The major premises of social exchange theory were derived with a goal of creating a mutually exclusive and exhaustive set of four almost lawlike generalizations: (1) exchange relationships result in economic or social outcomes (or both), (2) a cost-benefit analysis is performed on the outcomes received and compared with the potential costs and benefits of alternative exchange relationships, (3) the receipt of rewarding outcomes over time increases mutual trust and commitment in exchange relationships, and

(4) exchange norms and expectancies develop over time from rewarding exchange relationships (Popper, 1959; Rudner, 1966).

Researchers have defined social and economic exchanges as a type of choice behavior, although no formal bargaining or written contracts are involved. Parties freely perform cost-benefit analyses regarding current or potential social exchanges (Molm, 1990). The satisfaction levels of the parties in the exchanges become the prime determinants of whether future exchanges will occur or not. However, parties do not make these considerations in isolation. Instead, a party's social network can help support or disrupt future exchanges. For example, if reciprocal obligations are not met, then social sanctions, such as moral disapproval, can result. However, social exchange theory has tended to view party satisfaction as the primary influence over exchange maintenance and to treat social sanctions as a secondary influence (Blau, 1994).

Social exchange research has evolved from two different traditions: the individualistic and the collectivistic (Makoba, 1993). The individualistic perspective stresses the individual psychological and economic self-interests involved in the exchange (Blau, 1964; Homans, 1961). The collectivistic perspective emphasizes the importance of the social needs of the group or of society (Befu, 1977). According to the collectivistic approach, society is assumed to have its own existence, and individuals are assumed to exist for the benefit of society (Sahlins, 1965; Mauss, 1967; Levi-Strauss, 1969; Ekeh, 1974). Researchers have tried to integrate the two approaches (for example, Makoba, 1993).

Reciprocity, or repaying obligations to another, is one of the best-known exchange rules in social exchange theory, but there has been ambiguity in how this concept has been defined (Gouldner, 1960). For example, reciprocity can be defined as (1) interdependent exchanges, (2) cultural expectations, and (3) cultural norms of how people ought to and should behave. Sahlins (1972) created a continuum of levels of reciprocity that range from "negative" to "generalized." Generalized reciprocity is altruistic and refers to an indefinite reimbursement period, without defined equivalency in repayment and with low self-interest. Balanced reciprocity refers to a simultaneous exchange of equivalent resources. Negative reciprocity refers to timely and equal exchanges of resources with high self-interest. Other examples of exchange rules include individually negotiated rules, rationality, altruism, group gain, status consistency, and competition (Cropanzano & Mitchell, 2005).

Criticisms and Critiques of the Theory

Although social exchange theory is among the most influential theories for understanding organizational behavior (Cropanzano & Mitchell, 2005), the theory has not gone without criticism. Some critics have argued that, given the assumptions of the theory, all human interactions would have to be considered as social exchanges. Some researchers have treated social exchanges as a special case of human social interaction, and others have simply ignored distinctions between the two (Burgess & Neilsen, 1974; Molm & Takahashi, 2003). Coyle-Shapiro and Conway (2004) explored theoretical ambiguities, and Cropanzano, Rupp, Mohler, and Schminke (2001) expressed concern over frequent misunderstandings of the social exchange theory model.

Critics have argued that the concept of exchange relationships has not been well defined. For example, Cropanzano and Mitchell (2005) describe two types of relationships: (1) a series of interdependent exchanges and (2) the interpersonal attachments that result from the series of interdependent exchanges. To help resolve this dichotomy, Cropanzano and Mitchell provide a typology of transactions and relationships in social exchange.

Critics have argued that the theory oversimplifies human interactions by reducing them to only short-term, self-interested exchanges. Critics lament that humans are motivated to behave for any number of reasons and often maintain relationships that are not mutually beneficial when many other, more rewarding relationships are possible.

Measuring Variables in the Theory

Social and economic exchange scales. Shore, L. M., Tetrick, L. E., Lynch, P., & Barksdale, K. (2006). Social and economic exchange: Construct development and validation. *Journal of Applied and Social Psychology, 36*(4), 837–867.

Reciprocity scales. Wu, J. B., Hom, P. W., Tetrick, L., Shore, L. M., Jia, L., Li, C. P., & Song, L. J. (2006). The norm of reciprocity:

Scale development and validation in the Chinese context. *Management and Organization Review, 2,* 377–402.

Social exchange styles questionnaire. Leybman, M. E., Zuroff, D. C., Fournier, M. A., & Kelly, A. C. (2010). Social exchange styles: Measurement, validation, and application. *European Journal of Personality, 21,* 549–587.

Favor-doing, organizational citizenship behaviors, and other scales. Wayne, S. J., Shore, L. M., & Liden, R. C. (1997). Perceived organizational support and leader-member exchange: A social exchange perspective. *Academy of Management Journal, 40,* 82–111.

Power, trust, and knowledge-sharing behavior measures. Liao, L.-F. (2008, October). Knowledge-sharing in R&D departments: A social power and social exchange theory perspective. *International Journal of Human Resource Management, 19,* 1881–1895.

Knowledge sharing measure. Bartol, K. M., Liu, W., Zeng, X., & Wu, K. (2009). Social exchange and knowledge sharing among knowledge workers: The moderating role of perceived job security. *Management and Organization Review, 5,* 223–240.

Suggestions for Further Research

1. Examine interdependencies that occur when individuals form multiple, simultaneous exchange relationships and the influence of these interdependencies on behaviors and other outcomes.
2. Explore exchange rule usage when the type of transaction and the type of relationship match or don't match, such as in social or economic transactions in a social or economic relationship.
3. Study time-limit expectations with regard to the meeting of expected reciprocal obligations, and subsequent behaviors.
4. Examine how people manage reciprocity balances and imbalances over time.
5. Look at demographic differences and support of the theory for societal-level outcomes and behaviors.

33

6. Compare differences in perceived exchange benefits for individuals versus groups or societies.
7. Explore demographic and other types of reactions to unmet reciprocal obligations in exchange relationships.
8. Examine differences across countries in terms of societal safeguards that protect workers from exchange imbalances and the impact of those safeguards on worker behaviors.
9. Look at the actual economic resources and social rewards provided by organizations in reciprocation for employee contributions and their influence on subsequent behaviors.
10. Compare differences between perceived and expected versus actual trading partner reciprocation levels and their influence on trading behaviors.

References to Know

Blau, P. (1964). *Exchange and power in social life*. Hoboken, NJ: Wiley.

Emerson, R. M. (1976). Social exchange theory. *Annual Review of Sociology, 2*, 335–362.

Gouldner, A. W. (1960). The norm of reciprocity: A preliminary statement. *American Sociological Review, 25*, 161–178.

Homans, G. C. (1961). *Social behavior: Its elementary forms*. New York: Harcourt Brace.

Thibaut, J. W., & Kelley, H. H. (1959). *The social psychology of groups*. Hoboken, NJ: Wiley.

Implications of the Theory for Managers

People will engage in reciprocal, mutually rewarding relationships only when they trust and believe in their trading partners. Your job as a manager is to help your employees establish long-term, rewarding exchange relationships with both their organization and their fellow employees. Help employees know and trust their company, and help your organization reward employees both through economic rewards (compensation, benefits, vacation time, and so on) and social rewards (praise, respect, appreciation, friendship, and so on, which don't cost the company anything).

Employees' perceptions about their long-term job prospects with their organization can influence their organizational behaviors. Research has shown that employees may not volunteer to help their organization, such as by sharing knowledge, when they have perceptions of low job security or when they do not picture themselves with their company in the future. However, employees were found to share knowledge when they had perceptions of high job security. Therefore, your job as a manager is to help foster employees' perceptions of a long-term trusting and mutually satisfying relationship between them and the organization. Help your employees see that when they invest in the company, the company likewise will invest in them and their future with the company.

33

34

Social Facilitation Theory

Social facilitation theory examines the influences of other people on the increases or decreases of an individual's performance level (Zajonc, 1965, 1968). For example, when other people are around and the task is easy, then performance is better than when the individual is performing the task alone; if the task is hard, then the person's performance is worse than when he or she is performing the task alone (for example, Feinberg & Aiello, 2006; Geen, 1989).

The history of social facilitation research began with the work of Triplett (1898), who noticed differences in cyclists' performance times based on the presence or absence of other riders. Triplett reported that the fastest riding times always occurred during simultaneous competition. The next-fastest times occurred during paced races, and the slowest times occurred when riders performed alone. Triplett explained this result as a "theory of dynamogenesis" in which "the bodily presence of another rider is a stimulus to the racer in arousing the competitive instinct" (p. 516), and asserted that another rider can help the performer release nervous energy that could not otherwise be released.

Burnham (1910) concluded that the presence of others could either increase or decrease an individual's performance level, noting that (1) the presence of the group influences concentration of attention on task performance, (2) the group serves as a disturbing stimulus that influences task performance, and (3) the type of work being done can influence task performance. For example, some kinds of work, especially where original thinking is demanded, are better performed alone.

Allport (1920) coined the term "social facilitation" and defined it as "an increase in response merely from the sight or sound of others making the same movements" (p. 169). Ever since then there has been confusion over the precise meaning of the term and its relationship to similar terms (Clayton, 1978). Crawford (1939) defined social facilitation as "any increment of individual activity which results from the presence of another individual" (p. 410).

Guerin (1993) created three categories of research to explain the theory: (1) drives, (2) social comparisons, and (3) cognitive processes. The first category involves increased drive or arousal in the presence of others. Zajonc (1965) presented two dimensions of social facilitation: audience effects and co-actor effects. Audience effects refer to the influence of the mere presence of passive spectators on a person's behavior. Co-actor effects refer to the influence of others performing the same task. Zajonc (1980) added that the presence of others can trigger an alertness for uncertainties that can in turn trigger higher energy levels.

The presence of other people during task performance can increase a person's psychological arousal level (or drive), which can influence task performance. Hull-Spence drive theory attempted to explain the relationship between arousal level and performance (Hull, 1952). Specifically, if a person has learned a task well, then his or her dominant response (what the person does more than half of the time) would be to perform the task well, at a high level. However, if a person has not learned a task well or the task still has to be learned, then the dominant response would be to perform the task poorly, at a low level (Broen & Storms, 1961; Landers, 1980; Spence & Spence, 1966).

However, other research has found that an increase in drive can also lead to a decrease in the dominant response. These results were found for both team performance (Baumeister & Steinhilber, 1984) and for individual task performance (McNamara & Fisch, 1964; Paul & Eriksen, 1964; Wine, 1971). To account for these contradictory results, a modified drive theory was proposed in which drive will result in performance increases up to a specific point, but then after that point is reached, further increases in drive will lead to performance decrements (Broen & Storms, 1961; Duffy, 1962; Easterbrook, 1959).

The second category of research involves concern over being compared or evaluated when others are present. People adjust their performance level when they expect to be evaluated positively (receive rewards) or negatively (experience punishments, threat, loss of face, embarrassment); this is referred to as "evaluation apprehension" (Cottrell, 1972; Cottrell, Wack, Sekerak, & Rittle, 1968; Feinberg & Aiello, 2010; Geen, 1991; Geen & Gange, 1977; Good, 1973; Henchy & Glass, 1968; Weiss & Miller, 1971). Harkins (2006; Jamieson & Harkins, 2007) advocated that people merely work harder, or exert more effort toward their prepotent (or dominant) response, when they expect to be evaluated, the "mere effort" effect of evaluation.

34

The third category of research involves cognitive processes that include distraction. Baron (1986) proposed the distraction-conflict theory in which co-actors or spectators create a mental distraction that in turn creates attentional conflict that can lead to either cognitive overload (causing lower performance levels) or increased drive or arousal (causing higher performance levels) (Sanders & Baron, 1975; Sanders, Baron, & Moore, 1978). However, the presence of a passive, nonevaluative confederate can be a distraction inhibitor (Sharma, Booth, Brown, & Huguet, 2010).

Baumeister (1984) examined "choking situations," in which people perform poorly despite incentives for optimal performance, and offered two explanations: (1) the explicit monitoring (self-focus) approach and (2) distraction approaches. High-pressure situations can cause a person to experience anxiety and high levels of self-consciousness, which then can cause him or her to focus on task skills and step-by-step control over those skills. Paying specific attention to each step can impede automated or proceduralized skills that could flow naturally if the person were not focusing so intensely on completing the task (Baumeister, 1984; Beilock, Kulp, Holt, & Carr, 2004; Lewis & Langer, 1997). Individuals high in working memory capacity can be harmed by performance pressure, whereas those low in working memory capacity may not be harmed (Beilock & Carr, 2005; Schmader & Johns, 2003).

Research has found that social facilitation effects extend beyond co-acting and audience members. For example, audiences can be familiar or unfamiliar, physically present or not, easily seen or heard or not, visible or invisible, and even human or virtually human (Criddle, 1971; Geen, 1973; Cohen & Davis, 1973).

Research on performance monitoring found social facilitation effects for electronic monitoring of performance (Thompson, Sebastianelli, & Murray, 2009) and for virtual humans watching performance (Park & Catrambone, 2007).

Borrowing from consumer psychology, researchers have shown that crowding can have socially facilitating effects on individuals. For example, a person may buy more of a product or a different one when swayed by the influence of a large, excited crowd. Also, in a process called "deindividuation," individuals can adopt the positive or negative characteristics of a crowd, which can result in behaviors that are highly productive and supportive or destructive and violent (Gaumer & LaFief, 2005).

Criticisms and Critiques of the Theory

Critics have complained that the distraction-conflict explanation for social facilitation may not be falsifiable (Feinberg & Aiello, 2006; Geen, 1981). When performance effects are not found when a performer is distracted, it is impossible to determine if the reason for the performance level was due to (1) the theory's being wrong, (2) an excess of distracting conflict for the individual, or (3) an insufficient amount of distracting conflict for the individual (Sanders & Baron, 1975). As a result of this falsifiability problem, critics have argued that the distraction-conflict explanation may not have very much predictive ability for performance levels (Feinberg & Aiello, 2006). Geen (1981) argued that if the theory is to advance, researchers need to more precisely define the conditions under which all four of the following occur: distraction, attentional conflict, mere presence, and learned drive.

A vital aspect of the theory is the definition and description of the full range of types of tasks. Critics have argued that the theory cannot be adequately tested until various types of tasks are more unequivocally classified than they have been so far (Beilock et al., 2004; Strauss, 2002). Zajonc (1965) focused on the importance of acquisition of skills in task performance. However, nearly every researcher since then has abandoned this important part of the theory and replaced it with more easily operationalized types of tasks. Most studies since then simply classify tasks as "simple" or "complex" (Wankel, 1972).

Another criticism of social facilitation research has been that it turns the type of task into a feature of the individual performing the task (Strauss, 2002). Researchers often ascertain higher and lower performance levels a posteriori. For instance, individuals perform a task, and those individuals who perform well are categorized as "well-learned" on the task, but those who perform poorly are labeled as "still to be learned" for the task. Then researchers conduct a median split and classify higher performers as experts and lower performers as nonexperts. Strauss (2002) argued that this approach is problematic because a task could be labeled as simple for some individuals and as complex for others.

The theory has been criticized for predicting a range of performance levels, instead of specific, desired, performance levels, under the effects of various social influences and conditions (Aiello & Douthitt, 2001; Kelley & Thibaut, 1954). Bond and Titus (1983) found that evaluation apprehension had little influence on performance, and the influences of the mere presence of other people on task performance have been found to be weak at best (Strauss, 2002).

Measuring Variables in the Theory

Thought control questionnaire. Wells, A., & Davies, M. I. (1994). The thought control questionnaire: A measure of individual differences in the control of unwanted thoughts. *Behaviour Research and Therapy, 32,* 871–878.

Spielberger State Anxiety Symptom Scale. Bech, P., Gormsen, L., Loldrup, D., & Lunde, M. (2009). The clinical effect of clomipramine in chronic idiopathic pain disorder revisited using the Spielberger State Anxiety Symptom Scale (SSASS) as outcome scale. *Journal of Affective Disorders, 119,* 43–51.

Suggestions for Further Research

1. Examine the influence of a range of levels and types of distraction on task performance levels.
2. Explore the influence of levels and types of evaluation on resulting task performance.

3. Look at a distraction orientation or evaluation orientation for some individuals and its influence on task performance.
4. Compare the changes in both attitudes and behaviors through social facilitation processes.
5. Examine various types of human and nonhuman monitoring, such as providing real-time feedback, and their effects on performance levels.
6. Look at the influences of electronic monitoring with a range of human-like characteristics on facilitation effects and performance.
7. Explore the anthropomorphization of targets or objects and the facilitating influences of those targets on task performance.
8. Look at the influence of the number of others (one, small group, mob, population) on performance levels.
9. Examine the influences of affiliation (stranger, friend, enemy) and the age of performers on task performance levels.
10. Explore the influence of age and gender-related group performance strategies on social facilitation effects and performance levels.
11. Examine the individual ability to multitask and its relationship with distraction and social facilitation effects.

References to Know

Aiello, J. R., & Douthitt, E. A. (2001). Social facilitation from Triplett to electronic performance monitoring. *Group Dynamics, 5,* 163–180.

Geen, R. G. (1991). Social motivation. *Annual Review of Psychology, 42,* 377–399.

Guerin, B. (1993). *Social facilitation.* Cambridge: Cambridge University Press.

Triplett, N. (1898, July). The dynamogenic factors in pacemaking and competition. *American Journal of Psychology, 9,* 507–533.

Zajonc, R. B. (1965, July). Social facilitation. *Science, 149,* 269–274.

Implications of the Theory for Managers

The performance of your employees does not depend solely on their own individual effort. Instead, social facilitation theory examines how the influences of other people affect a person's performance level. For example, the physical presence of spectators or co-actors can cause a person's behavior level to either increase or decrease. The influence of others on performance can occur whether those others are: familiar or unfamiliar, physically present or absent, easily seen or heard or not, visible or invisible, and human or virtually human.

The performance of your employees does not depend solely on their own individual efforts. Your job as a manager is to help them reach their highest possible performance levels for desired organizational outcomes. Use the influence of other people to help your employees perform at optimal levels. For example, make use of the "mere presence" of other people to influence performance. Some employees tend to perform better in the presence of others, and some do not. Some employees will enjoy working with others or having an audience, but some will prefer to work alone. Talk with your employees and determine how the influence of others can help their performance and, when possible, use that influence to design jobs and job spaces where employees can reach their highest levels of performance.

Remember that performance can suffer when people are afraid of being evaluated or compared with others. Talk about this potential problem with your employees, and if they have evaluation apprehension, then try to find ways to lessen their concerns about being evaluated.

Also remember that the level of distraction in the workplace can influence employee behavior. Some employees love to multi-task in a chaotic environment and will perform well, but others dislike a highly distracting environment, and their performance might suffer. Talk with your employees about their optimal level of distraction in the workplace and, when possible, tailor distractions to suit the needs of your employees.

34

35

Social Identity Theory

Tajfel (1972) introduced the concept of "social identity," which refers to a person's knowledge that he or she belongs to certain social groups and which involves emotional and value significance because of that group membership. A social group is defined as more than two people who (1) identify and evaluate themselves in the same way, (2) have the same definition of who they are and what attributes they have, and (3) follow the same patterns for how they interact with others who are not in their group (Hogg, 2006). Group membership refers to a collective sense of "us" versus "them," and self-identification refers to an individual sense of "me" versus "you."

Social identity refers to those aspects of an individual's self-image that derive from the social categories to which they perceive themselves as belonging (Tajfel & Turner, 1986). The theory is based on some general assumptions: (1) people strive to maintain and improve their self-esteem and a positive self-concept; (2) social group, or category, membership can enhance or lower someone's self-esteem and self-concept; and (3) people evaluate the positive or negative attributes of groups to which they belong compared to those of other groups to which they do not belong, such as for status and prestige.

These general assumptions lead to general theoretical principles of the theory: (1) people work to achieve and maintain a positive social identity; (2) positive social identity is based on favorable comparisons made among groups to which a person belongs (in-groups) and groups to which a person does not belong (out-groups); and (3) if social identity is unsatisfactory, then people strive to leave their current groups and join more favorable groups, or they try to make their current groups more satisfactory (Tajfel & Turner, 1979).

The basic premise of social identity theory is that people carry with them a repertoire of the categories to which they belong, such as gender, nationality, political affiliation, and sports teams. Each of these category memberships is continually present in a person's mind as a social identity that both describes and prescribes his or her attributes as a member of those groups. The various social categories or groups tell a member how to think, how to feel, and how to behave (Hogg, Terry, & White, 1995). When a specific social identity becomes salient, such as when a church member is in a church, then self-perceptions, thoughts, feelings, and behaviors occur according to the typical norms, patterns, and stereotypes for in-group members of that group or social category. For example, a church member might not talk loudly or run and might use better language when inside a church, but might do just the opposite when attending a football game.

Social identity theory has split into two distinct branches (Huddy, 2001). One is referred to as social identity theory (for example, Tajfel, 1981; Tajfel & Turner, 1979), the other as social categorization theory (Turner, Hogg, Oakes, Reicher, & Wetherell, 1987). Both branches acknowledge that social identity has its origins in cognitive and motivational factors, but each places a different emphasis on them (Hogg, 1996). Social identity theory primarily examines the psychological motivations involving how people support or refute group membership. Social categorization theory primarily examines how individuals come to identify themselves and act as a group.

Social identity research findings suggest three important consequences for organizations (Ashforth & Mael, 1989). First, employees tend to select and perform activities that are congruent with their social identities, and they tend to support organizations that support their social identities. For example, Mael and Ashforth (1992) found that positive identification with one's alma mater resulted in alumni's making donations, recruiting their children and others, attending alumni functions, and having high levels of satisfaction.

Second, social identification tends to influence important group outcomes, such as cohesion, cooperation, altruism, and positive evaluations of the group (Turner, 1982, 1984), and to be positively related to employee loyalty to and pride in the organization (Ashforth & Mael, 1989). Third, as employees come to increasingly identify with the organization, then the values, ideals, and practices of that organization can be perceived as more unique, distinctive, and positive compared to other organizations. These increasingly positive perceptions can lead to higher levels of employee loyalty and commitment to an organization and its culture.

Hogg (2006) noted that there are some misunderstandings about social identity theory. First, there is the mistaken belief that the social identity approach is only about intergroup relations and does not involve interactive groups. Second, Hogg refutes the notion that social identity theory has focused only on abstract categorization of group membership, such as in-group and out-group membership, and does not place any conceptual value on the meaning and value of social interaction and interdependence. Third, there has been a misunderstanding about identification's being a generative process as opposed to its being a cognitive structure. A person identifies more strongly with some groups than with others, which places them more centrally and more accessibly in his or her mind. However, the context that a person is in will make some group identifications more important than others.

Researchers have moved on to examine the salience of simultaneous, multiple identities in the same context. In real-life situations, people identify with a multitude of groups at the same time, such as family, work, and country. Little is known about how people successfully identify with multiple groups, such as subgroups and superordinate groups, within the same context or situation. Social identity theory research has begun to examine these important areas (Lam, Ahearne, Hu, & Schillewaert, 2010).

Criticisms and Critiques of the Theory

Critiques of social identity theory contend that the original studies on which the theory is based used highly contrived and unrealistic minimalistic groups in laboratory settings (Schiffmann & Wicklund, 1992). For example, subjects were placed in one of two anonymous groups with no interaction where they did not know any other group members, and were simply labeled as either "Blues" or "Greens" or as preferring the artwork of Kandinsky versus Klee. Subjects were told to allocate money to two other members of the two groups. The results showed that subjects tended to give more money to those labeled as being in their in-group compared to those labeled as being in the out-group.

These studies concluded that creating discriminatory behavior and modifying in-group and out-group perceptions of subjects even in short-term competitive intergroup situations can be done easily and with little effort. Critics contend that these studies removed the psychological variables that play an important part in real, interacting groups; that the study results merely reflected the conditions in which subjects were artificially placed and nothing else; and that subjects will always be content to adopt any social identity assigned to them (Schiffmann & Wicklund, 1992).

Similar studies (for example, Horwitz & Rabbie, 1982) found no differences in in-group and out-group behavior. In addition, when subjects' perceptions about who controlled their outcomes were changed, subjects were found to favor those in their out-group (Rabbie, Schot, & Visser, 1987), which goes against the tenets of social identity theory. In a laboratory study, subjects' long-term identities were not changed because they had been labeled as Green or Blue.

Another problem with the theory is that the terms "groups" and "social categories" are confused and are used interchangeably (Rabbie & Horwitz, 1988). Lewin (1948) advocated the theoretical necessity of distinguishing between the two concepts. A major problem with using social identity to explain intergroup behavior is that people can have a positive or negative view of one group or another without having to be a member of those groups (Rabbie & Horwitz, 1988).

Measuring Variables in the Theory

Organizational identity scale, perceived organizational prestige scale, and perceived organizational competition scale. Mael, F., & Ashforth, B. E. (1992). Alumni and their alma mater: A partial test of the reformulated model of organizational identification. *Journal of Organizational Behavior, 13,* 103–123.

Group identification measure. Doosje, B., Ellemers, N., & Spears, R. (1995). Perceived intragroup variability as a function of group status and identification. *Journal of Experimental Social Psychology, 31,* 410–436.

Various identity scales. Grice, T. A., Gallois, C., Jones, E., Paulsen, N. M., & Callan, V. J. (2006, November). "We do it, but they don't": Multiple categorizations and work team communication. *Journal of Applied Communication Research, 34*(4), 331–348.

Communication relationships measure, organizational identification measure, and intent to leave scale. Scott, C. R., Connaughton, S. L., Diaz-Saenz, H. R., Maguire, K., Ramirez, R., Richardson, B., Shaw, S. P., and Morgan, D. (1999, February). The impacts of communication and multiple identifications on intent to leave: A multimethodological exploration. *Management Communication Quarterly, 12,* 400–435.

35

Identity Distress Survey (IDS). Berman, S. L., Montgomery, M. J., & Kurtines, W. M. (2004). The development and validation of a measure of identity distress. *Identity: An International Journal of Theory and Research, 4*(1), 1–8.

Team identity scale. Heere, B., & James, J. D. (2007). Stepping outside the lines: Developing a multi-dimensional team identity scale based on social identity theory. *Sport Management Review, 10,* 65–91.

Suggestions for Further Research

1. Examine negative versus positive social identity perceptions and their influence on employee attitudes and behaviors.
2. Explore how people effectively structure their simultaneous, multiple identities and how that influences attitudes and behaviors.
3. Look at differences in performance between short-term artificial groups and long-term, real-life, interactive groups.
4. Study the meaning and value of membership in groups and how that influences in-group and out-group attitudes and behaviors.

5. Examine how people maintain and regulate multiple, simultaneous social identities and how that influences behavior.
6. Explore how static versus dynamic context and setting influence individual social identities.
7. Investigate how people make sense of their competing versus their cooperating social identities.
8. Examine how social identities change and adapt over time, age, experience, and life stage of the individual.
9. Explore undesirable behavior that can occur as a result of negative social identity perceptions in organizations.
10. Investigate how identity distress can influence attitudes and performance in the workplace and in other settings.

35

References to Know

Tajfel, H. (1978). The achievement of group differentiation. In H. Tajfel (Ed.), *Differentiation between social groups: Studies in the social psychology of intergroup relations* (pp. 77–98). London: Academic Press.

Tajfel, H. (1981). *Human groups and social categories: Studies in social psychology.* Cambridge: Cambridge University Press.

Tajfel, H., & Turner, J. C. (1986). The social identity of intergroup behavior. In S. Worchel & W. G. Austin (Eds.), *The psychology of intergroup relations* (2nd ed., pp. 7–24). Chicago: Nelson-Hall.

Turner, J. C. (1982). Towards a cognitive redefinition of the social group. In H. Tajfel (Ed.), *Social identity and intergroup relations* (pp. 15–40). Cambridge: Cambridge University Press.

Turner, J. C. (1984). Social identification and psychological group formation. In H. Tajfel (Ed.), *The social dimension: European developments in social psychology* (Vol. 2, pp. 518–538). Cambridge: Cambridge University Press.

Implications of the Theory for Managers

According to social identity theory, employees are continually looking for ways to improve their self-esteem and self-concept through the groups and organizations to which they belong. If employees do not see that their organization is helping improve their self-perceptions, then at best they will try to help change their organization, and at worst they will leave. When employees have a positive social identification with their groups and organization, this may help them internalize and support organizational norms, values, and goals, which can help enhance their overall attitudes and behaviors.

Your job as a manager is to help your employees see how their job, their work groups, and their organization help them improve important aspects of themselves, such as their reputation, their status, their prestige, and so on. One way to foster positive employee social identity is to create in-groups and out-groups, such as "our team" versus "their team" or "our company" versus "their company." Merely creating labels of "us" and "them" can improve positive feelings among group members. Creating strong in-group identification can help regulate positive employee attitudes and behaviors across all group members.

35

When employees identify with their organization, for example when they fully believe in the vision, mission, strategies, and goals of the company, then those employees tend to have higher levels of pride, commitment, loyalty, and performance and more positive attitudes compared to employees who don't identify with their organization. To help employees improve their identification with their organization, work with them to uncover their personal goals, values, and ideals, and show them how their organization can help them achieve these.

36

Social Network Theory

The basic notion of social network theory is that people tend to think and behave similarly because they are connected. The theory examines the set of ties or linkages among a defined set of actors (individuals, groups, or organizations), with the view that the system of linkages as a whole can be used to interpret the social behavior of the actors involved (Mitchell, 1969; Tichy, Tushman, & Fombrun, 1979). The network linkages can both connect and divide the actors. The theory enables analysis of a range of organizational phenomena at both the micro level (leadership, teams, power, trust, turnover, and so on) and the macro level (interfirm relations, alliances, network governance, and so on).

Many of the concepts in social network theory were derived from graph theory. A graph consists of a set of points and a set of lines or edges connecting the points (Freeman, 1978/1979). In social network theory, the points are the social actors, or nodes, and the lines are the ties or linkages among the social actors. A key concept is "centrality" (Bavelas, 1948, 1950; Leavitt, 1951), which means that being at the most center point in a social network is the most advantageous. People gain social capital through their position in social structures or social networks (Coleman, 1990; Portes, 1998; Lin, 2002).

Granovetter (1973) examined the strength of ties among individuals in social networks. Prior research had only studied the importance of strong ties among members within social networks, but Granovetter examined the strength of weak ties. He proposed that weak ties might actually be more important and more influential on member attitudes and behaviors than strong ties.

The strength of a tie is dependent on the amount of time spent, emotional intensity, mutual confiding, and reciprocal exchanges among individuals in a social network. Weak ties may help individuals make connections among social networks, bridging them together. Individuals may be able to support a dozen or so strong ties, but may be able to support an extremely large number of weak ties. Friedkin (1980) found that all local bridges among networks were weak ties, and that ties across groups tended to be weak ties.

Social network analysis focuses on the interactions among network members and the structure of those interactions (Wasserman & Faust, 1994). Social network studies have taken two different approaches when collecting data about networks (Marsden, 1990). Some studies gather complete and total network data for all ties that link elements of an entire population. Other studies gather what are called "egocentric" network data, which are data only for the set of ties for specifically sampled individuals.

Kilduff and Brass (2010) discussed the four leading inter-related ideas that dominate social network theory research: (1) relations between actors, (2) embeddedness, (3) structural patterning, and (4) the social utility of network connections. From the beginning, social network analysis has focused on the relations that connect or separate a set of actors (Tichy, Tushman, & Fombrun, 1979). Moreno (1934) argued that a person's location in a social network determined his or her behavior. Other researchers conducted experimental studies of actors in their social context (Heider, 1946; Lewin, 1936). Durkheim (1951) argued that social irregularities were not caused by the intentions of individuals but because human societies were like biological systems made up of interrelated components. Comte (1854) hoped to found a field of "social physics" or what he later called "sociology."

The second core assumption of social network theory is embeddedness, or the tendency to stay involved in a network and create, renew, and extend relationships over time (Baker & Faulkner, 2002; Granovetter, 1985). "Arm's length" ties are less powerful than "embedded" ties for trust, rich transfers of information, and problem-solving capabilities (Uzzi, 1996).

The third core idea in social network theory is that there are long-lasting patterns of clustering, connectivity, and centralization (Wellman, 1988; White, Boorman, & Breiger, 1976). Social network analysis simultaneously examines the whole and the parts of social networks (Moliterno & Mahony, 2011; Wellman, 1988).

The fourth core idea in the theory is the social utility of network connections, or that the social networks that actors create provide opportunities and constraints for outcomes that are important to those actors. Burt (1992, 2000) examined the idea of structural holes. A structural hole exists between two people in an individual's network if the two share a tie but are not connected with each other (Obstfeld, 2005). This approach suggests that unique ties to other individuals and firms can provide superior access to information and resources, which can result in greater opportunities to exert control.

Social network theory stresses the power of indirect ties and pathways. The theory posits that networks are more than just two people who interact. Instead, the planet is a diverse collection of indirect ties and pathways that connect all of us. Travers and Milgram (1969) asked volunteers in Nebraska to send mail to an unknown person in Boston by sending mail to people who had a better chance than they did of knowing that person. Results showed that it took about six intermediaries to reach the target person, which gave rise to the phrase "six degrees of separation." Small-world networks are highly locally clustered, have short path lengths among members, and can lead to extremely high levels of performance, such as collaboration and creativity (Feld, 1981; Watts, 1999). Performance levels increase in small-world networks up to a point, then the positive effects tend to reverse (Uzzi & Spiro, 2005).

As noted earlier, within a social network, a person's centrality, or position, is important. Centrality describes an actor's position relative to the entire social network (Freeman, 1978/1979). Closeness refers to the distance (such as the average distance) between an actor and all other actors in the network. Possible measures of centrality include degree, closeness, and betweenness (Stephenson & Zelen, 1989).

Network analysis can be traced back to Moreno (1934), who argued that a person's location in a social network determined his or her behavior. Moreno's concept of "sociometry" typically examined a single type of tie, namely cliques of tightly clustered

36

individuals, and chains of connectivity expressed in diagrams called "sociograms."

Older ideas of social network theory have become new again with the use of information technology. For example, Simmel (1908/1950) wrote about a stranger as being a member of a group in a spatial sense, but not a member of a group in a social sense. A stranger may be in a group but not of it, and may be both near and far and familiar and foreign. These ideas from over a century ago have become very relevant today due to rapid advances in communication and network technologies.

Newer roles in social networks are being examined, such as "brokers" (White, 1993; Burt, 2005). Brokers control access to resources, bridge gaps to nonredundant contacts, and exploit links for their own benefit. A *tertius iungens* (a third who joins) brings unconnected people together, whereas a *tertius gaudens* (a third who enjoys) is a broker who exploits others in the network for his or her own personal gain (Obstfeld, 2005).

Criticisms and Critiques of the Theory

One of the main criticisms of the theory is that social network researchers themselves dispute the manner in which important concepts are defined and operationalized, such as social structure, network centrality, distance, cohesion, and the term social network itself (Embirbayer & Goodwin, 1994).

A second criticism has to do with identifying which nodes to study. Researchers have to decide which nodes to include and exclude, a choice that can result in important social actors being left out (Laumann, Marsden, & Prensky, 1983). There is also considerable debate over what constitutes a tie among social actors, and to what extent nodes are connected or not (Borgatti & Halgin, in press).

Another criticism has been made over the use of categorical or individual differences in the social actors (Wellman, 1983). Some network analysts follow the "anticategorical imperative" that rejects all use of actor attributes (such as class, age, gender, social status, religion, ethnicity, and sexual orientation) to explain behaviors (Durkheim, 1951; Erickson, 1988) in favor of a network structural explanation. In contrast, researchers from a psychological perspective have focused on individual difference reasons (such as self-monitoring) to explain why some people maintain more favorable network positions over others (Kilduff & Krackhardt, 2008). Critics of this approach argue that it will require researchers to examine hundreds of individual difference variables and their influence on actor position and behavior in social networks (Kilduff & Brass, 2010).

There is also debate over why people join networks. People may form network ties that are only incidentally useful to them. However, people may also join networks for more strategic and instrumental reasons (Kilduff & Brass, 2010).

Measuring Variables in the Theory

Social pressure to use computers, and other scales. Frank, K. A., Zhao, Y., & Borman, K. (2004). Social capital and the diffusion of innovations within organizations: The case of computer technology in schools. *Sociology of Education, 77,* 148–171.

Strong ties, weak ties, and other measures. Tindall, D. B. (2002, November). Social networks, identification and participation in an environmental movement: Low-medium cost activism within the British Columbia wilderness preservation movement. *Canadian Review of Sociology and Anthropology, 39,* 413–452.

Convoy structure measure. Levitt, M. J., Guacci-Franco, N., & Levitt, J. L. (1993). Convoys of social support in childhood and early adolescence: Structure and function. *Developmental Psychology, 29,* 811–818.

Maximum relatedness subnetwork approach. Lee, S. H., Kim, P.-J., Ahn, Y.-Y., & Jeong, H. (2010). Googling social interactions: Web search engine based social network construction. *PLoS ONE, 5*(7), 1–11.

Suggestions for Further Research

1. Compare direct versus indirect managerial influences on employees' social networks and behaviors.
2. Examine the similarities and differences among strong and weak, positive and negative, and symmetrical and asymmetrical

ties among individuals in social networks, and their impact on outcomes.

3. Explore the range in the strength of ties among people and the causes for that range of strength, such as individual differences.

4. Look at the range in the number of strong and weak ties and methods used by people to manage and maintain those ties, and the impact of the number of ties on attitudes and behaviors.

5. Compare cross-national, cross-cultural versus same-country, same-culture aspects of social networks.

6. Examine the range of strangers, newcomers, acquaintances, friends, and intimates as being simultaneously near and far, familiar and foreign.

7. Explore network duration, such as how social networks form, grow, change, adapt, and finally die out over time.

8. Look at competition and cooperation among networks and how networks support and/or harm each other.

9. Study the way that people rationalize and maintain their relationships within competing and opposing networks.

10. Explore universal characteristics of random versus nonrandom social networks.

References to Know

Barnes, J. A. (1954). Class and committees in a Norwegian island parish. *Human Relations, 7,* 39–58.

Brass, D. J. (in press). A social network perspective on industrial/ organizational psychology. In S. Kozlowski (Ed.), *The Oxford handbook of industrial and organizational psychology.* New York: Oxford University Press.

Burt, R. (2005). *Brokerage and social closure.* Oxford: Oxford University Press.

Granovetter, M. (1973). The strength of weak ties. *American Journal of Sociology, 78,* 1360–1380.

Kilduff, M., & Brass, D. J. (2010, June). Organizational social network research: Core ideas and key debates. *Academy of Management Annals, 4,* 317–357.

36

Implications of the Theory for Managers

Social networks are vital for sustaining and improving employee attitudes, behaviors, and even health and well-being. A primary focus of social network theory is that social actors (individuals, groups, and organizations) are connected to others through strong or weak ties. These ties help shape the attitudes and behaviors of those in the network and can influence a number of outcomes that are important to the actors. As a manager, seek to connect with the powerful social networks in your organization so that you can benefit from these important connections, which can help enhance your own performance.

Help foster the creation and maintenance of social networks that work to improve and sustain important organizational outcomes. Weak ties can be important for bringing unrelated social networks together. Work to help build ties and bridges among important, but unrelated, social networks in your organization. Doing so may help more employees share in information and resource exchanges that can enable them to work more effectively than they would without such exchanges.

You can influence social networks either directly or indirectly. You can directly interact with employees, both face-to-face and through communication media. However, direct interaction can take a significant amount of time and energy. You can also use advocates, willing and able third parties who work on your behalf, to improve and sustain important social networks.

36

37

Stakeholder Theory

The traditional view of organizations is that they primarily care about improving the wealth of their shareholders, those who own shares in the company. In this view, the actions and decisions of the firm are primarily economic and are at the expense of other types of interests, such as society's best interests. Stakeholder theory goes against this traditional view of the corporation (Freeman, 2002).

The main idea in stakeholder theory is that organizations should focus on meeting a broader set of interests than just amassing shareholder wealth. Instead of focusing only on the firm's financial performance, organizations should also focus on their social performance. They should try to understand, respect, and meet the needs of all of those who have a stake in the actions and outcomes of the organization. According to stakeholder theory, involving stakeholders in corporate decisions is considered an ethical requirement and a strategic resource, both of which help provide organizational competitive advantages (Cennamo, Berrone, & Gomez-Mejia, 2009; Plaza-Ubeda, de Burgos-Jimenez, & Carmona-Moreno, 2010).

Stakeholders are individuals or groups who can affect, or are affected by, the actions and results of an organization (Freeman, 1984). This definition can be interpreted so broadly that anyone or any group can be seen as a company stakeholder. Therefore, stakeholder theory usually narrows the definition of a stakeholder to major, legitimate individuals or groups. For the most part, stakeholder theory has excluded the interests of stakeholders whose interests are far from the firm's operations or corporate objectives (Hillman & Keim, 2001; Walsh, 2005). If an organization were to focus on meeting the interests of those who have extremely different interests, then the organization might not survive economically (Mitchell, Agle, & Wood, 1997).

Sirgy (2002) developed a list of three categories of stakeholders: internal, external, and distal. Internal stakeholders include employees, executive staff, firm departments, and the board of directors. External stakeholders include shareholders, suppliers, creditors, the local community, and the environment. Distal stakeholders include rival firms, consumer and advocacy groups, government agencies, voters, and labor unions.

A central idea of stakeholder theory is that some corporate decision-making power and benefits should be taken away from the shareholders and given to the stakeholders (Stieb, 2008). Freeman (1984) was careful to note that any theory that refocuses decision-making power in such a way was open to abuse by nonshareholders, because power is being redirected from the wealthy shareholders to the usually less wealthy stakeholders. This type of redistribution of wealth could potentially harm the shareholders who have earned their corporate earnings.

Stakeholder theory can be categorized from three points of view: descriptive, instrumental, and normative (Donaldson & Preston, 1995). The descriptive perspective simply states that organizations have stakeholders. The role of organizations is to satisfy a wide range of stakeholders and not just the shareholders. Research has shown that a significant number of firms practice shareholder management, which involves balancing the needs of organizations with the needs of stakeholders (for example, Clarkson, 1991).

The instrumental perspective is that firms that consider their stakeholders' interests will be more successful than those that do not. Research in this area has examined the connection between stakeholder strategies and organizational performance. The assumption is that organizations that practice stakeholder management, assuming all other variables are held constant, will be relatively successful in terms of profitability, stability, growth, and so on.

The normative perspective examines why firms should give consideration to their stakeholders. This perspective has been the predominant view, or main core, in stakeholder theory (Donaldson

& Preston, 1995). The other two perspectives have been largely neglected by researchers (Egels-Zanden & Sandberg, 2010).

According to the normative perspective, stakeholders are individuals or groups who have legitimate interests in substantive aspects of the firm (Donaldson & Preston, 1995). Stakeholders are defined by their own interests in the organization, whether or not the organization has any corresponding interest in the stakeholders. The interests of the stakeholders are valuable to the organization for their own sake and not because addressing their interests could benefit any other group, such as the shareholders of the firm. Kaler (2003) developed a typology of stakeholder theories and concluded that there are only two permissible types: (1) theories in which firms have perfect responsibilities toward both shareholders and nonshareholders and (2) theories in which firms have perfect responsibilities toward shareholders, but imperfect ones toward nonshareholders.

Stakeholder theory has been continually fine-tuned and expanded, in such areas as differentiating between primary and secondary stakeholders (Clarkson, 1995), focusing on restricted (narrow) versus unrestricted (broad) stakeholder strategies (Greenwood, 2001), balancing diverse stakeholder orientations (Buono & Nichols, 1985), and assessing corporate performance from the perspective of different stakeholders (Donaldson & Preston, 1995).

Research also has focused on aspects of stakeholder integration, such as knowledge of stakeholders and their demands (Maignan & Ferrell, 2004), interaction among stakeholders and the firm (Payne & Calton, 2004), and making decisions that account for stakeholders' demands (Altman & Petkus, 1994). Knowledge of stakeholders refers to uncovering salient stakeholders and prioritizing their demands (Rowley, 1997). Firms must pay primary attention to stakeholders with power, legitimacy, urgent demands, or some combination of these. Interaction with stakeholders should involve mutually satisfying, reciprocal relationships among shareholders and the organization. Examples of stakeholder interactions with organizations include participation, consultation, cooperation, and information exchange (Grafe-Buckens & Hinton, 1998; Green & Hunton-Clarke, 2003).

A recent debate in stakeholder theory has been over the moral and ethical obligations of managers to stakeholders.

Greenwood (2007) argued that stakeholder theory is morally neutral, in that engaging stakeholders and committing to considering their needs do not automatically obligate a firm to act in stakeholders' best interests.

Stakeholder research has begun to examine the extent to which managers have the power, freedom, and capacity—what is called managerial discretion—to act according to the wishes and desires of stakeholders (Hambrick & Finkelstein, 1987; Phillips, Berman, Elms, & Johnson-Cramer, 2010). Stakeholders themselves can be the source of both constraints and catalysts for managerial behavior. Research has also addressed the relationships between what managers do (behaviors) and why they do it (rationale) (Egels-Zanden & Sandberg, 2010).

Criticisms and Critiques of the Theory

Stakeholder theory continues to gain in popularity among both managers and academics (Agle et al., 2008). However, critics of the theory have claimed that it has not been operationalized in such a way that it allows scientific inspection (Key, 1999). Critics also have argued that a glaring shortcoming of the theory is the problem of identifying stakeholders (Freeman, 2004). The theory is often unable to distinguish between who is and who is not a stakeholder.

Another area of continuing criticism concerns identification of salient stakeholders. Managers may be unable to attend to all stakeholder needs, so they often narrow the field of stakeholders on the basis of such attributes as power, legitimacy, and urgency. Clifton and Amran (2011) argue that using power to categorize stakeholders has significant problems. Favoring one party over another simply due to power differentials is a violation of justice and fairness principles (Harrison, Bosse, & Phillips, 2010).

Critics of the theory have condemned the notion that corporate profits must be sacrificed in order to meet various stakeholder needs. Shareholders invest in a firm because they want it to stay in business and make a profit. Some researchers have contended that both financial and social performance should be stressed, but others have focused purely on the importance of primarily meeting the needs of all relevant stakeholders, even if that is at the expense of profits.

37

Stakeholder theory posits that the interests of all persons or groups with legitimate interests in an organization should be considered. However, critics argue that there is no prima facie priority of one group's interests and benefits over those of another (for example, Donaldson & Preston, 1995).

Measuring Variables in the Theory

Influence ratings of stakeholders' scale and importance ratings of values concerns scale. Hosseini, J. C., & Brenner, S. N. (1992). The stakeholder theory of the firm: A methodology to generate value matrix weights. *Business Ethics Quarterly, 2,* 99–119.

Managerial perception of stakeholder satisfaction measure, environmental management measure, knowledge of stakeholders measure, stakeholder interactions measure, behaviors of adaptation measure. Plaza-Ubeda, J. A., de Burgos-Jimenez, J., & Carmona-Moreno, E. (2010). Measuring stakeholder integration: Knowledge, interaction and adaptational behavior dimensions. *Journal of Business Ethics, 93,* 419–442.

Observed unethical behavior measure. Kaptein, M. (2008). Developing a measure of unethical behavior in the workplace: A stakeholder perspective. *Journal of Management, 34,* 978–1008.

37

Principles of corporate citizenship measure. Davenport, K. (2002). Corporate citizenship: A stakeholder approach for defining corporate social performance and identifying measures for assessing it. *Business and Society, 39,* 210–219.

Stakeholder attributes measure. Agle, B. R., Mitchell, R. K., & Sonnenfeld, J. A. (1999). Who matters to CEOs? An investigation of stakeholder attributes and salience, corporate performance, and CEO values. *Academy of Management Review, 42,* 505–525.

Suggestions for Further Research

1. Examine the point at which shareholders leave when firms sacrifice too much financially for the sake of stakeholder interests.

2. Explore the process through which firms learn about salient stakeholder interests and how firms prioritize those interests.
3. Create a typology of how organizations create value for stakeholders.
4. Look at how stakeholders assess value created for them by organizations.
5. Examine how firms create a single-value objective function through which stakeholder interests are subordinated to the firm's interests.
6. Study how firms simultaneously manage competing stakeholder demands from multiple stakeholder sources.
7. Examine the full relationships among stakeholder attributes, stakeholder salience, and firm social and financial performance.
8. Explore the dynamics of managerial discretion, orientation, and stakeholder behavior.
9. Look at the variations in behaviors of high- versus low-discretion managers in terms of firm social and financial performance.
10. Examine the relationship between what managers do and why they do it, with regard to meeting the needs of stakeholders.
11. Look at the extent to which there are conflicts and similarities between stakeholder and shareholder interests.

37

References to Know

Donaldson, T., & Preston, L. (1995). The stakeholder theory of the corporation: Concepts, evidence, and implications. *Academy of Management Review, 20,* 65–91.

Freeman, R. E. (1984). *Strategic management: A stakeholder approach.* Boston: Pitman.

Freeman, R. E. (2004). The stakeholder approach revisited. *Zeitschrift für Wirtschafts und Unternehmensethik, 5,* 228–241.

Freeman, R. E. (2008). Managing for stakeholders. In T. Donaldson & P. Werhane (Eds.), *Ethical issues in business: A philosophical approach* (8th ed., pp. 39–53). Englewood Cliffs, NJ: Prentice Hall.

Parmar, B. L., Freeman, R. E., Harrison, J. S., Wicks, A. C., Purnell, L., & De Colle, S. (2010). Stakeholder theory: The state of the art. *Academy of Management Annals 4*, 403–445.

Implications of the Theory for Managers

Stakeholder theory explores the view that organizations should focus on a broader set of goals than simply improving shareholder wealth. The theory posits that organizations have to make money and stay in business, or else they won't be able to help meet anyone's needs. However, an organization should strive to meet the needs of both shareholders and stakeholders, so that both the financial performance and the social performance of the firm are enhanced.

A key implication of the theory for managers is the necessity of identifying your most important and relevant stakeholders. This is easier said than done. You will need to invest time and resources to identify those stakeholders who have the most powerful, legitimate, and urgent influences over your organization. Once you have identified your stakeholders, then you will need to establish a relationship and dialogue with them so that you can know and understand their needs and demands in relation to your organization.

You won't be able to address the needs and demands of all your stakeholders. You will have to create a way to prioritize some needs and demands over others. This may also be difficult to do. For example, some shareholders may not be happy about the firm sacrificing earnings for social causes. Finally, only you can decide how much power and authority you want to give to your stakeholders and how much you will allow stakeholders to constrain your management actions.

37

38

Structural Contingency Theory

The main premise in structural contingency theory is that there is no one best organizational structure; rather, the appropriate organizational structure depends on the contingencies facing the organization (Blau, 1970; Burns & Stalker, 1961; Chandler, 1962; Child, 1973; Galbraith, 1973; Rumelt, 1974; Thompson, 1967; Woodward, 1965). The theory posits that organizations will be effective if managers fit characteristics of the organization, such as its structure, with contingencies in their environment (Donaldson, 2001). Early work (Burns & Stalker, 1961; Woodward, 1965; Lawrence & Lorsch, 1967) supported the theory, and later theoretical developments helped explain those results (Thompson, 1967; Galbraith, 1977).

Contingency theory was a move away from the universalist theories (Tosi & Slocum, 1984), which advocated that there was only one way to organize, meaning that the highest level of organizational performance could only be obtained from the maximum level of an organizational structural variable, such as formalization or specialization (Taylor, 1947; Brech, 1957). Contingency theory posits that organizational success does not mean adopting the maximum level, but adopting the appropriate level of structural variables that depend on some level of the contingency variable (Donaldson, 2001).

One of the most important concepts in the theory is fit (Drazin & Van de Ven, 1985). Linguistic substitutes for fit have included alignment, co-alignment, match, conform, consistent with, and appropriate for (Umanath, 2003). An organization whose characteristics (for example, needs, demands, goals, objectives, and structures) fit with the contingencies in its situation will perform more effectively compared to an organization whose characteristics do not fit with the contingencies in its situation (Nadler & Tushman, 1980). Fit can be operationalized as conditional or unconditional association between variables (Umanath, 2003; Venkatraman, 1989).

Umanath (2003) provided three classifications of fit: congruence, contingency, and holistic configuration. Congruence means that a variable of interest, such as information technology, is related to organizational factors, without assessing whether this relationship affects performance. Contingency means that the effect of one variable x on another variable y depends on the level of a third variable z. Thus the effect of x on y when z is low is different than the effect of x on y when z is high. In other words, the influence of x on y depends on z or is contingent on the level of z. Variable z moderates the relationship of variables x and y (Donaldson, 2001). Holistic configuration refers to overall internal coherence of a set of organizational attributes, or to simultaneous interdependencies among variables that are subject to multiple contingencies (Cao, Wiengarten, & Humphreys, 2011).

There are two different concepts of fit (Umanath, 2003). Traditional approaches have focused on fit as a bivariate relationship in which context and structure covary independently (Fry & Smith, 1987). However, systems-based approaches have focused on more systemic, holistic approaches to simultaneous interaction among multiple variables and contingencies (Miller, 1981).

According to the theory, there are two main contingencies: organizational size and organizational task. Size has been operationalized most often as the approximate number of employees (Pugh, Hickson, Hinings, & Turner, 1969; Pugh & Hinings, 1976). A low level of bureaucracy fits a smaller organization, whereas a high level of bureaucracy fits a larger organization (Child, 1975). Other contingencies are specialization, formalization, differentiation, and decentralization (Donaldson, 2001).

The task contingency comprises two components: task uncertainty and task interdependence. For example, as task uncertainty increases through increased product or service innovation, there is typically a reduction in organizational formalization and an increase in decentralized decision making (Donaldson, 2001).

The following researchers examined how organizational structure relates to task uncertainty and the environment. Burns and Stalker (1961) distinguished between organic and mechanistic organizational structures. Mechanistic structures emphasize hierarchy, with the task divided into specialized roles and knowledge of the task by a few. Organic structures are fluid, dynamic networks in which many people share task knowledge and information. Hage (1965) argued that organizational efficiency is maximized when the structure has centralized decision making, has formal rules, and is not complex. However, innovation occurs with the opposite structure (decentralized, informal, and complex). Lawrence and Lorsch (1967) stressed organizational integration versus differentiation (departmental differences in goals, time frame, formality, and interpersonal orientation). The greater the differentiation, then the greater the need for devices (hierarchy, rules, individuals, departments) that bring the organization together.

Miles and Snow (1978) proffered that company strategies arise from the way that organizations address three types of problems: entrepreneurial (managing market share), engineering (implementing the solution to the entrepreneurial problem), and administrative (how a company structures itself to solve the first two problems). On the basis of this reasoning, they postulated four strategic types of organizations: prospector (locate and exploit new product and market opportunities), defender (maintain stable market share), analyzer (be a prospector and a defender), and reactor (make no plans, merely respond to sudden changes).

Regarding task interdependence, three main researchers examined the need for organizations to adopt organic structures following from the contingency of technology: Perrow (1967), Thompson (1967), and Woodward (1958, 1965). For example, according to Thompson, task interdependence refers to how organizational activities are connected to each other: pooled (only indirect connection), sequential (direct, one-way connection), and reciprocal (direct, two-way connection).

Morgan (1989) profiled ranges of organizational characteristics to determine their degree of congruence or noncongruence with six organizational subsystems: (1) environment (stable and certain to turbulent and unpredictable); (2) strategic (defensive, operational, and goal setting to proactive with learning systems);

38

(3) technological (routine, low-discretion roles to complex, high-discretion roles); (4) human/cultural (economic, instrumental orientation to work to self-actualizing orientation to work); (5) structural (mechanistic and bureaucratic to organic); and (6) managerial (authoritarian, Theory X, to democratic, Theory Y).

The theory has been applied recently to outsourcing, multinational corporations (MNCs), information technology systems (Cao et al., 2011), nonprofit firms (Tucker, 2010), enterprise resource planning (Morton & Hu, 2008), transnational professional service firms (Greenwood & Miller, 2010), and dynamic equilibria (Smith & Lewis, 2011). Thompson (1967) posited that highly interdependent organizational activities should be located physically, structurally, and temporally close together, so as not to tax the information-processing capacity of the social unit. Hui, Davis-Blake, and Broschak (2008) extended this idea to the interorganizational level and found that subtle differences in structuring of outsourcing projects can prevent the gain of expected outsourcing benefits and can lead to higher cost overruns and control problems. Donaldson (2009) and Qiu and Donaldson (2010) developed a cubic contingency model that explored a comprehensive international strategy-structure model for MNCs.

Criticisms and Critiques of the Theory

The theory has received a great deal of criticism (Mohr, 1971; Pennings, 1975; Schoonhoven, 1981). Critics argue that the theory is a tautology, or true by definition and therefore employing circular reasoning, because of the concept of fit. The theory holds that fit produces high performance, but at the most abstract level this relationship is true by definition, so cannot be tested. Donaldson (2001) defended the theory, arguing that even Darwin's survival of the fittest argument (1909–1914) is a tautology. Darwin's evolutionary theory advocates "survival of the fittest," but tautologically answers the question "Why are they the fittest?" with "Because they survive."

Another criticism of the theory is that it is deterministic (Perrow, 1980, 1984). The theory posits that an organization reacts to changes in its contingencies, which changes its environment, which changes its contingencies; thus the organization's structure is determined solely by its situation. Critics of the theory argue that managerial free choice opposes contingency theory (Schreyogg, 1980). Child (1972) offered a middle ground, strategic choice, giving managers some freedom to make decisions within a contingency framework. De Rond and Theitart (2007) added the concept of chance, referring to an event that happens for no known cause or that is irrelevant to any present organizational need.

Critics have argued extensively about two main problems with the theory: the concepts are unclear, and the relationships among the concepts have not been clearly defined (Miller, 1981; Schoonhoven, 1981; Drazin & Van de Ven, 1985; Tosi & Slocum, 1984). In order to solve these problems, Tosi and Slocum helped further define the concepts: effectiveness (the degree to which an environment obtains a limited number of highly desirable outcomes), environment (for example, homogeneous or heterogeneous and stable or shifting) (Jurkovich, 1974; Thompson, 1967), and congruency (a proper match between environment and structure) (Randolph & Dess, 1984).

Measuring Variables in the Theory

Operational performance measure. Tenhiala, A. (2011). Contingency theory of capacity planning: The link between process types and planning methods. *Journal of Operations Management, 29,* 65–77.

Centralization, formalization, and fairness scales. Schminke, M., Cropanzano, R., & Rupp, D. E. (2002). Organization structure and fairness perceptions: The moderating effects of organization level. *Organizational Behavior and Human Decision Processes, 89,* 881–905.

Environmental, structural, and effectiveness measures. Pennings, J. M. (1987). Structural contingency theory: A multivariate test. *Organization Studies, 8,* 223–240.

Routine to nonroutine technology scale. Mohr, L. B. (1971, December). Organizational technology and organizational structure. *Administrative Science Quarterly, 16,* 444–459.

Suggestions for Further Research

1. Examine how the task environment of contracting parties influences the effectiveness of different contract types.
2. Explore why researchers advocate increasingly more complex structures, yet practitioners still tend to rely on much simpler methods and structures.
3. Look at how the unsuccessful structuring of outsourcing ventures has led to organizations' bringing those activities back in-house.
4. Study how developments in technology have led to greater numbers of globalized and offshore organizational structures.
5. Examine the complementarity of informal and formal structures on the effectiveness of organizational success measures.
6. Explore the impact of differences in front-office versus back-office structures on MNC performance and effectiveness measures.
7. Compare successes and failures in transplanting organizational structures from the private to the nonprofit sector.
8. Across a range of organizations, examine how environment, managerial choice, and chance influence organizational structure.
9. Explore variations in fit and misfit, systems fit and misfit, holistic fit and misfit, and information technology in terms of firm success.
10. Examine the effects of variation in the rate of firm reorganization and contingencies on organizational performance variables.

38

References to Know

Burns, T., & Stalker, G. (1961). *The management of innovation.* London: Tavistock.

Chandler, A. D., Jr. (1962). *Strategy and structure: Chapters in the history of the industrial enterprise.* Cambridge, MA: MIT Press.

Donaldson, L. (2001). *The contingency theory of organizations.* Thousand Oaks, CA: Sage.

Lawrence, P., & Lorsch, J. (1967). Differentiation and integration in complex organizations. *Administrative Science Quarterly, 12,* 1–30.

Miles, R. E., & Snow, C. C. (1978). *Organizational strategy, structure, and process.* Tokyo: McGraw-Hill Kogakusha.

Implications of the Theory for Managers

Structural contingency theory argues that organizations can't be their most effective if they don't have the right structure. However, finding the perfect structure for an organization is a difficult, ongoing, and time-consuming process. Organizational structures are difficult to create because they tend to form through (1) managerial hard work and strategic decision making, (2) environmental variables, and (3) chance. There is no one correct structure for every organization. Instead, the most effective structure depends on, or is contingent on, both internal and external variables facing that specific organization.

A contingency means that the influence of one variable on another variable depends on the level of a third variable. For example, the influence of an organizational structure on organizational performance depends on such variables as the level of technology used in the organization. According to the theory, organizational performance is a consequence of the fit among several factors: structure, people, technology, strategy, and culture. Organizations that have better fit will have higher levels of performance; those that have worse fit will have lower levels of performance. Uncover what variables affect your organization, and work hard to create the perfectly fitting structure that will result in optimal levels of performance for your organization.

Talk with your employees about the effectiveness of your current organizational structure. If there are problem areas, then work together to create an organizational structure that will better enable everyone to accomplish the organization's vision, mission, and goals. Be proactive in creating your organization's structure, rather than allow your environment to create your organizational structure for you.

38

39

Structuration Theory

The central theme of structuration theory is that individuals are members of social structures, and those structures support continued performance of routines over time (Giddens, 1976, 1979, 1984). The theory focuses on the fundamental circularity (recursiveness) of social life. It assumes that the structural properties of social systems are composed of the practices of individuals and of the outcomes of those practices (Giddens, 1979).

Further, the theory examines (1) the extent to which the voluntary behaviors of people create and shape social structures (agency) and (2) the extent to which social structures shape, constrain, and enable the behaviors of individuals, or what Giddens (1984) called the "duality of structure and action." Thus social structures are both the medium and the outcome of people's behaviors. Social structures are also the result of unanticipated human actions.

The theory has been described as a very ambitious effort to integrate two opposing schools of thought in social theory (Callinicos, 1985). It tries to preserve the view that social relations are the result of intentional human activity (advocated by Weber, Schutz, and ethnomethodology). It also tries to preserve the view that social structures shape human behavior (advocated by Marxists, Parsonian sociologists, and structuralists).

Giddens (1984) defined social structures as the rules and resources that influence each other in the reproduction of social systems, that exist or are "instantiated" through recurrent social practices (p. 25). For example, language rules help someone speak a sentence, and at the same time, speaking the sentence can influence language rules.

An analogy can be made with the game of football (Schneidewind & Petersen, 1998). A game of football cannot happen without the players and cannot happen without the rules of the game and the necessary resources, such as footballs and goalposts. Both the structure of the game and the players in the game must interplay for the activity to take place. Also, the rules and the resources of the game have been developed over time to make the game safer and more enjoyable. The same is true in society, where the rules and resources of social structures have been changed over time.

The theory identifies three types of actions (interactions) that interplay with three types of social structures. People perform (produce and reproduce) three specific types of interactions: (1) understandable communication, (2) exercise of power, and (3) sanctioning of one another. There are three types of social structures: (1) signification, (2) domination, and (3) legitimation. Signification involves the effective use of language. Domination involves control of materials and resources. Legitimation involves moral rules that determine the appropriateness of behaviors. The three interactions correspond separately with the three social structures: (1) signification interplays with communication, (2) domination interplays with power, and (3) legitimation interplays with sanction.

According to the theory, people access structures in order to help them determine what to do and what to say to each other. However, people do not access structures directly. Instead, they use modalities, and there is a separate modality for each interaction-structure pairing: (1) interpretive scheme connects signification and communication, (2) facility connects domination with power, and (3) norms connect legitimation and sanction. The modality of interpretive scheme includes language and non-verbal codes. The modality of facility includes capacities and capabilities. The modality of norms includes values and moral rules. People use all three of these modalities to help them decide what to do and what to say.

People access social structures to help guide their behavior. However, all people do not access social structures in the same way. Every person accesses his social structures differently through

39

the unique position that he holds within those structures. Some people have better or worse positions within their social structures compared to other people. For example, some people have more or less knowledge or resources compared to others in their network. A person's position in her social structure can both enable and constrain her behaviors.

Social structures advocate that individuals perform specific behaviors, or routines. Routines are typical, habitual behaviors that are taken for granted over time. The performance of routines helps reinforce the social structures. If groups of routines or practices become deeply embedded in social structures, then they can become "traditions" and then can become "institutions" (Giddens, 1976, 1979, 1984).

People are motivated to perform routines in order to obtain ontological security, which includes comfort, order, stress management, and anxiety and tension reduction. Ontological refers to one's sense of being or existing. The performance of routines also provides people with a sense of self-identity and esteem (Giddens, 1991).

The theory advocates that social structures help bind together human practices across time and space. The theory explores how history is characterized by a "time-space distanciation," meaning that societal influences can stretch out across time and space due to ever-increasing communication sophistication. The theory also distinguishes societies on the basis of their "presence-availability," or the extent to which face-to-face interactions are prevalent.

In order to apply the concepts of structuration theory to a specific situation, two types of analysis must be conducted: (1) strategic conduct analysis and (2) institutional analysis. Strategic conduct analysis involves exploring how various routines are related and interconnected; entrenched through traditions and institutions; and able to provide individuals with a sense of ontological security, self-identity, and esteem. Institutional analysis involves exploring how the three types of social structures (signification, domination, and legitimation) influence, mediate, or contradict each other, and how they influence the three types of interactions (communication, power, and sanction). Typically the interplay between interactions and structures evolves slowly over time. However, researchers should pay specific attention to events

39

that disrupt routines and that alter traditions and institutions, which Giddens (1979, 1984) called "critical situations."

The theory has been adapted and extended. DeSanctis and Poole (1994) adapted the theory for specific use with the interaction of groups and information technology in organizations, and called it adaptive structuration. Strong structuration theory (Stones, 2005) was developed to explore empirical applications of the theory and includes four distinct components: (1) external structures (conditions of action); (2) internal structures within the agent (how and what the person knows); (3) action-active agency (when, how, and why individuals use what they know); and (4) outcomes (how external and internal structures are either reproduced or changed) (Greenhalgh & Stones, 2010). Outcomes influence the other three levels in adaptive structuration theory.

Criticisms and Critiques of the Theory

One of the strengths of structuration theory is that it tried to integrate the views of "individualists" (who see individuals as essentially having control over their own actions) with those of the "structuralists" or "collectivists" (who see society or structures as essentially determining an individual's behaviors) (Gane, 1985). Giddens envisioned structuration theory as an alternative to Marxist social theory, arguing that the theory avoided structural determinism of human behavior, and instead focused on the interplay between structure and agency. However, critics have argued that theory retains this divide rather than overcomes it (Archer, 1990). Further, critics contend that the theory contains three contradictory epistemological forces (those regarding the nature, presuppositions, and foundations of knowledge): an explicit subject-centered humanism, an explicit subjectless structuration, and an implicit subject-centered structuralism (Gane, 1985). Thus critics have argued that the theory does not bring the closure that it sought to produce.

Critics have argued that the theory's assumptions about rules and resources are incorrect (Callinicos, 1985). In the theory, structures have been reduced to mere rules and resources, but may be more complex than merely rules and resources. Critics have argued that rules serve to generate practices only in a very weak sense.

The theory has been criticized for the "exorbitation of language," or comparing the structures and rules of language with those of society (Anderson, 1983, p. 40). Anderson argued that language was not a proper model for other human practices. Linguistic structures change very slowly and exist through individualistic and not collective agents. Therefore, critics have argued that the language example does not provide support for the theory.

Measuring Variables in the Theory

Adaptive structuration measures. Chin, W. W., Gopal, A., & Salisbury, W. D. (1997). Advancing the theory of adaptive structuration: The development of a scale to measure faithfulness of appropriation. *Information Systems Research, 8,* 342–367.

Strong structuration theory questions. Greenhalgh, T., & Stones, R. (2010). Theorising big IT programmes in healthcare: Strong structuration theory meets actor-network theory. *Social Science and Medicine, 70,* 1285–1294.

Rules and resources understanding questions. Hoffman, M. F., & Cowan, R. L. (2010). Be careful what you ask for: Structuration theory and work/life accommodation. *Communication Studies, 61,* 205–223.

Suggestions for Further Research

1. Examine ways in which societies, organizations, or individuals abolish and replace old routines.
2. Explore how unacceptable social behaviors, such as rudeness and lack of privacy, have become acceptable over time.
3. Compare the influence of local societies versus global ad hoc collectives and the interplay of individual agents on behaviors.
4. Look at how semantic rules, moral norms, and authorization and allocation of resources change over time in societies.
5. Create a classification of critical situations or disruptive events that resulted in changes to routinized behaviors in structures.

39

6. Examine the characteristics of individuals that helped bring about the most significant changes to social structures.
7. Explore types of communication needed to influence production of routines, thus creating a sense of safety, self-identity, and esteem.
8. Look at the influence of conflicting structures (signification, domination, and legitimation) on performance of routines.
9. Examine why people do not make use of organizational benefits, such as vacation time, even though those benefits are approved of.
10. Study the extent to which employees understand the rules and resources for day-to-day behaviors.
11. Examine which approaches for challenging rules result in the most significant changes to routines and structures over time.

References to Know

Cohen, I. J. (1989). *Structuration theory: Anthony Giddens and the constitution of social life.* London: Macmillan.

Giddens, A. (1976). *New rules of sociological method: A positive critique of interpretative sociologies.* London: Hutchinson.

Giddens, A. (1979). *Central problems in social theory: Action, structure, and contradiction in social analysis.* London: Macmillan.

Giddens, A. (1984). *The constitution of society: Outline of the theory of structuration.* Cambridge, UK: Polity Press.

Poole, M. S. (1996). The structuration of group decisions. In R. Y. Hirokawa & M. S. Poole (Eds.), *Communication and group decision making* (2nd ed., pp. 114–146). Thousand Oaks, CA: Sage.

Implications of the Theory for Managers

39

Structuration theory examines how social structures influence individual behaviors and how individual behaviors, in turn, influence social structures over time. At the firm level, organizational practices are recurrent employee activities that emerge and develop over time, which shape and are shaped by organizational structures. Organizational practices become routinized, or standardized, over time. When routines become deeply embedded in the organization, then they become traditions. Collections of traditions become institutions. Structures of significance (language), domination (allocation and authorization of resources), and legitimation (moral norms) help ensure that employees follow specific routines. Routines develop over long periods of time. For example, employees can feel secure and understand their place in the organization by performing routines in which they have been (1) told the rules (signification structures); (2) given necessary resources (domination structures); and (3) received moral approval (legitimation structures).

People are motivated to perform routines because they seek a sense of safety and security, self-identity, and esteem. People often take routines for granted and do not question whether or not they should be performed. If your organization wants behaviors to stay the same, then social structures in your organization can help ensure that the routine behaviors will be followed.

However, if your organization wants behaviors to change in some way, then routines can prevent changes from taking place. If behavioral changes are desired, then your task as a manager is to help employees change the routines and change the social structures that keep those routines from changing. Routines will change only if (1) people are told about the rules that should be followed (communication); (2) people are given the authority and resources they need to perform the new behaviors (power); and (3) new norms for performing the new behaviors are established (sanction). Then, over time, the new behaviors can become routinized, and the behaviors will continue to be performed without question.

39

40

Transaction Cost Theory

Transaction cost theory examines whether firms should make something or buy it instead (Coase, 1937; Williamson, 1998). If a firm could obtain resources and produce a product all alone, then the firm would not need to make arrangements with other companies. However, this is usually not the case, and it is often advantageous for firms to enter into trading or other types of agreements with other companies.

The basic unit of analysis in transaction cost theory is the transaction. A transaction has occurred when a good or service is transferred across an organizational boundary. All transactions contain conflict, mutuality, and order (Williamson, 2002). Commons (1934) introduced a tripartite classification of transactions: bargaining, managing, and rationing. Bargaining transactions transfer ownership of wealth between equals by voluntary agreements. Managerial transactions create wealth by commands of legal superiors and authorities. Rationing transactions apportion the benefits and burdens of wealth creation processes through the actions of legal superiors and authorities.

The theory assumes that two trading companies are risk neutral; deal with each other basically as equals; have extensive business experience; and employ specialized managerial, legal, technical, and financial experts. With these assumptions, rather than focus on differences in the trading partners (such as experienced versus naïve), the theory focuses on differences in contracting issues between the trading partners and on the costs involved in those contracts (Williamson, 1998).

40

Focusing on transaction costs was a major shift in economics research, as prior to that time the costs of running a business were mainly for production, and the costs of contracts and transactions were assumed to be zero (Coase, 1937). The costs of transactions are usually not measured directly, but are estimated using proxies of critical dimensions of transactions (Jobin, 2008). Transaction costs include negotiating, monitoring, and enforcing contracts (Hill, 1990) and the costs of planning, adapting, and monitoring task completion (Williamson, 1985).

According to the theory, transactions differ in a number of ways, such as the degree to which each party's relationship-specific assets are involved, the amount of uncertainty about the other party's actions and about the future in general, the complexity of the trading agreement, and the frequency with which transactions occur. These differences help a firm decide which governance structures are preferable. Asset specificity is particularly important and refers to (1) the extent to which assets that support a transaction are tailored to it and (2) the amount of opportunity costs for using these same assets for the next-best alternative, or for alternative users, should the transaction be prematurely terminated (Williamson, 1985).

Williamson (1985) identified four types of asset specificity: site, physical, human, and dedicated. Site specificity refers to highly immobile assets that remain in place to save transportation and inventory costs. Physical specificity refers to equipment and machinery that are specific to this relationship. Human specificity refers to human capital or other employee education and training that is specific to this relationship. Dedicated specificity refers to substantial investments that were made only for this transaction and have no value outside this transaction. When one party has specific assets, then it triggers opportunistic behaviors, which puts a firm at risk and requires costly contractual safeguards to deter those negative behaviors (Poppo & Zenger, 1998).

Transactions must be governed, designed, and carried out by institutional arrangements or contracts between firms. Forms of governance structures have been described as existing along a spectrum from market prices at one end to a fully integrated firm at the other end. For example, at one end lies the spot market, whose prices are used for simple transactions involving sales of commodities. At the other end of the spectrum lies a fully integrated firm where trading partners are under unified control and ownership. In the middle lie all kinds of hybrid modes, such as complex contracts, partial ownership, and other types of arrangements between firms (Shelanski & Klein, 1995).

The central idea in transaction cost theory is that organizations change because managers seek to economize their transaction costs (Williamson, 1985). The theory examines the costs of transactions in one governance structure versus another. Organizations will perform the best when they use governance structures that are the least expensive possible.

If parties to transactions are bilaterally dependent on each other, meaning that neither party can easily make alternative arrangements, then the parties are vulnerable. In response, the parties create value-preserving governance structures among the parties. These structures infuse order, which helps mitigate conflict and allows the firms to realize mutual gain.

Transaction cost theory examines how trading companies protect themselves from the hazards associated with exchange relationships with other companies (Williamson, 1975, 1985). According to the theory, trading partners choose the most cost-effective arrangement or agreement that offers the best protection for their relationship-specific investments. Firms with lower transaction costs are higher performers than are firms with higher transaction costs (Williamson, 1985).

One of the main concepts in transaction cost theory is integration. The theory examines the costs involved in the merger of firm A with firm B. The benefits of firm A merging with firm B derive from the ability of the manager of firm A to give orders to the manager of firm B (a quantity mode) (Coase, 1937). Conversely, if firm A does not merge with (integrate with) firm B, then the manager of firm A must pay or have a contract with the manager of firm B in order to influence the manager of firm B to perform (a price mode). When two firms integrate, they move from a price mode to a quantity mode. When the quantity mode is more advantageous than the price mode, then the two firms will be more likely to integrate. There are conditions when the quantity mode is less efficient than the price mode. Under these circumstances, such as costs of increased bureaucracy and greater likelihood of managerial error in larger firms (Hart, 1988), the firms will tend not to integrate.

40

Transaction cost theory originally focused on the dichotomy between "make it" and "buy it." However, more recent research has focused on collaborative arrangements, called relational governance, or alliances (Dyer, 1997). Relational or alliance governance exchanges may be more beneficial and practicable than other types of governance, such as when the market fails. However, relational governance exchanges may be hard to legally enforce as they are often open ended and require such mechanisms as trust, mutual dependence, parallel expectations, and fairness to sustain them. Geyskens, Steenkamp, and Kumar (2006) found strong support for transaction cost theory for both make-versus-buy and ally-versus-buy decisions.

Transaction cost research has begun to examine how firms align their transactions so as to pursue multiple goals. Firms often assign different goals for different organizational units. These various goals can lead to complicated decisions about whether to make, buy, or use allies. Multiple decisions that are made by multiple entities can result in organizational transaction misalignment, which can impede organizational performance (Bidwell, 2010).

Criticisms and Critiques of the Theory

Transaction cost theory has not yet been fully formalized (Williamson, 2010). Despite a large body of work and much research support for transaction cost theory, there continue to be a number of gaps in the literature (noted, for example, by Macher & Richman, 2008). For example, there is a lack of consensus regarding definitions of key terms and concepts in the theory. Inconsistencies and difficulties in measuring such terms as opportunism, asset specificity, and uncertainty make it difficult to interpret results among various studies.

A second criticism of the theory is of its assumption that humans always behave opportunistically, meaning with self-interest and without morality. Therefore, transactions must always be governed by harshly specific contracts, because trading partners will always be out to harm each other, and discovering avenues of harm after the fact will always be extremely costly (Williamson, 1975).

40

Ghoshal and Moran (1996) argue that there are self-fulfilling prophecy problems with transaction cost theory. As opportunism is always possible and often cannot be predicted, then it must always be expected. As a result, trading partners must always distrust each other and create contracts with as many controls as possible so that there will be enhanced behavior from both trading partners.

Finally, critics have argued that transaction cost theory is biased toward the benefits of integration and explicit contract safeguards (Poppo & Zenger, 2002). The theory has not been able to explain anomalies, or situations where organizations can exist quite successfully without typical governance structures (Chiles & McMackin, 1996).

Measuring Variables in the Theory

Coordination, search, contracting, monitoring, and enforcement costs measures. Jobin, D. (2008). A transaction-cost based approach to partnership performance evaluation. *Evaluation, 14,* 437–465.

Trust and transaction cost measures. Dyer, J. H., & Chu, W. (2003). The role of trustworthiness in reducing transaction costs and improving performance: Empirical evidence from the United States, Japan, and Korea. *Organization Science, 14,* 57–68.

Extent of trust-based governance, assessing reputations, and other scales. Carson, S. J., Madhok, R., & John, G. (2003). Information processing moderators of the effectiveness of trust-based governance in interfirm R&D collaboration. *Organization Science, 14,* 45–56.

Volume uncertainty scale. John, G., & Weitz, B. A. (1988). Forward integration into distribution: An empirical test of transaction cost analysis. *Journal of Law, Economics, and Organizations, 4,* 337–355.

Asset specificity and measurement difficulty scales. Poppo, L., & Zenger, T. (2002). Do formal contracts and relational governance function as substitutes or complements? *Strategic Management Journal, 23,* 707–725.

40

Suggestions for Further Research

1. Examine the relative importance of various transaction dimensions and their impact on organizational behaviors and governance choices.
2. Compare similarities and differences in single-party cost minimization efforts versus relational governance cost minimization efforts.
3. Explore organizational performance differences for purposeful versus random governance choice.
4. Look at how firms align their transactions to accomplish multiple goals.
5. Examine how firms respond when they perceive that their transactions are misaligned.
6. Explore how contracts are written that manage both governance and production problems both internally and externally.
7. Compare governance choices and firm performance for partnerships versus nonpartnerships.
8. Look at the range of demographic differences in managerial opportunistic behavior during contracting events and their influence on organizational performance.
9. Explore situations and conditions where firms can transact successfully without the need for governance structures.
10. Examine the details of contracts, both internal and external to the firm, and their impact on boundary decisions.

References to Know

Coase, R. H. (1937, November). The nature of the firm. *Economica, 4,* 386–405.

Williamson, O. E. (1975). *Markets and hierarchies: Analysis and antitrust implications.* New York: Free Press.

Williamson, O. E. (1985). *The economic institutions of capitalism.* New York: Free Press.

Williamson, O. E. (2002). The theory of the firm as governance structure: From choice to contract. *Journal of Economic Perspectives, 16*(3), 171–195.

Williamson, O. E. (2010, June). Transaction cost economics: The natural progression. *American Economic Review, 100,* 673–690.

40

Implications of the Theory for Managers

Transaction cost theory examines the importance of costs not directly related to the production of goods and services. When you are budgeting for specific projects, be sure to include all of the extra costs involved for you that are not directly related to producing your product or services, such as searching, bargaining, monitoring, and enforcing your contracts with others. For example, if you are buying a product, include the purchase price, but also include in your costs the time you spent searching stores, comparing products, and making your purchasing decision.

Be aware of how your trading partners act toward you. For instance, do you have to treat them harshly and include as many controls and constraints in your contracts as possible in order to prevent bad behaviors, or are your trading partners fun and easy so that it is a pleasure to do business with them? Can you create trusting, mutually beneficial trading relationships without contracts, where both sides thrive, or is it not possible for you to do so? The more you know about your trading partners and what it costs you to maintain relationships with them, the better you will be able to reduce your costs yet create trading conditions under which everyone can benefit.

40

Conclusion

The three main goals of this book are to help you (1) learn about the most important theories in the field of management and organization, (2) apply that knowledge to real organizational problems and situations, and (3) conduct your own research projects that advance the management and organization literature. I will explore each of these goals in this conclusion.

Learn About the Field of Management and Organization

The first main goal of this book is to help students, faculty, practicing managers, and consultants learn about the field of management and organization. Toward that end, I will discuss two important topics with regard to theories in this field: (1) the levels of analysis in theories and (2) the chronology of theory creation.

Levels of Analysis

The level of analysis in a theory refers primarily to what the theory is examining, or the "focal unit" of the theory (Mathieu & Chen, 2011). A number of different levels of analysis are possible: individual, group, unit, division, organization, industry, region, society, culture, nation, continent, international, intercontinental, global, and universal. Theories in the field of management and organization tend to follow one of two major categories of analysis: micro or macro. Micro refers to an individual person or group level of analysis. Macro refers to an organization, industry, or nation level of analysis.

The appropriate level of analysis for a theory is open to debate. Some researchers argue for the strict separation of the different levels and for the strict separation of micro versus macro theories. For example, Turner (2006) argued for strict distinctions among micro, meso, and macro levels of analysis, stating that "they are the way reality actually unfolds" (p. 353). However, other researchers argue for the growing necessity of multilevel or meso-level research (House, Rousseau, & Thomas-Hunt, 1995; Kavanagh, 1991; Klein & Kozlowski, 2000).

Some researchers believe that there is a great divide or conflict between researchers who primarily explore micro levels of analysis and those who primarily explore macro levels of analysis (Huselid & Becker, 2011), although others believe that there is less of a divide than is often assumed (Rousseau, 2011). However, researchers agree that one of the most critical challenges in the field of management and organization research is finding ways to integrate micro- and macro-level research methods and theories (Aguinis, Boyd, Pierce, & Short, 2011). One of my goals in writing this book is to help integrate all the theories of management and organization. To help accomplish this goal, I specifically do not label any of the theories as primarily micro or macro level in focus. I want to avoid perpetuating the divide.

Some theorists have argued for examining theories from multiple perspectives. For example, the topic of authentic leadership has almost always been examined on an individual level of analysis, but researchers have advocated a meso-level or multilevel approach (for example, Yammarino, Dionne, Schriesheim, & Dansereau, 2008). Similarly, goal setting has almost always been examined at the individual level of analysis, but recent developments in goal setting theory include moving to a macro level (Locke & Latham, 2006).

My view is that all forty theories can and should be examined at all possible levels of analysis. Management and organization researchers have argued that one of the most important strengths of the field is that the research could be conducted at multiple levels of analysis (Roberts et al., 1990). Some researchers have already started doing this for some of the theories. Two examples of multilevel approaches are social network theory and social capital theory. Moliterno and Mahony (2011) argue for a multi-level approach to social network theory. Payne, Moore, Griffis, and Autry (2011) explore how social capital theory has already been examined from individual, group, organization, and multiple levels. Researchers have already explored how an organization can develop a sustained competitive advantage over other organizations by developing its resources, knowledge, dynamic capabilities, and absorptive capacities. These same theories could be applied to show how individuals and groups can develop sustained competitive advantages over other individuals and groups.

A Chronology of the Theories

An important part of learning about management and organization theories involves knowing when the theories were created, understanding the order in which they were created, and exploring how they have developed over time. To assist in that effort, I have created a chronologically ordered list of the forty theories included in this book. To create this chronology, I examined the five most important references to know for each theory and made note of the earliest date of those five references. This list presents an approximate time frame of theory creation and can help show how management and organization theoretical approaches have developed and evolved over time.

Theory	Date
Ethical theory	350 B.C.
Agency theory	1776
Social facilitation theory	1898
Efficient market theory	1900
Transaction cost theory	1937
Field theory	1943
Game theory	1944
Balance theory	1946
Social comparison theory	1954
Social network theory	1954
Social exchange theory	1959
Structural contingency theory	1961
Agenda setting theory	1963

Knowledge-based theory	1966
Attachment theory	1967
Attribution theory	1967
Diffusion of innovations theory	1969
Planned behavior theory	1975
Structuration theory	1976
Institutional theory	1977
Organizational ecology theory	1977
Social cognitive theory	1977
Social identity theory	1978
Prospect theory	1979
Role theory	1979
Sensemaking theory	1979
Mental models theory	1980
Self-determination theory	1980
Control theory	1981
Media richness theory	1981
Goal setting theory	1984
Stakeholder theory	1984
Resource-based theory	1984
Actor-network theory	1986
Social capital theory	1986
Organizational justice theory	1987
Absorptive capacity theory	1989
Image theory	1990
Psychological contract theory	1994
Dynamic capabilities theory	1997

When you are learning about and using management and organization theories, keep in mind when they were created, the order in which they were created, and the level of analysis they use.

Apply Your Knowledge About Management and Organization

The second main goal of this book is to help you apply your new knowledge about management and organizations. Whether or not you are ready to apply what you have learned depends on your current level of learning. There are six levels of learning that relate to the theories: (1) remembering, (2) understanding, (3) applying, (4) analyzing, (5) evaluating, and (6) creating (Anderson & Krathwohl, 2001; Pohl, 2000). I will describe each of these six levels separately in terms of how they relate to applying what you have learned.

The first level of learning is remembering. Remembering involves recalling, recognizing, listing, and describing information. The first step in learning the management and organization theories involves remembering their names, the five most important works for each theory, the general description of each theory, the main criticisms of each theory, and the implications for managers for each theory. Each theory has its own terms and jargon that you will need to memorize. This is probably the most time-consuming aspect of learning about a field of study, but arguably the most important step. Most every person who is knowledgeable about the field of management and organization expects every other person who is knowledgeable about this field to have memorized all of this important information, even if they have not learned about every theory themselves.

The second level of learning is understanding. Understanding involves interpreting, summarizing, paraphrasing, and explaining ideas and concepts. This step involves going beyond the mere ability to describe the theories. To use these theories in your daily life, you will need to be able to explain them to others, to compare them, and to understand the point of view of each.

The third level of learning is applying. Applying involves using information in the theories in other familiar situations and implementing the relevant ideas. Every theory offers you a perspective, an approach, and a framework through which you can identify problems, discuss important issues, and create solutions with other people who are also knowledgeable about the field of management and organization. One of the most amazing and helpful things about learning forty theories of management is that from then on you will be able to look at every problem you face from forty different points of view.

The fourth level of learning is analyzing. Analyzing involves breaking down information into smaller parts to explore various relationships, and comparing, organizing, and deconstructing the theories.

Once you have mastered the ability to see every problem and issue from forty different theoretical points of view, then you can analyze the strengths and weaknesses of different courses of action that you face in organizations. A goal of management is to help organizations operate more efficiently and more effectively. After you have learned the theories, then you can analyze your problems from each of these differing perspectives, which will enable you to create better and more effective solutions for your employees and for your organization.

The fifth level of learning is evaluating. Evaluating involves justifying a decision or a course of action, and critiquing, experimenting, and testing ideas and concepts. Once you have gained practice at analyzing issues, problems, and challenges from the forty different theoretical points of view, the next step is to evaluate the strengths and weaknesses of different courses of action or plans of attack. After you are used to applying the different theoretical points of view, you will be able to see the advantages and disadvantages of different options or approaches that you or others are deciding to take.

The sixth and last level of learning is creating. Creating involves generating new ideas or new ways of seeing things, and designing, constructing, or inventing new theories. Once you have worked your way through the first five levels of learning, the next step is to create your own theories of management and organization. (The next section of this conclusion examines the processes involved in creating your own theories.)

When you are learning the theories of management and organization, keep in mind the six levels of learning. Learning about an academic field of study is not an easy and simple process. The more time and energy that you spend learning the theories and the more time and effort that you put in to practicing the application and analysis of problems, issues, and challenges, the better the manager you can be and the more efficient and effective your organization can become.

Conduct Your Own Research on Management and Organization

The third main goal of this book is to help you conduct your own research in the field of management and organization. As I've noted elsewhere, this book can be a valuable resource for under-graduate students who want to conduct a research project, master's and MBA students who want to write a master's thesis, PhD students who want to write a dissertation, and faculty members who want to conduct their own research as part of a research stream. This book also can help practicing managers and consultants who want to conduct and publish their own research in the field of management and organization. You might want to create your own brand-new theory for the field of management and organization.

This last section of the book looks at the three steps to conducting research: (1) selecting a theory that interests you, (2) determining the type of research that you would like to conduct, and (3) creating your own theories.

Select a Theory That Interests You

In order to conduct your own research, you will first need to select one or more management and organization theories that interest you. Read through all forty theories in the book, and as you read them, make note of which ones you find interesting or intriguing, or which ones simply seem to stand out from the others. There may be more than one theory that interests you, but to conduct your own research, you will need to follow the steps in the following process for each theory.

It is vital that you select a theory that you like, because you will be spending a great deal of time working on it. Some researchers also believe that it is important to find a theory that is a good personal fit for you, because in some ways, the theory that you select will reflect on your personal identity, or ideally you will become personally associated with that theory.

After you have selected a theory that interests you, the next step is to "take a bath" in your theory, or find out everything that you can about it. Start by reading the five most important (or seminal) works for that theory, which are listed in this book. Then find out what has been published for that theory over the last five to ten years. Use an academic database, such as EBSCO (Academic Search Complete, Business Source Complete, or both), and search for everything that has been published for your theory. Print out and read all of those articles. Make a list of the constructs or variables in each article and record the definitions for each; be sure to record the full reference for each item. If you record the reference right when reading each article, it will save you tons of time trying to go back and find that reference later on. You might want to draw a picture or diagram of how the constructs and variables are related to each other in the theory. Also make note of any boundaries, or limits, specified by existing research. It will take you some time to create this reference for yourself, but it will be an invaluable tool for you to use for all the research projects that you want to perform.

Determine the Type of Research That You Would Like to Conduct

Once you have become immersed in your theory, the next step is to decide what type of research project you would like to conduct. There are a number of ways that you can contribute to the literature in the field of management and organization. For instance, there are at least ten ways that you can help advance management and organization theory: (1) reviewing, (2) clarifying, (3) replicating, (4) extending and elaborating, (5) reformulating, (6) criticizing, (7) borrowing, (8) blending, (9) integrating, and (10) refocusing. In the following sections, I briefly describe each of these ten ways to contribute to management and organization theory.

Reviewing Theory

The review and summary of theoretical and empirical knowledge of existing work is of great value to the field of management and organization theory (LePine & King, 2010). However, simply reviewing the existing literature is typically not enough for a review to get published (Kilduff, 2007). You can maximize your review's potential contribution to the literature by doing the following: (1) challenging or clarifying existing relationships and interrelationships in the theory; (2) conveying the shortcomings and challenges for the theory; (3) identifying theoretical gaps, holes, or problems; (4) highlighting, analyzing, and critiquing relationships among the constructs in the theory; and (5) synthesizing the latest research findings into a coherent whole (LePine & King). Two great examples of review articles for a specific theory are the following: Eisenhardt, 1989, for agency theory and Payne et al., 2011, for social capital theory.

Clarifying Theory

Another way to contribute to management and organization theory is by clarifying existing work. For example, you can compare and clarify definitions for important constructs and variables in the theory. You can also compare and clarify the important relationships, interrelationships, mediators, and moderators in the theory. To maximize the likelihood that this type of work will be published, be sure to point out and offer solutions for any contradictions, contrasts, or disagreements within the existing research.

Replicating Research Findings

Replicating existing work means to conduct the same tests and analyses that were used in an original test of a theory. Some journals specialize in publishing work that replicates existing research findings. However, some journals will not publish pure replications, so check with desired journals before you begin a project to ensure that they are able to publish a replication. Further, if you want to publish in a specific journal, then it is highly advised that you determine which types of research that journal tends to publish and which theories that journal tends to include. If that journal has never published an article on your theory, then you might want to select a different journal as an outlet for your research.

To maximize the chances that your own replication study will be published, you might want not only to replicate the original work but also to change or alter something about the original work in a new way. For example, if the original work focused on only male subjects, then you might want to focus your replication on both males and females.

Extending and Elaborating Theory

Researchers specify the constructs and their relationships when a theory is initially developed. However, rarely is a theory established all at once in a flash of brilliance (Smith & Hitt, 2005). Instead, theories tend to evolve over time through extensions and elaborations. Subsequent research helps refine the relevant variables and their relationships. Work that extends and elaborates a theory can be messy, as people attempt to stretch the boundaries of a theory in new and different directions. To maximize your chances of getting an extension study published, you might try extending your favorite theory in the same way that another researcher extended a different theory in an article that has already been published, then reference that other study in yours.

An additional way to extend and elaborate a theory is by following a method of asking contrasting questions (Tsang & Ellsaesser, 2011). There are two main methods of asking contrasting questions: (1) allomorph and (2) fact and foil. An allomorph refers to a different aspect of an event, and suggests that there might be different research questions for you to address depending on which word or words are stressed in your question. For example, when considering the question, "Why did the chicken cross the road?" you would conduct an entirely different research study if you focused on the chicken rather than focusing on the road or on the verb "to cross." "Why was it a chicken and not some other type of animal?" focuses on the chicken. "Why was it a road and not some other type of transportation system?" focuses on the road. "Why did the animal cross the road, instead of walk beside it, turn away from it, or have some other animal cross it for him?" focuses on crossing.

Another way to extend or elaborate on an existing theory is by using the fact-and-foil method. A typical research question is "Why P rather than Q?" where P is called the fact and Q is called the foil (Tsang & Ellsaesser, 2011). For example, if we extend our research question to "Why did the chicken cross the road instead of taking a bus?" the first part of the question ("Why did the chicken cross the road") is the fact, and "instead of taking a bus?" is the foil. Creating a number of different foils to your original factual research question can be a great way to create new research questions for you to examine in your elaboration or extension of an existing theory.

Reformulating Theory

Reformulating a theory involves making a major change to the constructs and relationships in an existing theory. For example, if you notice that there is a problem or flaw in a theory, then you can offer a way to improve or change the theory to solve that problem or overcome that flaw. An example of reformulating a theory is the work of Zahra and George (2002), who reformulated absorptive capacity theory. To maximize the potential for this type of work, you will need to very clearly specify the current constructs and relationships in the theory and then very precisely specify how your changes to the theory help advance the theory in new and important ways.

Criticizing Theory

Another way to contribute to management and organization theory is to write a critique of existing work. Not every journal will publish criticisms or critiques, so be certain that a desired journal will accept such work before you spend time writing a critique and submitting it for review. Examples of critiques of management and organization theories include those addressing resource-based theory (Bromiley & Fleming, 2002), transaction cost theory (Ghoshal & Moran, 1996), and stakeholder theory (Key, 1999).

Borrowing from Other Theories

Borrowing theories or parts of theories from other disciplines is commonplace in the field of management and organization (Ilgen & Klein, 1989; Oswick, Fleming, & Hanlon, 2011; Whetten, Felin, & King, 2009). Borrowing theory is a one-way process of bringing a theory from a related discipline over to the management and organization field (Oswick et al., 2011). For instance, social network theory was brought over from the fields of economics and sociology, and structuration theory was brought over from sociology. If you want to borrow theories from other disciplines, then you will need to explore those disciplines and find interesting theories. Then you will need to find a way to apply those theories to an organization and management setting or perspective.

Blending Theories

Borrowing theory is a one-way process, but blending theory involves a two-way, back-and-forth movement of theory between two or more fields. Oswick et al. (2011) discuss the use of four types of reasoning as ways to blend theories from different fields: (1) disanalogous reasoning (focus on dissimilarities in similar fields); (2) ironic reasoning (compare inverse or diametrically opposed fields on their similarities); (3) counterfactual reasoning (juxtapose work from fields that are similar but have discernable differences); and (4) anomalous reasoning (compare unrelated or dissimilar domains on the basis of their similarities).

Integrating Theories

Another way that you can contribute to management and organization theory is to integrate two or more theories. Look for similar constructs and approaches in one or more theories, then look for ways to integrate or combine those theories into a new, unified approach. An example of an integrative approach is the work of Klein (1989).

Refocusing Theory

A last way that you can conduct your own research to extend theory in the management and organization field is by refocusing a theory. To refocus a theory means to adopt different lenses from within or outside the field and combine them in a new way (Okhuysen & Bonardi, 2011). Theory building that combines lenses has an important role to play in advancing theory in management and organization (Gioia & Pitre, 1990). An example of combining lenses is the new research area of behavioral economics. Researchers took the lens of cognitive and emotional factors of individuals from the field of psychology and combined it with the lens of making investments in finance. This new field looks at individual difference variables in how people interact with the financial markets. Look for ways to combine lenses from both similar and different fields into new approaches in the management and organization field.

Create Your Own Theories

The field of management and organization needs new, bold, great theories (Suddaby, Hardy, & Huy, 2011; Weick, 1999), so why shouldn't it be you who creates them? To help you better understand how new theories are created, the next sections examine three important aspects of theory creation: (1) characteristics of the theorist, (2) stages of theory development, and (3) roles of the theorist (Smith & Hitt, 2005).

Characteristics of the Theorist

Creating new theories requires some specific and important talents: passion, creative and innovative thinking skills, confidence, persistence, and discipline. If you want to be a theorist, then you will need to have passion for the field. Having passion means that you are energized and excited about exploring important issues involving management and organizations. For example, when you go to a bookstore, you are naturally drawn to the business management section, and you typically find yourself flipping through the books there.

If you want to be a theorist, then you will need to have the skills to think innovatively and creatively; you will also need to be able to see the overall "big picture" of a situation. Theorists are also able to conceive how various elements relate to each other and fit together over time.

You will need to have a great deal of confidence if you want to be a theorist. There is a fine line between genius and insanity. When you invent new theories, some people will love your ideas, and others will hate them. You will need to have a great deal of confidence in both yourself and your ideas if you are to succeed in coping with the criticism and defending your ideas from the attacks of others.

If you want to be a theorist, you will need to be persistent. Becoming a theorist takes time and perseverance. You will need to learn the field, take a bath in your theory, come up with new ideas, and carefully write about your new theory, all of which requires a great deal of time, patience, and personal motivation. Writing and publishing research takes time, so you will need to be persistent and conscientious as you see your ideas through to publication.

Finally, if you want to be a theorist, you will need to have discipline. You will need to be committed to your work and to spend many long hours and days working on your ideas. I was once told that conducting a research project involves doing a thousand little things one at a time. You will need to have discipline in order to accomplish all of the thousands of things that are required to publish your new theoretical ideas.

Stages of Theory Development

Smith and Hitt (2005) identified four main stages that occur when creating new theories: (1) phenomenon/tension, (2) search, (3) elaboration and research, and (4) proclamation/presentation.

Phenomenon/tension. The idea for a new theory can arise in several ways. For example, a theorist might notice some phenomenon and wonder why it occurred. For instance, agenda-setting theory was started when a researcher wondered why some stories ended up on the evening news or on the front page of a newspaper, but others did not. You might notice something occurring in an organization or having to do with an organization and decide to pursue a new theory to help explain that phenomenon. Another way that new theories can start is by disagreeing with current theories or experiencing some tension about the explanation given by some theories for some aspect of an organization or about some management activity. Many ideas for new theories arise when a person thinks, "That's not exactly how things work in my organization."

Search. Once you have identified some sort of phenomenon or tension that you would like to explore further, the next stage involves searching for a solution to explain that phenomenon or to reduce that tension. For most theorists, their knowledge, skills, abilities, background, and experiences help them find some solution to their tension or for their phenomenon. Searching for answers can involve conducting research and talking with others, such as researchers, theorists, and managers. Theorists report that they sometimes find answers through mere chance.

Elaboration and research. After you have found your approach to solving your problem, the next step is to get those ideas down on paper. You will need to describe your constructs and explain the relationships among those constructs. Some theorists create outlines; some draw diagrams to better organize their thoughts and to help them include all relevant information in their theory. You might also need to conduct research projects in order to test out some of your ideas.

Proclamation/presentation. The last stage of theory development is showing your theory to others. Many theorists report that this can be a difficult part of theory development. Some people may like your new theoretical approach and some may not. Some theorists have noted that not all journals are appreciative of brand-new theoretical approaches. Sometimes theorists have had to resort to writing books to elaborate their new theories after the major journals refused to publish their new ideas.

Roles of the Theorist

Smith and Hitt (2005) described five important roles that are played by theorists who create new management and organization theories: (1) creator, (2) codifier, (3) disseminator, (4) researcher, and (5) advocate.

The first role of a theorist is that of creator. A theorist should invent a new theory that helps us see the world in new and different ways that surprise us and change our perceptions. In your second role, you codify your ideas. Codification involves summarizing your ideas, organizing your thoughts, differentiating your theory from other theories, positioning your theory among related theories, and periodically updating your theory over time as new advances are made. The third role is to be a disseminator. Dissemination includes communicating your ideas to a wide audience through multiple and varied communication channels. The fourth role, that of researcher, entails conducting research to further analyze and test your theoretical ideas. This research could involve all sorts of methodologies, such as field or laboratory studies and qualitative or quantitative approaches. The fifth role is to be an advocate for your theory. You must promote, market, sell, and defend the theory if it is to be adopted, supported, and used by others.

Final Thoughts

I was inspired to write *Management and Organization Theory* by my observation that students, faculty, practicing managers, and consultants need a reference book to help them learn about the major theories in the field of management and organization.

I sincerely hope that this book inspires you to learn about the field, get out there and improve managerial performance and organizational functioning, get busy conducting your own research projects, and create your own new theories in the field of management and organization.

References

Introduction

Abend, G. (2008, June). The meaning of "theory." *Sociological Theory, 26,* 173–199.

Bacharach, S. B. (1989). Organizational theories: Some criteria for evaluation. *Academy of Management Journal, 14,* 496–515.

Colquitt, J. A., & Zapata-Phelan, C.P.H (2007). Trends in theory building and theory testing: A five-decade study of *Academy of Management Journal. Academy of Management Journal, 50,* 1281–1303.

Corley, K. G., & Gioia, D. A. (2011). Building theory about theory building: What constitutes a theoretical contribution? *Academy of Management Review, 36,* 12–32.

Gioia, D. A., & Pitre, E. (1990). Multiparadigm perspectives on theory building. *Academy of Management Review, 15,* 584–602.

Hambrick, D. C. (2007). The field of management's devotion to theory: Too much of a good thing? *Academy of Management Journal, 50,* 1346–1352.

LePine, J. A., & Wilcox-King, A. W. (2010). Editors' comments: Developing novel theoretical insight from reviews of existing theory and research. *Academy of Management Review, 35,* 506–509.

Lewin, K. (1945, May). The research center for group dynamics at Massachusetts Institute of Technology. *Sociometry, 8,* 126–136.

Miner, J. B. (1984). The validity and usefulness of theories in an emerging organizational science. *Academy of Management Review, 9,* 296–306.

Miner, J. B. (2003). The rated importance, scientific validity, and practical usefulness of organizational behavior theories: A quantitative review. *Academy of Management Learning and Education, 2,* 250–268.

Suddaby, R. (2010). Construct clarity in theories of management and organization. *Academy of Management Review, 35,* 346–357.

Sutton, R. I., & Staw, B. M. (1995, September). What theory is *not. Administrative Science Quarterly, 40,* 371–384.

Whetten, D. A. (1989). What constitutes a theoretical contribution? *Academy of Management Review, 14,* 490–495.

1: Absorptive Capacity Theory

Baker, T., Miner, A. S., & Eesley, D. (2003). Improvising firms: Bricolage, retrospective interpretation and improvisational competencies in the founding process. *Research Policy, 32*, 255–276.

Cohen, W. M., & Levinthal, D. A. (1989, September). Innovation and learning: The two faces of R & D. *Economic Journal, 99*(397), 569–596.

Cohen, W. M., & Levinthal, D. A. (1990, March). Absorptive capacity: A new perspective on learning and innovation. *Administrative Science Quarterly, 35*(1, Special Issue), 128–152.

Gavetti, G., & Levinthal, D. (2000). Looking forward and looking backwards: Cognitive and experiential search. *Administrative Science Quarterly, 45*, 113–137.

Glass, A. J., & Saggi, K. (1998). International technology transfer and the technology gap. *Journal of Development Economics, 55*, 369–398.

Keller, W. (1996). Absorptive capacity: On the creation and acquisition of technology in development. *Journal of Development Economics, 49*, 199–227.

March, J. G., & Simon, H. A. (1958). *Organizations.* Hoboken, NJ: Wiley.

Murovec, N., & Prodan, J. (2009). Absorptive capacity, its determinants, and influence on innovation output: Cross-cultural validation of the structural model. *Technovation, 29*, 859–872.

Schumpeter, J. A. (1942). *Capitalism, socialism, and democracy.* New York: Harper & Row.

Todorova, G., & Durisin, B. (2007). Absorptive capacity: Valuing a reconceptualization. *Academy of Management Review, 32*, 774–786.

Tripsas, M., & Gavetti, G. (2000). Capabilities, cognition and inertia: Evidence from digital imaging. *Strategic Management Journal, 21*, 1147–1162.

Volberda, H. W., Foss, N., & Lyles, M. A. (2010, July-August). Absorbing the concept of absorptive capacity: How to realize its potential in the organization field. *Organization Science, 21*, 931–951.

Zahra, S. A., & George, G. (2002). Absorptive capacity: A review, reconceptualization, and extension. *Academy of Management Review, 27*, 185–203.

2: Actor-Network Theory

Alcadipani, R., & Hassard, J. (2010). Actor-network theory, organizations and critique: Toward a politics of organizing. *Organization, 17*, 419–435.

Bryson, J. M., Crosby, B. C., & Bryson, J. K. (2009). Understanding strategic planning and the formulation and implementation of strategic plans as a way of knowing: The contributions of actor-network theory. *International Public Management Journal, 12,* 172–207.

Calas, M. B., & Smirich, L. (1999). Past postmodernism? Reflections and tentative directions. *Academy of Management Review, 24,* 649–671.

Callon, M. (1986). Some elements of a sociology of translation: Domestication of the scallops and the fishermen of St. Brieuc Bay. In J. E. Law (Ed.), *Power, action, and belief: A new sociology of knowledge* (pp. 196–223). London: Routledge.

Callon, M., & Latour, B. (1981). Unscrewing the big leviathan: How actors macro-structure reality and how sociologists help them do so. In K. Knorr-Cetina & A. V. Cicourel (Eds.), *Advances in social theory and methodology* (pp. 277–303). London: Routledge & Kegan Paul.

Chateauraynaud, F. (1991, June-July). Forces et faiblesses de la nouvelle anthropologie des sciences (Strengths and weaknesses of the new anthropology of science). *Critique, 529–530,* 458–478.

Grint, K. (1998). *The sociology of work.* Cambridge: Polity.

Habers, H., & Koenis, S. (1996). The political eggs of the chicken debate. *EASST Review, 15*(1), 9–15.

Hanseth, O., Aanestad, M., & Berg, M. (2004). Guest editor's introduction: Actor-network theory and information systems: What's so special? *Information, Technology and People, 17,* 116–123.

Krarup, T. M., & Blok, A. (2011). Unfolding the social: Quasi-actants, virtual theory, and the new empiricism of Bruno Latour. *Sociological Review, 59*(1), 42–63.

Latour, B. (1987). *Science in action: How to follow scientists and engineers through society.* Cambridge, MA: Harvard University Press.

Latour, B. (1996). *Aramis, or the love of technology.* Cambridge, MA: MIT Press.

Latour, B. (1999). On recalling ANT. In J. Law & J. Hassard (Eds.), *Actor network theory and after* (pp. 15–25). Oxford: Blackwell.

Latour, B. (2004, Winter). Why has critique run out of steam? From matters of fact to matters of concern. *Critical Inquiry, 30,* 225–248.

Latour, B. (2005). *Reassembling the social: An introduction to actor-network theory.* Oxford: Oxford University Press.

Law, J. (1994). *Organizing modernity.* Oxford: Blackwell.

Law, J. (1999). After ANT: Complexity, naming and topology. In J. Law & J. Hassard (Eds.), *Actor network theory and after* (pp. 1–14). Oxford: Blackwell.

Law, J., & Hassard, J. (Eds.). (1999). *Actor network theory and after.* Oxford: Blackwell.

Lee, N., & Brown, S. (1994). Otherness and the actor network: The undiscovered continent. *American Behavioral Scientist, 36,* 772–790.

McLean, C., & Hassard, J. (2004). Symmetrical absence/symmetrical absurdity: Critical notes on the production of actor-network accounts. *Journal of Management Studies, 41,* 493–519.

Newton, T. (1999). Power, subjectivity, and British industrial and organizational sociology: The relevance of the work of Norbert Elias. *Sociology, 33,* 411–440.

Newton, T. (2002). Creating the new ecological order? Elias and actor-network theory. *Academy of Management Review, 27,* 523–540.

Oppenheim, R. (2007). Actor-network theory and anthropology after science, technology, and society. *Anthropological Theory, 7,* 471–493.

Reed, M. I. (1997). In praise of duality and dualism: Rethinking agency and structure in organizational analysis. *Organization Studies, 18,* 21–42.

Savage, M. (2009). Contemporary sociology and the challenge of descriptive assemblage. *European Journal of Social Psychology, 12,* 155–174.

Walsham, G. (1997). Actor-network theory and IS research: Current status and future prospects. In A. Lee, J. Liebenau, & J. DeGross (Eds.), *Information systems and qualitative research* (pp. 466–480). London: Chapman and Hall.

Whittle, A., & Spicer, A. (2008). Is actor network theory critique? *Organization Studies, 29,* 611–629.

Young, D., Borland, R., & Coghill, K. (2010, July). An actor-network theory analysis of policy innovation for smoke-free places: Understanding change in complex systems. *American Journal of Public Health, 100,* 1208–1217.

3: Agency Theory

Arrow, K. J. (1985). The economics of agency. In J. W. Pratt & R. J. Zeckhauser (Eds.), *Principals and agents: The structure of business* (pp. 37–51). Boston, MA: Harvard Business School Press.

Barney, J., & Ouchi, W. (Eds.). (1986). *Organizational economics.* San Francisco: Jossey-Bass.

Berle, A., & Means, G. (1932). *The modern corporation and private property.* New York: Macmillan.

Dalton, D. R., Daily, C. M., Certo, S. T., & Roengpitya, R. (2003). Meta-analyses of financial performance and equity. Fusion or confusion? *Academy of Management Journal, 46,* 13–26.

Dalton, D. R., Hitt, M. A., Certo, S. T., & Dalton, C. M. (2007). The fundamental agency problem and its mitigation. In J. F. Walsh &

A. P. Brief (Eds.), *Academy of Management Annals* (Vol. 1, pp. 1–64). Mahwah, NJ: Erlbaum.

Davies, M., & Prince, M. (2010, Spring). Advertising agency compensation, client evaluation and switching costs: An extension of agency theory. *Journal of Current Issues and Research in Advertising, 32*(1), 13–31.

Eisenhardt, K. M. (1989). Agency theory: An assessment and review. *Academy of Management Review, 14*, 57–74.

Ellis, R. S., & Johnson, L. W. (1993, September-October). Observations: Agency theory as a framework for advertising agency compensation decisions. *Journal of Advertising Research, 33*, 75–80.

Fama, E. F. (1980). Agency problems and the theory of the firm. *Journal of Political Economy, 88*, 288–307.

Fama, E. F., & Jensen, M. C. (1983). Separation of ownership and control. *Journal of Law and Economics, 26*, 301–325.

Ghoshal, S. (2005). Bad management theories are destroying good management practices. *Academy of Management Review, 4*, 75–91.

Hirsch, P., & Friedman, R. (1986). Collaboration or paradigm shift? Economic vs. behavioral thinking about policy? In J. Pearce & R. Robinson (Eds.), *Best paper proceedings* (pp. 31–35). Chicago: Academy of Management.

Hirsch, P., Michaels, S., & Friedman, R. (1987). "Dirty hands" versus "clean models": Is sociology in danger of being seduced by economics? *Theory and Society, 16*, 317–336.

Holmstrom, B. (1979). Moral hazard and observability. *Bell Journal of Economics, 10*, 74–91.

Jensen, M. C. (1983). Organization theory and methodology. *Accounting Review, 58*, 319–339.

Jensen, M. C., & Meckling, W. H. (1976). Theory of the firm: Managerial behavior, agency costs, and ownership structure. *Journal of Financial Economics, 3*, 305–360.

Kiser, E. (1999). Comparing varieties of agency theory in economics, political science, and sociology: An illustration from state policy implementation. *Sociological Theory, 17*, 146–170.

Lan, L. L., & Heracleous, L. (2010). Rethinking agency theory: The view from law. *Academy of Management Review, 35*, 294–314.

Mitnick, B. M. (1988). Agency theory. In R. E. Freeman, & P. H. Werhane (Eds.), *The Blackwell encyclopedic dictionary of business ethics* (pp. 12–15). Malden, MA: Blackwell.

Nyberg, A. J., Fulmer, I. S., Gerhart, B., & Carpenter, M. A. (2010). Agency theory revisited: CEO return and shareholder interest alignment. *Academy of Management Review, 53*, 1029–1049.

Perrow, C. (1986). *Complex organizations.* New York: Random House.

Petersen, T. (1993). The economics of organizations: The principal-agent relationship. *Acta Sociologica, 36*, 277–293.

Ross, S. (1973). The economic theory of agency: The principal's problem. *American Economic Review, 63*, 134–139.

Shapiro, S. P. (2005). Agency theory. *Annual Review of Sociology, 31*, 263–284.

Smith, A. (1952). An inquiry into the nature and causes of wealth of nations (1776). In R. M. Hutchins (Ed.), *Great books of the Western world* (Vol. 39, pp. 291–376). Chicago: Encyclopedia Britannica (Originally published 1776).

4: Agenda Setting Theory

Baumgartner, F. R., & Jones, B. D. (1993). *Agendas and instability in American politics.* Chicago: University of Chicago Press.

Berger, B. K. (2001). Private issues and public policy: Locating the corporate agenda in agenda-setting theory. *Journal of Public Relations Research, 13*, 91–126.

Brosius, H. B., & Eps, P. (1995). Prototyping through key events: News selection in the case of violence against aliens and asylum seekers in Germany. *European Journal of Communication, 10*, 391–412.

Cobb, R. W., & Elder, C. D. (1983). *Participation in American politics: The dynamics of agenda-building.* Boston: Allyn & Bacon.

Cohen, B. (1963). *The press and foreign policy.* Princeton, NJ: Princeton University Press.

Dearing, J. W., & Rogers, E. M. (1996). *Communication concepts 6: Agenda-setting.* Thousand Oaks, CA: Sage.

Entman, R. M. (1993). Framing: Towards clarification of a fractured paradigm. *Journal of Communication, 43*, 51–58.

Fiske, S. T., & Taylor, S. E. (1991). *Social cognition.* New York: McGraw-Hill.

Fombrun, C. J. (1998). Indices of corporate reputation: An analysis of media rankings and social monitors' ratings. *Corporate Reputation Review, 1*, 327–340.

Fombrun, C. J., Gardberg, N. A., & Sever, J. M. (2001). The reputation quotient: A multi-stakeholder measure of corporate reputation. *Journal of Brand Management, 7*, 241–255.

Iyengar, S. (1988). New directions of agenda-setting research. In J. A. Anderson (Ed.), *Communication yearbook 11* (pp. 595–602). Thousand Oaks, CA: Sage.

Iyengar, S. (1990). The accessibility bias in politics: Television news and public opinion. *International Journal of Public Opinion Research, 2*(1), 1–15.

Iyengar, S., & Kinder, D. R. (1987). *News that matters*. Chicago: University of Chicago Press.

Kingdon, J. (1984). *Agendas, alternatives, and public policies* (2nd ed.). New York: HarperCollins.

Klapper, J. T. (1960). *The effects of mass communications*. New York: Free Press.

Kosicki, G. M. (1993). Problems and opportunities in agenda-setting research. *Journal of Communication, 43*, 100–127.

Lasswell, H. D. (1927). *Propaganda techniques in the World War*. New York: Knopf.

Leech, B. L., Baumgartner, F. R., Berry, J. M., Hojnacki, M., & Kimball, D. C. (2002). Organized interests and issue definition in policy debates. In A. J. Cigler & B. A. Loomis (Eds.), *Interest group politics* (6th ed., pp. 275–292). Washington, DC: CQ Press.

Lippman, W. (1922). *Public opinion*. New York: Macmillan.

MacKuen, M. B. (1981). Social communication and the mass policy agenda. In M. B. MacKuen & S. L. Coombs (Eds.), *More than news: Media power in public affairs* (pp. 17–44). Thousand Oaks, CA: Sage.

Matthes, J. (2009). What's in a frame? A content analysis of media framing studies in the world's leading communication journals, 1990–2005. *Journalism and Mass Communication Quarterly, 86*, 349–367.

McCombs, M. (2004). *Setting the agenda: The mass media and public opinion*. Cambridge: Polity.

McCombs, M., & Evatt, D. (1995). Issues and attributes: Exploring a new dimension in agenda setting. *Comunicacion y Sociedad, 8*(1), 7–32.

McCombs, M., & Ghanem, S. I. (2001). The convergence of agenda setting and framing. In S. D. Reese, O. H. Gandy Jr., & A. E. Grant (Eds.), *Framing public life: Perspectives on media and our understanding of the social world* (pp. 67–81). Mahwah, NJ: Erlbaum.

McCombs, M., & Shaw, D. L. (1972, Summer). The agenda-setting function of mass media. *Public Opinion Quarterly, 36*, 176–187.

McCombs, M., Shaw, D. L., & Weaver, D. (1997). *Communication and democracy: Exploring intellectual frontiers in agenda-setting theory*. Mahwah, NJ: Erlbaum.

McKelvey, R. D. (1981, March). A theory of optimal agenda design. *Management Science, 27*, 303–321.

Miller, J. N. (2007). Examining the mediators of agenda setting: A new experimental paradigm reveals the role of emotions. *Political Psychology, 28*, 689–717.

Pralle, S. (2006). The "mouse that roared": Agenda setting in Canadian pesticide politics. *Policy Studies Journal, 34*, 171–194.

Rochefort, D. A., & Cobb, R. W. (1994). *The politics of problem definition.* Lawrence: University Press of Kansas.

Rogers, E. M., Dearing, J. W., & Bregman, D. (1993). The anatomy of agenda-setting research. *Journal of Communication, 43,* 68–84.

Schattschneider, E. E. (1960). *The semisovereign people: A realist's view of democracy in America.* New York: Holt, Rinehart & Winston.

Scheufele, D. A. (1999). Framing as a theory of media effects. *Journal of Communication, 49,* 103–122.

Schlozman, K. L., & Tierney, J. T. (1986). *Organized interests and American democracy.* New York: Harper & Row.

Staw, B. M., & Epstein, L. D. (2000). What bandwagons bring: Effects of popular management techniques on corporate performance, reputation, and CEO pay. *Administrative Science Quarterly, 45,* 557–590.

Stone, D. (1988). *Policy paradox and political reason.* Glenview, IL: Scott, Foresman.

Takeshita, T. (2005). Current problems in agenda-setting research. *International Journal of Public Opinion Research, 18,* 275–296.

Useem, M. (1980). Which business leaders help govern? In G. W. Domhoff (Ed.), *Power structure research* (pp. 199–226). Thousand Oaks, CA: Sage.

Wartick, S. L., & Mahon, J. F. (1994). Toward a substantive definition of the corporate issue construct: A review and synthesis of the literature. *Business and Society, 33,* 293–311.

Weaver, D. H. (1977). Political issues and voter need for orientation. In D. L. Shaw & M. E. McCombs (Eds.), *The emergence of American political issues: The agenda-setting function of the press* (pp. 107–119). St. Paul, MN: West.

Weaver, D. H. (1980). Audience need for orientation and media effects. *Communication Research, 7,* 361–376.

Zhou, Y., & Moy, P. (2007). Parsing framing processes: The interplay between online public opinion and media coverage. *Journal of Communication, 57,* 79–98.

5: Attachment Theory

Adshead, G. (2010). Becoming a caregiver: Attachment theory and poorly performing doctors. *Medical Education, 44,* 125–131.

Ainsworth, M.D.S. (1967). *Infancy in Uganda: Infant care and the growth of love.* Baltimore, MD: Johns Hopkins University Press.

Ainsworth, M.D.S. (1969). Object relations, dependency and attachment: A theoretical review of the infant-mother relationship. *Child Development, 40,* 969–1025.

Ainsworth, M.D.S., & Bell, S. M. (1970). Attachment, exploration, and separation: Illustrated by the behavior of one-year-olds in a strange situation. *Child Development, 41,* 49–67.

Ainsworth, M.D.S., Blehar, M., Waters, E., & Wall, S. (1978). *Patterns of attachment: A psychological study of the strange situation.* Mahwah, NJ: Erlbaum.

Ainsworth, M.D.S., & Bowlby, J. (1991, April). An ethological approach to personality development. *American Psychologist, 46,* 333–341.

Albert, L. S., & Horowitz, L. M. (2009). Attachment styles and ethical behavior: Their relationship and significance in the marketplace. *Journal of Business Ethics, 87,* 299–316.

Bartholomew, K., & Horowitz, L. M. (1991). Attachment styles among young adults: A test of a four-category model. *Journal of Personality and Social Psychology, 61,* 226–244.

Bowlby, J. (1969). *Attachment and loss: Vol. 1. Attachment.* New York: Basic Books.

Bowlby, J. (1973). *Attachment and loss: Vol. 2. Separation: Anxiety and anger.* New York: Basic Books.

Bowlby, J. (1980). *Attachment and loss: Vol. 3. Loss: Sadness and depression.* New York: Basic Books.

Bowlby, J. (1988). *A secure base: Clinical applications of attachment theory.* London: Routledge.

Buelow, S. A., Lyddon, W. J., & Johnson, J. T. (2002). Client attachment and coping resources. *Counseling Psychology Quarterly, 15,* 145–152.

Davidovitz, R., Mikulincer, M., Shaver, P. R., Izsak, R., & Popper, M. (2007). Leaders as attachment figures: Leaders' attachment orientations predict leader-related mental representations and followers' performance and mental health. *Journal of Personality and Social Psychology, 93,* 632–650.

Field, T. (1996). Attachment and separation in young children. *Annual Review of Psychology, 47,* 541–561.

Harris, J. R. (1998). *The nurture assumption: Why children turn out the way they do.* New York: Free Press.

Harris, J. R. (2009). Beyond the nurture assumption: Testing hypotheses about the child's environment. In J. G. Borkowski, S. Landesman Ramey, & M. Bristol-Power (Eds.), *Parenting and the child's world: Influences on academic, intellectual, and socio-emotional development* (pp. 3–20). Mahwah, NJ: Erlbaum.

Hawkins, A. C., Howard, R. A., & Oyebode, J. R. (2007). Stress and coping in hospice nursing staff: The impact of attachment styles. *Psycho-Oncology, 16,* 563–572.

Lee, H.-Y., & Hughley, K. F. (2001). The relationship of psychological separation and parental attachment to the career maturity of college freshmen from intact families. *Journal of Career Development,* *27*, 279–293.

Lorenz, K. (1935). Der kumpan in der umwelt des vogels. Der artgenosse als auslösendes moment sozialer verhaltensweisen (The sidekick in the environment of the bird. Fellow species as a triggering moment of social behaviors). *Journal für Ornithologie, 83,* 137–215, 289–413.

Mikulincer, M., Shaver, P. R., Gillath, O., & Nitzberg, R. A. (2005). Attachment, caregiving, and altruism: Boosting attachment security increases compassion and helping. *Journal of Personality and Social Psychology, 89,* 817–839.

Popper, M., & Mayseless, O. (2003). Back to basics: Applying a parenting perspective to transformational leadership. *Leadership Quarterly, 14,* 41–65.

Popper, M., Mayseless, O., & Castelnovo, O. (2000). Transformational leadership and attachment. *Leadership Quarterly, 11,* 267–289.

Renfro-Michel, E. L., Burlew, L. D., & Robert, T. (2009, March). The interaction of work adjustment and attachment theory: Employment counseling implications. *Journal of Employment Counseling, 46,* 18–26.

Richards, D. A., & Schat, A.C.H. (2011). Attachment at (not to) work: Applying attachment theory to explain individual behavior in organizations. *Journal of Applied Psychology, 96,* 169–182.

Rutter, M. (1979, June). Maternal deprivation, 1972–1978: New findings, new concepts, new approaches. *Child Development, 50,* 283–305.

Smith, E. R., Murphy, J., & Coats, S. (1999). Attachment to groups: Theory and measurement. *Journal of Personality and Social Psychology, 77,* 94–110.

Suomi, S. J., Harlow, H. F., & Domek, C. J. (1970). Effect of repetitive infant-infant separation of young monkeys. *Journal of Abnormal Psychology, 76,* 161–172.

van Ecke, Y. (2007, June). Attachment style and dysfunctional career thoughts: How attachment style can affect the career counseling process. *Career Development Quarterly, 55,* 339–350.

Wolfe, J. B., & Betz, N. E. (2004, June). The relationship of attachment to career decision-making self-efficacy and fear of commitment. *Career Development Quarterly, 52,* 363–369.

Wright, S. L., & Perrone, K. M. (2008). The impact of attachment and career-related variables. *Journal of Career Development, 35,* 87–106.

6: Attribution Theory

Anderson, C. A. (1983). The causal structure of situations: The generation of plausible causal attributions as a function of type of event situation. *Journal of Experimental Social Psychology, 19,* 185–203.

Bradley, G. W. (1978). Self-serving biases in the attribution process: A reexamination of the fact or fiction question. *Journal of Personality and Social Psychology, 36,* 56–71.

Burger, J. M. (1991). Changes in attributions over time: The ephemeral fundamental attribution error. *Social Cognition, 9,* 182–193.

Buss, A. R. (1978). Causes and reasons in attribution theory: A conceptual critique. *Journal of Personality and Social Psychology, 36,* 1311–1321.

Chattopadhyay, R. (2007). Attribution style and entrepreneurial success: A study based on Indian culture. *Journal of Enterprising Culture, 15,* 301–316.

DiVitto, B., & McArthur, L. Z. (1978). Developmental differences in the use of distinctiveness, consensus, and consistency information for making causal attributions. *Developmental Psychology, 14,* 474–482.

Ellis, A. P. J., Ilgen, D. R., & Hollenbeck, J. R. (2006). The effects of team leader race on performance evaluations. *Small Group Research, 37,* 295–332.

Forsyth, D. R., & Schlenker, B. R. (1977). Attributing the causes of group performance: Effects of performance quality, task importance, and future testing. *Journal of Personality, 45,* 220–236.

Goncalo, J. A., & Duguid, M. M. (2008). Hidden consequences of the group-serving bias: Causal attributions and the quality of group decision making. *Organizational Behavior and Human Decision Processes, 107,* 219–233.

Greitemeyer, T., & Weiner, B. (2008). Asymmetrical effects of reward and punishment on attributions of morality. *Journal of Social Psychology, 148,* 407–420.

Harvey, P., & Martinko, M. J. (2009). An empirical examination of the role of attributions in psychological entitlement and its outcomes. *Journal of Organizational Behavior, 30,* 459–476.

Hegarty, P., & Golden, A. M. (2008). Attributional beliefs about the controllability of stigmatized traits: Antecedents or justifications of prejudice? *Journal of Applied Social Psychology, 38,* 1023–1044.

Heider, F. (1958). *The psychology of interpersonal relationships.* Hoboken, NJ: Wiley.

Jeong, S.-H. (2009). Public's responses to an oil spill accident: A test of the attribution theory and situational crisis communication theory. *Public Relations Review, 35,* 307–309.

Johns, G. (1999). A multi-level theory of self-serving behavior in and by organizations. In R. I. Sutton & B. M. Staw (Eds.), *Research in organizational behavior* (Vol. 21, pp. 1–38). Greenwich, CT: JAI Press.

Jones, E. E. (1979). The rocky road from acts to dispositions. *American Psychology, 34,* 107–117.

Jones, E. E., & Harris, V. A. (1967). The attribution of attitudes. *Journal of Experimental Social Psychology, 3,* 1–24.

Jones, E. E., & Nisbett, R. E. (1971). *The actor and the observer: Divergent perceptions of the causes of behavior.* New York: General Learning Press.

Kelley, H. H. (1967). Attribution theory in social psychology. In D. Levine (Ed.), *Nebraska symposium on motivation* (Vol. 15, pp. 192–238). Lincoln: University of Nebraska Press.

Kelley, H. H. (1973, February). The processes of causal attribution. *American Psychologist, 28,* 107–128.

Lam, W., Huang, X., & Snape, E. (2007). Feedback-seeking behavior and leader-member exchange: Do supervisor-attributed motives matter? *Academy of Management Journal, 50,* 348–363.

Martinko, M. J., Harvey, P., & Dasborough, M. T. (2011). Attribution theory in the organizational sciences: A case of unrealized potential. *Journal of Organizational Behavior, 32,* 144–149.

Martinko, M. J., Harvey, P., & Douglas, S. C. (2007). The role, function, and contribution of attribution theory to leadership: A review. *Leadership Quarterly, 18,* 561–585.

Miller, D. T., & Ross, M. (1975). Self-serving bias in attribution of causality: Fact or fiction? *Psychological Bulletin, 82,* 213–225.

Orvis, B. R., Cunningham, J. D., & Kelley, H. H. (1975). A closer examination of causal inference: The roles of consensus, distinctiveness, and consistency information. *Journal of Personality and Social Psychology, 32,* 605–616.

Riess, M., Rosenfeld, P., Melburg, P., & Tedeschi, J. T. (1981). Self-serving attributions: Biased private perceptions and distorted public perceptions. *Journal of Personality and Social Psychology, 41,* 224–231.

Ross, L. (1977). The intuitive psychologist and his shortcomings: Distortions in the attribution process. In L. Berkowitz (Ed.), *Advances in experimental social psychology* (Vol. 10, pp. 173–240). New York: Academic Press.

Rotter, J. B. (1966). Generalized expectancies for internal versus external control of reinforcement. *Psychological Monographs, 80,* 1–28.

Ryan, W. (1976). *Blaming the victim.* New York: Vintage Books.

Salancik, G. R., & Meindl, J. R. (1984). Corporate attributions as strategic illusions of management control. *Administrative Science Quarterly, 29,* 238–254.

Sjovall, A. M., & Talk, A. C. (2004). From actions to impressions: Cognitive attribution theory and the formation of corporate reputation. *Corporate Reputation Review, 7,* 269–281.

Staw, B. M., McKechnie, P. I., & Puffer, S. M. (1983). The justification of organizational performance. *Administrative Science Quarterly, 28,* 582–600.

Tessarolo, I. F., Pagliarussi, M. S., & Mattos da Luz, A. T. (2010). The justification of organizational performance in annual report narratives. *Brazilian Administration Review, 7,* 198–212.

Truchot, D., Maure, G., & Patte, S. (2003). Do attributions change over time when the actor's behavior is hedonically relevant to the perceiver? *Journal of Social Psychology, 143,* 202–208.

Weiner, B. (Ed.). (1974). *Cognitive views of human motivation.* New York: Academic Press.

Weiner, B. (1985). An attributional theory of achievement motivation and emotion. *Psychological Review, 92,* 548–573.

Weiner, B. (1986). *An attributional theory of motivation and emotion.* New York: Springer.

Weiner, B. (2000). Intrapersonal and interpersonal theories of motivation from an attributional perspective. *Educational Psychology Review, 12,* 1–14.

Weiner, B. (2010). The development of an attribution-based theory of motivation: A history of ideas. *Educational Psychologist, 45,* 28–36.

Weiner, B., Frieze, I. H., Kukla, A., Reed, L., Rest, S., & Rosenbaum, R. M. (1971). *Perceiving the causes of success and failure.* Morristown, NJ: General Learning Press.

Wong, P. T. P., & Weiner, B. (1981). When people ask "why" questions, and the heuristics of attributional search. *Journal of Personality and Social Psychology, 40,* 650–663.

7: Balance Theory

Burdick, H. A., & Burnes, A. J. (1958). A test of "strain toward symmetry" theories. *Journal of Abnormal and Social Psychology, 57,* 367–370.

Cacioppo, J. T., & Petty, R. E. (1981). Effects of extent of thought on the pleasantness ratings of *p-o-x* triads: Evidence for three judgmental tendencies in the evaluating of social situations. *Journal of Personality and Social Psychology, 40,* 1000–1009.

Cartwright, D., & Harary, F. (1956). Structural balance: A generalization of Heider's theory. *Psychological Review, 63,* 277–293.

Chaiken, S., & Eagly, A. H. (1983). Communication modality as a determinant of persuasion: The role of communicator salience. *Journal of Personality and Social Psychology, 45,* 241–256.

Festinger, L. (1957). *A theory of cognitive dissonance.* Evanston, IL: Row, Peterson.

Festinger, L., & Hutte, H. A. (1954). An experimental investigation of the effect of unstable interpersonal relations in a group. *Journal of Abnormal Psychology*, *49*, 513–522.

Fournier, S. (1998). Consumers and their brands: Developing relationship theory in consumer research. *Journal of Consumer Research*, *24*, 343–373.

Heider, F. (1946). Attitudes and cognitive organization. *Journal of Psychology*, *21*, 107–112.

Heider, F. (1958). *The psychology of interpersonal relations*. Hoboken, NJ: Wiley.

Homburg, C., & Stock, R. M. (2005, May). Exploring the conditions under which salesperson work satisfaction can lead to customer satisfaction. *Psychology & Marketing*, *22*, 393–420.

Hovland, C. I., Janis, I. L., & Kelley, H. H. (1953). *Communication and persuasion*. New Haven, CT: Yale University Press.

Insko, C. A., & Adewole, A. (1979). The role of assumed reciprocation of sentiment and assumed similarity in the production of attraction and agreement effects in *p-o-x* triads. *Journal of Personality and Social Psychology*, *37*, 790–808.

Insko, C. A., Sedlak, A. J., & Lipsitz, A. (1982). A two-valued logic or two-valued balance resolution of the challenge of agreement and attraction effects in *p-o-x* triads, and a theoretical perspective on conformity and hedonism. *European Journal of Social Psychology*, *12*, 143–167.

Jordan, N. (1953). Behavioral forces that are a function of attitude and cognitive organization. *Human Relations*, *6*, 273–287.

Jordan, N. (1963, Spring). Cognitive balance, cognitive organization, and attitude change: A critique. *Public Opinion Quarterly*, *27*, 123–132.

Newcomb, T. M. (1953). An approach to the study of communicative acts. *Psychological Review*, *60*, 393–404.

Newcomb, T. M. (1968). Interpersonal balance. In R. P. Abelson, W. J. Aronson, T. M. McGuire, T. M. Newcomb, M. J. Rosenberg, & P. H. Tannenbaum (Eds.), *Theories of cognitive consistency: A source book* (pp. 28–51). Chicago: Rand McNally.

Osgood, C. E., & Tannenbaum, P. H. (1955). The principle of congruity in the prediction of attitude change. *Psychological Review*, *62*, 42–55.

Peterson, R. T. (2006). Improving relationships with small business buyers: Potential contributions of balance theory. *Journal of Marketing Channels*, *13*, 63–77.

Sampson, E. E., & Insko, C. A. (1964). Cognitive consistency and performance in the autokinetic situation. *Journal of Abnormal and Social Psychology*, *2*, 184–192.

Taylor, H. F. (1967). Balance and change in two-person groups. *Sociometry*, *30*, 262–279.

Treadway, D. C., Ferris, G. R., Duke, A. B., Adams, G. L., & Thatcher, J. B. (2007). The moderating role of subordinate political skill on supervisors' impressions of subordinate ingratiation and ratings of subordinate interpersonal facilitation. *Journal of Applied Psychology, 92,* 848–855.

Tsai, J. L., & Levenson, R. W. (1997). Cultural influences of emotional responding: Chinese American and European American dating couples during interpersonal conflict. *Journal of Cross-Cultural Psychology, 28,* 600–625.

Zajonc, R. B. (1960, Summer). The concepts of balance, congruity, and dissonance. *Public Opinion Quarterly, 24*(2, Special Issue: Attitude Change), 280–296.

Zajonc, R. B. (1968a, June). Attitudinal effects of mere exposure. *Journal of Personality and Social Psychology, 9*(2, Part 2), 1–27.

Zajonc, R. B. (1968b). Cognitive theories in social psychology. In G. Lindzey & E. Aronson (Eds.), *The handbook of social psychology* (Vol. 1, 2nd ed., pp. 320–411). Reading, MA: Addison-Wesley.

8: Control Theory

Cannon, W. B. (1929). Organization for physiological homeostasis. *Physiological Review, 9,* 399–431.

Carver, C. S., & Scheier, M. F. (1981). *Attention and self-regulation: A control theory approach to human behavior.* New York: Springer.

Carver, C. S., & Scheier, M. F. (1982). Control theory: A useful conceptual framework for personality—social, clinical, and health psychology. *Psychological Bulletin, 92,* 111–135.

Fellenz, M. R. (1997). *Control theory in organizational behavior: Review, critique, and prospects.* Unpublished manuscript, Trinity College, Dublin.

Klein, H. J. (1989). An integrated control theory model of work motivation. *Academy of Management Review, 14,* 150–172.

Locke, E. A. (1991). Goal theory vs. control theory: Contrasting approaches to understanding work motivation. *Motivation and Emotion, 15,* 9–28.

Powers, W. T. (1973). *Behavior: The control of perception.* Chicago: Aldine.

Wiener, N. (1948). *Cybernetics: Control and communication in the animal and the machine.* Cambridge, MA: MIT Press.

9: Diffusion of Innovations Theory

Bass, F. M. (1969). A new product growth model for consumer durables. *Management Science, 15,* 215–227.

Coleman, J. S. (1966). *Medical innovation: A diffusion study.* New York: Bobbs-Merrill.

Goss, K. R. (1979, Winter). Consequences of diffusion of innovations. *Rural Sociology, 44,* 754–772.

Gouldner, A. W. (1957). Cosmopolitans and locals: Toward an analysis of latent social roles. *Administrative Science Quarterly, 2,* 281–306.

Hassinger, E. (1959, March). Stages in the adoption process. *Rural Sociology, 24,* 52–53.

Mahler, A., & Rogers, E. M. (1999). The diffusion of interactive communication innovations and the critical mass: The adoption of telecommunications services by German banks. *Telecommunications Policy, 23,* 719–740.

March, J. G. (1981). Footnotes to organizational change. *Administrative Science Quarterly, 26,* 563–577.

Merton, R. K. (1957). *Social theory and social structure.* New York: Free Press.

Peres, R., Muller, E., & Mahajan, V. (2010). Innovation diffusion and new product growth models: A critical review and research directions. *International Journal of Research in Marketing, 27,* 91–106.

Robertson, T. S., & Wind, Y. (1983). Organizational cosmopolitanism and innovativeness. *Academy of Management Journal, 26,* 332–338.

Rogers, E. M. (1962). *Diffusion of innovations.* New York: Free Press.

Rogers, E. M. (1983). *Diffusion of innovations* (3rd ed.). New York: Free Press.

Rogers, E. M. (2002). Diffusion of preventive innovations. *Addictive Behaviors, 27,* 989–993.

Rogers, E. M. (2004). A prospective and retrospective look at the diffusion model. *Journal of Health Communication, 9,* 13–19.

Rogers, E. M., & Kincaid, D. L. (1981). *Communication networks: Toward a new paradigm for research.* New York: Free Press.

10: Dynamic Capabilities Theory

Arend, R. J., & Bromiley, P. (2009). Assessing the dynamic capabilities view: Spare change, everyone? *Strategic Organization, 7,* 75–90.

Argote, L. (1999). *Organizational learning: Creating, retaining, and transferring knowledge.* Boston: Kluwer Academic.

Collins, J. C. (2001). *Good to great: Why some companies make the leap and others don't.* New York: Harper Business.

Collis, D. J. (1994, Winter). Research note: How valuable are organizational capabilities? *Strategic Management Journal, 15,* 143–152.

Di Stefano, G., Peteraf, M., & Verona, G. (2010). Dynamic capabilities deconstructed: A bibliographic investigation into the origins, development, and future directions of the research domain. *Industrial and Corporate Change, 19,* 1187–1204.

Dunning, J. H., & Lundan, S. M. (2010). The institutional origins of dynamic capabilities in multinational enterprises. *Industrial and Corporate Change, 19,* 1225–1246.

Eisenhardt, K. M., & Martin, J. A. (2000). Dynamic capabilities: What are they? *Strategic Management Journal, 21,* 1105–1121.

Ettlie, J., & Pavlou, P. A. (2006). Technology-based new product development partnerships. *Decision Sciences, 37,* 117–148.

Galunic, D. C., & Eisenhardt, K. M. (2001). Architectural innovation and modular corporate forms. *Academy of Management Journal, 44,* 1229–1249.

Helfat, C. E., Finkelstein, S., Mitchell, W., Peteraf, M., Singh, H., Teece, D., & Winter, S. G. (Eds.). (2007). *Dynamic capabilities: Understanding strategic change in organizations.* Oxford: Blackwell.

Helfat, C. E., & Peteraf, M. A. (2009). Understanding dynamic capabilities: Progress along a developmental path. *Strategic Organization, 7,* 91–102.

Henderson, R., & Cockburn, I. (1994, Winter). Measuring competence? Exploring firm effects in pharmaceutical research. *Strategic Management Journal, 15,* 63–84.

Macher, J. T., & Mowery, D. C. (2009). Measuring dynamic capabilities: Practices and performance in semiconductor manufacturing. *British Journal of Management, 20,* S41–S62.

March, J. G. (1991). Exploration and exploitation in organizational learning. *Organization Science, 2,* 71–87.

Nelson, R. R., & Winter, S. G. (1982). The Schumpeterian trade-off revisited. *American Economic Review, 72,* 114–132.

Parayitam, S., & Guru, K. (2010). Economics of resource based and dynamic capabilities view: A contemporary framework. *Academy of Strategic Management Journal, 9*(1), 83–93.

Pavlou, P. A., & El Sawy, O. A. (2006). From IT to competence to competitive advantage in turbulent environments: The case of new product development. *Information Systems Research, 17,* 198–227.

Pavlou, P. A., & El Sawy, O. A. (2011, February). Understanding the elusive black box of dynamic capabilities. *Decision Sciences, 42,* 239–273.

Penrose, E. T. (1959). *The theory of growth of the firm.* London: Blackwell.

Peters, T. J., & Waterman, R. H. (1982). *In search of excellence: Lessons from America's best-run companies.* New York: Harper & Row.

Ricardo, D. (1817). *The principles of political economy and taxation.* London: Dent.

Rindova, V. P., & Kotha, S. (2001). "Continuous morphing": Competing through dynamic capabilities, form, and function. *Academy of Management Journal, 44,* 1263–1280.

Romme, A.G.L., Zollo, M., & Berends, P. (2010). Dynamic capabilities, deliberate learning and environmental dynamism: A simulation model. *Industrial and Corporate Change, 19,* 1271–1299.

Schumpeter, J. A. (1934). *The theory of economic development: An inquiry into profits, capital, credit, interest, and the business cycle.* Cambridge, MA: Harvard University Press. (Original work published 1911)

Teece, D. (2007). Explicating dynamic capabilities: The nature and microfoundations of (sustainable) enterprise performance. *Strategic Management Journal, 28,* 1319–1350.

Teece, D., Pisano, G., & Shuen, A. (1997). Dynamic capabilities and strategic management. *Strategic Management Journal, 18,* 509–533.

Williamson, O. E. (1999). Strategy research: Governance and competence perspectives. *Strategic Management Journal, 20,* 1087–1110.

Winter, S. G. (2003). Understanding dynamic capabilities. *Strategic Management Journal, 24,* 991–995.

Zahra, S. A., Sapienza, H. J., & Davidsson, P. (2006). Entrepreneurship and dynamic capabilities: A review, model and research agenda. *Journal of Management Studies, 43,* 917–955.

Zollo, M., & Winter, S. G. (2002, May-June). Deliberate learning and the evolution of dynamic capabilities. *Organization Science, 13,* 339–351.

11: Efficient Market Theory

Bachelier, L. (1900). *Théorie de la speculation (Theory of speculation).* Paris, France: Gauthier-Villars.

Ball, R. J., & Brown, P. (1968). An empirical evaluation of accounting income numbers. *Journal of Accounting Research, 6,* 159–178.

Cowles, A., III. (1933). Can stock market forecasters forecast? *Econometrica, 1,* 309–324.

Cross, F. (1973, November-December). The behavior of stock prices on Fridays and Mondays. *Financial Analysts Journal, 29,* 67–69.

De Bondt, W.F.M., & Thaler, R. (1985). Does the stock market overreact? *Journal of Finance, 40,* 793–805.

Dimson, E., & Mussavian, M. (2000). Market efficiency. *Current State of Business Disciplines, 3,* 959–970.

Fama, E. F. (1970). Efficient capital markets: A review of theory and empirical work. *Journal of Finance, 25,* 383–417.

Fama, E. F. (1991). Efficient capital markets: II. *Journal of Finance, 46,* 1575–1617.

Fama, E. F., Fisher, L., Jensen, M. C., & Roll, R. (1969). The adjustment of stock prices to new information. *International Economic Review, 10,* 1–21.

Grinblatt, M., & Keloharju, M. (2001). How distance, language, and culture influence stockholdings and trades. *Journal of Finance, 56,* 1053–1073.

Jensen, M. C. (1978). Some anomalous evidence regarding market efficiency. *Journal of Financial Economics, 6,* 95–101.

Jensen, M. C., & Ruback, R. S. (1983). The market for corporate control: The scientific evidence. *Journal of Financial Economics, 11,* 5–50.

Keim, D., & Stambaugh, R. (1984). A further investigation of the weekend effect in stock returns. *Journal of Finance, 37,* 883–889.

Klein, A. (1986). The timing and substance of divestiture announcements: Individual, simultaneous, and cumulative effects. *Journal of Finance, 41,* 685–696.

McConnell, J. J., & Muscarella, C. J. (1985). Corporate capital expenditure decisions and the market value of the firm. *Journal of Financial Economics, 14,* 399–422.

Okhuysen, G., & Bonardi, J.-P. (2011). The challenges of building theory by combining lenses. *Academy of Management Review, 36,* 6–11.

Pearson, K. (1905). The problem of the random walk. *Nature, 72,* 342.

Rozeff, M. S., & Kinney, W. R. (1976). Capital market seasonality: The case of stock returns. *Journal of Financial Economics, 3,* 379–402.

Seyhun, N. (1986). Insiders' profits, costs of trading, and market efficiency. *Journal of Financial Economics, 16,* 189–212.

Shiller, R. J. (2003). *The new financial order: Risk in the 21st century.* Princeton, NJ: Princeton University Press.

Shiller, R. J. (2006). Tools for financial innovation: Neoclassical versus behavioral finance. *Financial Review, 41,* 1–8.

Subrahmanyam, A. (2007). Behavioral finance: A review and synthesis. *European Financial Management, 14,* 12–29.

12: Ethical Theory

Ambrose, M. L., & Schminke, M. (1999). Sex differences in business ethics: The importance of perceptions. *Journal of Managerial Issues, 11,* 454–474.

Arnold, D. G., Audi, R., & Zwolinski, M. (2010). Recent work in ethical theory and its implications for business ethics. *Business Ethics Quarterly, 20,* 559–581.

Audi, R. (2004). *The good in the right: A theory of intuition and intrinsic value.* Princeton, NJ: Princeton University Press.

Bentham, J. (1996). *An introduction to the principles of morals and legislation* (J. Burns & H. L. A. Hart, Eds.). New York: Oxford University Press. (Original work published 1789)

Brady, F. N. (1985). A Janus-headed model of ethical theory: Looking two ways at business/society issues. *Academy of Management Review, 10,* 568–576.

Brady, F. N. (1990). *Ethical managing: Rules and results.* New York: Macmillan.

Brady, F. N., & Hart, D. (2007). An exploration into the developmental psychology of ethical theory with implications for business practice and pedagogy. *Journal of Business Ethics, 76,* 397–412.

Brewer, T. (2005, July). Virtues we can share: Friendship and Aristotelian ethical theory. *Ethics, 115,* 721–758.

Broad, C. D. (1959). *Five types of ethical theory.* Paterson, NJ: Littlefield, Adams.

Buckle, S. (2002). Aristotle's republic or, why Aristotle's ethics is not virtue ethics. *Royal Institute of Philosophy, 77,* 565–595.

Crane, A., Gilbert, D. U., Goodpaster, K. E., Miceli, M. P., Moore, G., Reynolds, S. J., Schminke, M., Waddock, S., Weaver, G. R., & Wicks, A. C. (2011, January). Comments on BEQ's twentieth anniversary forum on new directions for business ethics research. *Business Ethics Quarterly, 21,* 157–187.

Derry, R., & Green, R. (1989). Ethical theory in business ethics: A critical assessment. *Journal of Business Ethics, 8,* 521–533.

Fritzsche, D. J., & Becker, H. (1984). Linking management behavior to ethical philosophy—an empirical investigation. *Academy of Management Journal, 27,* 166–175.

Hodgson, B. J. (2001). Michalos and the theory of ethical theory. *Journal of Business Ethics, 29,* 19–23.

Hull, R. T. (1979, March 27). *The varieties of ethical theories.* Presented at the Buffalo Psychiatric Center, Buffalo, New York.

Hume, D. (2000). *A treatise of human nature* (D. F. Norton & M. J. Norton, Eds.). New York: Oxford University Press. (Original work published 1740)

Kant, I. (1993). *Groundwork of the metaphysics of morals* (3rd ed.). (J. W. Ellington, Trans.). Indianapolis, IN: Hackett. (Original work published 1785)

Kelly, E. I. (2005). Ethical disagreements in theory and practice. *Journal of Social Philosophy, 36,* 382–387.

Kohlberg, L. (1984). *The psychology of moral development.* San Francisco: Harper & Row.

Louden, R. B. (1996). Toward a genealogy of "deontology." *Journal of the History of Philosophy, 34,* 571–592.

Mill, J. S. (1998). *Utilitarianism* (R. Crisp, Ed.). Oxford: Oxford University Press. (Original work published 1863)

Moore, A. (2007). Ethical theory, completeness and consistency. *Ethical Theory and Moral Practice, 10,* 297–308.

Place, K. R. (2010). A qualitative examination of public relations practitioner ethical decision making and the deontological theory of ethical issues management. *Journal of Mass Media Ethics, 25,* 226–245.

Rawls, J. (1971). *A theory of justice.* Cambridge, MA: Belknap Press.

Ross, W. D. (1930). *The right and the good.* Oxford: Oxford University Press.

Sandler, R. (2010). Ethical theory and the problem of inconsequentialism: Why environmental ethicists should be virtue-oriented ethicists. *Journal of Agriculture and Environmental Ethics, 23,* 167–183.

Santas, G. (1993). Did Aristotle have a virtue ethics? *Philosophical Inquiry, 15*(3–4), 1–32.

Schminke, M. (1997). Gender differences in ethical frameworks and evaluations of others' choices in ethical dilemmas. *Journal of Business Ethics, 16,* 55–65.

Schminke, M., & Ambrose, M. L. (1997). Asymmetric perceptions of ethical frameworks of men and women in business and nonbusiness settings. *Journal of Business Ethics, 16,* 719–729.

Schminke, M., Ambrose, M. L., & Miles, J. A. (2003). The impact of gender and setting on perceptions of others' ethics. *Sex Roles, 48,* 361–375.

Schminke, M., Ambrose, M. L., & Noel, T. W. (1997). The effects of ethical frameworks on perceptions of organizational justice. *Academy of Management Journal, 40,* 1190–1207.

Sidgwick, H. (1981). *The method of ethics.* Indianapolis, IN: Hackett. (Original work published 1874)

Sim, M. (2010). Rethinking virtue ethics and social justice with Aristotle and Confucius. *Asian Philosophy, 20,* 195–213.

Velasquez, M. G. (1992). *Business ethics: Concepts and cases.* Englewood Cliffs, NJ: Prentice Hall.

13: Field Theory

Back, K. W. (1992). This business of typology. *Journal of Social Issues, 48,* 51–66.

Bourdieu, P. (1985). The genesis of the concepts of habitus and of field. *Sociocriticism, 2,* 11–24.

Bourdieu, P. (1988). *Homo academicus* (P. Collier, Trans.). Stanford, CA: Stanford University Press.

Brunswik, E. (1943). Organismic achievement and environmental probability. *Psychological Review, 50,* 255–272.

Burnes, B. (2004). Kurt Lewin and the planned approach to change: A re-appraisal. *Journal of Management Studies, 41,* 977–1002.

Deutsch, M. (1954). Field theory in social psychology. In G. Lindzey (Ed.), *Handbook of social psychology* (pp. 181–222). Reading, MA: Addison-Wesley.

Diamond, G. A. (1992). Field theory and rational choice: A Lewinian approach to modeling motivation. *Journal of Social Issues, 48,* 79–94.

Einstein, A., & Infeld, L. (1938). *The evolution of physics.* New York: Simon & Schuster.

Gold, M. (1992). Metatheory and field theory in social psychology: Relevance or elegance? *Journal of Social Issues, 48,* 67–78.

Haveman, H. A., Russo, M. V., & Meyer, A. D. (2001). Organizational environments in flux: The impact of regulatory punctuations on organizational domains, CEO succession, and performance. *Organization Science, 12,* 253–273.

Houston, M. B., Bettencourt, L. A., & Wenger, S. (1998, December). The relationship between waiting in a service queue and evaluations of service quality: A field theory perspective. *Psychology & Marketing, 15,* 735–753.

Jones, E. E. (1985). Major developments in social psychology during the past five decades. In G. Lindzey & E. Aronson (Eds.), *Handbook of social psychology* (Vol. 1, 3rd ed., pp. 47–107). New York: Random House.

Lewin, K. (1936). *Principles of topological psychology* (F. Heider & G. M. Heider, Trans.). New York: McGraw-Hill.

Lewin, K. (1943a). Defining the "field at a given time." *Psychological Review, 50,* 292–310.

Lewin, K. (1943b). Psychological ecology. In D. Cartwright (Ed.), *Field theory in social science* (pp. 170–187). London: Social Science Paperbacks.

Lewin, K. (1946). Behavior and development as a function of the total situation. In L. Carmichael (Ed.), *Manual of child psychology* (pp. 791–844). Hoboken, NJ: Wiley.

Lewin, K. (1947). Frontiers in group dynamics. *Human Relations, 1,* 143–153.

Lewin, K. (1951). *Field theory in social science* (D. Cartwright, Ed.). New York: Harper & Brothers.

Martin, J. L. (2003, July). What is field theory? *American Journal of Sociology, 109,* 1–49.

Maxwell, C. (1921). *Matter and motion.* New York: Macmillan.

Meyer, A. D., Gaba, V., & Colwell, K. A. (2005). Organizing far from equilibrium: Nonlinear change in organizational fields. *Organization Science, 16,* 456–473.

Riordan, D. A., & Riordan, M. P. (1993, April). Field theory: An alternative to systems theories in understanding the small family business. *Journal of Small Business Management,* 66–78.

Sauder, M. (2008). Interlopers and field change: The entry of *U.S. News* into the field of legal education. *Administrative Science Quarterly, 53,* 209–234.

Scott, W. R., Ruef, M., Mandel, P. J., & Caronna, C. A. (2000). *Institutional change and healthcare organizations.* Chicago: University of Chicago Press.

Sjovold, E. (2007). Systematizing person-group relations (SPGR): A field theory of social interaction. *Small Group Research, 38,* 615–635.

Thornton, P. H., & Ocasio, W. (1999). Institutional logics and the historical contingency of power in organizations: Executive succession in the higher education publishing industry, 1958–1990. *American Journal of Sociology, 105,* 801–843.

Wheatley, M. J. (2006). *Leadership and the new science: Discovering order in a chaotic world.* San Francisco: Berrett-Koehler.

14: Game Theory

Brandenburger, A., & Stuart, H. (2007). Biform games. *Management Science, 53,* 537–549.

Camerer, C. F. (1991). Does strategy research need game theory? *Strategic Management Journal, 12,* 137–152.

Fisher, L. (2008). *Rock, paper, scissors: Game theory in everyday life.* New York: Basic Books.

Green, K. C. (2002). Forecasting decisions in conflict situations: A comparison of game theory, role-playing, and unaided judgment. *International Journal of Forecasting, 18,* 321–344.

Harsanyi, J. C. (1967). Games with incomplete information played by "Bayesian" players, Part I. The basic model. *Management Science, 14,* 159–182.

Harsanyi, J. C. (1968a). Games with incomplete information played by "Bayesian" players, Part II. Bayesian equilibrium points. *Management Science, 14,* 320–334.

Harsanyi, J. C. (1968b). Games with incomplete information played by "Bayesian" players, Part III. Bayesian equilibrium points. *Management Science, 14,* 486–502.

Herbig, P. A. (1991). Game theory in marketing: Applications, uses and limits. *Journal of Marketing Management, 7,* 285–298.

Madhani, P. M. (2010, October–December). Salesforce compensation: Game theory. *SCMS Journal of Indian Management*, 7(4), 72–82.

Miller, J. D. (2003). *Game theory at work: How to use game theory to outthink and outmaneuver your competition.* Blacklick, OH: McGraw-Hill.

Nash, J. (1951, September). Non-cooperative games. *Annals of Mathematics*, 54, 286–295.

Rasmusen, E. (1989). *Games and information.* Oxford: Blackwell.

Roy, A. (2003). Game theory in strategic analysis: A comparative study of two Indian joint ventures. *Journal of Management Research*, 3, 127–138.

Scharlemann, J. P. W., Eckel, C. C., Kacelnik, A., & Wilson, R. K. (2001). The value of a smile: Game theory with a human face. *Journal of Economic Psychology*, 22, 617–640.

Thomadsen, R., & Bhardwaj, P. (2011, February). Cooperation in games with forgetfulness. *Management Science*, 57, 363–375.

Van Lange, P. A. M., Agnew, C. R., Harinck, F., & Steemers, E. M. (1997). From game theory to real life: How social value orientation affects willingness to sacrifice in ongoing close relationships. *Journal of Personality and Social Psychology*, 73, 1330–1344.

Von Neumann, J., & Morgenstern, O. (1944). *Theory of games and economic behavior.* Princeton, NJ: Princeton University Press.

15: Goal Setting Theory

Cheng, M., Subramanyam, K. R., & Zhang, Y. (2005). Earnings guidance and managerial myopia. Working paper. Los Angeles, CA: University of Southern California.

Earley, P. C. (1985). Influence of information, choice and task complexity upon goal acceptance, performance, and personal goals. *Journal of Applied Psychology*, 70, 481–491.

Galinsky, A. D., Mussweiler, T., & Medvec, V. H. (2002). Disconnecting outcomes and evaluations: The role of negotiator focus. *Journal of Personality and Social Psychology*, 83, 1131–1140.

Hollenbeck, J. R., & Brief, A. P. (1987). The effects of individual differences and goal origin on goal setting and performance. *Organizational Behavior and Human Decision Processes*, 40, 392–414.

Jackson, S. E., & Zedeck, S. (1982). Explaining performance variability: Contributions of goal setting, task characteristics, and evaluative contexts. *Journal of Applied Psychology*, 67, 759–768.

Larrick, R. P., Heath, C., & Wu, G. (2009). Goal-induced risk taking in negotiation and decision making. *Social Cognition*, 27, 342–364.

Latham, G. P., & Locke, E. A. (2006). Enhancing the benefits and overcoming the pitfalls of goal setting. *Organizational Dynamics*, 35, 332–340.

Locke, E. A. (1967). Motivational effects of knowledge of results: Knowledge or goal setting? *Journal of Applied Psychology*, *51*, 324–329.

Locke, E.A. (1968). Toward a theory of task motivation and incentives. *Organizational Behavior and Human Decision Processes*, *3*, 157–189.

Locke, E. A. (1996). Motivation through conscious goal setting. *Applied & Preventative Psychology*, *5*, 117–124.

Locke, E. A., & Latham, G. P. (1990). *A theory of goal setting and task performance*. Englewood Cliffs, NJ: Prentice Hall.

Locke, E. A., & Latham, G. P. (2002, September). Building a practically useful theory of goal setting and task motivation: A 35-year odyssey. *American Psychologist*, *57*, 705–717.

Locke, E. A., & Latham, G. P. (2006). New directions in goal-setting theory. *Current Directions in Psychological Science*, *15*, 265–268.

Locke, E. A., & Latham, G. P. (2009, February). Has goal setting gone wild, or have its attackers abandoned good scholarship? *Academy of Management Perspectives*, *23*(1), 17–23.

Locke, E. A., Latham, G. P., & Erez, M. (1988). The determinants of goal commitment. *Academy of Management Review*, *13*, 23–39.

Locke, E. A., Shaw, K. N., Saari, L. M., & Latham, G. P. (1981, July). Goal setting and task performance: 1969–1980. *Psychological Bulletin*, *90*, 125–152.

Ordoñez, L. D., Schweitzer, M. E., Galinsky, A. D., & Bazerman, M. H. (2009, February). Goals gone wild: The systematic side effects of overprescribing goal setting. *Academy of Management Perspectives*, *23*(1), 6–16.

Mussweiler, T., & Strack, F. (2000). The "relative self": Informational and judgmental consequences of comparative self-evaluation. *Journal of Personality and Social Psychology*, *79*, 23–38.

Shah, J. Y., Friedman, R., & Kruglanski, A. W. (2002). Forgetting all else: On the antecedents and consequences of goal shielding. *Journal of Personality and Social Psychology*, *83*, 1261–1280.

Staw, B. M., & Boettger, R. D. (1990). Task revision: A neglected form of work performance. *Academy of Management Journal*, *33*, 534–559.

Wood, R. E., Mento, A. J., & Locke, E. A. (1987). Task complexity as a moderator of goal effects: A meta-analysis. *Journal of Applied Psychology*, *72*, 416–425.

16: Image Theory

Beach, L. R., & Mitchell, T. R. (1987). Image theory: Principles, goals, and plans in decision making. *Acta Psychologica*, *66*, 201–220.

Beach, L. R., & Mitchell, T. R. (1990). A contingency model for the selection of decision strategies. *Academy of Management Review, 3,* 439–449.

Beach, L. R., & Mitchell, T. R. (2005). Image theory. In K. G. Smith & M. A. Hitt (Eds.), *Great minds in management* (pp. 36–54). Oxford: Oxford University Press.

Bissell, B. L., & Beach, L. R. (1996). Supervision and job satisfaction. In L. R. Beach (Ed.), *Decision making in the workplace: A unified perspective* (pp. 63–72). Mahwah, NJ: Erlbaum.

Dunegan, K. J. (1995). Image theory: Testing the role of image compatibility in progress decisions. *Organizational Behavior and Human Decision Processes, 62,* 79–86.

Dunegan, K. J. (2003, Winter). Leader-image compatibility: An image theory view of leadership. *Journal of Business and Management, 9,* 61–77.

Gilliland, S. W., Benson, L., III, & Schepers, D. H. (1998). A rejection threshold in justice evaluations: Effects on judgment and decision-making. *Organizational Behavior and Human Decision Processes, 76,* 113–131.

Mady, S., & Gopinath, M. (2008). Consumer ethical identity: The role of personal values in the service encounter. *Advances in Consumer Research, 8,* 374–375.

Mitchell, T. R., & Beach, L. R. (1990). "... Do I love thee? Let me count ..." Toward an understanding of intuitive and automatic decision making. *Organizational Behavior and Human Decision Processes, 47,* 1–20.

Richmond, S. M., Bissell, B. L., & Beach, L. R. (1998). Image theory's compatibility test and evaluations of the status quo. *Organizational Behavior and Human Decision Processes, 73,* 39–53.

17: Institutional Theory

Aldrich, H., & Fiol, M. (1994). Fools rush in? The institutional context of industry creation. *Academy of Management Review, 19,* 645–670.

Battilana, J., Leca, B., & Boxenbaum, E. (2009). How actors change institutions: Towards a theory of institutional entrepreneurship. *Academy of Management Annals, 3,* 65–107.

Berger, P. L., & Luckmann, T. (1967). *The social construction of reality.* New York: Doubleday.

Dacin, M. T., Goodstein, J., & Scott, W. R. (2002). Institutional theory and institutional change. *Academy of Management Journal, 45,* 45–57.

Deephouse, D. L. (1999). To be different, or to be the same? It's a question (and theory) of strategic balance. *Strategic Management Journal*, *20*, 147–166.

DiMaggio, P. (1988). Interest and agency in institutional theory. In L. Zucker (Ed.), *Institutional patterns and culture* (pp. 3–32). Cambridge, MA: Ballinger.

DiMaggio, P., & Powell, W. W. (1983). The iron cage revisited: Institutional isomorphism and collective rationality in organizational fields. *American Sociological Review*, *48*, 147–160.

Garud, R., Hardy, C., & Maguire, S. (2007). Institutional entrepreneurship as embedded agency: An introduction to the special issue. *Organization Studies*, *28*, 957–969.

Greenwood, R., & Hinings, C. R. (1996). Understanding radical organizational change: Bringing together the old and the new institutionalism. *Academy of Management Review*, *21*, 1022–1054.

Hardy, C., Lawrence, T. B., & Grant, D. (2005). Discourse and collaboration: The role of conversations and collective identity. *Academy of Management Review*, *30*, 58–77.

Hawley, A. (1968). Human ecology. In D. L. Sills (Ed.), *International encyclopedia of the social sciences* (pp. 328–337). New York: Macmillan.

Heugens, P.P.M.A.R., & Lander, M. W. (2009). Structure! Agency! (and other quarrels): A meta-analysis of institutional theories of organizations. *Academy of Management Journal*, *52*, 61–85.

Koelble, T. A. (1995). The new institutionalism in political science and sociology. *Comparative Politics*, *27*, 231–243.

Kostova, T., Roth, K., & Dacin, M. T. (2008). Institutional theory in the study of multinational corporations: A critique and new directions. *Academy of Management Review*, *33*, 994–1006.

Kraatz, M., & Zajac, E. (1996). Exploring the limits of new institutionalism: The causes and consequences of illegitimate organizational change. *American Sociological Review*, *61*, 812–836.

Landman, J. (1993). *Regret: The persistence of the possible*. New York: Oxford University Press.

Lincoln, J. R. (1995, March). [Review of the book *The new institutionalism in organizational research.*] *Social Forces*, *73*, 1147–1148.

Oliver, C. (1991). Strategic responses to institutional processes. *Academy of Management Review*, *16*, 145–179.

Oliver, C. (1997). Sustainable competitive advantage: Combining institutional and resource-based views. *Strategic Management Journal*, *18*, 697–713.

Peters, B. G. (2000). Institutional theory: Problems and prospects. *69 Political Science Series*. Vienna, Austria: Institute for Advanced Studies.

Phillips, D. J., & Zuckerman, E. (2001). Middle-status conformity: Theoretical restatement and empirical demonstration in two markets. *American Journal of Sociology, 107,* 379–429.

Phillips, N., Lawrence, T. B., & Hardy, C. (2004). Discourse and institutions. *Academy of Management Review, 29,* 635–652.

Scott, W. R. (1995). *Institutions and organizations.* Thousand Oaks, CA: Sage.

Selznick, P. (1957). *Leadership in administration.* New York: McGraw-Hill.

Selznick, P. (1996). Institutionalism "old" and "new." *Administrative Science Quarterly, 41,* 270–277.

Sonpar, K., Pazzaglia, F., & Kornijenko, J. (2009). The paradox and constraints of legitimacy. *Journal of Business Ethics, 95,* 1–21.

Suddaby, R. (2010). Challenges for institutional theory. *Journal of Management Inquiry, 19,* 14–20.

Yang, Y., & Konrad, A. M. (2010). Understanding diversity management practices: Implications of institutional theory and resource-based theory. *Group & Organization Management, 36,* 6–38.

18: Knowledge-Based Theory

Adler, P. S. (2001). Market, hierarchy, and trust: The knowledge economy and the future of capitalism. *Organization Science, 12,* 215–234.

Ancori, B., Bureth, A., & Cohendet, P. (2000). The economics of knowledge: The debate about codification and tacit knowledge. *Industrial and Corporate Change, 9,* 255–287.

Balconi, M., Pozzali, A., & Viale, R. (2007). The "codification debate" revisited: A conceptual framework to analyze the role of tacit knowledge in economies. *Industrial and Corporate Change, 16,* 823–849.

Brown, J. S., & Duguid, P. (2001). Knowledge and organization: A social-practice perspective. *Organization Science, 12,* 198–213.

Cabrita, M. R., & Bontis, N. (2008). Intellectual capital and business performance in the Portuguese banking industry. *International Journal of Technology Management, 43,* 212–237.

Conner, K. R. (1991). A historical comparison of resource-based theory and five schools of thought within industrial organization economics: Do we have a new theory of the firm? *Journal of Management, 17,* 121–154.

Conner, K. R., & Prahalad, C. K. (1996). A resource-based theory of the firm: Knowledge versus opportunism. *Organization Science, 7,* 477–501.

Dean, A., & Kretschmer, M. (2007). Can ideas be capital? Factors of production in the postindustrial economy: A review and critique. *Academy of Management Review, 32,* 573–594.

Felin, T., & Hesterly, W. S. (2007). The knowledge-based view, nested heterogeneity, and new value creation: Philosophical considerations on the locus of knowledge. *Academy of Management Review, 32,* 195–218.

Foss, N. J. (1996). Knowledge-based approaches to the theory of the firm: Some critical comments. *Organization Science, 7,* 470–476.

Foss, N. J. (2003). Bounded rationality and tacit knowledge in the organizational capabilities approach: An assessment and re-evaluation. *Industrial and Corporate Change, 12,* 185–201.

Gorman, M. E. (2002). Types of knowledge and their roles in technology transfer. *Journal of Technology Transfer, 27,* 219–231.

Grant, R. M. (1996a). Prospering in dynamically competitive environments: Organizational capability as knowledge integration. *Strategic Management Journal, 7,* 375–387.

Grant, R. M. (1996b, Winter). Toward a knowledge-based theory of the firm. *Strategic Management Journal, 17*(Special Issue), 109–122.

Grant, R. M., & Baden-Fuller, C. (1995). A knowledge-based theory of inter-firm collaboration. *Academy of Management Best Papers Proceedings* (pp. 17–21). New York: Academy of Management.

Hakanson, L. (2007). Creating knowledge: The power and logic of articulation. *Industrial and Corporate Change, 16,* 51–88.

Hakanson, L. (2010). The firm as an epistemic community: The knowledge-based view revisited. *Industrial and Corporate Change, 19,* 1801–1828.

Kogut, B. (2000). The network as knowledge: Generative rules and the emergence of structure. *Strategic Management Journal, 21,* 405–425.

Kogut, B., & Zander, U. (1992). Knowledge of the firm, combinative capabilities, and the replication of technology. *Organization Science, 3,* 384–397.

Kogut, B., & Zander, U. (1993). Knowledge of the firm and the evolutionary theory of the multinational corporation. *Journal of International Business Studies, 24,* 625–645.

Kogut, B., & Zander, U. (1996). What firms do? Coordination, identity and learning. *Organization Science, 7,* 502–518.

Liebeskind, J. P. (1996). Knowledge, strategy, and the theory of the firm. *Strategic Management Journal, 17,* 93–107.

Madhok, A. (1996). The organization of economic activity: Transaction costs, firm capabilities and the nature of governance. *Organization Science, 7,* 577–590.

Martin-de-Castro, G., Delgado-Verde, M., Lopez-Saez, P., & Navas-Lopez, J. E. (2011). Towards an intellectual capital view of the firm: Origins and nature. *Journal of Business Ethics, 98*, 649–662.

Nahapiet, J., & Ghoshal, S. (1998). Social capital, intellectual capital and the organizational advantage. *Academy of Management Review, 23*, 242–266.

Nelson, R. R., & Winter, S. G. (1982). *An evolutionary theory of economic change.* Cambridge, MA: Harvard University Press.

Nickerson, J. A., & Zenger, T. R. (2004). A knowledge-based theory of the firm—the problem-solving perspective. *Organization Science, 15*, 617–632.

Nonaka, I. (1994). A dynamic theory of organizational knowledge creation. *Organization Science, 5*, 14–37.

Phelan, S. E., & Lewin, P. L. (2000). Arriving at a strategic theory of the firm. *International Journal of Management Reviews, 2*, 305–323.

Polanyi, M. (1966). *The tacit dimension.* New York: Doubleday.

Reed, R., & DeFillipi, R. J. (1990). Causal ambiguity, barriers to imitation, and sustainable competitive advantage. *Academy of Management Review, 15*, 88–102.

Schulz, M., & Jobe, A. (2001). Codification and tacitness as knowledge management strategies: An empirical exploration. *Journal of High Technology Management Research, 12*, 139–165.

Simon, H. A. (1991). Bounded rationality and organizational learning. *Organization Science, 2*, 125–134.

Soo, C. T., Devinney, D., Midgley, D., & Deering, A. (2002). Knowledge management: Philosophy, processes and pitfalls. *California Management Review, 44*, 129–150.

Tsoukas, R. (1996, Winter). The firm as a distributed knowledge system: A constructionist approach. *Strategic Management Journal, 17*(Special Issue), 11–25.

Williamson, O. E. (1999). Strategy research: Competence and governance perspectives. *Strategic Management Journal, 20*, 1087–1108.

Winkin, Y. (1996). *Anthropologie de la communication. De la theorie au terrain (Anthropology of communication. In the theory of the field.)* Brussells, Belgium: De Boeck Université.

19: Media Richness Theory

Bodensteiner, W. D. (1970). *Information channel utilization under varying research and development project conditions: An aspect of interorganizational communication channel usages.* Unpublished PhD dissertation, University of Texas, Austin.

Carlson, J. R., & Zmud, R. W. (1999). Channel expansion theory and the experiential nature of media richness perceptions. *Academy of Management Journal, 42,* 153–170.

Daft, R. L., & Lengel, R. H. (1984). Information richness: A new approach to managerial behavior and organization design. In B. M. Staw & L. L. Cummings (Eds.), *Research in organizational behavior* (Vol. 6, pp. 191–233). Greenwich, CT: JAI Press.

Daft, R. L., & Lengel, R. H. (1986). Organizational information requirements, media richness and structural design. *Management Science, 32,* 554–571.

Daft, R. L., Lengel, R. H., & Trevino, L. K. (1987). Message equivocality, media selection, and manager performance: Implications for information systems. *MIS Quarterly, 11,* 355–366.

Daft, R. L., & Macintosh, N. B. (1981, June). A tentative exploration into the amount and equivocality of information processing in organizational work units. *Administrative Science Quarterly, 26,* 207–224.

Davis, F., Bagozzi, R., & Warshaw, P. (1989). User acceptance of computer technology: A comparison of two theoretical models. *Management Science, 35,* 982–1003.

Fulk, J. (1983). Social construction of communication technology. *Academy of Management Journal, 36,* 921–950.

Fulk, J., Steinfeld, C. W., Schmitz, J., & Power, J. G. (1987). A social information processing model of media use in organizations. *Communication Research, 14,* 529–552.

Habermas, J. (1979). *Communication and the evolution of society.* London: Heinemann.

Habermas, J. (1984). *The theory of communicative action: Vol. 1. Reason and rationalization of society.* Boston: Beacon Press.

Habermas, J. (1987). *The theory of communicative action: Vol. 2. Lifeworld and social system.* Boston: Beacon Press.

Kock, N. (2005, June). Media richness or media naturalness? The evolution of our biological communication apparatus and its influence on our behavior toward e-communication tools. *IEEE Transactions on Professional Communication, 48,* 117–130.

Kock, N. (2009, June). Information systems theorizing based on evolutionary psychology: An interdisciplinary review and theory integration framework. *MIS Quarterly, 33,* 395–418.

Lan, Y.-F., & Sie, Y.-S. (2010). Using RSS to support mobile learning based on media richness theory. *Computers and Education, 55,* 723–732.

Lengel, R. H., & Daft, R. L. (1988). The selection of communication media as an executive skill. *Academy of Management Executive, 2,* 225–232.

Markus, M. L. (1987). Toward a "critical mass" theory of interactive media. *Communication Research, 14*, 491–511.

Markus, M. L. (1994). Electronic mail as the medium of managerial choice. *Organization Science, 5*, 502–511.

Mohan, K., Kumar, N., & Benbunan-Fich, R. (2009, March). Examining communication media selection and information processing in software development traceability: An empirical investigation. *IEEE Transactions on Professional Communication, 52*, 17–39.

Ngwenyama, O. K., & Lee, A. S. (1997). Communication richness in electronic mail: Critical social theory and the contextuality of meaning. *MIS Quarterly, 21*, 145–167.

Rice, R. (1983). Media appropriateness: Using social presence theory to compare traditional and new organizational media. *Human Communication Research, 19*, 451–484.

Robert, L. P., & Dennis, A. R. (2005). Paradox of richness: A cognitive model of media choice. *IEEE Transactions on Professional Communication, 48*, 10–21.

Russ, G. S., Daft, R. L., & Lengel, R. H. (1990, November). Media selection and managerial characteristics in organizational communications. *Management Communication Quarterly, 4*, 151–175.

Schmitz, J., & Fulk, J. (1991). Organizational colleagues, media richness, and electronic mail. *Communication Research, 18*, 487–523.

Shannon, C., & Weaver, W. (1949). *The mathematical theory of communication.* Urbana: University of Illinois Press.

Suh, K. S. (1999). Impact of communication medium on task performance and satisfaction: An examination of media richness theory. *Information and Management, 35*, 295–312.

Weick, K. E. (1979). *The social psychology of organizations* (2nd ed.). Reading, MA: Addison-Wesley.

20: Mental Models Theory

Axelrod, R. (Ed.). (1976). *The structure of decision: The cognitive maps of political elites.* Princeton, NJ: Princeton University Press.

Bara, B. G., Bucciarelli, M., & Lombardo, V. (2001). Model theory of deduction: A unified computational approach. *Cognitive Science, 25*, 839–901.

Cockburn, I. M., Henderson, R. M., & Stern, S. (2000, October-November). Untangling the origins of competitive advantage. *Strategic Management Journal, 21*(Special Issue), 1123–1145.

Craik, K. (1943). *The nature of explanation.* Cambridge, MA: Cambridge University Press.

Cyert, R. M., & March, J. G. (1992). *A behavioral theory of the firm* (2nd ed.). Malden, MA: Blackwell.

Dean, J. W., & Sharfman, M. P. (1993). Procedural rationality in the strategic decision making process. *Journal of Management Studies, 30,* 587–610.

Doyle, J. K., & Ford, D. N. (1998, Spring). Mental models concepts for system dynamics research. *System Dynamics Review, 14,* 3–29.

Doyle, J. K., & Ford, D. N. (1999, Winter). Mental models concepts revisited: Some clarifications and a reply to Lane. *Systems Dynamics Review, 15,* 411–415.

Dutton, J. E. (1993). Interpretations on automatic: A different view of strategic issue diagnosis. *Journal of Management Studies, 30,* 339–357.

Eden, C., Jones, S., & Sims, D. (1979). *Thinking in organizations.* London: Macmillan.

Fetzer, J. H. (1993). The argument for mental models is unsound. *Behavioral and Brain Sciences, 16,* 347–348.

Fetzer, J. H. (1999). Deduction and mental models. *Minds and Machines, 9,* 105–110.

Friedman, L. A., & Neumann, B. R. (1980). The effects of opportunity costs on project investment decisions: A replication and extension. *Journal of Accounting Research, 18,* 407–419.

Gary, M. S., & Wood, R. E. (2011). Mental models, decision rules, and performance heterogeneity. *Strategic Management Journal, 32,* 569–594.

Gentner, D., & Stevens, A. L. (Eds.). (1983). *Mental models.* Mahwah, NJ: Erlbaum.

Haley, U. C. V., & Stumph, S. A. (1989). Cognitive traits in strategic management decision-making: Linking theories of personalities and cognitions. *Journal of Management Studies, 26,* 477–497.

Johnson-Laird, P. N. (1983). *Mental models.* Cambridge, MA: Harvard University Press.

Johnson-Laird, P. N. (2006). Models and heterogeneous reasoning. *Journal of Experimental and Theoretical Artificial Intelligence, 18,* 121–148.

Kiesler, S., & Sproull, L. (1982). Managerial response to changing environments: Perspectives on problem sensing from social cognition. *Administrative Science Quarterly, 27,* 548–570.

March, J. G., & Simon, H. A. (1958). *Organizations.* Hoboken, NJ: Wiley.

Mathieu, J., Maynard, M. T., Rapp, T., & Gilson, L. (2008). Team effectiveness 1997–2007: A review of recent advances and a glimpse into the future. *Journal of Management, 34,* 410–476.

Mohammed, S., Ferzandi, L., & Hamilton, K. (2010). Metaphor no more: A 15-year review of the team mental model construct. *Journal of Management*, 36, 876–910.

Peirce, C. S. (1931–1958). *Collected papers of Charles Sanders Peirce* (Vols. 1–9). (C. Hartshorne, P. Weiss, & A. Burks, Eds.). Cambridge, MA: Harvard University Press.

Tolman, E. C. (1948). Cognitive maps in rats and men. *Psychological Review*, 55, 189–208.

Turner, J., & Belanger, F. (1996). Escaping from Babel: Improving the terminology of mental models in the literature of human-computer interaction. *Canadian Journal of Information and Library Science*, 21, 35–58.

Von Hecker, U. (2004, Winter). Disambiguating a mental model: Influence of social context. *Psychological Record*, 54, 27–43.

Westbrook, L. (2006). Mental models: A theoretical overview and preliminary study. *Journal of Information Science*, 32, 563–579.

Zhang, Y. (2010). Dimensions and elements of people's mental models of an information-rich web space. *Journal of the American Society for Information Science and Technology*, 61, 2206–2218.

21: Organizational Ecology Theory

Aldrich, H., & Auster, E. R. (1986). Even dwarfs started small: Liabilities of age and size and their strategic implications. In L. L. Cummings & B. M. Staw (Eds.), *Research in organizational behavior* (Vol. 8, pp. 165–198). Greenwich, CT: JAI Press.

Aldrich, H., & Ruef, M. (2006). *Organizations evolving* (2nd ed.). Thousand Oaks, CA: Sage.

Barron, D. N., West, E., & Hannan, M. T. (1994). A time to grow and a time to die: Growth and mortality of credit unions in New York City: 1914–1990. *American Journal of Sociology*, 100, 381–421.

Basil, D., Runte, M., Basil, M., & Usher, J. (2011). Company support for employee volunteerism: Does size matter? *Journal of Business Research*, 64, 61–66.

Baum, J. A. C. (1989). Liabilities of newness, adolescence, and obsolescence: Exploring age dependence in the dissolution of organizational relationships and organizations. *Proceedings of the Administrative Science Association of Canada*, 10(5), 1–10.

Baum, J. A. C., & Oliver, C. (1991). Institutional linkages and organizational mortality. *Administrative Science Quarterly*, 36, 187–218.

Baum, J. A. C., & Singh, J. V. (1994a). Organizational niches and the dynamics of organizational founding. *Organization Science*, 5, 483–501.

Baum, J. A. C., & Singh, J. V. (1994b, September). Organizational niches and the dynamics of organizational mortality. *American Journal of Sociology, 100*, 346–380.

Bruderl, J., & Schussler, R. (1990). Organizational mortality: The liabilities of newness and adolescence. *Administrative Science Quarterly, 35*, 530–547.

Carroll, G. R. (1983). A stochastic model of organizational mortality: Review and reanalysis. *Social Sciences Research, 12*, 303–329.

Carroll, G. R., & Delacroix, J. (1982). Organizational mortality in newspaper industries of Argentina and Ireland: An ecological approach. *Administrative Science Quarterly, 27*, 169–198.

Carroll, G. R., & Swaminathan, A. (1991). Density dependent organizational evolution in the American brewing industry from 1633 to 1988. *Acta Sociologica, 34*, 155–175.

Darwin, C. (1859/2003). *The origin of species.* New York: Random House.

Fichman, M., & Levinthal, D. A. (1991). Honeymoons and the liability of adolescence: A new perspective on duration dependence in social and organizational relationships. *Academy of Management Review, 16*, 442–468.

Freeman, J., & Audia, P. G. (2006). Community ecology and the sociology of organizations. *Annual Review of Sociology, 32*, 145–169.

Freeman, J., Carroll, G. R., & Hannan, M. T. (1983). The liability of newness: Age dependence in organizational death rates. *American Sociological Review, 48*, 692–710.

Freeman, J., & Hannan, M. T. (1983). Niche width and the dynamics of organizational populations. *American Journal of Sociology, 88*, 1116–1145.

Freeman, J., & Hannan, M. T. (1987). The ecology of restaurants revisited. *American Journal of Sociology, 92*, 1214–1220.

Greiner, L. E. (1972, July–August). Evolution and revolution as organizations grow. *Harvard Business Review, 50*(4), 37–46.

Hannan, M. T., Carroll, G. R., & Polos, L. (2003). The organizational niche. *Sociological Theory, 21*, 309–340.

Hannan, M. T., & Freeman, J. (1977, March). The population ecology of organizations. *American Journal of Sociology, 82*, 929–964.

Hannan, M. T., & Freeman, J. (1984). Structural inertia and organizational change. *American Sociological Review, 49*, 149–164.

Hannan, M. T., & Freeman, J. (1987). The ecology of organizational founding: American labor unions, 1836–1985. *American Journal of Sociology, 92*, 910–943.

Hannan, M. T., & Freeman, J. (1988). The ecology of organizational mortality: American labor unions, 1836–1985. *American Journal of Sociology, 94*, 25–52.

Hannan, M. T., & Freeman, J. (1989). *Organizational ecology.* Cambridge, MA: Harvard University Press.

Hawley, A. H. (1950). *Human ecology: A theory of community structure.* New York: Ronald.

Hawley, A. H. (1968). Human ecology. In D. L. Sills (Ed.), *International encyclopedia of the social sciences* (pp. 328–337). New York: Macmillan.

Hutchinson, G. E. (1978). *An introduction to population ecology.* New Haven, CT: Yale University Press.

Ingram, P. L. (1993, August). *Old, tired, and ready to die: The age dependence of organizational mortality reconsidered.* Paper presented at the 66th annual meeting of the Academy of Management, Atlanta, GA.

Lomi, A., Larsen, E. R., & Freeman, J. (2005). Things change: Dynamic resource constraints and system-dependent selection in the evolution of organizational populations. *Management Science, 51,* 882–903.

McKelvey, B. (1982). *Organizational systematics: Taxonomy, evolution, classification.* Berkeley: University of California Press.

Monge, P., & Poole, M. S. (2008). The evolution of organizational communication. *Journal of Communication, 58,* 679–692.

Núñez-Nickel, M., & Moyano-Fuentes, J. (2006). New size measurements in population ecology. *Small Business Economics, 26,* 61–81.

Peli, G., & Nooteboom, B. (1999). Marketing partitioning and the geometry of the resource space. *American Journal of Sociology, 104,* 1132–1153.

Reydon, T. A. C., & Scholz, M. (2009). Why organizational ecology is not a Darwinian research program. *Philosophy of the Social Sciences, 39,* 408–439.

Rich, P. (1992). The organizational taxonomy: Definition and design. *Academy of Management Review, 17,* 758–781.

Scheitle, C. P. (2007). Organizational niches and religious markets: Uniting two literatures. *Interdisciplinary Journal of Research on Religion, 3,* 1–29.

Scholz, M., & Reydon, T. A. C. (2010). Organizational ecology: No Darwinian evolution after all: A rejoinder to Lemos. *Philosophy of the Social Sciences, 40,* 504–512.

Singh, J. V., Tucker, D. J., & House, R. J. (1986). Organizational legitimacy and the liability of newness. *Administrative Science Quarterly, 31,* 171–193.

Sorenson, O., McEvily, S., Ren, C. R., & Roy, R. (2006). Niche width revisited: Organizational scope, behavior and performance. *Strategic Management Journal, 27,* 915–936.

Stinchcombe, A. L. (1965). Organizations and social structure. In J. G. March (Ed.), *Handbook of organizations* (pp. 142–193). Chicago: Rand McNally.

Strauss, G. (1974). Adolescence in organization growth: Problems, pains, possibilities. *Organizational Dynamics, 2,* 3–17.

Young, R. C. (1988). Is population ecology a useful paradigm for the study of organizations? *American Journal of Sociology, 94,* 1–24.

22: Organizational Justice Theory

Adams, J. S. (1963). Toward an understanding of inequity. *Journal of Abnormal and Social Psychology, 47,* 422–436.

Adams, J. S. (1965). Inequity in social exchange. In L. Berkowitz (Ed.), *Advances in experimental social psychology* (Vol. 2, pp. 267–299). New York: Academic Press.

Ambrose, M. L., & Arnaud, A. (2005). Are procedural justice and distributive justice conceptually distinct? In J. Greenberg & J. A. Colquitt (Eds.), *Handbook of organizational justice* (pp. 59–84). Mahwah, NJ: Erlbaum.

Ambrose, M. L., & Schminke, M. (2009). The role of overall justice judgments in organizational justice research: A test of mediation. *Journal of Applied Psychology, 94,* 491–500.

Bies, R. J. (1987). The predicament of injustice: The management of moral outrage. In L. L. Cummings & B. M. Staw (Eds.), *Research in organizational behavior* (Vol. 9, pp. 289–319). Greenwich, CT: JAI Press.

Bies, R. J. (2005). Are procedural justice and interactional justice conceptually distinct? In J. Greenberg & J. A. Colquitt (Eds.), *Handbook of organizational justice* (pp. 85–112). Mahwah, NJ: Erlbaum.

Bies, R. J., & Moag, J. S. (1986). Interactional justice: Communication criteria of fairness. In R. J. Lewicki, B. H. Sheppard, & M. H. Bazerman (Eds.), *Research on negotiation in organizations* (pp. 43–55). Greenwich, CT: JAI Press.

Bies, R. J., & Shapiro, D. L. (1987). Interactional fairness judgments: The influence of causal accounts. *Social Justice Research, 1,* 199–218.

Choi, J. (2008). Event justice perceptions and employees' reactions: Perceptions of social entity justice as a moderator. *Journal of Applied Psychology, 93,* 513–528.

Colquitt, J. A. (2001). On the dimensionality of organizational justice: A construct validation measure. *Journal of Applied Psychology, 86,* 386–400.

Colquitt, J. A., Conlon, D. E., Wesson, M. J., Porter, C.O.L.H., & Ng, K. Y. (2001). Justice at the millennium: A meta-analytic review of 25 years of organizational justice research. *Journal of Applied Psychology, 86,* 425–445.

Colquitt, J. A., Greenberg, J., & Zapata-Phelan, C. P. (2005). What is organizational justice? A historical overview. In J. Greenberg & J. A. Colquitt (Eds.), *Handbook of organizational justice* (pp. 3–56). Mahwah, NJ: Erlbaum.

Cropanzano, R., & Ambrose, M. L. (2001). Procedural and distributive justice are more similar than you think: A monistic perspective and a research agenda. In J. Greenberg & R. Cropanzano (Eds.), *Advances in organizational justice research* (pp. 119–151). Lexington, MA: New Lexington Press.

Cropanzano, R., Byrne, Z. S., Bobocel, D. R., & Rupp, D. E. (2001). Moral virtues, fairness heuristics, social entities, and other denizens of organizational justice. *Journal of Vocational Behavior, 58,* 164–209.

Folger, R., & Cropanzano, R. (1998). *Organizational justice and human resource management.* Thousand Oaks, CA: Sage.

Folger, R., & Cropanzano, R. (2001). Fairness theory: Justice as accountability. In J. Greenberg & R. Folger (Eds.), *Advances in organizational justice* (pp. 1–55). Lexington, MA: New Lexington Press.

Fryxell, G. E., & Gordon, M. E. (1989). Workplace justice and job satisfaction predictors of satisfaction with union and management. *Academy of Management Journal, 32,* 851–866.

Greenberg, J. (1988). Cultivating an image of justice: Looking fair on the job. *Academy of Management Executive, 2,* 155–158.

Greenberg, J. (1990). Organizational justice: Yesterday, today, and tomorrow. *Journal of Management, 16,* 399–432.

Greenberg, J. (2009). Promote procedural and interactional justice to enhance individual and organizational outcomes. In E. A. Locke (Ed.), *Handbook of principles of organizational behavior* (2nd ed., pp. 255–271). Hoboken, NJ: Wiley.

Lind, A. (2001). Fairness heuristic theory: Justice judgments as pivotal cognitions in organizational relations. In J. Greenberg & R. Folger (Eds.), *Advances in organizational justice* (pp. 56–88). Lexington, MA: New Lexington Press.

Martocchio, J. J., & Judge, T. A. (1995). When we don't see eye to eye: Discrepancies between supervisors and subordinates in absence disciplinary decisions. *Journal of Management, 21,* 251–278.

Shapiro, D. L. (1993). Reconciling theoretical differences among procedural justice researchers by re-evaluating what it means to have one's views "considered": Implications for third-party managers. In R. Cropanzano (Ed.), *Justice in the workplace: Approaching fairness in human resource management* (pp. 51–78). Mahwah, NJ: Erlbaum.

Thibaut, J., & Walker, L. (1975). *Procedural justice: A psychological analysis.* Hoboken, NJ: Wiley.

Thibaut, J., & Walker, L. (1978). A theory of procedure. *California Law Review, 66*, 541–566.

23: Planned Behavior Theory

Ajzen, I. (1985). From intentions to actions: A theory of planned behavior. In J. Kuhland & J. Beckman (Eds.), *Action-control: From cognitions to behavior* (pp. 11–39). Heidelberg: Springer.

Ajzen, I. (1991). The theory of planned behavior. *Organizational Behavior and Human Decision Processes, 50*, 179–211.

Ajzen, I. (2001). Nature and operations of attitudes. *Annual Review of Psychology, 52*, 27–58.

Ajzen, I., & Driver, B. L. (1992). Application of the theory of planned behavior to leisure choice. *Journal of Leisure Research, 24*, 207–224.

Ajzen, I., & Fishbein, M. (1980). *Understanding attitudes and predicting social behavior.* Englewood Cliffs, NJ: Prentice Hall.

Ajzen, I., & Fishbein, M. (2000). Attitudes and the attitude-behavior relation: Reasoned and automatic processes. In W. Stroebe & H. Miles (Eds.), *European review of social psychology* (Vol. 11, pp. 17–33). Chichester, UK: Wiley.

Ajzen, I., & Madden, T. J. (1986). Prediction of goal-directed behavior: Attitudes, intentions, and perceived behavioral control. *Journal of Experimental Social Psychology, 22*, 453–474.

Armitage, C. J., & Conner, M. (1999a). The theory of planned behavior: Assessments of predictive validity and "perceived control." *British Journal of Social Psychology, 38*, 35–54.

Armitage, C. J., & Conner, M. (1999b). Distinguishing perceptions of control from self-efficacy: Predicting consumption of a low fat diet using the theory of planned behavior. *Journal of Applied Social Psychology, 29*, 72–90.

Armitage, C. J., & Conner, M. (2001). Efficacy of the theory of planned behavior: A meta-analytic review. *British Journal of Social Psychology, 40*, 471–499.

Askelson, N. M., Campo, S., Loew, J. B., Smith, S., Dennis, L. K., & Andsager, J. (2010). Using the theory of planned behavior to predict mothers' intentions to vaccinate their daughters against HPV. *Journal of School Nursing, 26*, 194–202.

Bandura, A. (1986). *Social foundations of thought and action.* Englewood Cliffs, NJ: Prentice Hall.

Bandura, A. (1992). On rectifying the comparative anatomy of perceived control: Comments on "cognates of personal control." *Applied and Preventative Psychology, 1*, 121–126.

Bandura, A., Adams, N. E., Hardy, A. B., & Howells, G. N. (1980). Tests of the generality of self-efficacy theory. *Cognitive Therapy and Research, 4,* 39–66.

Bargh, J. A. (1996). Automaticity in social psychology. In E. T. Higgins & A. W. Kruglanski (Eds.), *Social psychology: Handbook of basic principles* (pp. 169–183). New York: Guilford.

Bargh, J. A., Chen, M., & Burrows, L. (1996). Automaticity of social behavior: Direct effects of trait construct and stereotype activation on action. *Journal of Personality and Social Psychology, 71,* 230–244.

Beck, L., & Ajzen, I. (1991, September). Predicting dishonest actions using the theory of planned behavior. *Journal of Research in Personality, 25,* 285–301.

Conner, M., & Armitage, C. J. (1998). Extending the theory of planned behavior: A review and avenues for future research. *Journal of Applied Social Psychology, 28,* 1429–1464.

Conner, M., Sheeran, P., Norman, P., & Armitage, C. J. (2000). Temporal stability as a moderator of relationships in the theory of planned behaviour. *British Journal of Social Psychology, 39,* 469–493.

de Vries, H., Dijkstra, M., & Kuhlman, P. (1988). Self-efficacy: The third factor besides attitude and subjective norm as a predictor of behavioural intentions. *Heath Education Research, 3,* 273–282.

Doll, J., & Ajzen, I. (1992). Accessibility and stability of predictors in the theory of planned behavior. *Journal of Personality and Social Psychology, 63,* 754–765.

Fishbein, M., & Ajzen, I. (1975). *Belief, attitude, intention and behavior: An introduction to theory and research.* Reading, MA: Addison-Wesley.

French, D. P., & Cooke, R. (in press). Using the theory of planned behaviour to understand binge drinking: The importance of beliefs for developing interventions. *British Journal of Health Psychology, 16.*

Ganesh, G., & Barat, S. (2010). A theory-of-planned-behavior perspective on B2C e-commerce. *Review of Business Research, 10*(3), 92–99.

Godin, G., & Kok, G. (1996). The theory of planned behavior: A review of its applications to health-related behaviors. *American Journal of Health Promotion, 11,* 87–98.

Hagger, M. S., Chatzisarantis, N. L. D., & Biddle, S. J. H. (2002, March). A meta-analytic review of the theories of reasoned action and planned behavior in physical activity: Predictive validity and the contribution of additional variables. *Journal of Sport and Exercise Psychology, 24,* 133–150.

Harris, J., & Hagger, M. S. (2007). Do basic psychological needs moderate relationships within the theory of planned behavior? *Journal of Applied Biobehavioral Research, 12,* 43–64.

Kraft, P., Rise, J., Sutton, S., & Roysamb, E. (2005). Perceived difficulty in the theory of planned behaviour: Perceived behavioral control or affective attitude? *British Journal of Social Psychology, 44,* 479–496.

Kuhl, J. (1985). Volitional aspects of achievement motivation and learned helplessness: Toward a comprehensive theory of action control. In B. A. Maher (Ed.), *Progress in experimental personality research* (Vol. 13, pp. 99–171). New York: Academic Press.

Liska, A. E. (1984). A critical examination of the causal structure of the Fishbein/Ajzen attitude-behavior model. *Social Psychology Quarterly, 47,* 61–74.

Madden, T. J., Ellen, P. S., & Ajzen, I. (1992, February). A comparison of the theory of planned behavior and the theory of reasoned action. *Personality and Social Psychology Bulletin, 18*(1), 3–9.

McCarthy, A., & Garavan, T. (2006, Fall). Postfeedback development perceptions: Applying the theory of planned behavior. *Human Resource Development Quarterly, 17,* 245–267.

Moan, I. S., & Rise, J, (2006, December). Predicting smoking reduction among adolescents using an extended version of the theory of planned behavior. *Psychology and Health, 21,* 717–738.

Norwich, B., & Rovoli, I. (1993). Affective factors and learning behavior in secondary school mathematics and English lessons for average and low attainers. *British Journal of Educational Psychology, 63,* 308–321.

Orbell, S. (2003). Personality systems interactions theory and the theory of planned behaviour: Evidence that self-regulatory volitional components enhance enactment of studying behaviour. *British Journal of Social Psychology, 42,* 95–112.

Orbell, S., Hodgkins, S., & Sheeran, P. (1997). Implementation intentions and the theory of planned behavior. *Personality and Social Psychology Bulletin, 23,* 945–954.

Pellino, T. A. (1997). Relationships between patient attitudes, subjective norms, perceived control, and analgesic use following elective orthopedic surgery. *Research in Nursing and Health, 20,* 97–105.

Posner, M. I., & Synder, C. R. R. (1975). Attention and cognitive control. In R. L. Solso (Ed.), *Information processing and cognition: The Loyola symposium* (pp. 55–85). Mahwah, NJ: Erlbaum.

Rhodes, R. E., Courneya, K. S., & Hayduk, L. A. (2002). Does personality moderate the theory of planned behavior in the exercise domain? *Journal of Sport and Exercise Psychology, 24,* 120–132.

Rise, J., Sheeran, P., & Hukkelberg, S. (2010). The role of self-identity in the theory of planned behavior: A meta-analysis. *Journal of Applied Social Psychology, 40,* 1085–1105.

Sarver, V. T. (1983). Ajzen and Fishbein's "theory of reasoned action": A critical assessment. *Journal for the Theory of Social Behavior, 13,* 155–163.

Schifter, D. B., & Ajzen, I. (1985). Intention, perceived control, and weight loss: An application of the theory of planned behavior. *Journal of Personality and Social Psychology, 49,* 843–851.

Sheeran, P., & Orbell, S. (1999). Augmenting the predictive validity of the theory of planned behavior: Roles for anticipated regret and descriptive norms. *Journal of Applied Social Psychology, 29,* 2107–2142.

Sheeran, P., Orbell, S., & Trafimow, D. (1999). Does the temporal stability of behavioral intentions moderate intention-behavior and past behavior–future behavior relations? *Personality and Social Psychology Bulletin, 25,* 724–730.

Sheeran, P., & Taylor, S. (1999). Predicting intentions to use condoms: A meta-analysis and comparison of the theories of reasoned action and planned behavior. *Journal of Applied Social Psychology, 29,* 1624–1675.

Sheppard, B. H., Hartwick, J., & Warshaw, P. R. (1988). The theory of reasoned action: A meta-analysis of past research with recommendations for modifications and future research. *Journal of Consumer Research, 15,* 325–343.

Sparks, P., Shepard, R., & Frewer, L. J. (1995). Assessing and structuring attitudes toward the use of gene technology in food production: The role of perceived ethical obligation. *Basic and Applied Social Psychology, 16,* 267–285.

Sutton, S. (1998). Explaining and predicting intentions and behavior: How well are we doing? *Journal of Applied Social Psychology, 28,* 1318–1339.

Terry, D. J. (1993). Self-efficacy expectancies and the theory of reasoned action. In D. J. Terry, C. Gallois, & M. McCamish (Eds.), *The theory of reasoned action: Its application to AIDs-preventative behavior* (pp. 135–151). Oxford: Pergamon.

Terry, D. J., & Hogg, M. A. (1996). Group norms and the attitude-behavior relationship: A role for group identification. *Personality and Social Psychology Bulletin, 22,* 776–793.

Triandis, H. C. (1977). *Interpersonal behavior.* Monterey, CA: Brooks/Cole.

van den Putte, B. (1991). *Twenty years of the theory of reasoned action of Fishbein and Ajzen: A meta-analysis.* Unpublished manuscript, University of Amsterdam.

Wang, Y. J., Hong, S., & Wei, J. (2010). A broadened model of goal-directed behavior: Incorporating the conative force into consumer research. *Review of Business Research, 10,* 142–150.

Warshaw, P. R., & Davis, F. D. (1985). Disentangling behavioral intentions and behavioral expectations. *Journal of Experimental Social Psychology, 21,* 213–228.

Wegner, D. M., & Bargh, J. A. (1998). Control and automaticity in social life. In D. Gilbert, S. T. Fiske, & G. Lindzey (Eds.), *Handbook of social psychology* (4th ed., pp. 446–496). New York: McGraw-Hill.

24: Prospect Theory

Highhouse, S., & Paese, P. W. (1996). Problem domain and prospect frame: Choice under opportunity versus threat. *Personality and Social Psychology Bulletin, 22*, 124–132.

Kahneman, D., & Tversky, A. (1979). Prospect theory: An analysis of decision under risk. *Econometrica, 47*, 263–291.

Kanfer, R. (1990). Motivation theory. In M. Dunnette, & L. Houghs (Eds.), *Handbook of industrial and organizational psychology* (Vol. 1, 2nd ed., pp. 124–151). Palo Alto, CA: Consulting Psychologists Press.

Levy, M., & Levy, H. (2002). Prospect theory: Much ado about nothing? *Management Science, 48*, 1334–1349.

March, J. G., & Shapira, Z. (1987). Managerial perspective on risk and risk taking. *Management Science, 33*, 1404–1418.

Markowitz, H. M. (1952). Portfolio selection. *Journal of Finance, 7*, 77–91.

Mercer, J. (2005). Prospect theory and political science. *Annual Review of Political Science, 8*, 1–21.

Rieger, M. O., & Wang, M. (2006). Cumulative prospect theory and the St. Petersburg paradox. *Economic Theory, 28*, 665–679.

Steel, P., & Konig, C. J. (2006). Integrating theories of motivation. *Academy of Management Review, 31*, 889–913.

Swalm, R. O. (1966). Utility theory—insights into risk taking. *Harvard Business Review, 44*, 123–136.

Tversky, A., & Kahneman, D. (1981). The framing of decisions and psychology of choice. *Science, 211*, 453–458.

Tversky, A., & Kahneman, D. (1992). Advances in prospect theory: Cumulative representation of uncertainty. *Journal of Risk and Uncertainty, 5*, 297–323.

Wakker, P. P. (2003). The data of Levy and Levy (2002) "Prospect theory: Much ado about nothing?" actually support prospect theory. *Management Science, 49*, 979–981.

25: Psychological Contract Theory

Argyris, C. (1960). *Understanding organizational behavior.* Homewood, IL: Dorsey.

Blau, P. M. (1964). *Exchange and power in social life.* Hoboken, NJ: Wiley.

Dabos, G. E., & Rousseau, D. M. (2004). Mutuality and reciprocity in the psychological contracts of employee and employer. *Journal of Applied Psychology, 89,* 52–72.

Guest, D. E. (1998). Is the psychological contract worth taking seriously? *Journal of Organizational Behavior, 19,* 649–664.

Hallier, J., & James, P. (1997). Middle managers and the employee psychological contract: Agency, protection and advancement. *Journal of Management Studies, 34,* 703–728.

Levinson, H., Price, C. R., Munden, K. J., Mandl, H. J., Solley, C. M. (1962). *Men, management, and mental health.* Cambridge, MA: Harvard University Press.

McGaughey, S. L., & Liesch, P. W. (2002). The global sports-media nexus: Reflections on the "Super League Saga" in Australia. *Journal of Management Studies, 39,* 383–416.

McLean Parks, J., Kidder, D. L., & Gallagher, D. G. (1998). Fitting square pegs into round holes: Mapping the domain of contingent work arrangements onto the psychological contract. *Journal of Organizational Behavior, 19,* 697–730.

Morrison, E. W., & Robinson, S. L. (1997). When employees feel betrayed: A model of how psychological contract violation develops. *Academy of Management Review, 22,* 226–256.

Robinson, S. L., Kraatz, M. S., & Rousseau, D. M. (1994). Changing obligations and the psychological contract: A longitudinal study. *Academy of Management Journal, 37,* 137–152.

Rousseau, D. M. (1989). Psychological and implied contracts in organizations. *Employee Rights and Responsibilities Journal, 2,* 121–139.

Rousseau, D. M. (1990). New hire perceptions of their own and their employer's obligations: A study of psychological contracts. *Journal of Organizational Behavior, 11,* 389–400.

Rousseau, D. M. (1995). *Psychological contracts in organizations: Understanding written and unwritten agreements.* Thousand Oaks, CA: Sage.

Rousseau, D. M., & Greller, M. M. (1994). Human resource practices: Administrative contract makers. *Human Resource Management, 33,* 385–401.

Rousseau, D. M., & McLean Parks, J. (1993). The contracts of individuals and organizations. In L. L. Cummings and B. M. Staw (Eds.), *Research in organizational behavior* (Vol. 15, pp. 1–43). Greenwich, CT: JAI Press.

Rousseau, D. M., & Tijoriwala, S. A. (1998). Assessing psychological contracts: Issues, alternatives and measures. *Journal of Organizational Behavior, 19,* 679–695.

Schein, E. H. (1965). *Organizational psychology.* Englewood Cliffs, NJ: Prentice Hall.

Thompson, J. A., & Bunderson, J. S. (2003). Violations of principle: Ideological currency in the psychological contract. *Academy of Management Review, 28,* 571–586.

26: Resource-Based Theory

Armstrong, C. E., & Shimizu, K. (2007). A review of approaches to empirical research on the resource-based view of the firm. *Journal of Management, 33,* 959–986.

Barney, J. B. (1991). Firm resources and sustained competitive advantage. *Journal of Management, 17,* 99–120.

Barney, J. B., & Clark, D. N. (2007). *Resource-based theory: Creating and sustaining competitive advantage.* New York: Oxford University Press.

Bowman, C., & Ambrosini, V. (2000). Value creation versus value capture: Towards a coherent definition of value in strategy. *British Journal of Management, 11,* 1–15.

Bromiley, P., & Fleming, L. (2002). The resource-based view of strategy: A behavioral critique. In M. Augier & J. G. March (Eds.), *Change, choice and organization: Essays in memory of Richard M. Cyert* (pp. 319–336). Cheltenham, England: Elgar.

Caves, R. E. (1980). Industrial organization, corporate strategy and structure. *Journal of Economic Literature, 58,* 64–92.

Conner, K. R. (1991). A historical comparison of resource-based theory and five schools of thought within industrial organization economics: Do we have a new theory of the firm? *Journal of Management, 17,* 121–154.

Conner, T. (2002). The resource-based view of strategy and its value to practising managers. *Strategic Change, 11,* 307–316.

Fiol, C. M. (2001). Revisiting an identity-based view of sustainable competitive advantage. *Journal of Management, 27,* 691–699.

Helfat, C. E., & Peteraf, M. A. (2003). The dynamic resource-based view: Capability lifecycles. *Strategic Management Journal, 24,* 997–1010.

Hoopes, D. G., Madsen, T. L., & Walker, G. (2003). Guest editor's introduction to the special issue: Why is there a resource-based view? Toward a theory of competitive heterogeneity. *Strategic Management Journal, 24,* 889–902.

Kraaijenbrink, J., Spender, J.-C., & Groen, A. J. (2010). The resource-based view: A review and assessment of its critiques. *Journal of Management, 36,* 349–372.

Lockett, A., Thompson, S., & Morgenstern, U. (2009). The development of the resource-based view of the firm: A critical appraisal. *International Journal of Management Reviews, 11,* 9–28.

Makadok, R. (2001). Towards a synthesis of the resource-based and dynamic-capability views of rent creation. *Strategic Management Journal*, 22(5), 387–402.

Miller, D. (2003). An asymmetry-based view of advantage: Towards an attainable sustainability. *Strategic Management Journal*, 24, 961–976.

Newbert, S. L. (2007). Empirical research on the resource-based view of the firm: An assessment and suggestions for future research. *Strategic Management Journal*, 28, 121–146.

Oliver, C. (1997). Sustainable competitive advantage: Combining institutional and resource-based views. *Strategic Management Journal*, 18, 697–713.

Peteraf, M. A. (1993). The cornerstones of competitive advantage: A resource-based view. *Strategic Management Journal*, 14, 179–191.

Peteraf, M. A., & Barney, J. B. (2003). Unraveling the resource-based triangle. *Managerial and Decision Economics*, 24, 309–323.

Peteraf, M. A., & Bergen, M. E. (2003). Scanning dynamic competitive landscapes: A market-based and resource-based framework. *Strategic Management Journal*, 24, 1027–1041.

Porter, M. (1981). The contributions of industrial organization to strategic management. *Academy of Management Review*, 6, 609–620.

Priem, R. L., & Butler, J. E. (2001). Is the resource-based "view" a useful perspective for strategic management research? *Academy of Management Review*, 21, 22–40.

Rumelt, R. P. (1974). *Strategy, structure, and economic performance*. Cambridge, MA: Harvard University Press.

Teece, D., Pisano, G., & Shuen, A. (1997). Dynamic capabilities and strategic management. *Strategic Management Journal*, 18, 509–533.

Wernerfelt, B. (1984). A resource-based view of the firm. *Strategic Management Journal*, 5, 171–180.

27: Role Theory

Ashforth, B. E., & Johnson, S. A. (2001). Which hat to wear? The relative salience of multiple identities in organizational contexts. In M. A. Hogg & D. J. Terry (Eds.), *Social identity processes in organizational contexts* (pp. 31–48). Philadelphia: Psychology Press.

Biddle, B. J. (1979). *Role theory: Expectations, identities, and behaviors*. New York: Academic Press.

Biddle, B. J., & Thomas, E. (1979). *Role theory: Concepts and research*. Huntington, NY: Krieger.

Callero, P. L. (1994). From role-playing to role-using: Understanding role as a resource. *Social Psychology Quarterly*, 57, 228–243.

Collier, P. J., & Callero, P. L. (2005). Role theory and social cognition: Learning to think like a recycler. *Self and Identity, 4*, 45–58.

Connell, R. W. (1987). *Gender and power: Society, the person and sexual politics.* Stanford, CA: Stanford University Press.

Goffman, E. (1959). *The presentation of self in everyday life.* New York: Anchor Books.

Hall, D. T., & Richter, J. (1988). Balancing work life and home life: What can organizations do to help? *Academy of Management Executive, 2*, 213–223.

Hilbert, R. A. (1981). Toward an improved understanding of "role." *Theory and Society, 10*, 207–226.

Jackson, J. (1998, August). Contemporary criticisms of role theory. *Journal of Occupational Science, 5*(2), 49–55.

Linton, R. (1936). *The study of man.* New York: Appleton-Century.

Lynch, K. D. (2007). Modeling role enactment: Linking role theory and social cognition. *Journal for the Theory of Social Behavior, 37*, 379–399.

McCall, G., & Simmons, J. (1978). *Identities and interactions.* New York: Free Press.

Mead, G. H. (1934). *Mind, self, and society.* Chicago: University of Chicago Press.

Merton, R. K. (1957). *On theoretical sociology.* New York: Free Press.

Montgomery, J. D. (1998, July). Toward a role theoretic concept of embeddedness. *American Journal of Sociology, 104*, 92–125.

Montgomery, J. D. (2005). The logic of role theory: Role conflict and stability of the self-concept. *Journal of Mathematical Sociology, 29*, 33–71.

Moreno, J. L. (1934). *Who shall survive?* Washington, DC: Nervous and Mental Disease Publishing.

Parsons, T. (1951). *The social system.* New York: Free Press.

Turner, R. H. (1962). Role-taking: Process versus conformity. In A. M. Rose (Ed.), *Human behavior and social processes* (pp. 20–40). Boston: Houghton Mifflin.

Zurcher, L. A. (1983). *Social roles: Conformity, conflict and creativity.* Thousand Oaks, CA: Sage.

28: Self-Determination Theory

Brown, K. W., & Ryan, R. M. (2003). The benefits of being present: Mindfulness and its role in psychological well-being. *Journal of Personality and Social Psychology, 84*, 822–848.

Deci, E. L., & Ryan, R. M. (2000a). The "what" and "why" of goal pursuits: Human needs and the self-determination of behavior. *Psychological Inquiry, 11*, 227–268.

Deci, E. L., & Ryan, R. M. (2000b). The darker and brighter sides of human existence: Basic psychological needs as a unifying concept. *Psychological Inquiry, 11,* 319–338.

Deci, E. L., & Ryan, R. M. (2008). Facilitating optimal motivation and psychological well-being across life's domains. *Canadian Psychology, 49,* 14–23.

Deci, E. L., Ryan, R. M., Gagne, M., Leone, D. R., Usunov, J., & Kornazheva, B. P. (2001). Need satisfaction, motivation, and well-being in the work organizations of a former Eastern Bloc country. *Personality and Social Psychology Bulletin, 27,* 930–942.

Gagne, M., & Forest, J. (2008). The study of compensation systems through the lens of self-determination theory: Reconciling 35 years of debate. *Canadian Psychology, 49,* 225–232.

Hull, C. L. (1943). *Principles of behavior: An introduction to behavior theory.* New York: Appleton-Century-Crofts.

Kasser, T., & Ryan, R. M. (1993). A dark side of the American dream: Correlates of financial success as a life aspiration. *Journal of Personality and Social Psychology, 65,* 410–422.

Kasser, T., & Ryan, R. M. (1996). Further examining the American dream: Differential correlates of intrinsic and extrinsic goals. *Personality and Social Psychology Bulletin, 22,* 80–87.

Ryan, R. M., Chirkov, V. I., Little, T. D., Sheldon, K. M., Timoshina, E., & Deci, E. L. (1999). The American dream in Russia: Extrinsic aspirations and well-being in two cultures. *Personality and Social Psychology Bulletin, 25,* 1509–1524.

Ryan, R. M., & Connell, J. P. (1989). Perceived locus of causality and internationalization: Examining reasons for acting in two domains. *Journal of Personality and Social Psychology, 57,* 749–761.

Ryan, R. M., & Deci, E. L. (2000a). The darker and brighter sides of human existence: Basic psychological needs as a unifying concept. *Psychological Inquiry, 11,* 319–338.

Ryan, R. M., & Deci, E. L. (2000b, January). Self-determination theory and the facilitation of intrinsic motivation, social development, and well-being. *American Psychologist, 55,* 68–78.

Ryan, R. M., & Deci, E. L. (2002). An overview of self-determination theory: An organismic dialectical perspective. In E. L. Deci & R. M. Ryan (Eds.), *Handbook of self-determination research* (pp. 3–33). Rochester, NY: University of Rochester Press.

Ryan, R. M., & Frederick, C. M. (1997). On energy, personality, and health: Subjective vitality as a dynamic reflection of well-being. *Journal of Personality and Social Psychology, 65,* 529–565.

Ryan, R. M., Sheldon, K. M., Kasser, T., & Deci, E. L. (1996). All goals are not created equal: An organismic perspective on the nature of goals and their regulation. In P. M. Gollwitzer & J. A. Bargh (Eds.), *The psychology of action: Linking cognition and motivation to behavior* (pp. 7–26). New York: Guilford Press.

Sheldon, K. M. (2002). The self-concordance model of health goal striving: When personal goals correctly represent the person. In E. L. Deci & R. M. Ryan (Eds.), *Handbook of self-determination research* (pp. 65–86). Rochester, NY: University of Rochester Press.

Turban, D. B., Tan, H. H., Brown, K. G., & Sheldon, K. M. (2007). Antecedents and outcomes of perceived locus of causality: An application of self-determination theory. *Journal of Applied Social Psychology, 37,* 2376–2404.

Vansteenkiste, M., Simons, J., Lens, W., Sheldon, K. M., & Deci, E. L. (2004). Motivating learning, performance, and persistence: The synergistic effects of intrinsic goal contents and autonomy-supportive context. *Journal of Personality and Social Psychology, 87,* 246–260.

Vansteenkiste, M., Zhou, M., Lens, W., & Soenens, B. (2005). Experiences of autonomy and control among Chinese learners: Vitalizing or immobilizing? *Journal of Educational Psychology, 87,* 468–483.

White, R. W. (1959). Motivation reconsidered. *Psychological Review, 66,* 297–333.

29: Sensemaking Theory

Cantril, H. (1941). *The psychology of social movements.* Hoboken, NJ: Wiley.

Cornelissen, J. P., & Clarke, J. S. (2010). Imagining and rationalizing opportunities: Inductive reasoning and the creation and justification of new ventures. *Academy of Management Review, 35,* 539–557.

Daft, R. L., & Weick, K. E. (1984). Toward a model of organizations as interpretive systems. *Academy of Management Review, 9,* 284–295.

Dunbar, R. (1981). Designs for organizational control. In P. C. Nystrom & W. H. Starbuck (Eds.), *Handbook of organizational design* (Vol. 2, pp. 85–115). Oxford: Oxford University Press.

Dutton, J. E., & Duncan, R. B. (1987). The creation of momentum for change through the process of strategic issue diagnosis. *Strategic Management Journal, 8,* 279–295.

Gioia, D. A. (1986). Symbols, scripts, and sensemaking: Creating meaning in the organizational experience. In H. P. Sims Jr. & D. A. Gioia (Eds.), *The thinking organization* (pp. 49–74). San Francisco: Jossey-Bass.

Gioia, D. A., & Chittipeddi, K. (1991). Sensemaking and sensegiving in strategic change initiation. *Strategic Management Journal, 12,* 433–448.

Goleman, D. (1985). *Vital lies, simple truths: The psychology of self-deception.* New York: Simon & Schuster.

Kiesler, S., & Sproull, L. (1986). Managerial response to changing environments: Perspectives on problem sensing from social cognition. *Administrative Science Quarterly, 27,* 548–570.

Luscher, L. S., & Lewis, M. W. (2008). Organizational change and managerial sensemaking: Working through paradox. *Academy of Management Journal, 51,* 221–240.

Maitlis, S. (2005). The social processes of organizational sensemaking. *Academy of Management Journal, 48,* 21–49.

Maitlis, S., & Lawrence, T. B. (2007). Triggers and enablers of sensegiving in organizations. *Academy of Management Journal, 50,* 57–84.

Maitlis, S., & Sonenshein, S. (2010, May). Sensemaking in crisis and change: Inspiration and insights from Weick (1988). *Journal of Management Studies, 47,* 551–580.

Milliken, F. J. (1990). Perceiving and interpreting environmental change: An examination of college administrators' interpretation of changing demographics. *Academy of Management Journal, 33,* 42–63.

Rudolph, J. W., Morrison, J. B., & Carroll, J. S. (2009). The dynamics of action-oriented problem solving: Linking interpretation and choice. *Academy of Management Review, 34,* 733–756.

Schwandt, D. R. (2005). When managers become philosophers: Integrating learning with sensemaking. *Academy of Management Learning and Education, 4,* 176–192.

Sonenshein, S. (2007). The role of construction, intuition, and justification in responding to ethical issues at work: The sensemaking-intuition model. *Academy of Management Review, 32,* 1022–1040.

Starbuck, W. H., & Milliken, F. J. (1988). Executives' perceptual filters: What they notice and how they make sense. In D. C. Hambrick (Ed.), *The executive effect: Concepts and methods for studying top managers* (pp. 35–66). Greenwich, CT: JAI Press.

Taylor, S. E., & Crocker, J. (1981). Schematic bases of social information processing. In E. T. Higgins, C. P. Herman, & M. P. Zanna (Eds.), *Social cognition* (Vol. 1, pp. 89–133). Mahwah, NJ: Erlbaum.

Thomas, J. B., Clark, S. M., & Gioia, D. A. (1993). Strategic sensemaking and organizational performance: Linkages among scanning, interpretation, action, and outcomes. *Academy of Management Journal, 36,* 239–270.

Weick, K. E. (1979). *The social psychology of organizing* (2nd ed.). New York: Addison-Wesley.

Weick, K. E. (1993). The collapse of sensemaking in organizations. The Mann Gulch disaster. *Administrative Science Quarterly, 38,* 628–652.

Weick, K. E. (1995). *Sensemaking in organizations.* Thousand Oaks, CA: Sage.

Weick, K. E. (2010). Reflections on enacted sensemaking in the Bhopal disaster. *Journal of Management Studies, 47,* 537–550.

Weick, K. E., & Roberts, K. H. (1993). Collective mind in organizations: Heedful interrelating on flight decks. *Administrative Science Quarterly, 38,* 357–381.

Weick, K. E., Sutcliffe, K. M., & Obstfeld, D. (2005). Organizing and the process of sensemaking. *Organization Science, 16,* 409–421.

Whetten, D. A. (1984, November–December). Effective administrators: Good management on the college campus. *Change, 16*(8), 38–43.

30: Social Capital Theory

Adler, P. S., & Kwon, S.-W. (2002). Social capital: Prospects for a new concept. *Academy of Management Review, 27,* 17–40.

Arrow, K. (1999). Observations on social capital. In P. Dasgupta & I. Serageldin (Eds.), *Social capital: A multifaceted perspective* (pp. 3–5). Washington, DC: World Bank.

Baker, W. E. (1990). Market networks and corporate behavior. *American Journal of Sociology, 96,* 589–625.

Belliveau, M., O'Reilly, C., & Wade, J. (1996). Social capital at the top: Effects of social similarity and status on CEO compensation. *Academy of Management Journal, 39,* 1568–1593.

Bolino, M. C., Turnley, W. H., & Bloodgood, J. M. (2002). Citizenship behavior and the creation of social capital in organizations. *Academy of Management Review, 27,* 505–522.

Bourdieu, P. (1986). The forms of capital. In J. G. Richardson (Ed.), *Handbook of theory and research for the sociology of education* (pp. 241–258). New York: Greenwood Press.

Bourdieu, P., & Wacquant, L. (1992). *Invitation to reflexive sociology.* Chicago: University of Chicago Press.

Colclough, G., & Sitaraman, B. (2005). Community and social capital: What is the difference? *Sociological Inquiry, 75,* 474–496.

Coleman, J. S. (1988). Social capital in the creation of human capital. *American Journal of Sociology, 94*(Supplement), S95–S120.

Coleman, J. S. (1990). *Foundations of social theory.* Cambridge, MA: Belknap Press.

DeFilippis, J. (2002). Symposium on social capital: An introduction. *Antipode, 34,* 790–795.

Durkheim, E. (1960). *The division of labor in society.* New York: Free Press. (Original work published 1902)

Fine, B. (2001). *Social capital versus social theory: Political economy and social science at the turn of the millennium.* London: Routledge.

Fine, B. (2002a). They f**k you up those social capitalists. *Antipode, 34,* 796–799.

Fine, B. (2002b). It ain't social, it ain't capital, and it ain't Africa. *Studia Africana, 13,* 18–33.

Fischer, C. S. (2005). Bowling alone: What's the score? *Social Networks, 27,* 155–167.

Fischer, H. M., & Pollock, T. G. (2004). Effects of social capital and power on surviving transformational change: The case of initial public offerings. *Academy of Management Journal, 47,* 463–481.

Florin, J., Lubatkin, M., & Schulze, W. (2003). A social capital model of high-growth ventures. *Academy of Management Journal, 46,* 374–384.

Foley, M., & Edwards, R. (1999). Is it time to divest in social capital? *Journal of Public Policy, 19,* 141–173.

Fukuyama, F. (1995). *Trust: Social virtues and the creation of prosperity.* London: Hamilton.

Fulkerson, G. M., & Thompson, G. H. (2008). The evolution of a contested concept: A meta-analysis of social capital definitions and trends (1988–2006). *Sociological Inquiry, 78,* 536–557.

Granovetter, M. S. (1973). The strength of weak ties. *American Journal of Sociology, 78,* 1360–1380.

Hanifan, L. J. (1916, September). The rural school community center. *Annals of the American Academy of Political and Social Science, 67,* 130–138.

Hansen, M. T. (2002). Knowledge networks: Explaining effective knowledge sharing in multiunit companies. *Organization Science, 13,* 232–248.

Haynes, P. (2009). *Before going any further with social capital: Eight key criticisms to address.* (Ingenio working paper series: Instituto de Gestión de la Innovación y del Conocimiento). Valencia: La Universidad Politécnica de Valencia.

Inkpen, A. C., & Tsang, E. W. K. (2005). Social capital, networks, and knowledge transfer. *Academy of Management Review, 30,* 146–165.

Jacobs, J. (1965). *The death and life of great American cities.* London: Penguin Books.

Kostova, T., & Roth, K. (2003). Social capital in multinational corporations and a micro-macro model of its formation. *Academy of Management Review, 28,* 297–317.

Lin, N. (2001). *Social capital: A theory of social structure and action.* Cambridge: Cambridge University Press.

Loury, G. C. (1977). A dynamic theory of racial income differences. In P. A. Wallace & A. M. LaMonde (Eds.), *Women, minorities and employment discrimination* (pp. 153–186). Lexington, MA: Lexington Books.

Maraffi, M, (1994). [Review of the book *Making democracy work*]. *American Journal of Sociology, 99,* 1348–1349.

Mix, T. L. (2011, May). Rally the people: Building local-environmental justice grassroots coalitions and enhancing social capital. *Sociological Inquiry, 81*, 174–194.

Morlino, L. (1995). Italy's civic divide. *Journal of Democracy, 6*(1), 173–177.

Nahapiet, J., & Ghoshal, S. (1998). Social capital, intellectual capital, and the organizational advantage. *Academy of Management Journal, 23*, 242–266.

Portes, A. (1998). Social capital: Its origins and applications in modern sociology. *Annual Review of Sociology, 24*, 1–24.

Portes, A., & Landolt, P. (1996). The downside of social capital. *American Prospect, 26*, 18–22.

Portes, A., & Landolt, P. (2000). Social capital: Promise and pitfalls of its role development. *Journal of Latin American Studies, 32*, 529–547.

Portes, A., & Sensenbrenner, J. (1993). Embeddedness and immigration: Notes on the social determinants of economic action. *American Journal of Sociology, 98*, 1320–1350.

Putnam, R. (1993). The prosperous community: Social capital and public life. *American Prospect, 13*, 35–42.

Putnam, R. (1995). Bowling alone: America's declining social capital. *Journal of Democracy, 6*(1), 65–78.

Putnam, R. (2000). *Bowling alone: The collapse and revival of American community.* New York: Simon & Schuster.

Putnam, R., Leonardi, R., & Nanetti, R. (1993). *Making democracy work: Civic traditions in modern Italy.* Princeton, NJ: Princeton University Press.

Ritchie, L. A., & Gill, D. A. (2007). Social capital theory as an integrating theoretical framework in technological disaster research. *Sociological Spectrum, 27*, 103–129.

Simmel, G. (1971). *Georg Simmel on individuality and social forms* (D. N. Levine, Ed.). Chicago: University of Chicago Press.

Tönnies, F. (1957). *Community and society* (C. P. Loomis, Ed.). East Lansing: Michigan State University Press.

Uzzi, B. (1997). Social structure and competition in interfirm networks: The paradox of embeddedness. *Administrative Science Quarterly, 42*, 35–67.

31: Social Cognitive Theory

Bandura, A. (1986). *Social foundations of thought and action: A social cognitive theory.* Englewood Cliffs, NJ: Prentice Hall.

Bandura, A. (1988). Organizational applications of social cognitive theory. *Australian Journal of Management, 13*, 137–164.

Bandura, A. (1989, September). Human agency in social cognitive theory. *American Psychologist, 44,* 1175–1184.

Bandura, A. (1997). *Self-efficacy: The exercise of control.* New York: Freeman.

Bandura, A. (2001). Social cognitive theory: An agentic perspective. *Annual Review of Psychology, 52,* 1–26.

Bandura, A. (2002). Social cognitive theory in cultural context. *Applied Psychology: International Review, 51,* 269–290.

Bandura, A., & Locke, E. A. (2003). Negative self-efficacy and goal effects revisited. *Journal of Applied Psychology, 88,* 87–99.

Baumeister, R. F. (1990). Suicide as escape from self. *Psychological Review, 97,* 90–113.

Chatard, A., & Selimbegovic, L. (2011). When self-destructive thoughts flash through the mind: Failure to meet standards affects the accessibility of suicide-related thoughts. *Journal of Personality and Social Psychology, 100,* 587–605.

Chen, G., Gulley, S. M., & Eden, D. (2001, January). Validation of a new general self-efficacy scale. *Organizational Research Methods, 4,* 62–83.

Judge, T. A., Erez, A., Bono, J. E., & Thoresen, C. J. (2002). Are measures of self-esteem, neuroticism, locus of control, and generalized self-efficacy indicators of a common core construct? *Journal of Personality and Social Psychology, 83,* 693–710.

Scherbaum, C. A., Cohen-Charash, Y., & Kern, M. J. (2006, December). Measuring general self-efficacy: A comparison of three measures using item response theory. *Educational and Psychological Measurement, 66,* 1047–1063.

Stanley, K., & Murphy, M. (1997). A comparison of general self-efficacy with self-esteem. *Genetic, Social and General Psychology Monographs, 123,* 81–99.

Vancouver, J. B., Thompson, C. M., Tischner, E. C., & Putka, D. J. (2002). Two studies examining the negative effect of self-efficacy on performance. *Journal of Applied Psychology, 87,* 506–516.

Vancouver, J. B., Thompson, C. M., & Williams, A. A. (2001). The changing signs in the relationships among self-efficacy, personal goals, and performance. *Journal of Applied Psychology, 86,* 605–620.

Wood, R., & Bandura, A. (1989). Social cognitive theory of organizational management. *Academy of Management Review, 14,* 361–384.

32: Social Comparison Theory

Alicke, M. D., & Govorun, O. (2005). The better-than-average effect. In M. D. Alicke, D. A. Dunning, & J. I. Krueger (Eds.), *The self in social judgment* (pp. 85–106). New York: Psychology Press.

Aspinwall, L. G., & Taylor, S. E. (1993). Effects on social comparison direction, threat, and self-esteem on affect, self-evaluation, and expected success. *Journal of Personality and Social Psychology, 64,* 708–722.

Blanton, H. (2001). Evaluating the self in the context of another: The three-selves model of social comparison assimilation and contrast. In G. B. Moskowitz (Ed.), *Cognitive social psychology: The Princeton symposium on the legacy and future of social cognition* (pp. 75–87). Mahwah, NJ: Erlbaum.

Blanton, H., & Stapel, D. A. (2008). Unconscious and spontaneous and . . . complex: The three selves model of social comparison assimilation and contrast. *Journal of Personality and Social Psychology, 94,* 1018–1032.

Brown, D. J., Ferris, D. L., Heller, D., & Keeping, L. M. (2007). Antecedents and consequences of the frequency of upward and downward social comparisons at work. *Organizational Behavior and Human Decision Processes, 102,* 59–75.

Buunk, A. P., Collins, R. L., Taylor, S. E., VanYperen, N. W., & Dakof, G. A. (1990). The affective consequence of social comparison: Either direction has its ups and downs. *Journal of Personality and Social Psychology, 59,* 1238–1249.

Buunk, A. P., & Gibbons, F. X. (2007). Social comparison: The end of a theory and the emergence of a field. *Organizational Behavior and Human Decision Processes, 102,* 3–21.

Buunk, A. P., Zurriaga, R., & Peiro, J. M. (2010, March). Social comparison as a predictor of changes in burnout among nurses. *Anxiety, Stress, and Coping, 23,* 181–194.

Collins, R. L. (1996). For better or worse: The impact of upward social comparison on self-evaluations. *Psychological Bulletin, 119,* 51–69.

Festinger, L. (1954). A theory of social comparison. *Human Relations, 7,* 117–140.

Gibbons, F. X., & Buunk, A. P. (1999). Individual differences in social comparison: Development and validation of a measure of social comparison orientation. *Journal of Personality and Social Psychology, 76,* 129–142.

Gilbert, D. T., Giesler, R. B., & Morris, K. A. (1995). When comparisons arise. *Journal of Personality and Social Psychology, 69,* 227–236.

Goethals, G. R., & Darley, J. M. (1977). Social comparison theory: An attributional approach. In J. M. Suls & R. L. Miller (Eds.), *Social comparison processes: Theoretical and empirical perspectives* (pp. 259–278). Washington, DC: Hemisphere.

Goffin, R. D., Jelley, R. B., Powell, D. M., & Johnston, N. G. (2009). Taking advantage of social comparisons in performance appraisal:

The relative percentile method. *Human Resource Management, 48,* 251–268.

Goodman, P. S., & Haisley, E. (2007). Social comparison processes in an organizational context: New directions. *Organizational Behavior and Human Decision Processes, 102,* 109–125.

Gordijn, E. H., & Stapel, D. A. (2006). Behavioural effects of automatic interpersonal versus intergroup social comparison. *British Journal of Social Psychology, 45,* 717–729.

Hertel, G., Niemeyer, G., & Clauss, A. (2008). Social indispensability or social comparison: The why and when of motivation gains of inferior group members. *Journal of Applied Social Psychology, 35,* 1329–1363.

Hoorens, V., & Buunk, B. P. (1993). Social comparison of health risks: Locus of control, the person-positivity bias, and unrealistic optimism. *Journal of Applied Social Psychology, 23,* 291–302.

James, W. (1890). *The principles of psychology* (Vol. 1). New York: Holt, Rinehart & Winston.

Koch, E. J., & Metcalfe, K. P. (2011). The bittersweet taste of success: Daily and recalled experiences of being an upward social comparison target. *Basic and Applied Social Psychology, 33,* 47–58.

Kruglanski, A. W., & Mayseless, O. (1990). Classic and current social comparison research: Expanding the perspective. *Psychological Bulletin, 108,* 195–208.

Larrick, R. P., Burson, K. A., & Soll, J. B. (2007). Social comparison and confidence: When thinking you're better than average predicts overconfidence (and when it does not). *Organizational Behavior and Human Decision Processes, 102,* 76–94.

Levine, J. M., & Moreland, R. L. (1987). Social comparison and outcome evaluation in group contexts. In J. C. Masters & W. P. Smith (Eds.), *Social comparison, social justice, and relative deprivation: Theoretical, empirical, and policy perspectives* (pp. 105–127). Mahwah, NJ: Erlbaum.

Mahler, H. I. M., Kulik, J. A., Gerrard, M., & Gibbons, F. X. (2010). Effects of upward and downward social comparison information on the efficacy of an appearance-based sun protection intervention: A randomized, controlled experiment. *Journal of Behavioral Medicine, 33,* 496–507.

Moore, D. A. (2007). Not so above average after all: When people believe they are worse than average and its implications for theories of bias in social comparison. *Organizational Behavior and Human Decision Processes, 102,* 42–58.

Pyszczynski, T., Greenberg, J., & LaPrelle, J. (1985). Social comparison after success and failure: Biased search for information consistent with a self-serving conclusion. *Journal of Experimental Social Psychology, 21,* 195–211.

Santor, D. A., & Yazbek, A. A. (2004). Soliciting unfavorable social comparison: Effects of self-criticism. *Personality and Individual Differences, 40,* 545–556.

Schwinghammer, S. A., & Stapel, D. A. (2011). Measure by measure: When implicit and explicit social comparison effects differ. *Self and Identity, 10,* 166–184.

Sharp, M., Voci, A., & Hewstone, M. (2011). Individual difference variables as moderators of the effect of extended cross-group friendship on prejudice: Testing the effects of public self-consciousness and social comparison. *Group Processes and Intergroup Relations, 14,* 207–221.

Stapel, D. A., & Blanton, H. (2004). From seeing to being: Subliminal social comparisons affect implicit and explicit self-evaluations. *Journal of Personality and Social Psychology, 87,* 468–481.

Stapel, D. A., & Suls, J. (2004). Method matters: Effects of explicit versus implicit social comparisons on activation, behavior, and self-views. *Journal of Personality and Social Psychology, 87,* 860–875.

Suls, J. (1986). Notes on the occasion of social comparison theory's thirtieth birthday. *Personality and Social Psychology Bulletin, 12,* 289–296.

Suls, J., & Wheeler, L. (Eds.). (2000). *Handbook of social comparison.* New York: Plenum/Kluwer Academic.

Taylor, S. E., & Lobel, M. (1989). Social comparison activity under threat: Downward evaluation and upward contacts. *Psychological Bulletin, 96,* 569–575.

Willis, T. A. (1981). Downward comparison principles in social psychology. *Psychological Bulletin, 90,* 245–271.

Wood, J. V. (1989). Theory and research concerning social comparisons of personal attributes. *Psychological Bulletin, 106,* 231–248.

Wood, J. V. (1996). What is social comparison and how should we study it? *Personality and Social Psychology Bulletin, 22,* 520–537.

Zell, E., & Alicke, M. D. (2009). Self-evaluative effects of temporal and social comparison. *Journal of Experimental Social Psychology, 45,* 223–227.

Zell, E., & Alicke, M. D. (2010). Comparisons over time: Temporal trajectories, social comparison, and self-evaluation. *European Journal of Social Psychology, 40,* 375–382.

33: Social Exchange Theory

Befu, H. (1977). Social exchange. *Annual Review of Anthropology, 6,* 255–281.

Blau, P. M. (1955). *The dynamics of bureaucracy: A study of interpersonal relations in two government agencies.* Chicago: University of Chicago Press.

Blau, P. M. (1960, May). A theory of social integration. *American Journal of Sociology, 65,* 545–556.

Blau, P. M. (1964). *Exchange and power in social life.* Hoboken, NJ: Wiley.

Blau, P. M. (1968). Interaction: Social exchange. *International Encyclopedia of the Social Sciences, 7,* 452–458.

Blau, P. M. (1994). *Structural context of opportunities.* Chicago: University of Chicago Press.

Burgess, R., & Neilsen, J. (1974). An experimental analysis of some structural determinants of equitable and inequitable exchange relations. *American Sociological Review, 39,* 427–443.

Coyle-Shapiro, J. A.-M., & Conway, N. (2004). The employment relationship through the lens of social exchange theory. In J. Coyle-Shapiro, L. M. Shore, M. S. Taylor, & L. E. Tetrick (Eds.), *The employment relationship: Examining psychological and contextual perspectives* (pp. 5–28). Oxford: Oxford University Press.

Cropanzano, R., & Mitchell, M. S. (2005). Social exchange theory: An interdisciplinary review. *Journal of Management, 31,* 874–900.

Cropanzano, R., Rupp, D. E., Mohler, C. J., & Schminke, M. (2001). Three roads to organizational justice. In J. Ferris (Ed.), *Research in personnel and human resources management* (Vol. 20, pp. 1–113). Greenwich, CT: JAI.

Ekeh, P. P. (1974). *Social exchange theory.* Cambridge, MA: Harvard University Press.

Emerson, R. M. (1962, February). Power-dependence relations. *American Sociological Review, 27,* 31–41.

Emerson, R. M. (1976). Social exchange theory. *Annual Review of Sociology, 2,* 335–362.

Gouldner, A. W. (1960). The norm of reciprocity: A preliminary statement. *American Sociological Review, 25,* 161–178.

Holmes, J. G. (1981). The exchange process in close relationships: Microbehavior and macromotives. In M. J. Lerner & S. C. Lerner (Eds.), *The justice motive in social behavior* (pp. 261–284). New York: Plenum.

Homans, G. C. (1958). Social behavior as exchange. *American Journal of Sociology, 63,* 597–606.

Homans, G. C. (1961). *Social behavior: Its elementary forms.* New York: Harcourt Brace.

Lawler, E. J., & Thye, S. R. (1999). Bringing emotions into social exchange theory. *Annual Review of Sociology, 25,* 217–244.

Levi-Strauss, C. (1969). *The elementary structure of kinship.* Boston: Beacon Press.

Makoba, J. W. (1993). Toward a general theory of social exchange. *Social Behavior and Personality, 21,* 227–240.

Mauss, M. (1967). *The gift: Forms and functions of exchange in archaic societies.* New York: Norton.

Molm, L. G. (1990). Structure, action, and outcomes: The dynamics of power in social exchange. *American Sociological Review, 55,* 427–447.

Molm, L. G., & Takahashi, N. (2003). In the eye of the beholder: Procedural justice in social exchange. *American Sociological Review, 68,* 128–152.

Popper, K. R. (1959). *The logic of scientific discovery.* New York: Harper & Row.

Rudner, R. (1966). *Philosophy of social science.* Englewood Cliffs, NJ: Prentice Hall.

Sahlins, M. D. (1965). On the sociology of primitive exchange. In M. Banton (Ed.), *The relevance of models for social anthropology* (pp. 139–236). London: Tavistock.

Thibaut, J. W., & Kelley, H. H. (1959). *The social psychology of groups.* Hoboken, NJ: Wiley.

34: Social Facilitation Theory

Aiello, J. R., & Douthitt, E. A. (2001). Social facilitation from Triplett to electronic performance monitoring. *Group Dynamics, 5,* 163–180.

Allport, F. H. (1920, June). The influence of the group upon association and thought. *Journal of Experimental Psychology, 3,* 159–182.

Baron, R. S. (1986). Distraction-conflict theory: Progress and problems. In L. Berkowitz (Ed.), *Advances in experimental social psychology* (Vol. 19, pp. 1–40). New York: Academic Press.

Baumeister, R. F. (1984). Choking under pressure: Self-consciousness and paradoxical effects of incentives on skillful performance. *Journal of Personality and Social Psychology, 46,* 610–620.

Baumeister, R. F., & Steinhilber, A. (1984). Paradoxical effects of supportive audiences on performance under pressure: The home field disadvantage in sports championships. *Journal of Personality and Social Psychology, 47,* 85–93.

Beilock, S. L., & Carr, T. H. (2005). When high-powered people fail: Working memory and "choking under pressure" in math. *Psychological Science, 16,* 101–105.

Beilock, S. L., Kulp, C. A., Holt, L. E., & Carr, T. H. (2004). More on the fragility of performance: Choking under pressure in mathematical problem solving. *Journal of Experimental Psychology: General, 133,* 584–600.

Bond, C. F., Jr., & Titus, L. J. (1983). Social facilitation: A meta-analysis of 241 studies. *Psychological Bulletin, 94,* 265–292.

Broen, W. E., Jr., & Storms, L. H. (1961). A reaction potential ceiling and response decrements in complex situations. *Psychological Review, 68,* 405–415.

Burnham, W. H. (1910, May). The group as a stimulus to mental activity. *Science, 31,* 761–767.

Clayton, D. A. (1978). Socially facilitated behavior. *Quarterly Review of Biology, 53,* 373–392.

Cohen, J. L., & Davis, J. H. (1973). Effects of audience status, evaluation, and time of action on performance with hidden-word problems. *Journal of Personality and Social Psychology, 27,* 74–85.

Cottrell, N. B. (1972). Social facilitation. In N. B. McClintock (Ed.), *Experimental social psychology* (pp. 185–236). New York: Holt, Rinehart and Winston.

Cottrell, N. B., Wack, D. L., Sekerak, G. J., & Rittle, R. H. (1968). Social facilitation of dominant responses by the presence of an audience and the mere presence of others. *Journal of Personality and Social Psychology, 9,* 245–250.

Crawford, M. P. (1939, June). The social psychology of the invertebrates. *Psychological Bulletin, 36,* 407–446.

Criddle, W. D. (1971). The physical presence of other individuals as a factor in social facilitation. *Psychonomic Science, 22,* 229–230.

Duffy, E. (1962). *Activation and behavior.* Hoboken, NJ: Wiley.

Easterbrook, J. A. (1959). The effect of emotion on cue utilization and the organization of behavior. *Psychological Bulletin, 13,* 363–385.

Feinberg, J. M., & Aiello, J. R. (2006). Social facilitation: A test of competing theories. *Journal of Applied Social Psychology, 36,* 1087–1109.

Feinberg, J. M., & Aiello, J. R. (2010). The effect of challenge and threat appraisals under evaluative presence. *Journal of Applied Social Psychology, 40,* 2071–2104.

Gaumer, C. J., & LaFief, W. C. (2005). Social facilitation: Affect and application in consumer buying situations. *Journal of Food Products Marketing, 11*(1), 75–82.

Geen, R. G. (1973). Effects of being observed on short- and long-term recall. *Journal of Experimental Social Psychology, 100,* 395–398.

Geen, R. G. (1981). Evaluation apprehension and social facilitation: A reply to Sanders. *Journal of Experimental and Social Psychology, 17,* 252–256.

Geen, R. G. (1989). Alternative conceptions of social facilitation. In P. B. Paulus (Ed.), *Psychology of group influence* (pp. 15–51). Mahwah, NJ: Erlbaum.

Geen, R. G. (1991). Social motivation. *Annual Review of Psychology, 42,* 377–399.

Geen, R. G., & Gange, J. J. (1977). Drive theory of social facilitation: Twelve years of theory and research. *Psychological Bulletin, 84*, 1267–1288.

Good, K. J. (1973). Social facilitation: Effects of performance anticipation, evaluation, and response competition on free association. *Journal of Personality and Social Psychology, 28*, 270–275.

Guerin, B. (1993). *Social facilitation.* Cambridge: Cambridge University Press.

Harkins, S. G. (2006). Mere effort as the mediator of the evaluation-performance relationship. *Journal of Personality and Social Psychology, 91*, 436–455.

Henchy, T., & Glass, D. C. (1968). Evaluation apprehension and the social facilitation of dominant and subordinate responses. *Journal of Personality and Social Psychology, 10*, 446–454.

Hull, C. L. (1952). *A behavior system.* New Haven, CT: Yale University Press.

Jamieson, J. P., & Harkins, S. G. (2007). Mere effort and stereotype threat performance effects. *Journal of Personality and Social Psychology, 93*, 544–564.

Kelley, H. H., & Thibaut, J. W. (1954). Experimental studies of group problem solving and process. In G. Lindzey (Ed.), *Handbook of social psychology* (pp. 735–785). Reading, MA: Addison-Wesley.

Landers, D. M. (1980). The arousal-performance relationship revisited. *Research Quarterly for Exercise and Sport, 51*, 77–90.

Lewis, B. P., & Langer, D. E. (1997). Thinking about choking? Attentional processes and paradoxical performance. *Personality and Social Psychology Bulletin, 23*, 937–944.

McNamara, H. J., & Fisch, R. I. (1964). Effect of high and low motivation on two aspects of attention. *Perceptual and Motor Skills, 19*, 571–578.

Park, S., & Catrambone, R. (2007, December). Social facilitation effects for virtual humans. *Human Factors, 49*, 1054–1060.

Paul, G. L., & Eriksen, C. W. (1964). Effects of test anxiety on time and untimed intelligence tests. *Journal of Consulting and Clinical Psychology, 33*, 240–244.

Sanders, G. S., & Baron, R. S. (1975). The motivating effect of distraction on task performance. *Journal of Personality and Social Psychology, 32*, 956–963.

Sanders, G. S., Baron, R. S., & Moore, D. L. (1978). Distraction and social comparison as mediators of social facilitation. *Journal of Experimental Social Psychology, 14*, 291–303.

Schmader, T., & Johns, M. (2003). Converging evidence that stereotype threat reduces working memory capacity. *Journal of Personality and Social Psychology, 85*, 440–452.

Sharma, D., Booth, R., Brown, R., & Huguet, P. (2010). Exploring the temporal dynamics of the social facilitation in the Stroop task. *Psychonomic Bulletin & Review, 17,* 52–58.

Spence, J. T., & Spence, K. W. (1966). The motivational components of manifest anxiety: Drive and drive stimuli. In C. D. Spielberger (Ed.), *Anxiety and behavior* (pp. 291–326). New York: Academic Press.

Strauss, B. (2002). Social facilitation in motor tasks: A review of research and theory. *Psychology of Sport and Exercise, 3,* 237–256.

Thompson, L. F., Sebastianelli, J. D., & Murray, N. P. (2009). Monitoring online training behaviors: Awareness of electronic surveillance hinders e-learners. *Journal of Applied Social Psychology, 39,* 2191–2212.

Triplett, N. (1898, July). The dynamogenic factors in pacemaking and competition. *American Journal of Psychology, 9,* 507–533.

Wankel, L. M. (1972). Competition in motor performance: An experimental analysis of motivational components. *Journal of Experimental Social Psychology, 8,* 427–437.

Weiss, R. F., & Miller, F. G. (1971). The drive theory of social facilitation. *Psychological Review, 78,* 44–57.

Wine, J. (1971). Test anxiety and direction of attention. *Psychological Bulletin, 76,* 92–104.

Zajonc, R. B. (1965, July). Social facilitation. *Science, 149,* 269–274.

Zajonc, R. B. (1968). Social facilitation in cockroaches. In E. C. Simmel, R. A. Hoppe, & G. A. Milton (Eds.), *Social facilitation and imitative behavior* (pp. 73–90). Boston: Allyn & Bacon.

Zajonc, R. B. (1980). Compresence. In P. B. Paulus (Ed.), *Psychology of group influence* (pp. 35–60). Mahwah, NJ: Erlbaum.

35: Social Identity Theory

Ashforth, B. E., & Mael, F. (1989). Social identity theory and the organization. *Academy of Management Review, 14,* 20–39.

Hogg, M. A. (1996). Social identity, self-categorization, and the small group. In E. H. Witte & J. H. Davis (Eds.), *Understanding group behavior, Vol. 2: Small group processes and interpersonal relations* (pp. 227–253). Mahwah, NJ: Erlbaum.

Hogg, M. A. (2006). Social identity theory. In P. J. Burke (Ed.), *Contemporary social psychological theories* (pp. 111–136). Stanford, CA: Stanford University Press.

Hogg, M. A., Terry, D. J., & White, K. M. (1995). A tale of two theories: A critical comparison of identity theory with social identity theory. *Social Psychology Quarterly, 58,* 255–269.

Horwitz, M., & Rabbie, J. M. (1982). Individuality and membership in intergroup system. In H. Tajfel (Ed.), *Social identity and intergroup relations* (pp. 241–274). Cambridge: Cambridge University Press.

Huddy, L. (2001). From social to political identity: A critical examination of social identity theory. *Political Psychology, 22*, 127–156.

Lam, S. K., Ahearne, M., Hu, Y., & Schillewaert, N. (2010, November). Resistance to brand switching when a radically new brand is introduced: A social identity theory perspective. *Journal of Marketing, 74*, 128–146.

Lewin, K. (1948). *Resolving social conflicts.* New York: Harper & Row.

Mael, F., & Ashforth, B. E. (1992). Alumni and their alma mater: A partial test of the reformulated model of organizational identification. *Journal of Organizational Behavior, 13*, 103–123.

Rabbie, J. M., & Horwitz, M. (1988). Categories versus groups as explanatory concepts in intergroup relations. *European Journal of Social Psychology, 18*, 117–123.

Rabbie, J. M., Schot, J., & Visser, L. (1987, July 16–18). *Instrumental intragroup cooperation and intergroup competition in the minimal group paradigm.* Paper presented at the Conference on Social Identity at the University of Exeter.

Schiffmann, R., & Wicklund, R. A. (1992). The minimal group paradigm and its minimal psychology: On equating social identity with arbitrary group membership. *Theory & Psychology, 2*, 29–50.

Tajfel, H. (1972). Social categorization. In S. Moscovici (Ed.), *Introduction to social psychology* (Vol. 1, pp. 272–302). Paris: Larousse.

Tajfel, H. (1981). *Human groups and social categories: Studies in social psychology.* Cambridge: Cambridge University Press.

Tajfel, H., & Turner, J. C. (1979). An integrative theory of intergroup conflict. In W. G. Austin & S. Worchel (Eds.), *The social psychology of intergroup relations* (pp. 33–47). Monterey, CA: Brooks-Cole.

Tajfel, H., & Turner, J. C. (1986). The social identity of intergroup behavior. In S. Worchel & W. G. Austin (Eds.), *The psychology of intergroup relations* (2nd ed., pp. 7–24). Chicago: Nelson-Hall.

Turner, J. C. (1982). Towards a cognitive redefinition of the social group. In H. Tajfel (Ed.), *Social identity and intergroup relations* (pp. 15–40). Cambridge: Cambridge University Press.

Turner, J. C. (1984). Social identification and psychological group formation. In H. Tajfel (Ed.), *The social dimension: European developments in social psychology* (Vol. 2, pp. 518–538). Cambridge: Cambridge University Press.

Turner, J. C., Hogg, M. A., Oakes, P. J., Reicher, S. D. & Wetherell, M. S. (1987). *Rediscovering the social group.* Oxford, England: Basil Blackwell.

36: Social Network Theory

Baker, W. E., & Faulkner, R. R. (2002). Interorganizational networks. In J. A. C. Baum (Ed.), *The Blackwell companion to organizations* (pp. 520–540). Oxford: Blackwell.

Bavelas, A. (1948). A mathematical model for group structures. *Human Organization, 7,* 16–30.

Bavelas, A. (1950). Communication patterns in task oriented groups. *Journal of the Acoustical Society of America, 22,* 271–282.

Borgatti, S. P., & Halgin, D. (in press). On network theory. *Organization Science.*

Burt, R. S. (1992). *Structural holes: The social structure of competition.* Cambridge, MA: Harvard University Press.

Burt, R. S. (2000). The network structure of social capital. In R. I. Sutton & B. M. Staw (Eds.), *Research in organizational behavior* (Vol. 22, pp. 345–423). Greenwich, CT: JAI Press.

Burt, R. (2005). *Brokerage and social closure.* Oxford: Oxford University Press.

Coleman, J. S. (1990). *Foundations of social theory.* Cambridge, MA: Belknap Press.

Comte, A. (1854). *The positive philosophy* (Vol. 2). (H. Martineau, Trans.). New York: Appleton.

Durkheim, E. (1951). *Suicide: A study in sociology.* New York: Free Press.

Embirbayer, M., & Goodwin, J. (1994, May). Network analysis, culture, and the problem of agency. *Administrative Science Quarterly, 99,* 1411–1454.

Erickson, B. H. (1988). The relational basis of attitudes. In B. Wellman & S. D. Berkowitz (Eds.), *Social structures: A network approach* (pp. 99–121). New York: Cambridge University Press.

Feld, S. (1981). The focused organization of social ties. *American Journal of Sociology, 86,* 1015–1035.

Freeman, L. C. (1978/1979). Centrality in social networks: Conceptual clarification. *Social Networks, 1,* 215–239.

Friedkin, N. (1980). A test of structural features of Granovetter's strength of weak ties theory. *Social Networks, 2,* 411–422.

Granovetter, M. (1973). The strength of weak ties. *American Journal of Sociology, 78,* 1360–1380.

Granovetter, M. (1985). Economic action and social structure: The problem of embeddedness. *American Journal of Sociology, 91,* 481–510.

Heider, F. (1946). Attitudes and cognitive organization. *Journal of Psychology, 21,* 107–121.

Kilduff, M., & Brass, D. J. (2010, June). Organizational social network research: Core ideas and key debates. *Academy of Management Annals, 4,* 317–357.

Kilduff, M., & Krackhardt, D. (2008). *Interpersonal networks in organizations.* New York: Cambridge University Press.

Laumann, E. O., Marsden, P. V., & Prensky, D. (1983). The boundary specification problem in network analysis. In R. S. Burt & M. J. Minor (Eds.), *Applied network analysis.* Thousand Oaks, CA: Sage.

Leavitt, H. J. (1951). Some effects of communication patterns on group performance. *Journal of Abnormal and Social Psychology, 46,* 38–50.

Lewin, K. (1936). *Principles of topological psychology.* New York: McGraw-Hill.

Lin, N. (2002). *Social capital.* New York: Cambridge University Press.

Marsden, P. V. (1990). Network data and measurement. *Annual Review of Sociology, 16,* 435–463.

Mitchell, J. C. (1969). The concept and use of social networks. In J. C. Mitchell (Ed.), *Social networks in urban situations* (pp. 1–50). Manchester, England: University of Manchester Press.

Moliterno, T. P., & Mahony, D. M. (2011, March). Network theory of organization: A multilevel approach. *Journal of Management, 37,* 443–467.

Moreno, J. L. (1934). *Who shall survive?* Washington DC: Nervous and Mental Disease Publishing.

Obstfeld, D. (2005). Social networks, the tertius iungens orientation, and involvement innovation. *Administrative Science Quarterly, 50,* 100–130.

Portes, A. (1998). Social capital: Its origins and applications in modern sociology. *Annual Review of Sociology, 24,* 1–24.

Simmel, G. (1950). *The sociology of Georg Simmel* (K. H. Wolff, Trans.). New York: Free Press. (Original work published 1908)

Stephenson, K., & Zelen, M. (1989). Rethinking centrality: Methods and examples. *Social Networks, 11,* 1–37.

Tichy, N. M., Tushman, M. L., & Fombrun, C. (1979). Social network analysis for organizations. *Academy of Management Review, 4,* 507–519.

Travers, J., & Milgram, S. (1969). An experimental study of the "small world" problem. *Sociometry, 32,* 425–443.

Uzzi, B. (1996). The sources and consequences of embeddedness for the economic performance of organizations: The network effect. *American Sociological Review, 61,* 674–698.

Uzzi, B., & Spiro, J. (2005). Collaboration and creativity: The small world problem. *American Journal of Sociology, 111,* 447–504.

Wasserman, S., & Faust, K. (1994). *Social network analysis: Methods and applications.* Cambridge: Cambridge University Press.

Watts, D. J. (1999). *Small worlds: The dynamics of networks between order and randomness.* Princeton, NJ: Princeton University Press.

Wellman, B. (1983). Network analysis: Some basic principles. In R. Collins (Ed.), *Sociological theory* (pp. 155–200). San Francisco: Jossey-Bass.

Wellman, B. (1988). Structural analysis: From method and metaphor to theory and substance. In B. Wellman & S. D. Berkowitz (Eds.), *Social structures: A network approach* (pp. 19–61). New York: Cambridge University Press.

White, H. C. (1993). *Careers and creativity.* Boulder, CO: Westview Press.

White, H. C., Boorman, S. A., & Breiger, R. L. (1976). Social structures from multiple networks: Blockmodels of roles and positions. *American Journal of Sociology, 81,* 730–779.

37: Stakeholder Theory

Agle, B. R., Donaldson, T., Freeman, R. E., Jensen, M. C., Mitchell, R. K., & Wood, D. J. (2008). Dialogue: Toward superior stakeholder theory. *Business Ethics Quarterly, 18,* 153–190.

Altman, J. A., & Petkus, J. R. (1994). Toward a stakeholder-based policy process: An application of the social marketing perspective to environmental policy development. *Policy Sciences, 27,* 37–51.

Buono, A. F., & Nichols, L. T. (1985). *Corporate policy, values and social responsibility.* New York: Praeger.

Cennamo, C., Berrone, P., & Gomez-Mejia, L. R. (2009). Does stakeholder management have a dark side? *Journal of Business Ethics, 89,* 491–507.

Clarkson, M. B. E. (1991). Defining, evaluating, and managing corporate social performance: A stakeholder management model. In J. E. Post (Ed.), *Research in corporate social performance and policy* (Vol. 12, pp. 331–358). Greenwich, CT: JAI Press.

Clarkson, M. B. E. (1995). A stakeholder framework for analyzing and evaluating corporate social performance. *Academy of Management Review, 20,* 92–117.

Clifton, D., & Amran, A. (2011). The stakeholder approach: A sustainability perspective. *Journal of Business Ethics, 98,* 121–136.

Donaldson, T., & Preston, L. E. (1995). The stakeholder theory of the corporation: Concepts, evidence, and implications. *Academy of Management Review, 20,* 65–91.

Egels-Zanden, N., & Sandberg, J. (2010, January). Distinctions in descriptive and instrumental stakeholder theory: A challenge for empirical research. *Business Ethics, 19,* 35–49.

Freeman, R. E. (1984). *Strategic management: A stakeholder approach.* Boston: Pitman.

Freeman, R. E. (2002). Stakeholder theory of the modern corporation. In T. Donaldson & P. Werhane (Eds.), *Ethical issues in business: A philosophical approach* (7th ed., pp. 38–48). Englewood Cliffs, NJ: Prentice Hall.

Freeman, R. E. (2004). The stakeholder approach revisited. *Zeitschrift für Wirtschafts- und Unternehmensethik, 5,* 228–241.

Grafe-Buckens, A., & Hinton, A.-F. (1998). Engaging the stakeholder: Corporate views and current trends. *Business Strategy and the Environment, 7,* 124–133.

Green, A. O., & Hunton-Clarke, L. (2003). A typology of stakeholder participation for company environmental decision-making. *Business Strategy and the Environment, 12,* 292–299.

Greenwood, M. (2001, Spring). The importance of stakeholders according to business leaders. *Business and Society Review, 106,* 29–49.

Greenwood, M. (2007). Stakeholder engagement: Beyond the myth of corporate responsibility. *Journal of Business Ethics, 74,* 315–327.

Hambrick, D. C., & Finkelstein, S. (1987). Managerial discretion: A bridge between polar views of organizational outcomes. In L. L. Cummings & B. M. Staw (Eds.), *Research in organizational behavior* (Vol. 9, pp. 369–406). Greenwich, CT: JAI Press.

Harrison, J. S., Bosse, D. A., & Phillips, R. A. (2010). Managing for stakeholders, stakeholder utility, and competitive advantage. *Strategic Management Journal, 31,* 58–74.

Hillman, A. J., & Keim, G. D. (2001). Shareholder value, shareholder management, and social issues: What's the bottom line? *Strategic Management Journal, 22,* 125–139.

Kaler, J. (2003). Differentiating stakeholder theories. *Journal of Business Ethics, 46,* 71–83.

Key, S. (1999). Toward a new theory of the firm: A critique of stakeholder "theory." *Management Decision, 37,* 317–328.

Maignan, I., & Ferrell, O. (2004). Corporate social responsibility and marketing: An integrative framework. *Academy of Marketing Science, 32,* 3–19.

Mitchell, R., Agle, B. R., & Wood, D. J. (1997). Toward a theory of stakeholder identification and salience: Defining the principles of who and what really counts. *Academy of Management Review, 22,* 853–886.

Payne, S., & Calton, J. (2004). Exploring research potentials and applications for multi-stakeholder learning dialogues. *Journal of Business Ethics, 55,* 71–78.

Phillips, R. A., Berman, S. L., Elms, H., & Johnson-Cramer, M. E. (2010). Strategy, stakeholders, and managerial discretion. *Strategic Organization, 8,* 176–183.

Plaza-Ubeda, J. A., de Burgos-Jimenez, J., & Carmona-Moreno, E. (2010). Measuring stakeholder integration: Knowledge, interaction and adaptational behavior dimensions. *Journal of Business Ethics, 93,* 419–442.

Rowley, T. J. (1997). Moving beyond dyadic ties: A network theory of stakeholder influences. *Academy of Management Review, 22,* 887–910.

Sirgy, M. J. (2002). Measuring corporate performance by building on the stakeholder model of business ethics. *Journal of Business Ethics, 35,* 143–162.

Stieb, J. A. (2008). Assessing Freeman's stakeholder theory. *Journal of Business Ethics, 87,* 401–414.

Walsh, J. P. (2005). Taking stock of stakeholder management. *Academy of Management Review, 30,* 426–438.

38: Structural Contingency Theory

Blau, P. M. (1970). A formal theory of differentiation in organizations. *American Sociological Review, 35,* 201–218.

Brech, E. F. L. (1957). *Organisation: The framework of management.* London: Longmans, Green.

Burns, T., & Stalker, G. (1961). *The management of innovation.* London: Tavistock.

Cao, G., Wiengarten, F., & Humphreys, P. (2011). Towards a contingency resource-based view of IT business value. *Systemic Practice and Action Research, 24,* 85–106.

Chandler, A. D., Jr. (1962). *Strategy and structure: Chapters in the history of the industrial enterprise.* Cambridge, MA: MIT Press.

Child, J. (1972). Organizational structure, environment and performance: The role of strategic choice. *Sociology, 6,* 1–22.

Child, J. (1973). Parkinson's progress: Accounting for the number of specialists in organizations. *Administrative Science Quarterly, 18,* 328–348.

Child, J. (1975). Managerial and organizational factors associated with company performance, part 2: A contingency analysis. *Journal of Management Studies, 12,* 12–27.

Darwin, C. R. (1909–1914). *The origin of species.* Harvard Classics, Vol. 11. New York: Collier.

De Rond, M., & Theitart, R.-A. (2007). Choice, change, and inevitability in strategy. *Strategic Management Journal, 28,* 535–551.

Donaldson, L. (2001). *The contingency theory of organizations.* Thousand Oaks, CA: Sage.

Donaldson, L. (2009). In search of the matrix advantage: A re-examination of the fit of matrix structures to transnational strategy in MNEs. In J. Cheng, E. Maitland, & S. Nicholas (Eds.), *Managing subsidiary dynamics: Headquarters role, capacity development, and China strategy* (pp. 3–26). Bingley, England: Emerald.

Drazin, R., & Van de Ven, A. H. (1985). Alternative forms of fit in contingency theory. *Administrative Science Quarterly, 30,* 514–539.

Fry, L., & Smith, D. A. (1987). Congruence, contingency and theory building. *Academy of Management Review, 12,* 117–132.

Galbraith, J. (1973). *Designing complex organizations.* Reading, MA: Addison-Wesley.

Galbraith, J. (1977). *Organizational design.* Reading, MA: Addison-Wesley.

Greenwood, R., & Miller, D. (2010, November). Tackling design anew: Getting back to the heart of organizational theory. *Academy of Management Perspectives, 24*(4), 78–88.

Hage, J. (1965). An axiomatic theory of organizations. *Administrative Science Quarterly, 10,* 289–320.

Hui, P. P., Davis-Blake, A., & Broschak, J. P. (2008, February). Managing interdependence: The effects of outsourcing structure on the performance of complex projects. *Decision Sciences, 39,* 5–31.

Jurkovich, R. (1974). A core typology of organizational environments. *Administrative Science Quarterly, 19,* 380–394.

Lawrence, P., & Lorsch, J. (1967). Differentiation and integration in complex organizations. *Administrative Science Quarterly, 12,* 1–30.

Miles, R. E., & Snow, C. C. (1978). *Organizational strategy, structure, and process.* Tokyo: McGraw-Hill Kogakusha.

Miller, D. (1981). Toward a new contingency approach: The search for organizational gestalts. *Journal of Management Studies, 18,* 1–26.

Mohr, L. B. (1971). Organizational technology and organizational structure. *Administrative Science Quarterly, 16,* 444–459.

Morgan, G. (1989). *Creative organization theory: A resource book.* Thousand Oaks, CA: Sage.

Morton, N. A., & Hu, Q. (2008). Implications of the fit between organizational structure and ERP: A structural contingency theory perspective. *Information Management, 28,* 391–402.

Nadler, D., & Tushman, M. (1980). A model for diagnosing organizational behavior. *Organizational Dynamics, 9,* 35–51.

Pennings, J. (1975). The relevance of the structural-contingency model for organizational effectiveness. *Administrative Science Quarterly, 30,* 393–410.

Perrow, C. (1967). A framework for the comparative analysis of organizations. *American Sociological Review, 32*, 194–208.

Perrow, C. (1980). *Organization theory in a society of organizations.* Unpublished manuscript, Red Feather Institute for Advance Studies in Sociology, State University of New York at Stony Brook.

Perrow, C. (1984). *Normal accidents: Living with high-risk technologies.* New York: Basic Books.

Pugh, D. S., Hickson, D. J., Hinings, C. R., & Turner, C. (1969). The context of organizational structure. *Administrative Science Quarterly, 14*, 91–114.

Pugh, D. S., & Hinings, C. R. (1976). *Organizational structure: Extensions and replications: The Aston Programme II.* Farnborough, England: Saxon House.

Qiu, J. X., & Donaldson, L. (2010, Autumn). The cubic contingency model: Towards a more comprehensive international strategy-structure model. *Journal of General Management, 36*(1), 81–100.

Randolph, W. A., & Dess, G. G. (1984). The congruence perspective of organization design: A conceptual model and multivariate research approach. *Academy of Management Review, 9*, 114–127.

Rumelt, R. (1974). *Strategy, structure and economic performance.* Boston: Division of Research, Graduate School of Business Administration, Harvard University.

Schoonhoven, C. B. (1981). Problems with contingency theory: Testing assumptions hidden within the language of contingency "theory." *Administrative Science Quarterly, 26*, 349–377.

Schreyogg, G. (1980). Contingency and choice in organization theory. *Organization Studies, 1*, 305–326.

Smith, W. K., & Lewis, M. W. (2011). Toward a theory of paradox: A dynamic equilibrium model of organizing. *Academy of Management Review, 36*, 381–403.

Taylor, F. W. (1947). *Scientific management.* New York: Harper. (Original work published 1911)

Thompson, J. (1967). *Organizations in action.* New York: McGraw-Hill.

Tosi, H. L., & Slocum, J. W., Jr., (1984). Contingency theory: Some suggested directions. *Journal of Management, 10*, 9–26.

Tucker, B. (2010). Through which lens? Contingency and institutional approaches to conceptualizing organizational performance in the not-for-profit sector. *Journal of Applied Management Accounting Research, 8*(1), 17–33.

Umanath, N. S. (2003). The concept of contingency beyond "it depends": Illustrations from IS research stream. *Information and Management, 40*, 551–562.

Venkatraman, N. (1989). The concept of fit in strategy research: Toward verbal and statistical correspondence. *Academy of Management Review, 14,* 423–444.

Woodward, J. (1958). *Management and technology.* London: H.M.S.O.

Woodward, J. (1965). *Industrial organization: Theory and practice.* Oxford: Oxford University Press.

39: Structuration Theory

Anderson, P. (1983). *In the tracks of historical materialism.* London: Verso.

Archer, M. (1990). Human agency and social structure: A critique of Giddens. In J. Clark, C. Modgil, & S. Modgil (Eds.), *Anthony Giddens: Consensus and controversy* (pp. 73–84). Brighton, England: Falmer.

Callinicos, A. (1985). Anthony Giddens: A contemporary critique. *Theory and Society, 14,* 133–166.

DeSanctis, G., & Poole, M. S. (1994, May). Capturing the complexity in advanced technology use: Adaptive structuration theory. *Organization Science, 5,* 121–147.

Gane, M. (1985). Anthony Giddens and the crisis of social theory. *Economy and Society, 12,* 368–398.

Giddens, A. (1976). *New rules of sociological method: A positive critique of interpretative sociologies.* London: Hutchinson.

Giddens, A. (1979). *Central problems in social theory: Action, structure, and contradiction in social analysis.* London: Macmillan.

Giddens, A. (1984). *The constitution of society: Outline of the theory of structuration.* Cambridge: Polity.

Giddens, A. (1991). *Modernity and self-identity: Self and society in the late modern age.* Stanford, CA: Stanford University Press.

Greenhalgh, T., & Stones, R. (2010). Theorising big IT programmes in healthcare: Strong structuration theory meets actor-network theory. *Social Science and Medicine, 70,* 1285–1294.

Schneidewind, U., & Petersen, H. (1998, Winter). Changing the rules—NGO partnerships and structuration theory. *Greener Management International, 24,* 105–114.

Stones, R. (2005). *Structuration theory.* Basingstoke, England: Palgrave-Macmillan.

40: Transaction Cost Theory

Bidwell, M. (2010). Problems deciding: How the structure of make-or-buy decisions leads to transaction misalignment. *Organization Science, 21,* 362–379.

Chiles, T. H., & McMackin, J. F. (1996). Integrative variable risk preferences, trust, and transaction cost economies. *Academy of Management Review*, *21*, 73–99.

Coase, R. H. (1937, November). The nature of the firm. *Economica*, *4*, 386–405.

Commons, J. R. (1934). *Institutional economics: Its place in political economy.* Madison: University of Wisconsin Press.

Dyer, J. H. (1997). Effective interfirm collaboration: How firms minimize transaction costs and maximize transaction value. *Strategic Management Journal*, *18*, 535–556.

Dyer, J. H., & Chu, W. (2003). The role of trustworthiness in reducing transaction costs and improving performance: Empirical evidence from the United States, Japan, and Korea. *Organization Science*, *14*, 57–68.

Geyskens, I., Steenkamp, J.-B. E. M., & Kumar, N. (2006). Make, buy, or ally: A transaction cost theory meta-analysis. *Academy of Management Journal*, *49*, 519–543.

Ghoshal, S., & Moran, P. (1996). Bad for practice: A critique of the transaction cost theory. *Academy of Management Review*, *21*, 13–47.

Hart, O. D. (1988, Spring). Incomplete contracts and the theory of the firm. *Journal of Law, Economics, and Organization*, *14*, 119–139.

Hill, C. W. L. (1990). Cooperation, opportunism, and the invisible hand: Implications for transaction cost theory. *Academy of Management Journal*, *15*, 500–513.

Jobin, D. (2008). A transaction cost-based approach to partnership performance evaluation. *Evaluation*, *14*, 437–465.

Macher, J. T., & Richman, B. D. (2008). Transaction cost economics: An assessment of empirical research in the social sciences. *Business and Politics*, *10*(1), 1–63.

Poppo, L., & Zenger, T. (1998). Testing alternative theories of the firm: Transaction cost, knowledge-based, and measurement explanations for make-or-buy decisions in information services. *Strategic Management Journal*, *19*, 853–877.

Poppo, L., & Zenger, T. (2002). Do formal contracts and relational governance function as substitutes or complements? *Strategic Management Journal*, *23*, 707–725.

Shelanski, H. A., & Klein, P. G. (1995, October). Empirical research in transaction cost economies: A review and assessment. *Journal of Law, Economics, and Organization*, *11*, 335–361.

Williamson, O. E. (1975). *Markets and hierarchies: Analysis and antitrust implications.* New York: Free Press.

Williamson, O. E. (1985). *The economic institutions of capitalism.* New York: Free Press.

Williamson, O. E. (1998). Transaction cost economics: How it works; where it is headed. *De Economist, 146,* 23–58.

Williamson, O. E. (2002). The theory of the firm as governance structure: From choice to contract. *Journal of Economic Perspectives, 16*(3), 171–195.

Williamson, O. E. (2010, June). Transaction cost economics: The natural progression. *American Economic Review, 100,* 673–690.

Conclusion

Aguinis, H., Boyd, B. K., Pierce, C. A., & Short, J. C. (2011, March). Walking new avenues in management: Research methods and theories: Bridging micro and macro domains. *Journal of Management, 37,* 395–403.

Anderson, L. W., & Krathwohl, D. R. (2001). *A taxonomy of learning, teaching and assessing: A revision of Bloom's taxonomy.* New York: Longman.

Bromiley, P., & Fleming, L. (2002). The resource-based view of strategy: A behavioral critique. In M. Augier & J. G. March (Eds.), *Change, choice and organization: Essays in memory of Richard M. Cyert* (pp. 319–336). Cheltenham, England: Elgar.

Eisenhardt, K. M. (1989). Agency theory: An assessment and review. *Academy of Management Review, 14,* 57–74.

Ghoshal, S., & Moran, P. (1996). Bad for practice: A critique of the transaction cost theory. *Academy of Management Review, 21,* 13–47.

Gioa, D. A., & Pitre, E. (1990). Multiparadigm perspectives on theory building. *Academy of Management Review, 15,* 584–602.

House, R., Rousseau, D. M., & Thomas-Hunt, M. (1995). The meso paradigm: A framework for the integration of micro and macro organizational behavior. In L. L. Cummings & B. M. Staw (Eds.), *Research in organizational behavior* (Vol. 17, pp. 71–114). Greenwich, CT: JAI Press.

Huselid, M. A., & Becker, B. E. (2011, March). Bridging micro and macro domains: Workforce differentiation and strategic human resource management. *Journal of Management, 37,* 421–428.

Ilgen, D. R., & Klein, H. J. (1989). Organizational behavior. *Annual Review of Psychology, 40,* 327–351.

Kavanagh, M. J. (1991, March). Our field of management has been suffering recently! *Group and Organization Studies, 16*(1), 3–4.

Key, S. (1999). Toward a new theory of the firm: A critique of stakeholder "theory." *Management Decision, 37,* 317–328.

Kilduff, M. (2007). Editor's comments: The top ten reasons why your paper might not be sent out for review. *Academy of Management Review, 32,* 1199–1228.

Klein, H. J. (1989). An integrated control theory model of work motivation. *Academy of Management Review, 14,* 150–172.

Klein, K. J., & Kozlowski, S. W. J. (2000). From micro to meso: Critical steps in conceptualizing and conducting multilevel research. *Organizational Research Methods, 3,* 211–236.

LePine, J. A., & King, A. W. (2010). Editor's comments: Developing novel theoretical insight from reviews of existing theory and research. *Academy of Management Review, 35,* 506–509.

Locke, E. A., & Latham, G. P. (2006). New directions in goal-setting theory. *Current Directions in Psychological Science, 15,* 265–268.

Mathieu, J. E., & Chen, G. (2011, March). The etiology of the multilevel paradigm in management research. *Journal of Management, 37,* 610–641.

Moliterno, T. P., & Mahony, D. M. (2011, March). Network theory of organization: A multilevel approach. *Journal of Management, 37,* 443–467.

Okhuysen, G., & Bonardi, J.-P. (2011). Editor's comments: The challenges of building theory by combining lenses. *Academy of Management Review, 36,* 6–11.

Oswick, C., Fleming, P., & Hanlon, G. (2011). From borrowing to blending: Rethinking the processes of organizational theory building. *Academy of Management Review, 36,* 318–337.

Payne, G. T., Moore, C. B., Griffis, S. E., & Autry, C. W. (2011, March). Multilevel challenges and opportunities for social capital research. *Journal of Management, 37,* 491–520.

Pohl, M. (2000). *Learning to think, thinking to learn.* Cheltenham, Victoria, Australia: Hawker Brownlow.

Roberts, K. H., Glick, W., Weissenberg, P., Bedeian, A., Whetten, D., Miller, H., Pearce, J., & Klimoski, R. (1990). Reflections on the field of organizational behavior. *Journal of Management Systems, 2*(1), 25–38.

Rousseau, D. M. (2011, March). Reinforcing the micro/macro bridge: Organizational thinking and pluralistic vehicles. *Journal of Management, 37,* 429–442.

Smith, K. G., & Hitt, M. A. (2005). Epilogue: Learning how to develop theory from the masters. In K. G. Smith (Ed.), *Great minds in management* (pp. 572–588). Oxford: Oxford University Press.

Suddaby, R., Hardy, C., & Huy, Q. N. (2011, April). Special topic forum—theory development introduction: Where are the new theories of organization? *Academy of Management Review, 36,* 236–246.

Tsang, E. W. K., & Ellsaesser, F. (2011). How contrastive explanation facilitates theory building. *Academy of Management Review, 36,* 404–419.

Turner, J. H. (2006). The state of theorizing in sociological social psychology: A grand theorist's view. In P. J. Burke (Ed.), *Contemporary social psychological theories* (pp. 353–373). Stanford, CA: Stanford University Press.

Weick, K. E. (1999). Theory construction as a disciplined reflexivity: Tradeoffs in the 1990s. *Academy of Management Review, 24,* 797–806.

Whetten, D. A., Felin, T., & King, B. G. (2009). The practice of theory borrowing in organizational studies: Current issues and future directions. *Journal of Management, 35,* 537–563.

Yammarino, F. J., Dionne, S. D., Schriesheim, C. A., & Dansereau, F. (2008). Authentic leadership and positive organizational behavior: A meso, multi-level perspective. *Leadership Quarterly, 19,* 693–707.

Zahra, S. A., & George, G. (2002). Absorptive capacity: A review, reconceptualization, and extension. *Academy of Management Review, 27,* 185–203.

Name Index

Subject Index

A

Ability (internal, stable), 58
Absorptive capacities, 18, 339
Absorptive capacity theory: criticisms and critiques of, 19–221; further research and references on, 21–23; implications for managers, 23; measuring variables in the, 21; on organization use of new knowledge, 17–23; reformulation of, 347
Academy of Management journals, 6–7
Achievement outcome causes, 58
Actants, 26, 128
Action: actor process of coordinating, 26–27; actor-network theory translating, 25–27; deontological perspective of, 106–107; of employees to become ideal self; hidden action model on, 34; how goals impact, 129–130; institutionalized, 146–147; interplaying in social structure, 322; intuitionism perspective of, 107; irrational, 123; life as goal-oriented, 129–135; sensemaking stress on, 245; social cognitive theory on factors causing, 257–263; teleological perspective of, 106; theory of reasoned, 193–194. *See also* Behavior
Action-active agency, 324
Action Control Scale (ACS-90), 76
Actor-network theory: criticisms and critiques of the, 27–29; further research and references on, 29–30; implications for managers of, 30–31; measuring variables in the, 29; as "sociology of translation," 25; translating relationships and actions, 25–27
Actor-observer effect, 59
Actors: actor-network theory on relationships between, 27–31; field

theory on activities of, 115; linkages among set of, 297–303; process of coordinating actions by, 26–27
Administrative problems, 315
Adopters, 83
Adoption decisions, 138, 139
Adult-child attachment, 49–50
Adverse selection, 34, 35
Advocate of theory, 351
Affective element, 74
Age: behavior and, 195, 286, 294, 300; of organizations, 178–179
Agency: action-active, 324; being agent of change through, 259; structuration theory on social structures created by, 321; three different modes of, 259–260. *See also* Choice (individual)
Agency problem: definition of the, 34; three main ways to minimize the, 34–35
Agency theory: criticisms and critiques of the, 36–37; future research and references on, 37–39; implications for managers of, 39; measuring variables in the, 37; positivist branch of, 35, 36; principal-agent branch of, 35; on the principal-agent relationship, 33–36
Agenda setting theory: criticisms and critiques of the, 44–45; framing as essential part of, 43; further research and references on, 46–47; on how mass media coverage affects public opinion, 41–44; implications for managers, 47; measuring variables in the, 45–46
Agents: definition of, 33; moral hazard of, 34; relationship between principal and, 33–36
Agreements: confidentiality, 155, 159; employment, 209; exchange, 209; exchange with other firms, 329. *See also* Contracts